The Academic Administrator Grid®

A Guide to Developing
Effective Management Teams

Robert R. Blake

Jane Srygley Mouton

Martha Shipe Williams

The Academic Administrator Grid®

Jossey-Bass Publishers
San Francisco • Washington • London • 1982

THE ACADEMIC ADMINISTRATOR GRID®
A Guide to Developing Effective Management Teams
by Robert R. Blake, Jane Srygley Mouton, and
Martha Shipe Williams

Copyright © 1981 by: Jossey-Bass Inc., Publishers
433 California Street
San Francisco, California 94104

Jossey-Bass Limited
28 Banner Street
London EC1Y 8QE

Robert R. Blake
and Jane Srygley Mouton

Library of Congress Cataloging in Publication Data

Blake, Robert Rogers, 1918-
      The academic administrator grid.

      Bibliography: p. 389
      Includes index.
      1. School administrators. I. Mouton, Jane Srygley,
joint author. II. Williams, Martha Shipe, joint
author. III. Title.
LB2806.B56   371.2   80-8908
ISBN 0-87589-492-5

Manufactured in the United States of America

JACKET DESIGN BY WILLI BAUM

FIRST EDITION
    First printing: March 1981
    Second printing: October 1982

Code 8106

The Jossey-Bass
Series in Higher Education

Preface

For many years, colleges and universities have not only contributed to the expansion of pure knowledge and the growth and development of individual students but they have also been the source of principles, theories, and empirical facts that have had an enlivening effect on government, business and industry, the practice of medicine, and other professions. A new development that has occurred, however, is that tested theories, concepts, facts, and techniques have become available for universities themselves to use in solving their own administrative problems and enhancing their contributions to society.

This book contains such ideas for those who administer and conduct the affairs of higher education institutions. It centers around what we have termed the *Grid approach*—a systematic way of understanding administrative leadership in terms of its two major and essential qualities: concern for *institutional performance* and concern for *people*. Based on extensive behavioral science theory and research, the Grid approach is a way of assuring team leadership in achieving excellence and as the means for bringing about consensus and cooperation on changes essential to such achievement.

In our view, a basic difficulty underlying many of the serious problems of academic administration is the inability to deal effectively with conflict among administrators, between administrators and faculty members, among the faculty, between faculty and students, and between representatives of the institution and the external constituencies with whom they must deal. When those responsible for institutional policy are able to focus and resolve conflicts arising from different ideologies, values, and vested interests, it is possible for decision making and problem solving to be governed by commitment to the pursuit of academic excellence.

The Academic Administrator Grid, then, is aimed at leaders in universities, colleges, and community colleges—at presidents, vice-presidents, deans, institute heads, department chairs, researchers, and those faculty members who exercise significant committee responsibility. It examines effective and ineffective conflict resolution from many different perspectives. It contains dozens of examples from university life that provide an x-ray view of the range and character of current approaches to academic administration. It illustrates how leaders can apply their concern both for institutional performance and for people to enhance institutional achievement. It shows how these leaders can reduce the disagreements and frustrations that arise from extensive faculty and staff meetings and the committee work so essential for mobilizing the human resources of the university. In addition, this book offers an understanding about the conduct of university affairs to students who seek involvement in policy formation and decision making; for administrators of large city school systems, it presents interesting parallels between university and school administration.

Because issues of academic administration are so unique, the organization of this book differs from others written around the Grid idea, and its contents are entirely original, having been prepared by the three of us based on research and our own experiences as university professors, researchers, and administrators. We deal with the behavioral science principles of effective human interaction: relationships based on trust and respect, confronting conflict to establish collaborative problem solving, encouraging open and candid communication, using critiques as the basis of personal learning, and promoting shared participation that leads to decisions based on understanding and agreement. These issues are dealt with in the context of such operational problems as implementing institutional mission, supporting teaching and learning, establishing the curriculum, supporting research and scholarly activity, encouraging community and institutional service, managing resources, supervising personnel, coordinating student affairs, managing external relations, and assuring basic operations. After analyzing different approaches to these administrative tasks, we offer specific suggestions for using the Grid approach as the basis for organization development.

It is our hope that this book will help readers see the problems of conducting the affairs of the university in a new and clearer light and that it will enable those who lead the affairs of universities and colleges to initiate programs of change that bring human resources to bear more effectively on the pursuit of academic excellence.

Austin, Texas   Robert R. Blake

Jane Srygley Mouton

Martha Shipe Williams

Contents

xiii

Contents

xiii

The Authors

Robert R. Blake is president of Scientific Methods, Inc., a behavioral science firm specializing in organization development. He received his B.A. degree in psychology from Berea College (1940), his M.A. degree in psychology from the University of Virginia (1941), and his Ph.D. degree in psychology from the University of Texas at Austin (1947), where he was a professor until 1964. He has lectured at Harvard, Oxford, and Cambridge universities; worked on special extended assignments at the Tavistock Clinic, London, as a Fulbright Scholar; and has served as a consultant with governments, industries, and universities in forty countries. He is a diplomate in Industrial and Organizational Psychology, American Board of Professional Psychology; a fellow of the American Psychological Association; and a member of the International Association of Applied Social Scientists, Phi Kappa Phi, Pi Gamma Mu, and Sigma Xi.

Blake is a pioneer in organizational dynamics, having initiated the first organization development effort in a major American corporation. Here he perfected the internationally known Grid approach to organization development and demonstrated its ability to promote organization excellence. Blake is the author of thirty books, including *The New Managerial Grid* (1978), *Consultation* (1976), and *Making Experience Work* (1978). The original Grid book, *The Managerial Grid* (1964), has sold in excess of one million copies and is available in ten languages.

Jane Srygley Mouton is vice-president and co-founder of Scientific Methods, Inc., and was the co-developer of the concepts of the Grid. Mouton received her B.S. degree in pure mathematics at the University of Texas at Austin (1950), her M.S. degree in psychology from Florida State University (1951), and her Ph.D. degree in psychology from the University of Texas at Austin (1957), where she also was a faculty member. She is an associate of the American Psychological Association; a diplomate in Industrial and Organizational Psychology, American Board of Professional Psychology; and a member of the American Association for the Advancement of Science, the International Association of Applied Social Scientists, Phi Kappa Phi, and Sigma Xi.

Mouton has consulted with government leaders, executives, and academic and other administrators from over forty countries. In addition to her work in executive management and organization development, she has engaged in research on conformity, dynamics of win-lose conflict, and creative decision making. She is coauthor with Robert Blake of twenty-nine books, including *The Marriage Grid* (1971), *Instrumented Team Learning* (1975), and *Managing Intergroup Conflict in Industry* (1964). Among other assignments, Blake and Mouton have served as consultants to the U.S. Senate on the structure and functioning of presidential commissions.

Martha Shipe Williams is professor of social work at the University of Texas at Austin and assistant director of the Institute of Higher Education Management, located in the University of Texas System administration. She received her B.A. (1957), M.A. (1961), and Ph.D. (1963) degrees in psychology from the University of Texas at Austin. Her university career has spanned twenty-three years, and she has been a staff and faculty member in a number of disciplines, including law, psychology, education, social work, and business administration.

Williams is a member of the American Psychological Association, Industrial and Organizational Psychology division, and Sigma Xi. She has authored sixty articles and monographs primarily in the areas of organization research and training and the administration of social services. She has also served on a number of university committees, including the Faculty Senate and Graduate Assembly, and has taught courses in organization theory, research methods, and administration. Currently Williams is a technical consultant to the Governor's Effectiveness Program in Texas.

The Academic Administrator Grid®

A Guide to Developing
Effective Management Teams

Chapter One

Seeing Yourself in the Academic Leadership Mirror

When you assume an administrative role, you do not leave your personality and general way of dealing with others behind. Instead, you bring to your new position the values and interpersonal skills you have acquired throughout a lifetime. Furthermore, the increased demands and extra stresses of administration are likely to reveal your personal strengths and weaknesses in bold relief. Therefore, we begin this book by asking you to reflect on your own typical approaches to handling specific administrative tasks in order to provide you with a personal framework for reading the remaining chapters.

Administrative Styles

To identify your own administrative style, rank the following paragraphs from most typical to least typical as descriptions of your behavior; with 5 as the most typical, 4 as the next most typical, and so on to 1, as the least typical. When you finish ranking the paragraphs, there should be only one of each number from 5 to 1. There can be no ties.

Before starting, a word of caution: Self-deception is likely to occur as you select your answers. The deception is caused by the tendency of people to confuse the way they *want* to administer with the way they actually *do*. The first step in accurate self-assessment is to strip away self-deception in order to see your underlying assumptions. Some self-deception is probably unavoidable, but it can be reduced by selecting answers which reflect on your actual performance as an administrator in the recent past.

_____ A. I accept the decisions of others with indifference. I avoid taking sides by not revealing my opinions, attitudes, and ideas. When conflict arises, I try to remain neutral. By remaining uninvolved, I rarely get stirred up. My humor is seen as rather pointless. I put out enough to get by.

_____ B. I support decisions that promote good relations. I embrace the opinions, attitudes, and ideas of others rather than push my own. I avoid generating conflict; but, when it does appear, I try to soothe feelings to keep people together. Because of the disapproval tensions can produce, I react to others in a warm and friendly way. My humor shifts attention away from the serious side. I prefer to support others rather than initiate action.

_____ C. I search for workable, even though not perfect, decisions. When others hold ideas, opinions, or attitudes different from my own, I try to meet them halfway. When conflict arises, I try to find fair solutions that accommodate others. Under tension, I feel unsure and anxious about how to meet others' expectations. My humor sells me or my position. I seek to maintain a steady pace.

_____ D. I expect decisions I make to be treated as final. I stand up for my ideas, opinions, and attitudes even though this sometimes results in stepping on toes. When conflict arises, I try to cut it off or win my position. When things are not going as I feel they should, I defend, resist, and come back with counterarguments. My humor is hard hitting. I drive myself and others.

_____ E. I place high value on sound, creative decisions that result in understanding and agreement. I listen for and seek out ideas, opinions, and attitudes different from my own. I have strong convictions, but respond to sounder ideas than my own by changing my mind. When conflict arises, I try to identify reasons for it and seek to resolve its underlying causes. When aroused, I reexamine my own and others' motives and assumptions in an effort to achieve a better understanding of the tensions being produced. My humor fits the situation and gives perspective; I retain a sense of humor even under pressure. I exert vigorous effort and others join in.

Elements of Interaction

The differences among these administrative styles can be isolated by examining in turn each of the six elements of behavior in an administrator's daily interactions that they highlight: (1) making decisions, (2) holding convictions, (3) managing conflict, (4) controlling temper, (5) expressing humor, and (6) exerting effort. Your own individual *modus operandi* regarding these elements of interaction reflects basic assumptions about your relationships with others.

Read the five sentences listed below for each of these elements and then check the sentence that is most typical of your behavior. Be straightforward with yourself: check your most typical *actual* behavior, not your ideal behavior. (The sentence that you check is likely to be from the paragraph that you ranked as most descriptive of your administrative style, but it may be from another one.)

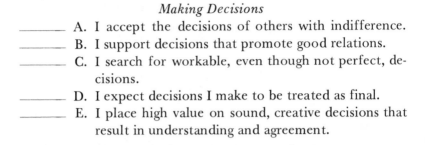

Making Decisions
_____ A. I accept the decisions of others with indifference.
_____ B. I support decisions that promote good relations.
_____ C. I search for workable, even though not perfect, decisions.
_____ D. I expect decisions I make to be treated as final.
_____ E. I place high value on sound, creative decisions that result in understanding and agreement.

Once you have checked one of these sentences as the best for describing your decisions, consider the following ideas about decision making: Reaching a decision is fundamental to any action. Many discussions in administration have to do with reaching a decision so that next steps can be taken. The point where administrators commit themselves to one course of action over others indicates their degree of certainty in choosing that specific alternative. Many times a decision cannot be changed once it has been made. Administrators who are decisive and can solve problems are viewed as effective leaders, confident and capable. Their confidence promotes respect. Administrators who are wishy-washy, who reverse themselves or fluctuate, are viewed as weak. They are seen as having no consistent agendas, no policies, and even no ethical standards. Others lack confidence in their leadership.

Holding Convictions
_____ A. I avoid taking sides by not revealing my opinions, attitudes, and ideas.
_____ B. I embrace the opinions, attitudes, and ideas of others rather than push my own.
_____ C. When others hold ideas, opinions, or attitudes different from my own, I try to meet them halfway.
_____ D. I stand up for my ideas, opinions, and attitudes

even though this sometimes results in stepping on toes.

_____ E. I listen for and seek out ideas, opinions, and attitudes different from my own.

Once you have checked one of these sentences, consider the following ideas: In an academic environment, administrators are expected to think for themselves, and the most highly respected are those who have sound convictions that are strongly held. An administrator with clear convictions is viewed as having a grasp of the problem, a sense of purpose, and the ability to give direction to others. An individual without convictions, or one who easily abandons positions, is seen as uncertain, anxious, indifferent, or even incapable of addressing the real issues.

Managing Conflict

_____ A. When conflict arises, I try to remain neutral.

_____ B. I avoid generating conflict; but, when it does appear, I try to soothe feelings to keep people together.

_____ C. When conflict arises, I try to find fair solutions that accommodate others.

_____ D. When conflict arises, I try to cut it off or win my position.

_____ E. When conflict arises, I try to identify reasons for it and seek to resolve its underlying causes.

Conflict is inevitable in a setting where people have different points of view and freedom of expression is encouraged. The effects of conflict can be either disruptive and destructive or creative and constructive, depending upon whether the persons involved can work toward mutual understanding or simply an agreement to differ without disrespect. Inability to cope with conflict constructively and creatively leads to increased hostility, antagonism, and divisiveness. Clear thinking disintegrates, and prejudice and dogmatism come to prevail. This is the antithesis of the university norm of "reasoned discourse."

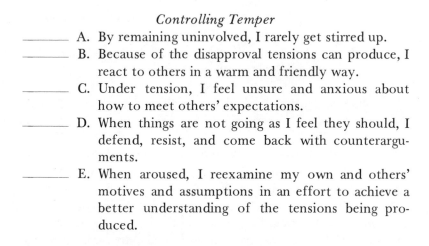

Controlling Temper

_____ A. By remaining uninvolved, I rarely get stirred up.

_____ B. Because of the disapproval tensions can produce, I react to others in a warm and friendly way.

_____ C. Under tension, I feel unsure and anxious about how to meet others' expectations.

_____ D. When things are not going as I feel they should, I defend, resist, and come back with counterarguments.

_____ E. When aroused, I reexamine my own and others' motives and assumptions in an effort to achieve a better understanding of the tensions being produced.

Temper is an emotional reaction to stress, tension, and strain. Often, loss of control means that reason has been abandoned and that strong, negative emotions now reign unchecked. The emotional tone of a person has contagious effects on others. Anger, for example, can spread like wildfire. When a person maintains a steady, even control over his or her emotions, however, others have confidence in that person's ability to reason and to cope with events. Respect for leadership is enhanced. At the same time, a person who shows no emotion or who is socialized to the extent that he or she never manifests negative feelings is likely to become suspect. This lack of feeling or inappropriate reaction can thus signal that the person does not fully appreciate the gravity of the situation or has no empathy or concern for others.

Expressing Humor

_____ A. My humor is seen as rather pointless.

_____ B. My humor shifts attention away from the serious side.

_____ C. My humor sells me or my position.

_____ D. My humor is hard hitting.

_____ E. My humor fits the situation and gives perspective; I retain a sense of humor even under pressure.

Humor lubricates social affairs by providing perspective and bringing unexpressed attitudes or feelings into focus. Humor can neutralize emotions, break impasses, and give richness to contradictory events. An individual with a sound sense of humor contributes to the enjoyment of others and builds a sense of spirit in the pursuit of goals. One who is humorless is lifeless and no fun to be around. A good sense of humor is the mark of a creative thinker who can stimulate others and create feelings of goodwill.

Exerting Effort

_____ A. I put out enough to get by.
_____ B. I prefer to support others rather than initiate action.
_____ C. I seek to maintain a steady pace.
_____ D. I drive myself and others.
_____ E. I exert vigorous effort and others join in.

Healthy, productive people have the capacity for utilizing their energies in positive and constructive ways without becoming "workaholics." Their enthusiasm is contagious, and others tend to match their pace and effort. This produces a "can do" spirit of optimism and progress. When administrators do not have enthusiasm, however, others lose their energy or become complacent. Conversely, when administrators work in a frantic way, others react by becoming hopelessly overwhelmed or defensive and complacent. The attitude might be "Why try?" or "If you want it done so much, do it yourself."

Assessing Your Grid Style

Before turning to the remaining chapters in this book, which interpret these styles of administration and elements of interaction, jot down in the left-hand column (on p. 8) the ranks that you assigned to each of the five preceding paragraphs; note in the right-hand column the letters that identify the sentences you checked as most typical of your behavior:

Paragraphs Depicting	*Sentences Illustrating*	
Administrative Styles	*Elements of Interaction*	
A _____	Making Decisions	_____
B _____	Holding Convictions	_____
C _____	Managing Conflict	_____
D _____	Controlling Temper	_____
E _____	Expressing Humor	_____
	Exerting Effort	_____

We will return to these rankings in Chapter Ten, where we will evaluate their implications for your effectiveness and identify alternative ways of administering so as to gain greater success while simultaneously deepening your sense of satisfaction from work. First, however, Chapter Two describes the Academic Administrator Grid—a device to aid your understanding of your own assumptions and administrative style and of why others respond to you as they do. Chapter Three highlights the major responsibilities involved in university administration and provides a picture of the context within which your administrative style must be viewed. And Chapters Four through Nine illustrate the distinctive styles of administration revealed by the Academic Administrator Grid and epitomized by the above paragraphs.

Chapter Two

The Academic
Administrator Grid

The Academic Administrator Grid is a systematic framework for ordering and compressing into usable form behavioral science theory and research significant for understanding and improving the exercise of leadership in college and university administration.

Two fundamental aspects of the exercise of leadership come to mind whenever an academic administrator thinks about his or her responsibilities: (1) concern for institutional performance and (2) concern for people. On the one hand, an administrator is concerned with institutional outcomes and with achieving institutional goals. This means that the administrator is concerned with getting results, either directly or through others. On the other hand, an administrator is concerned with people—other administrators, faculty members, students, benefactors, the public—whomever the administrator deals with on a day-in and day-out basis.

We know that these two concerns are not always present in the same amount. Each of them ranges through a scale of quantity. Some administrators may be less concerned than others with institutional performance, just as some may be less concerned than others with the people they work with in day-to-day activities. For example, an administrator's concern for institutional performance can be thought of as falling somewhere on a scale of degrees that ranges from 1, a very low concern, to 9, a very high concern:

Figure 1. Concern for Institutional Performance

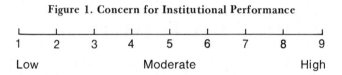

1	2	3	4	5	6	7	8	9
Low				Moderate				High

Concern for people also ranges through a number of degrees and can also be plotted on a nine-point scale, ranging from 1, a very low degree of concern, to 9, a very high degree of concern:

Figure 2. Concern for People

High   9

8

7

6

Moderate   5

4

3

2

Low   1

Leaders can be described in terms of their concern for performance and for people and how they deal with these two basic dimensions. The variety of ways in which administrative authority is exercised can be illustrated by placing these two dimensions at right angles to one another in the form of a matrix or Grid:

Figure 3.

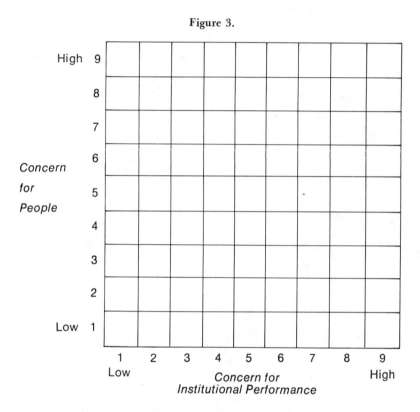

Eighty-one possible combinations of concerns are represented on the Grid. For example, one administrator may conceive of himself or herself (or be ranked by his or her associates) as having very little concern for either institutional performance or for people, and this concern can be represented at the bottom left corner of the Grid by the position 1,1. Another administrator may express the highest possible concern for institutional performance (9) but have very little concern for people (1), and this orientation can be represented at the bottom right corner of the Grid as position 9,1. A third administrator may hold a low concern for institutional performance (1) but a great concern for people (9) and thus rank at the upper left corner in position 1,9. Other administrators may rank at any one of the other seventy-eight points.

We have found, however, that it is most useful to discuss five major administrative styles out of all possible eighty-one; namely, the five that are represented in the extreme four corners—1,1, 9,1, 1,9, and 9,9—and in the very middle—5,5—of the Grid. Thus, we use the five main Grid styles as broadly descriptive of the most distinctive approaches to administration. Of course, when we talk about a "1,1" style of administration or about "Caretaker Administration," as we label this major approach on the Academic Administrator Grid illustrated below,

Figure 4. The Academic Administrator Grid

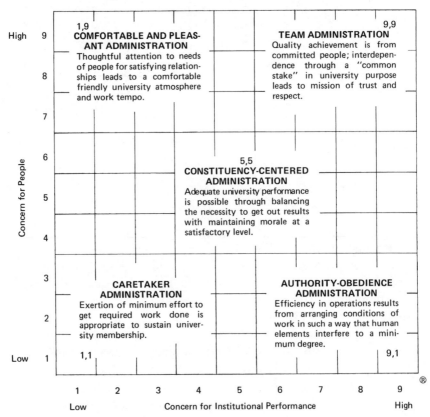

we are aware that 1,1 is only a shade away from 2,1 or 1,2 or 2,2. But all these neighboring combinations point in broadly similar ways to a Caretaker Administration approach. The same is true for ratings close to the 9,1 approach of "Authority-Obedience Administration," to the 1,9 approach of "Comfortable and Pleasant Administration," to the 9,9 approach of "Team Administration," or, in the very center of the Grid, to the 5,5 approach of "Constituency-Centered Administration."

The Academic Administrator Grid briefly describes the orientation or attitude typical of administrators who employ these different approaches, and the paragraphs that follow describe each of the approaches in greater detail. As may be evident, we believe that the behavioral patterns represented in Chapter One by Paragraph A are often typical of 1,1 or Caretaker Administration. Those of Paragraph D are often associated with 9,1 or Authority-Obedience Administration. Those of Paragraph B express 1,9 or Comfortable and Pleasant Administration. Those of Paragraph C represent 5,5 or Constituency-Centered Administration, and those of Paragraph E typify 9,9 or Team Administration.

Five Major Grid Styles

1,1: Caretaker Administration. Little concern for institutional performance is the defining characteristic of a 1,1-oriented administrator, and low involvement in exercising power and authority is typical of this administrative style. Such an administrator desires little, strives for little, gives little, gets little, and cares little, one way or the other. The concern or involvement of the administrator's associates or subordinates is also likely to be low because of the lack of leadership. The exception is the eager subordinate who either misinterprets the administrator's indifference and accepts it as delegation, or, seeing it as indifference, seizes the "delegation" anyway—a tactic particularly characteristic of 9,1-oriented subordinates.

9,1: Authority-Obedience Administration. The lower right corner of the Grid, represented by 9,1, is where a high concern for institutional performance comes together with a low concern for the people with whom one is dealing. An administrator acting under these assumptions concentrates on getting results by exercising power and authority in a unilateral way and by extracting obedience from those with whom he or she deals. A person with a 9,1 orientation thus is deeply involved and committed to institutional mission and drives himself or herself and others in the interest of results. But this kind of administrator views subordinates as little more than agents whose job it is to carry out the dictates of his or her will. The effect of the administrator's 9,1 orientation on the involvement of subordinates is likely to be adverse. Because they are likely to see the administrator's behavior as thoughtless and arbitrary and to look upon themselves as being "used," they may employ foot dragging and other work hindrances, if not out-and-out antiorganization tactics, as a means of discharging their resentments.

1,9: Comfortable and Pleasant Administration. This orientation occurs where concern for institutional performance is low and concern for people is all-important. The administrator working according to these assumptions believes that when people are happy, results will take care of themselves and that there will be little or no need for supervision. The 1,9-oriented administrator sees "togetherness" as a way of getting approval and wants subordinates to feel themselves to be part of one big happy family. Such an administrator goes all out to see that subordinates are satisfied with working conditions in order to avoid being rejected by them. Low concern for production and high concern for acceptance help generate subordinate identification with the work group and enjoyment of its social activities, both on the job and beyond. Administrative focus is on the human dimension, with performance deemphasized. This situation is found when high concern for morale is coupled with low concern for productivity.

5,5: Constituency-Centered Administration. The 5,5 orientation occurs where a moderate concern for institutional performance is coupled with a moderate concern for people. The 5,5-oriented administrator maintains a balance between results and people, so that neither concern dominates the other, and goes along with the majority, hoping to avoid being seen as unreasonable in the exercise of power and authority. The 5,5-oriented administrator attempts to gain acceptable results by doing whatever is expected by his or her superiors, while simultaneously avoiding actions that might upset the applecart and lead to criticism. He or she tries to be a constituency builder, and this attempt may reflect a personal need to be popular and "in." This kind of administrator is unlikely to be deeply committed to institutional performance and thus run the risk of being censured. To avoid embarrassing the administrator, subordinates are expected to put forth appropriate effort and to conform.

9,9: Team Administration. A 9,9 orientation involves an integration of concerns: a high concern for institutional performance combined with a high concern for people. This integration is carried out in ways that encourage subordinates to achieve the highest possible performance in terms of quality, quantity, and personal satisfaction. The consequences of 9,9-oriented administration are that subordinates also develop a personal commitment to organizational achievement. Involvement is generated in people who are able to mesh their individual efforts for the accomplishment of meaningful goals that are both sound and creative.

Dominant and Backup Grid Styles

Does an administrator have just one Grid strategy or does he or she skip over the Grid, shifting and adapting according to how the situation is seen?

All but a very few administrators have styles that are characteristic or typical of them. This is their dominant style. Each administrator's basic approach resembles one that is founded on either 1,1; 9,1; 1,9; 5,5; or 9,9 assumptions. But how can the idea that a person has a dominant Grid style be squared with the fact that administrators do shift and change from their tried and true methods? A way to answer the question is this: not only does an administrator have a dominant style but he or she often has a backup strategy and sometimes even a third strategy to utilize. A backup strategy is used when a dominant strategy fails or when an administrator is feeling the strain of tension, frustration, or conflict. This can happen when initial efforts meet resistance; for example, an administrator's zeal may stimulate stubborn reluctance in those with whom he or she is dealing.

Any Grid style can back up any other. For example, a 1,9-oriented administrator, when sharply challenged, might turn sulky and go into a 9,1 orientation. Again, an administrator who normally acts in a 9,9 manner may meet continued opposition. Unable to find a way of getting on, he or she may shift to a 5,5 approach, negotiating some kind of compromise in which both sides are partially satisfied. There are few "natural" links between one particular Grid style and another in terms of dominant-to-backup. It all depends on the individual and the situation. Sometimes a person who habitually comes on in a 9,1-oriented way will, after first pressing hard, then break off, crestfallen. He or she has switched to a different set of assumptions and moved back to a 1,1 state of resignation, reacting to events with a sense of powerlessness.

In addition, while pure Grid styles share the common, basic attribute of authenticity, some managerial behavior is dishonest. It can be described as a *facade*. Whether conscious or not, a managerial facade is a cover for deception, intrigue, trickery, or a way to avoid showing to others one's true assumptions and motives. There are facades which project each of the major Grid approaches and appear as a pure Grid style, but the motivation that underlies the behavior is inconsistent with this style, as when a 9,1-oriented administrator masks his or her real motivation of control, mastery, and domination by projecting the facade of a 9,9-oriented desire to contribute. Because facades are so common, it is important to evaluate constantly whether underlying motivations are congruent with observed behavior.

Assumptions Behind Different Grid Styles

These different orientations or approaches to administration are determined largely by the often unspoken assumptions and motivations that administrators use in dealing with other people. Assumptions are what we take for granted as being true or reliable. Administrators approaching a situation are usually not acting according to the objective reality of the situation but according to their subjective appraisal of it, including their assumptions about such situations. The objective reality and the subjective appraisal may be quite close together or far apart in that the assumptions one acts on may or may not be based on what has been repeatedly and objectively demonstrated to be sound. Either way, however, the assumptions have become part of the person's beliefs or attitudes.

Each of us tends to respond to circumstances in the light of assumptions, since these assumptions control our view of experience. They constitute our personal theory of behavior and thus guide our behavior. Our premise is that acting on assumption A will result in consequence B. For example, a university administrator concludes that in order to get compliance with a new policy, it will be necessary to specify in detail how the policy is to be executed. The unstated or unexamined assumption behind this conclusion may be that people are indifferent and make the minimum effort to get by. Therefore, in order to achieve compliance, the administrator develops and distributes a manual of procedure. Reports are required to demonstrate compliance. When reports are submitted with indications of mistakes, the administrator tightens up and issues a manual of procedures to cover procedures.

There are many examples of the ways that assumptions control behavior in different cultures. Assumptions about illness lead to treatment by magic in one culture and to cure through scientific medicine in another. Some cultures operate on the assumption that communism is the one best way to organize the activities of an entire people. The belief of others is that constitutional democracy or limited monarchy is the one best way. Other examples of assumptions about relationships apply to marriage. The general practice in the Western world is that monogamy is the ideal way to organize marriage and family life, but other societies favor polygamy. The assumptions held in one culture may be shared by all its members but appear foreign and unreasonable to outsiders. The point is that assumptions organize relationships and ways of conducting affairs. When those assumptions are shared by members of a culture, they may be subject to "culture blindness"—an inability to realistically see the forces that influence behavior.

If an assumption we make is also being made by those around us, for all practical purposes it becomes an article of faith, taking on the status of an "absolute." It becomes the basis for action and is not to be questioned. Other possible assumptions are either ignored or are tested for validity against the "absolute"; in this way the absolute eliminates courses of action that are inconsistent with it.

We learned many of our assumptions for getting results with and through others as we grew up. "I have to be a tough character [or a nice person or a strict disciplinarian] to get what I want" is the kind of assumption that may persist into adult life. Administrators act on the assumptions they hold, even though it is rare for any given administrator to put them into words. The same set of assumptions usually underlies a whole range of attitudes and activities. For example, a 1,9-oriented administrator who wants to please those with whom he or she deals may be quite inventive in finding all sorts of ways to show personal warmth. Keeping those with whom he or she deals happy and closely related dominates his or her concern. This kind of administrator's core assumptions are remarkably consistent—to avoid unpleasantness and to win appreciation.

Assumptions are a necessary part of administration. Were a person to act without assumptions, behavior would be random, purposeless; it would make no sense in any predictable way. Even so, it is not enough just to *have* a set of assumptions. Faulty assumptions can ruin an administrator, while sound assumptions can enhance work and enrich life on the job as well as elsewhere. When individuals understand their own Grid assumptions, this knowledge can aid them in predicting the impact of their behavior on those with whom they deal. Thus, learning the Grid framework helps an administrator to understand what kinds of actions are likely to lead to what kinds of results.

It is important to understand one's assumptions regarding institutional performance and other people not only because such assumptions have the character of self-fulfilling prophecies but also because they operate silently and their central role in controlling administrative practice is likely to be unseen. The administrator may become a victim of his or her own web of assumptions and be unable to untangle the pattern and see the situation from a more objective perspective. Aiding those who manage a university to become more aware of their assumptions and how these control their problem solving and decision making, as well as how different assumptions can lead to sounder action, is the key to increasing administrative effectiveness. A first step is to become aware of the assumptions one holds and acts upon in working with and through people.

Sometimes, of course, we do become aware of the assumptions that are controlling our behavior. Far more often, however, the assumptions that underlie our conduct remain outside our awareness. As a result we are sometimes as blind about why we do things as others are baffled in trying to explain our actions from their vantage point. Without new experiences that challenge our assumptions, we could not identify these assumptions even if we wanted to. With new experiences and with feedback from others as to what assumptions they see behind our actions, change becomes possible. When we become aware of the depth and character of our assumptions, we can analyze them and identify the good and bad consequences of actions based on them. We can consider alternative assumptions that may provide a sounder basis for our actions and practice applying them as we work with other people until they become characteristic of us.

What criteria can administrators use to test the assumptions on which they act? There are several possibilities. One is testing their own assumptions against those of colleagues. The limitation in this approach is that, because administrators in the same organization are likely to think somewhat alike, each may be confirming the soundness of the others' assumptions. Under these conditions all can agree and all can be wrong, because consensual validation is not necessarily the criterion of soundness. A second possibility is to test one's assumptions against results. The limitation in this is to be found in the self-fulfilling

prophecy mentioned above. Another possibility is to copy the behavior of a model, but one may then come to embrace assumptions of the model without being aware that one is doing so. Because a person reveres and likes another, the identification with the model is likely to be based on subjective feelings that may or may not lead a person to embrace sound assumptions. A fourth possibility is to derive one's assumptions from an ideology such as the Protestant ethic, communism, or oriental mysticism or from philosophical tracts, such as those of Rousseau and Locke.

An alternative to deriving assumptions from one closed system or another, however, is the open system model based on experimental methods as applied in the behavioral sciences. Behavioral science research has described the principles of sound behavior as well as the consequences of deviating from them. The Grid is a framework for bringing into coherent form both the various behavioral science theories one might utilize and the predictable consequences of administrative action. The Grid permits individuals to test their assumptions against the various alternatives and determine whether and how their own actions vary from what is considered sound practice according to valid research.

Personal Motivations Affecting Grid Styles

Before showing how the Grid can be applied to actual episodes of administrative conduct and can be used by administrators in examining their own assumptions as they conduct the affairs of a college or university, we must consider the role of personal motivation in academic leadership. A significant dimension of how we think and feel about institutional performance and about people involves the question "How are we motivated in life and work?" Since personal motivations have never been well understood or sorted out, administrators have found it difficult to know what motivations are best for getting people actively involved in quality institutional performance. As we all know from everyday life, people are motivated in different ways. When our motivations and those of our associates square with sound principles of behavior, we can expect to work with and through others in ways that solve problems, create positive involvement, build morale, and make us healthier in mental and physical terms.

The Grid framework provides a basis for understanding personal motivations. With it, we can answer the question "What are the personal motivations of an administrator who leads according to each Grid style?" As Figure 5 illustrates, this

Figure 5. Personal Motivations Influencing Grid Styles

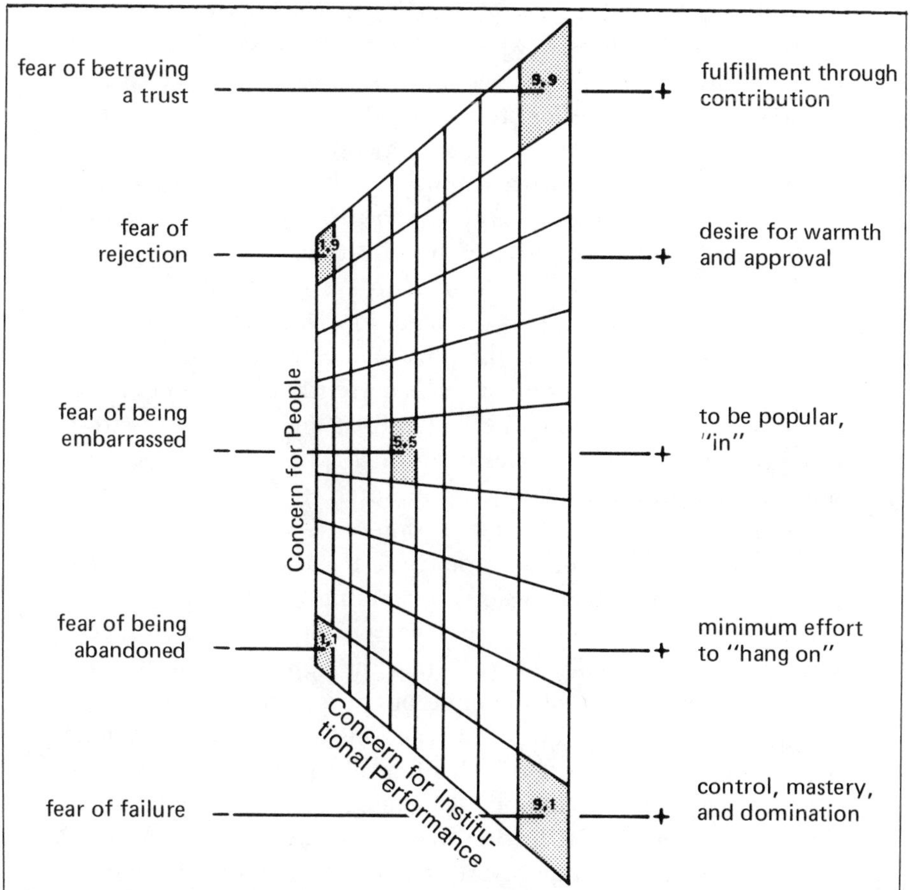

fear of betraying a trust −	+ fulfillment through contribution
fear of rejection −	desire for warmth and approval +
fear of being embarrassed −	to be popular, "in" +
fear of being abandoned −	minimum effort to "hang on" +
fear of failure −	control, mastery, and domination +

Concern for People

Concern for Institutional Performance

9,9 1,9 5,5 1,1 9,1

motivational dimension intersects the Grid at a right angle to it. And rather than running from a low of 1 to a high of 9, as do the scales of Concern for Institutional Performance and Concern for People, this dimension has two ends that are the opposite of one another: positive and negative. The midpoint of this scale, which is the neutral position, is centered on the Grid. The negative end is on the left side and the positive end on the right side of the page. Thus this scale moves from a negative pole through a neutral zone to a positive pole and shows that motivations are "bipolar."

The positive or plus (+) end tells what activities in life "pull" a person, that is, what he or she strives to reach. The negative or minus (−) end is what he or she seeks to avoid. These scales do not reflect traits an individual possesses. Rather they are scales that register how people perceive pertinent events in the environment, calibrate them, evaluate them for their personal significance, and respond to them. There are five of these scales. One relates to each Grid style.

1,1: Minimum Effort Needed to "Hang on" Versus Fear of Being Abandoned. The dominant motivations of a 1,1-oriented administrator are, at the plus or positive (+) side, to continue whatever activities he or she is currently engaged in but to do so by applying minimum effort and, at the minus or negative (−) pole, to avoid activities that might reveal that the 1,1-oriented person has become so uninterested that he or she would be asked to leave the institution.

An administrator adopting a $1,1^+$ orientation increases the likelihood of "hanging on" by taking on the correct outward behavior trappings, applauding on cue but without personal feeling for the action to which the applause is given. The expected response is forthcoming but it is without conviction. By giving the socially approved reactions on signal, a person at $1,1^+$ avoids drawing attention to himself or herself and in this way increases the likelihood of hanging on, even though emotions of positive identification may long since have been withdrawn. This kind of administrator may be prepared to take on trivial tasks in order to make his or her presence necessary.

A person anchored toward the $1,1^-$ end is likely to let

things slide, unaware of the extent to which a sense of hopeless-ness and helplessness has blinded him or her to the realities of administration. Only under sharp and jolting recognition of how far out he or she has gone is this kind of administrator likely to take efforts to avoid being replaced.

9,1: Need for Control, Mastery, and Domination Versus Fear of Failure. What a 9,1-oriented administrator strives posi-tively for is control, mastery, and domination—seeking to come out on top, using people as tools in the pursuit of results. The minus end is fear of failure; for this kind of administrator, de-feat in getting what he or she goes after is tantamount to accepting weakness and personal inadequacy. Activities in be-tween, around zero (0), are not important for proving oneself one way or the other.

An administrator who leads at the extreme of $9,1^+$ and for whom $9,1^-$ is an underdeveloped motivation is likely to take risks and to be ready to go for "broke," gambling all in pursuit of domination, mastery, and control. To gamble and to lose may be a demonstration of failure to others, but for the administrator who leads in a $9,1^+$ orientation, failure only spurs a more total, all-out effort: "if at first you try and don't suc-ceed, try, try again" is the motto here.

The opposite is characteristic for a person who is an-chored at the extreme of $9,1^-$. For this person, to fail is tanta-mount to self-destruction. Risk, in the sense of gambling or tak-ing a chance on an outcome, is far too threatening. The person in a $9,1^-$ mode prefers to avoid failure and in this way to "prove" strength. Thus, we see two administrators who appear different, yet both administer according to 9,1 assumptions. At $9,1^+$ we see administrators who are daring and unconventional, and at $9,1^-$ we see administrators who are cautious and conser-vative. Both give close supervision because both distrust others. The $9,1^+$-oriented person is prepared to gamble, but he or she alone calls the shots and expects compliance. The $9,1^-$-oriented person is unprepared to gamble and wants to ensure that no one beneath rolls the dice either.

1,9: Need for Warmth and Approval Versus Fear of Re-jection. For the 1,9-oriented administrator, the dominant plus motivation is to gain the warmth and approval of others. This is the consuming interest. The fear of suffering rejection is the dominant minus motivation. Rejection demonstrates to 1,9-oriented administrators that they are unworthy. Thus the same "objective" event may create different perceptions and produce different responses depending on one's dominant motivation. Giving a gift may stem from the positive motivation of gaining warmth and approval. The person to whom the gift is given expresses pleasure, appreciation, gratitude, or thanks, and the giver perceives himself or herself as being loved and approved of, that is, of achieving $1,9^+$. In contrast, the same gift might stem from the negative motivation of avoiding rejection. As a second example, a $1,9^+$-oriented administrator may be late for an appointment because he or she is trapped by a phone call important for self-approval. Under similar circumstances, the $1,9^-$, or negatively motivated, administrator may anticipate and calibrate the reactions of rejection yet cuts the call short and is at the same time unable to ask the caller to call back. The late appointment that results provokes the anticipated feelings of rejection and being misunderstood. No matter which way this administrator turns, rejection is the consequence.

The motivational axis of $1,9^+$ and $1,9^-$ brings out distinguishing features among academic administrators who have the same basic orientation. The administrator whose orientation is $1,9^+$ actively pursues love, affection, and approval. When the wanted response is not forthcoming, this person feels compelled to be even more charming and ingratiating and to do whatever is essential for increasing the likelihood of gaining support from others. The administrator whose orientation is $1,9^-$ meets the first evidence of rejection as proof of unworthiness. This leads to greater and greater efforts to reduce further rejection by avoiding repetition of whatever is thought to have caused the initial rejection. A person in a $1,9^-$ orientation is likely to be immobilized or to move backward in order to "stop" whatever has produced rejection.

5,5: Need for Popularity Versus Fear of Being Embarrassed. For a 5,5-oriented administrator, the plus pole involves doing whatever is necessary to be socially accepted and popular

—an "in-group" person. Satisfaction is derived from status and prestige rewards that originate within the system. Being in good standing with one's colleagues and feeling secure, confident, and even elated at one's own prestige result in a sense of well-being. A $5,5^+$ orientation lets a person develop the social attributes of a "hail fellow, well met." Such a person does whatever others suggest or request in support of good membership; he or she may even initiate activities that are appealing to others in order to elicit a "what a great guy" or "what a great gal" reaction.

The minus pole of the 5,5 orientation entails fear of embarrassment and feelings of anxiety regarding the possibility of criticism and censure or of jeopardizing membership. Social demotion is what a person with this orientation most dreads. He or she tries to avoid any statement or action that could result in ridicule or becoming the butt of others' jokes—anything, in other words, that might push him or her beyond the margin of membership. The person with a $5,5^-$ orientation avoids taking a separate stand or cracking a joke, the point of which might not be evident, or drawing subtle inferences that might be seen as wrong. The administrator with a $5,5^-$ orientation who has no membership identity feels totally at sea.

9,9: Fulfillment Through Contribution Versus Fear of Betraying a Trust. The plus pole of a 9,9 orientation involves contributing to important life goals and outcomes with and through others. The minus pole (−) relates to fear of betraying a trust, including failing to exercise responsibility, to deliver on commitments, or to think through the implications of an action.

Fulfillment through contribution can be considered from two perspectives. One involves what the individual is able to contribute to a given situation. The other involves enabling others to contribute their resources toward being effective in the fullest possible way. When an administrator acts according to a sense of purpose and in a spontaneous, self-generating, and self-directing way, organizational goals and the individual's commitment to contributing are integrated.

A person who manages in a $9,9^+$ orientation is characterized by a "can do" spirit of confidence, ready to design experiments to find best solutions, and such a person is therefore seen as creative and capable of innovation. This person is likely to regard his or her contributions in an objective way and to take no undeserved credit, as well as to make real efforts to share credit for achievement with others whose participation and contributions made it possible. A $9,9^+$ orientation, in other words, is likely to result in an administrator's being seen as exceptional. He or she may achieve this less through native intelligence than skill in learning to be effective in working with and through others.

An administrator who supervises in a $9,9^-$ orientation tries to avoid betraying the trust of others. A person with a $9,9^-$ orientation sees ideal actions to take but is likely to do so in the interest of being sure that whatever is done is "perfect." He or she feels that it would be letting others down not to give one's fullest effort and therefore is likely to continuously defer action.

Conclusion

These positive and negative motivations, applied to the major approaches to administration identified by the Grid, constitute the "striving to reach" and "seeking to avoid" that characterize administrative behavior in modern society. When they are put together on the three-dimensional Grid (Figure 5), we can see the variety and complexity of administrative assumptions and motivations in a way that allows us to understand and study them as they apply to each of us as individuals, to our administrative associates and those whom we supervise, and to our institutions.

Thus the Grid can be used by administrators in analyzing the assumptions they operate under and their motivations in conducting institutional affairs. With it, they can identify their own Grid styles and see how these translate into specific administrative behavior. They can refer to it in checking their assumptions as decisions are being made. They can ask themselves, "Are the assumptions I am applying in this situation the best for fulfilling the university's mission, or is there a stronger and more effective way to proceed?" And where everyone who shoulders administrative responsibilities knows the Grid, it can be used to change the character of the leadership of an entire college or university.

In Chapters Four through Nine we analyze each of the five major Grid styles, along with their various combinations, and apply them to actual episodes of administrative conduct as seen in common activities of college and university administration. First, however, we need to examine these common activities of academic administration.

Chapter Three

Responsibilities of Academic Leaders

The single greatest hope for coming to grips with the endless variety of problems confronting modern society, while also adding to the enrichment of living, is education. In the final analysis it is through an educated citizenry that true leadership can be exercised in solving society's problems and bringing about new developments. Educational institutions, especially colleges and universities, are potentially the primary agents of change in an unfolding world. When academic institutions measure themselves against standards of excellence, they can fulfill their primary change role most effectively. The reason for the central importance of colleges and universities is that governments, corporations, service organizations, and individuals can apply only what is already known. Universities contribute to society by creating a knowledge base. Apart from this practical side, learning has intrinsic value, involving as it does the pursuit of knowledge and beauty.

To attain excellence a college or university must develop an organizational model for itself. A university cannot be led or managed like a business, a hospital, a service agency, a political party, or a family. Universities cannot follow the organizational models of other institutions because universities have a very different role to play. In a broad sense, such an organizational model for universities would be one that brought forth the administrative practices essential for spurring the creativity, commitment, and convictions essential for the pursuit of excellence.

No agreed-upon model exists at the present time, and the result is that various observers of the university scene contradict one another in their picturing of it. Some see it as a political organization, others as a bureaucracy, others as a quasi-informal gathering of colleagues, and still others as an input-throughput-output system. It also has been pictured as an institution that seeks to maintain a quasi-stationary equilibrium with its environment and to be a mirror of the society that surrounds it. Each of these views in some measure portrays the way that different colleges and universities operate today, but none provides us with an ideal model of how a college or university should operate.

What is needed in order to develop a model of excellence is the use of the behavioral sciences as illustrated here by the Grid theory for diagnosing and describing how universities actually function in the modern world and how they would operate if they were meeting criteria of excellence. The application of the ideas about administrative assumptions and motivation expressed in Chapter Two to academic administration provides a practical model for the pursuit of academic excellence. For this model to be useful, however, we need to identify the major activities in which academic administrators engage as they conduct the affairs of a university. What, in fact, are their major activities? What is the administrator expected to do? How does the administrator in the modern university allocate his or her time? What is he or she trying to accomplish?

One way of describing these activities would be to break them into the five functions of planning, organizing, directing, controlling, and staffing that administrators in higher education perform. But these administrative functions are not unique to higher education. For academic administrators, it would be more helpful to identify their primary responsibilities and apply the Grid theory to each of them. The ten activities listed below represent a job description for academic administration, and the major leadership styles discussed in the chapters that follow are depicted by showing how academic administrators interact with one another in the process of dealing with these ten major tasks.

In one way or another, academic administrators are responsible for:

1. Establishing and implementing an implicit or explicit mission and administering the activities that result;
2. Supporting the teaching and learning process;
3. Establishing and supporting the curriculum;
4. Creating a climate for high-quality research;
5. Encouraging service to the university and community and beyond;
6. Acquiring and distributing financial resources through budgetary management;
7. Managing the academic personnel function;
8. Coordinating student affairs;
9. Managing external relations in order to secure and maintain the allegiance of various outside groups; and
10. Maintaining the physical plant and basic operations to provide necessary support services.

These activities are dealt with in one way or another by academic administrators. The key to understanding how an administrator actually is performing, however, is hidden in the words "one way or another." How "one way or another" is executed is basic in determining whether a college or university is excellent, good, mediocre, or poor in achieving its mission.

Implementing Institutional Mission

The mission of a college or a university needs to be examined in two quite different ways. One is related to the stated formulation of academic mission, as set by the board of overseers, regents, or trustees. The other is the actual day-to-day exercise of leadership that brings the stated mission into existence through thousands of decisions, every one of which is an interpretation by an administrator of his or her understanding—or lack of it—of the stated mission. The mission and the administrator's understanding of it can be closely congruent or widely divergent.

For the great majority of colleges and universities the mission is stated in general terms that often express lofty ideals, such as to be a "university of the first class," or "a strong liberal arts college," or "a college that serves the educational needs of the area or region." These broad statements of mission describe the general character of the institution, and for this reason they are important. But the interpretation of mission by presidents, vice-presidents, deans, chairs, faculty members, and students is what gives a college or university its actual direction. Administrators are particularly important in establishing direction because it is they who must interpret the mission and in their actions demonstrate how it is to be carried out.

Supporting Teaching and Learning

Instruction is the mainstay of any college or university. Students come to a campus to be educated, and instruction is the primary means of contributing to students' learning goals. Formal instruction may or may not be supplemented by homework, library research, tutoring, or other secondary aids, but the process of instruction remains at the very heart of the matter.

In the typical college the show goes on at eight o'clock on Monday morning in early September. Teachers must be available to teach given subjects. Students must be counseled about careers in their majors if they are to make informed choices. By mid August most administrators have returned from vacation and are back on duty. The registration and class assignment process has ended, and the implementation of the schedule is on track. After classes begin, the administrator sits back to await the usual brushfires: "Professor Jones didn't tell us how he was going to grade us in his class." "Dr. Brown couldn't find a parking place and missed the first session; do you have his course outline?" "I should have been registered for English 402 but my adviser registered me for 404, which is full of English majors." "I'm a computer science major and I work afternoons. That is the only time the computer lab is open to underclassmen. Can I use a terminal at some other time? Professor Smith said I should talk to you."

Although planning can alleviate some of these problems, it never eliminates all of them, and the administrator deals with various matters related to the teaching process in one way or another throughout the year. Some of these brushfires can involve feelings and emotions: "Mike Smith and five other seniors from Dr. Rowe's class want to switch to Dr. Monroe's class. They say Dr. Monroe is a much better teacher. But Dr. Monroe's class is bursting at the seams, and Dr. Rowe will not have an adequate class size to continue if these six students are permitted to switch. They are insisting on their rights. They say they cannot endure another class with Dr. Rowe. What should I tell them?" The administrator is expected to take some action and decide whether to permit a transfer or not; to speak to Dr. Brown about missing the first class or not; to permit a different schedule in the computer lab or not.

The quality of teaching in the classroom also is of significance. One faculty member in the course of his or her career is likely to come into classroom contact with thousands of students and may be responsible for millions of research dollars. A faculty member may not remember all the students' names, but most students definitely remember the faculty member's name, his or her appearance, political views, whether he or she smoked, was absent a lot, or spoke in complete sentences. All these observations come back to haunt the faculty member when the teaching evaluation forms are completed at the end of the semester. Furthermore, these evaluations haunt the administrator who chose that faculty member and promised him or her lab space and equipment, a summer teaching assignment, freedom to pursue research interests, and a salary higher than that of his or her colleagues if the faculty member would accept one of the few positions open at the administrator's university.

These kinds of decisions are included in the daily activities of academic administrators. Does the administrator have time to contemplate the important teaching and learning issues, such as encouraging faculty to utilize new teaching methods, does he prefer these kinds of problems, or does he or she deal with neither administrative nor academic issues? How much do students *really* learn in that freshman English course from the first of the semester to the last day? Are there differences in learning as a result of different teaching methods? What can be done to improve the learning atmosphere for minority students? Should admissions policies be reconsidered now that Scholastic Aptitude Test (SAT) scores are shifting? How can we tell if students are really learning to *think* as opposed to just regurgitating facts? Who should be given a merit increase for good teaching: Dr. Smith, who seems to force students to learn biology against their will, or Dr. Lightfoot, whose popular biology classes are replete with media presentations and classical music in the background? These weighty issues may or may not be dealt with in the face of the daily pressures for minor fine tuning of the educational mechanism.

Establishing the Curriculum

The curriculum is what is "taught," but since the arts and sciences and all applied areas have vastly expanded in the past few years, there are many topics, subjects, and skill areas beyond the limits of any one academic division or department to cover. It is for this reason that decisions regarding the curriculum are so central, for not only do they determine the subject areas to which students will or will not be exposed, but they also determine whether or not faculty members will be able to instruct in their preferred areas. In addition, because at this time many disciplines have a pure and an applied aspect, there are numerous curriculum decisions regarding how the content should be organized, what material should be required or optional, and so on.

Matching people to a curriculum plan can be a frustrating effort, but letting a curriculum evolve according to the natural preferences of faculty can lead to duplication, territorial disputes, gaps, and even criticism from accreditation bodies, as well as from students and other campus constituencies that feel they are not being served. The administrator has two main choices: lead a tedious curriculum-planning process with the associated inevitable revisions, or let individual faculty choices govern course offerings, thereby rubber-stamping a menu of courses with no requirements, prerequisites, continuity, integration, or sequence. The administrator makes his or her curriculum philosophy known through daily decisions if not in formal debates or active planning efforts. Faculty, students, and others quickly learn where the weaknesses are, whatever approach the administrator chooses, and continually advocate change.

Then there is the problem of the curriculum on paper versus the curriculum as presented. Course objectives can be interpreted very differently by any two faculty members, and each can argue for a different version of the "way it should be." The right to curriculum management can be the strongest of power bases on a campus. A faculty member selected to head a major curriculum area can argue persuasively that a given person should not be hired, that a summer course should be taught by person X, that students should be required to take course A and not B.

Territorial fights usually revolve around curriculum decisions, yet the uninitiated are unlikely to realize the gamesmanship involved. The administrator unconcerned with curriculum will never have a real feel for university administration and will never know whether curriculum decisions are leading the school forward, backward, or sideways or leaving it stagnant. Beyond the departmental level, whole careers and units can be at stake. The simple question "Should we require two years of a foreign language?" raised at a faculty senate meeting can cause a storm throughout the campus. Each department's livelihood rests on intrauniversity marketing. "Can we corner the freshman market by installing a prerequisite course in the business degree program? We can assure three faculty members full-time teaching loads if we can get the curriculum committee to accept that course." On the surface the argument involves high-sounding ideological and value-laden imperatives, but a power struggle is going on beneath the surface.

To employ a faculty member is to hire years of study about some knowledge area. Few faculty are so adaptable that they can adjust to new teaching assignments at the last minute, especially when the assignment is not in the area of their original training. There is room for some adaptation, but generally when a faculty member is hired, a curriculum is also hired. "Now that Professor Gray has retired, should we continue to teach the history of psychology, or should we add a new faculty member who can work more closely with the speech and hearing center?" But when a financial pinch comes, it must be dealt with in one way or another. The most adaptable and cooperative faculty member may be asked to make the sacrifice. "We've got to cover the research methods course, and you know that no one else around here would be able to step into that slot. Do it just this year and next year we'll recruit strenuously for someone to pick up that area." This is the kind of bargaining that colors the curriculum-building process.

Supporting Research and Scholarly Productivity

The pursuit of knowledge, which is one of the most important facets of the professorial job description, is only feasible when the individual faculty member has developed those skills essential for formulating problems, developing research designs, and gathering and interpreting data, as well as the skills needed for reporting and interpreting findings in the broader context of the knowledge area in which the research is embedded. Many areas involving the pursuit of knowledge do not lend themselves to scientific inquiry, but contributions that advance these areas and disciplines are no less important than scientific findings. Works of art and music, literary contributions, architectural designs, treatments of history, philosophical formulations, and so on cannot be judged by the same standards as scientific discoveries. But in each case these contributions come about from an attitude of inquiry, and criteria, even though subjective, are available for evaluation of merit in all of them.

Not all of higher education places equal emphasis on the research function. Some major universities incorporate research as a central component of their fundamental mission. Others see it as secondary and define the primary and most important mission as teaching in the liberal arts tradition, while still others regard themselves as service institutions and concentrate on technological and vocational skills. However, new knowledge must be developed somewhere. Luckily the products of this new knowledge are usually readily accepted, and it is the process of research, not its products, that is generally misunderstood. The public is quite happy to hear about a cure for cancer, a new energy source, a major archeological find, an important interpretative analysis of a war, or a better method for teaching math to elementary school students.

Often, however, an avenue of research interest does not bear fruit for twenty or thirty years, and some research directions may bear no fruit at all. It is difficult for the average citizen to see the connection between basic research and final outcomes. Senator Proxmire's Golden Fleece Award has done nothing to encourage public understanding or trust. How can an uninformed citizen tolerate the study of the love life of a bug when it is not explained that such studies may be related to control of pests that destroy crops? The public is even less sure of the value of the social sciences; at least the hard sciences have a reasonable track record.

The academic administrator deals in one way or another with the issue of creative research, and decisions related to research dictate the direction that an institution will take in the advancement of knowledge. The administrator either supports or fails to support the research efforts of the faculty. Such administrative actions have an impact on resources, from something as small as the hiring of a ten-hour research assistant to something as large as the installation of a major observatory on a mountain. They influence attendance at professional research meetings, the degree to which research findings are shared with colleagues, and whether or not a faculty member will have leave for a year to study a special technique, to obtain subjects for study, or to make trips to field sites to collect data. Computers may or may not be available to analyze the data collected.

Faculty members need time to write for journals to acquaint the scientific community with their findings, and such time may or may not be made available. In the arts, performances and exhibits must be organized if they are to be given at all. Auditoriums and buildings with special lighting and acoustics must be designed and constructed. How administrators deal with these issues will influence the college's future contribution to an evolving society in important ways.

Encouraging Community and Institutional Service

Service is one of those activities expected of members of a college or university. It includes all those activities outside of research and teaching that a university faculty member is expected to engage in from time to time. These activities include serving as liaison persons on committees related to the college or university and representing the university in activities external to it. Sometimes this might mean testifying to legislative bodies on behalf of the university, serving on federal commissions, accepting the editorship of a journal, or serving as an elected officer in an association.

Externally, faculty service involves consulting with corporations, governmental agencies, and other organizations about special problems, teaching through continuing education programs, speaking to various groups on specialized subjects, serving on boards and commissions, and conducting the affairs of professional associations. It also often involves applied research. Administrators evaluate the costs and benefits of such service in terms of the faculty member's time commitments, and in some cases recommend or withhold recommendation of faculty for choice consultative assignments that can benefit or harm the college or university.

Inside the university, faculty members may serve on campus-wide committees and perform special administrative tasks within their areas of expertise. The university administrator may or may not organize groups and committees to accomplish a special mission or to develop proposals for submission to the upper administration. University committees may or may not be formed to represent the wide variety of university interests (student, faculty, staff, administration) and in line with special needs for expertise (for example, an engineer on the energy conservation committee or a lawyer on the affirmative action committee). Such committee service is usually an extra assignment for an already active faculty member. Should the administrator reward or ignore this service?

The administrator must also provide logistical support for these committees, such as "a clerk typist three hours a week" or a "room to meet in every Thursday at nine o'clock." Some university departments have very large and complicated committee structures to ensure that democracy is practiced in all decision making. Others have very few committees, and decisions are made more unilaterally. The administrator must deal in one way or another with the question of balance between burdensome, time-consuming democracy and unilateral action and accept the predictable consequences in hard feelings and grumbling, whatever balance is struck. Given that the administrator often chooses a committee approach, he or she must live with the product of committee deliberations and then convey accurately any proposals to higher levels, knowing that many features of these proposals will be viewed as impractical or "counter" to the views of the president's executive group, the regents, the board, or some other august body. Thus, the administrator may review the document and then either advocate it or work toward modifying and softening it over the objections of the original committee that produced it. He or she may forward it with comments or table it to die a natural death. But the grumbling will continue: "If you didn't want to know what we thought, why did you ask us?" "I understand that Dean Valentine made a persuasive argument for a similar proposal last year in *his* division and it was approved." "If they can spend all that money on the football team, why can't they consider a new minority student loan program? What are the priorities around here anyway. . . ? ? ?"

Managing Resources

Education is not free, and the resources available seem always to fall short of what is needed. Buildings, computers, teachers, audiovisual equipment, desks, secretaries, telephones, utilities, microscopes, cyclotrons, paper, stamps, azaleas, television studios, blood pressure kits, and books cost money. In even the smallest colleges, the basic facilities and equipment needed in science laboratories alone would boggle the mind of Thomas Jefferson.

To say that no college or university has as much money available for conducting its affairs as it would like to have is a truism, and on many campuses money is becoming the scarcest of resources. Funding decisions today can significantly influence the direction and quality of an institution for years to come. Because there are so many good reasons to spend money, an administrator is often left with the difficult task of reducing or not approving funds for some obviously worthwhile programs. How administrators manage financial resources can significantly impede or promote an institution's pursuit of its actual mission.

The formal system of resource allocation is through the mechanisms of a budget. Many times the budget appears to be a rational, systematic expression of how the college or university is expected to function over a given time period. Beneath the surface, however, the budget is an instrument of human expression that can reflect administrative statesmanship, an administrator's reward and punishment system, his or her efforts to buy popularity, or his or her need to gain as much love and approval as possible; a budget can also cover up for an administrator's loss of will to manage. The budget, in other words, reflects an administrator's assumptions as they relate to his or her personal predilections toward the use of power and authority. It is for this reason that the budget should be viewed not as a mechanical, cut-and-dried process but as a living document that provides a summation of the style of an academic administrator.

Supervising Personnel

The personnel who populate a university are unique. Their uniqueness lies in their academic qualifications. Most hold advanced degrees, and many have completed postdoctoral work. These facts create problems of personnel management that universities share with very few other institutions beyond an occasional research and development laboratory. Even in this comparison, however, a distinction is important. Only at the college and university level is it expected of employees that they probe the frontiers of knowledge. They need not concentrate on issues that have relevance to application and are free to be impractical.

Individuals capable of advancing knowledge are clearly of unusual calibre. Their presence on the campus creates one of the most difficult aspects of academic administration. In employment decisions, for example, how is an academic administrator to assess an individual's qualifications to make unique contributions in the years ahead? When it comes to promotion, how does one calibrate another person's qualifications for tenure in the few short years during which his or her great ideas may be incubating? How does one assess a professor's teaching qualifications before that professor has begun to teach and particularly before students have had a chance to demonstrate the effect that he or she might have had upon them?

Another problem is burnout. Some tenured professors lose their commitment to academic pursuits years before retirement. Once lost, can commitment be reactivated? If so, how does an academic administrator go about doing this? If it is not practical to reinvolve a professor, is the academic administrator discharging his or her responsibility to students and to the future of a university if he or she permits a person to sit in a professorial chair doing nothing? If his employment were to be terminated, another professor might fill it with distinction.

Selection, promotion, counseling, development, and termination decisions with regard to such uniquely qualified personnel as academic professors call for a rare quality of administrative acumen. The tighter the job market, moreover, the longer the administrator has to live with his or her choices and the more competition there is for the really outstanding scholars. Stick around any university for six years and someone will discover that you don't know everything. Stick around another ten years and the students will claim that you have forgotten everything. Thus we can see that this "one way or another" as to how administrators deal with issues of selection, promotion, and tenure is all-important to the matter of excellence.

One should not forget the other personnel on a campus—the staff groups. Many of these are interested in, or have already engaged in, collective bargaining. The turnover rates for these employees are high, and inadequate salaries often prevent the hiring of well-trained personnel. At any rate the administrator has to set wages, classify jobs, deal with training programs, performance evaluations, and grievances against supervisors, and establish personnel and benefits policies. The academic administrator usually has two quite different management systems, one dealing with the faculty and another with the staff personnel, but he or she is responsible for both.

Coordinating Student Affairs

Students are campus citizens. As such, they are expected to be active in developing and regulating the culture of campus life. Some of the rules and requirements that give guidance and direction to student affairs are set by the administration, while other aspects are set and regulated through student government. Here we are concerned with those aspects of student life that are regulated by the academic administration.

A typical campus has a heterogeneous student body. Forty-five-year-old empty-nest mothers are returning to school. There are fifteen-year-old child prodigies. There are students rebelling against strict parents, and there are students who work twenty-five to thirty hours a week off campus and still carry a full load of courses. There is the perennial student who has taken one course a semester for two decades. There is the deaf student who needs special assistance. There is the musically talented student who can't afford a good string instrument. There is the student driving his father's Cadillac to all his freshman classes and skipping classes every chance he gets. (Of course his father is a prominent lawyer who serves as staff assistant on the education committee.) The list of unique students with special problems and talents is as long as the latest student body count.

Besides these there are the students whose admission is pending, or who are on probation, or who have been suspended, or who have dropped out for awhile and will return in a year or two. The administrator deals with all these students in one way or another. Furthermore, he or she is expected to organize essential services to assist students and to create a climate of trust among students, faculty, and administration. During some years the administrator may anticipate student unrest, scorching editorials in the student newspaper, and the impact of off-campus events, for example, the draft, inflation, nuclear power scares, and distracting fads such as "streaking." In addition, administrators are expected to participate in student social life on the campus. A dean is expected to attend graduation ceremonies and at least a few graduate student parties. An administrator is expected to meet with special student groups that want to express their collective concerns. At times, an administrator is expected to communicate really difficult information to a student or a parent: "Your son has been involved in an accident." "You have failed to earn the required grade points and must consider another career choice, perhaps work for awhile." "You must pay for these library books before you register this fall."

In addition, there are many points at which organized student groups have an impact on the university. These cover a range of potentially controversial activities, including student government, the campus newspaper, student organizations, the bringing of speakers onto the campus, and the use of campus facilities for social and other affairs.

On many campuses the dean of students is the person who is expected to interpret mission as it applies to students. But many other administrators are involved in interpreting university policies and procedures, as well as in managing aspects of university life relative to specific student interests.

Managing External Relations

Colleges or universities are conspicuous institutions because of the numerous activities of their administrators, faculty, and students. Academic personnel publish papers that sometimes are controversial. Faculty make presentations to professional bodies and in public forums. They appear on television. They are on the radio. As national and international events

an administrator manages these dimensions under each of the five major leadership styles that were described in Chapter Two. These chapters provide a framework for understanding the ways that different academic administrators go about dealing with these issues. By using them to analyze academic problem solving and decision making, we can discover how to strengthen university administration. When these activities of administration are dealt with in a sound way, the administrator is laying the foundation for excellence; but when they are dealt with in unsound ways, the administrator is reducing the university's prospects of achieving its mission of providing teaching, research, and service in an excellent manner.

After analyzing the different approaches to administration, the reader is likely to conclude that some approaches are better than others. The question then arises as to whether administrators can shift their approaches in a way that will support a model of excellence. The book thus concludes with an analysis of why some administrators resist change and how resistance can be reduced to bring a model of excellence into existence throughout the administrative system of a university.

Chapter Four

Caretaker Administration: 1,1

Though emotionally resigned and indifferent, the 1,1-oriented administrator (represented in the lower left corner of the Academic Administrator Grid of Chapter Two) is motivated to stay in the system. This means doing enough to build seniority but without making an effort to meaningfully contribute in a way that would benefit colleagues, students, or the university as a whole. Expecting little and giving little, the 1,1-oriented administrator is prepared to put up with the situation and to go through the motions of administration routinely and with a hollow commitment to the academic enterprise.

A combination of neutrality and physical presence is the key to preventing one's noncommitment from provoking undue resentment in others. Being visible yet inconspicuous protects one from being controversial, having enemies, or getting shuffled aside. A somewhat preoccupied attitude keeps others at arm's length. The degree to which passivity, non-

46

responsiveness, and uninvolvement is maintained is governed by the acceptable minimum others are prepared to tolerate. By not becoming emotionally entangled with people, this kind of administrator avoids coming to grips with their inadequacies and inabilities. His or her motto is "See no evil, speak no evil, and hear no evil, and you will be protected by not being noticed." It is possible for an institution to persist in ignoring its "deadwood," and silent expectations operate in some universities to guarantee job security after a few years. An administrator is then safe until retirement.

A 1,1-oriented administrator usually rationalizes nonperformance by putting the blame on something or someone else. For example, "The university has become so mammoth that nothing can be done about it." The "onslaught of technology" is blamed for bringing about a "dehumanizing way of life." Fingers are pointed at "the money-crazed" or the "vicious, competitive rat race for research money." These rationalizations serve the purpose of justifying indifference, passivity, and a "can't do" spirit and make it unnecessary for the administrator to admit that he or she is not involved. The chairman or dean says, "Nobody wanted this job and so they put it on me. It's a thankless task and one where it's impossible to get people's cooperation. There's nothing to be done beyond the minimum to keep people together." When left alone, the 1,1-oriented administrator is content to monitor the routine and ignore the rest.

The goal of this administrator is to maintain organizational membership and continuity for his or her own personal advantage. The administrator beats a strategic withdrawal from active participation. On the negative side, the motivation is to "hold on" and to avoid abandonment. To do so, the cast and form of acceptable behavior are maintained. Withdrawal leaves an empty shell. There is a vacuum within, but the exterior trappings that put personal behavior into conformance with that of associates remain as they were. The organization becomes the means for maintaining a socially acceptable role and for discharging the minimum of citizenship requirements. Position, status, and pay come from the organization, but only minimum effort is given in exchange.

Dynamics of the 1,1 Orientation

A dominant 1,1 orientation does not always originate early in life. Its origins may be in the adult years and related to the work situation itself. Consider the individual who does well in grammar school, high school, and in the first years of college. For the next two or three years, however, he becomes an academic vagabond, and people start to say that he will never amount to anything. Understanding a 1,1 orientation, however, we can appreciate that something may have happened in his sophomore year that caused him to pull back and stop trying. For the time being he has retreated from a dominant 9,9, 9,1, 5,5, or 1,9 style into a 1,1 orientation.

After a period he returns to college, picks up where he left off, graduates with flying colors, and enters graduate school also doing well. How can we understand this interruption? There are several possible causes. One is that the vagabond period permitted him to avoid a threat to his private image. Greater maturity provides the understanding and insight that now permit him to proceed with a career without facing the same personal threat. He is now able to grasp quickly what, as a sophomore, had been incomprehensible. His sense of personal adequacy may have increased so that now requirements for performance have a different meaning. Now they do not communicate the same threat or feeling of undue risk. The dominant orientation has shifted again, either back to the original style or to some other.

Another example involves the person who gets in over her head. This person may have had an outstanding record, particularly when provided with close supervision or when taken under the wing of a mentor, as can happen in predoctoral research. Because past performance was excellent, she was given responsibility for a section or a unit. Now, because of less supervision, her performance is visible to all. Personal competence to operate autonomously is exposed, possibly for the first time. At this point she becomes immobilized, unable to move. As a graduate student operating under precise instructions, she was acting on behalf of someone else rather than under her own motivation and inspiration. If she failed, it was not *personal* judgment that was in error, but faculty instructions. Internal values are not exposed when acting on behalf of others. When promoted, however, she has to act on her own initiative, with thinking and judgments exposed to the risk of being proved inadequate. We can understand how a person can perform with competence as a subordinate and yet be unable to act under personal responsibility as an autonomous faculty member or academic administrator.

Exposure to a 1,1 orientation can be found at all levels, not just at the point of entry. Because of unusual qualifications or academic or technical preparation, a person might be assigned as an assistant to a university president or vice-president. Talent in carrying out assignments is conspicuous. Performance draws attention. He or she receives an important line appointment, thus arriving at a high position long before peers do. Things go well during the learning period, that is, while the individual is still not personally responsible. But the more he or she comes to feel personal responsibility for decisions and results, the less he or she is able to initiate. Decisions about capital budget are postponed until "further studies are completed." When these studies are completed, additional unanswered questions that must be explored remain. Decisions are never put to the test. He or she becomes unreachable and unteachable.

As another example, a committed administrator may press others for a positive action on a favorite program or project. Unsuccessful, the administrator takes the defeat very personally and proceeds to back off, seemingly unable or unwilling to reenter the fray. A 1,1 orientation that may have been a backup has now become dominant, and this may remain the case for an extended period. When those responsible for the administrator's defeat have passed out of the scene, she may bounce back to her former style.

Another case is the department chair who has been, at some point in his career, heavily committed to departmental excellence but has withdrawn and is presently administering according to 1,1 assumptions: a case of a backup style becoming dominant. This individual is likely to have been one whose dominant style was 9,1 and who, rather than face defeat and failure, withdrew from the fight or caved in from pressures, rationalizing that his contributions were not appreciated. As an example, a person may perform quite well up to age forty or forty-five. Then he or she "burns out," losing interest in a job that has become empty and has ceased to be challenging, feeling drained and wanting to spend more time with family and friends. The actual causes of burnout are usually quite varied. During the early years of successful performance an administrator's dreams of control, mastery, and domination may be far away from what is actually achieved in day-by-day performance. The years go by, and now, as a mid-level administrator, he or she faces middle age, knowing that he or she is never going to be president. How can he or she avoid recognizing that performance has not matched aspirations? The myth can be maintained by avoiding the risk of self-revelation and "backing off" through rationalizations of the kind introduced earlier: "The challenge has gone out of the job . . . I've lost interest . . . I want to spend more time with my family." A dominant style has receded, and a 1,1 orientation has replaced it.

A 1,1-oriented administrator assigns whatever tasks must be done to others and gives them more or less full discretion in completing the tasks. That this is more abdication than delegation is shown by the following ways of viewing responsibilities:

- *Planning:* "I give broad assignments though without specifying goals or schedules when possible. Each subordinate is responsible for himself or herself."
- *Organizing:* "If left alone, they carry out assignments, as they know their own jobs and their capabilities better than anyone else."
- *Directing:* "I carry the message from those above to those below. I pass the story as straight as I can and with as little editing, embroidery, or interpretation as possible."
- *Controlling:* "I make the rounds, but I take little on-the-spot action. They like it that way. I do, too."
- *Staffing:* "I take whoever comes along."

The administrator avoids interfering not for the reason that others need the opportunity to be autonomous and to learn from their own efforts, but out of personal lack of involvement. A remark such as "I don't make decisions, I only work here" communicates a 1,1 sense of withdrawal from responsibility. Thus, this kind of administrator occupies his or her position in only a superficial way. The approach is to do whatever needs to be done to keep from losing the position. He or she passes like a shadow over the ground, leaving no permanent mark on the organization. Neither does the organization leave its mark on him or her.

Implementing Institutional Mission

The 1,1-oriented approach to university mission, goals, and objectives is "What's the big fuss about?" The administrator doesn't get involved in what he or she sees as meaningless debates about nothing. Talk is cheap. The university mechanism has a life of its own. A change in the stated "mission" seldom goes anywhere. Abdication, deferral, and default are this administrator's approaches to decision making. Alternatively, effort is concentrated on nominal decisions that keep the administrator busy or occupied but have little impact on university direction.

To this way of thinking, presidents, vice-presidents, deans come and go—the university as an institution remains and moves along at its own pace. A thousand small decisions made daily are more important than rhetoric. One should not get embroiled in trying to shape the institution. One must take it as it is and learn to live with it. An administrator who tries to shift the institution, or even a division or unit of it, probably has an inordinate need for power. The university is best left to its own evolutionary processes. Things will work out if people will just learn not to tinker too much with the internal workings.

On a daily level the administrator may make a long "to do" list: "Call Joe about the maintenance contract on the IBM typewriter in 402"; "Send memo out on holiday schedule"; "Inquire about the rules regarding parking privileges for Faith

Arnold (arthritis)"; "Meet with graduate students about serving on the curriculum committee." He or she fills the days with these kinds of "goals and objectives." This is what university life is all about, isn't it—the nitty-gritty? The rationalization is that it is all-important to get the sand out of the wheels.

In the situation presented below, the 1,1-oriented administrator is a vice-president, and he is speaking with the director of institutional research. The university is faced with a dramatic shift in the pattern of student enrollment in various divisions. The vice-president treats this major challenge to the university's present concept of its mission as if it were a ripple on a quiet sea. He minimizes the shift as just one more small task on his "to do" list. After all, he doesn't want to be the one to say that the sky is falling in on the university. A little adjustment to the clutch, a little oil in the gears, and the engine will be running as smoothly as ever.

Vice-President: Where are all these people coming from? These new enrollees in the business school?

Director: Well, about half of them are transfers from other departments. Some are part time. It's as though everybody is jumping on the bandwagon for a degree in business. Next year it'll be something else, I suppose.

Vice-President: Where have the enrollment declines come from?

Director: Oh, we see some real shifts away from the social sciences and from liberal arts. They're just not finding jobs the way they once did.

Vice-President: What are we going to do? We have a real imbalance in our teaching loads.

Director: I think we're in pretty good shape this year, but soon it is going to be worse. It may get to the point where we need to come up with some kind of new solution.

Vice-President: Oh, well, if we're talking about a year or two away, I'm not going to get into it yet. For all we know, some big national issue will come along and shift us back to where we were yesterday.

Director: Well, I think this is a longer-term, more basic shift than that.

Vice-President: Oh, I've seen these things come and go during my years. We usually find some solution. We may have to move some of the faculty for awhile to teaching part time in some of the other departments and get those people in the business school to recognize that they shouldn't be hiring new people when they can retrain or use faculty from other departments. You'd be surprised how many faculty can teach in more than one area.

Director: Well, then, we better start preparing them now for teaching in some field other than their own. That would require some kind of training program or something, wouldn't it?

Vice-President: Oh, no, not really. All you have to do is give them the name of a course. They prepare it. Most of our people really are generalists when you come right down to it. Students can't tell the difference.

Director: They may be generalists, but I'm not sure that's what they want to be.

Vice-President: (changing the subject) Let's move on to another issue, shall we? How is that idea you had about our new admissions procedures turning out?

Director: I was surprised at how well that turned out. I wish I could hatch a good idea like that more than once every six months.

Vice-President: Does it make any difference dollarwise?

Director: Yes. Maybe I've got a mind for business.

Vice-President: Well, most scholars don't tend to think in those terms.

At first glance, this dialogue might not seem to reveal a 1,1 orientation to planning on the part of the vice-president. He brings up the issue, he tracks down the implications of the shifting trends, and even tests out these implications from the standpoint of the future. None of this on the surface might seem characteristic of a 1,1 orientation. Nonetheless, it is a 1,1 orientation because the vice-president procrastinates when it comes to acting on the implications of the emerging trend. Postponing action for a year or two makes it unnecessary to do anything now. Postponement is justified by the fact that trends come and go, it is hard to predict the future, and things may be back in place by the time a year or two rolls around. If the trend is real, eventually a decision will be found by circumstances; at that point the decision will be obvious to everybody, and thus there will be reduced resistance to change.

Furthermore, we see the 1,1 orientation in the vice-president's casual attitude toward professorial specialization: he sees no reason why professors can't be generalists and be moved into areas of student demand. This careless disregard of specialization fails to appreciate the depth of emotional loyalty to a subject that is characteristic of many professors and their repugnance at being moved about like pawns on a chessboard. For some, an assignment to a professional school would be equivalent to being packed off to Siberia.

We see still another aspect of his 1,1 orientation in his attempt to sideline the shifting enrollment problem without appearing to be uninterested in its implication for future administration and to move on to the related topic of admission procedures. The attitude of passivity and indifference indicates that he prefers to believe that the problem will go away if it is left alone.

Supporting Teaching and Learning

A 1,1-oriented attitude toward teaching involves the belief that the professor can do little but the student can do much to facilitate learning. This is based on the notion that no matter how much effort teachers apply to the classroom process, little real learning happens if students are uninterested, bored, resistant, or occupied by such matters as politics, international relations, athletic contests, or social activities. Under these conditions little reason exists to try to gain the attention of the academically uninvolved. An administrator who conceives of teaching in this way places little emphasis on faculty selection beyond meeting the minimum requirements of accrediting bodies. As long as the faculty is composed of its expected proportion of Ph.D.'s, as long as teaching facilities meet minimum standards, and as long as teaching loads are not in excess of pre-scribed limits, there is little more that an academic administra-tor can do to promote excellence in teaching.

Among faculty in a university of any size there are always at least a few incompetent teachers. An individual may even contribute a great deal to other aspects of departmental activity (research, administration, and so on) but still teach in an un-inspiring, dull way. The 1,1-oriented administrator makes no real effort to do anything to correct this type of problem. The attitude is "Don't dabble." Teaching to the 1,1-oriented admin-istrator means making out the schedules, ordering the text-books, turning in the grades, and filing the teacher evaluations. "It's not my business to look at the course outlines or to ques-tion a faculty member about theories of learning. It's not really possible to measure student achievement in any scientific way, so why turn over rocks?"

In the following dialogue, a chairperson is reacting to bad news about teaching incompetence in his department. A disser-tation student has completed a study of student learning in which fellow students were used as subjects. The chair is dis-cussing the abstract of the student's results with the dissertation supervisor, who is also a budget council member.

Faculty Member: Did you read the dissertation on student learning? I think it's quite interesting.
Chair: No, but I glanced at the abstract.
Faculty Member: Real surprise, isn't it?
Chair: Think the conclusions are correct?
Faculty Member: That's exactly how it is. The Tract 1 programs are in a mess. Quality of teaching in that section is the prob-lem.
Chair: But it draws the crowds. It certainly helps to have num-bers, formula funding being what it is!
Faculty Member: But the dissertation validates the bad situa-tion that we already know prevails.
Chair: That's an important content area. Is the teaching really as weak as all that?
Faculty Member: In my opinion, yes. You've got some cronies

in that section. Most of them graduated from the same school. It's pretty much a buddy system. None of them is really strong. Our big mistake is to allow each subsection to choose its own faculty without overall control other than a rubber stamping. That's what happens when a department gets as big as ours.

Chair: That may be so, but it's inevitable. As big as we are, there's no choice.

Faculty Member: Is there nothing we can do?

Chair: I'm afraid not. We'll have to live with it until a viable solution shows up.

The chair's 1,1 orientation to the administration of teaching is apparent here, and it comes through in his attitudes toward staffing in a very clear way. First of all, the chair assumes a minimal role. Dissertations are too wordy to read in full, and abstracts are sufficient. Second, he reacts to the problem only when the supervisor of the research mentions the findings and even then his 1,1 orientation is evident in his resigned acceptance of the research conclusions.

The chairperson indicates that a particular set of courses draws the crowds and that it is necessary to go along because of the formula-funding mechanism. This is followed by the proposition that impoverished teaching is inevitable when a department is large. When probed directly, he reduces the pressure by saying, "We'll live with it until a viable solution shows up." Even an empty promise has a certain ring of responsibility.

Establishing the Curriculum

A 1,1-oriented administrator is likely to see curriculum development as beyond effective management. Various professors embrace different educational philosophies, with the play of vested interests producing arguments as to what should or should not be taught. Constraints result from funding, minimum teaching loads, and so on. It is beyond realistic possibility that curriculums can be developed in a sensible, coherent, logical manner. The only realism is to recognize the situation for what it is and to put out enough to counter the criticism that one is putting out nothing.

If at all possible, the administrator delegates decision making to a committee of persons who are ready to take the responsibility. He or she may attend meetings or even chair sessions but is likely to limit participation to the procedural level. Thus, he or she can take an active part but avoid getting involved in the content of deliberations. The 1,1-oriented chair elects to accept a curriculum committee's recommendations without even attempting to find out what the issues are. The curriculum is seen by the chair as the territory of feudal lords— the faculty. You don't cross the moats into someone's palace without very good cause. Sometimes the battles rage at the borders of the fiefdoms. In such situations the administrator can divert attention from the main game. Usually, as the weather turns crisp, the curriculum problems settle down, not to reemerge until the spring thaws.

In the following scene the 1,1-oriented chair avoids being dragged into a dispute between one faculty member and the curriculum committee.

Faculty Member: Ol' Martin was pretty hard on you at that faculty meeting the other day.

Chair: Yeah, I don't know what brought that on.

Faculty Member: I think he was hot about a lot of things.

Chair: I don't even understand what he was saying, but he'll get over it.

Faculty Member: He wants a decision from the curriculum committee about the course he is teaching.

Chair: What's he want me to do about it? I'm not on the curriculum committee. It's up to them.

Faculty Member: He thinks you have influence, and he blames you when things don't go right.

Chair: Why doesn't he blame the curriculum committee? That's their job. If they don't want him to teach that course according to the objectives he proposed, then let them fight it out. I've got other things to worry about. I'm an administrator, not a boxing referee.

Faculty Member: Well, he thinks we should all get into this. He says it's a major problem with the entire curriculum and not just a committee issue.

Chair: Nobody else has brought up evidence that this is a problem. Maybe it's just his opinion.

Faculty Member: Others feel this way too, and this is an area about which he's quite knowledgeable. I'm on the curriculum committee. What do you want me to tell them?

Chair: Nothing in particular. They should do whatever is right. I do believe in delegation. Just tell them to write me a note when they decide this issue that Martin thinks is so important. I can't send over the papers until someone tells me what the decision is.

The chair's 1,1 orientation is seen in his maintaining distance from the committee's problem. Rather than allowing "old Martin" to trap him into taking sides, he suggests to the faculty member that it is a matter for the committee to decide, not him, and he further affirms his "deep convictions" by saying he wants the committee to do whatever is right.

All this is justified in the name of delegation, which absolves the chair from any need to exercise initiative or to influence the outcome. By slipping out from under the exercise of direction, he will not be involved in the decision and therefore he cannot be held accountable for the outcome.

Supporting Research and Scholarly Productivity

The attitude of the 1,1-oriented administrator toward research and scholarly publications is neither positive nor negative. He or she circulates the announcements of available research funds but lacks the involvement to stimulate the curiosity of other faculty about someone's specific research project or latest ideas. Research constitutes an activity in which professors may engage as long as it does not encroach on teaching and campus and community services. Faculty will hold their own in research if they know what they are doing. Some people have the "gene" for it; some don't. If the formal system requires it, an accounting is made without exercising judgment as to whether research and scholarly publications meet acceptable criteria. If there is no such requirement, research activities are simply disregarded.

In the situation below, the 1,1-oriented president of a health science institution is discussing a research need with a president of another university within the state system. His lack of genuine commitment to research is seen as he quickly shifts away from lending support to a major research project when he meets resistance from his colleague.

President 1: It would be helpful to us if we could use your hospital staff for some research that we would like to conduct. I'll follow up our discussion with a formal letter of request, but I thought I'd let you know ahead of time what the idea is and how we might cooperate.

President 2: Yeah, I'd like to hear more.

President 1: We need a facility we can use as a control in a research project on the management of teaching hospitals. Emergency services are the first part of the study. We're making some major changes in emergency services and some of the other services of the hospital. We need a control hospital with which to compare our results. Naturally, it can't be widely known that one is experimental and one is the control.

President 2: What does this involve?

President 1: A series of interviews with your key staff at two different times. That is, in the prestage, and then in about a year, in the poststage of the research. In the intervening time we'll be making some of the changes in our experimental hospital. We need then to compare our results with yours over the same period. In no other way would we be interrupting or interfering with regular operations at your facility.

President 2: That sounds reasonable. I see no problem. We would be interested in the research results, of course.

President 1: Well, I'm not really up on the details, but one of our key people has received this research grant on hospital administration. He asked me if I could locate a comparable facility for him, and you are the first person I thought of.

President 2: Well, our two hospitals are quite comparable. I think it's a good plan. Of course I'll have to get the hospital administrator's approval, and he will no doubt want to know a bit more of the details. There may be sensitivities involved if it makes any invidious comparisons.

President 1: Oh, we don't want that. I've already asked the grant recipient to make the thing as unburdensome as possible. I got him to cut down on some of the objectives that are too ambitious. Now it's at a reasonable size where it can be carried out without disruption, at either the experimental or the control hospital. As you know, this kind of research can create a lot of discussion if it affects too many people at once, and we want to avoid that.

President 2: Well, this sounds as though it's getting more interesting. Can you give me a little more detail?

(The first president narrates some of the details of the research study. The second president begins to back off from his original commitment.)

President 2: I am getting concerned, now that I see what you're trying to do. I wonder if it wouldn't be a good idea if we put our two heads together and whittled down this research a little more. I see no reason why all employees have to be surveyed. Why not a random sample of thirty or so? They could be screened to gain voluntary cooperation and to assure confidentiality of patient records. That's the way to avoid trouble. That would be adequate.

President 1: I agree. I see no reason why that can't be done.

President 2: And also, although you're going to change some of your management procedures and services in the experimental program, some of those experimental services may create a pressure for funding that may not be reasonable in the future.

President 1: I see what you mean. Maybe we ought to put this on hold. I'm not sure the project director has thought through the problem of setting expectations for funding that maybe we can't deliver on in the next few years. We don't want to squash research, but we also don't want it to have a disrupting effect on our institutions. Maybe we'd better let it die a natural death.

The first president speaks of his interest in research and of how to help it along until the implications of what is involved begin to raise administrative problems. When this happens, we see his underlying attitude toward research in his readiness to back off and sacrifice research rather than to help it by getting the support necessary for the success of the project. His attitude toward organizing is, "Don't do it if it's going to take any significant effort. It's just not worth it." Now he can go back to the research project director and say that he explored the use of another facility as a control but ran into numerous obstacles. If the researcher continues to press, the president can have similar perfunctory contacts with others. This continues until the researcher gives up and eliminates the control condition and thus weakens the study design. The president cannot be accused of being uncooperative, and yet the character of his participation contributes nothing to the research outcome.

Encouraging Community and Institutional Service

Administrators and faculty are constantly being called on to devote time and energy to activities that are with little real merit when viewed from the perspective of the total academic context. The university mission applauds service as one of the trinity, equal in importance with research and teaching. To frown upon it is to reflect unfavorably on the college or university and to mark it as an unresponsive institution. To a 1,1-oriented administrator, service borders on being a necessary evil, but much of the inconvenience can be avoided by lip service and double-talk.

The 1,1-oriented administrator accepts appointments to committees or advisory groups and then attends meetings only frequently enough to create a sense of presence. The administrator's attitude toward service beyond the campus may not be clearly evident by his or her behavior. A trip to Washington or

New York or Los Angeles or attendance at a special committee of a professional association may be "talked up" when actually it serves to relieve the administrator from campus responsibilities. Therefore, such shifts of scenery offer welcome diversions. When away from the campus, however, the administrator is likely to have spotty attendance and his or her participation limited to meeting the requirements of form and protocol.

Many university administrators are ambivalent about the service function of the university. The value of "serving the community" is respected. The problem facing the administrator is to differentiate *real* service from a whole host of other outside activities faculty might engage in for fun or profit. To clarify the ambiguity is costly because explicitness can create controversy; drawing a line anywhere means protecting the borders. The 1,1-oriented administrator gives lip-service support to "service" but hopes no one questions his or her concept of it in depth. What "counts" is best left to each person's discretion: "Write on the activity report anything you think appropriate and of course it will be considered in merit and promotion decisions."

In the episode reported next, a 1,1-oriented dean is being asked to organize a meeting to clarify service criteria. The dean, not being inclined to court controversy, chooses to keep a light beam out of this corner. "Let's just feel our way" is the 1,1-oriented attitude that can be seen in this transaction.

The dean reads a letter from a budget council:

> "Dear Dean: One of the topics of repeated discussion in our budget council is over a set of agreed-upon criteria for evaluating faculty with respect to community service. We have no guidelines across departments about how to rate this important aspect of faculty performance. We have reason to believe that other budget councils have the same problem.
>
> "We suggest a meeting among several budget councils be organized in order to discuss standards for this area more fully."

The dean then telephones the budget council chairman who sent the letter.

Dean: I have your letter. Same old chronic problem, right?

Chair: My budget council has been arguing about this for years so I wrote the letter. As you know, I have tended to de-emphasize community service in assigning merit money, but I can see that it would be a good idea to get criteria clarified on an across-departments basis. Departments do it quite differently, I think, and that's what's behind the letter. But on the other hand, my budget council feels I have deemphasized public service too much, so in one sense this is a conflict between us as well.

Dean: You know what happens to neighbors who get involved in family fights.

Chair: On this we'd welcome the broadening of the battle front. We need a university-wide approach.

Dean: It may not be such a problem in other departments. Let me check around. If no one feels it's really of general interest, then I'd suggest you continue your battle in private.

(The dean and chair are discussing the question at a later time.)

Dean: The other departments don't want to touch it. Lots of spilt blood over it. It's too tender to tackle right now. I'll write a letter to you indicating that this does not seem to be an important issue at this time. Perhaps that will satisfy your budget council. Of course we might consider such a joint meeting in the future, perhaps next year, if there is increased readiness to deal with it.

Chair: Is that the best way for us to resolve such a tender issue?

Dean: I agree with you that it is a difficult and perennial issue but to tackle it now might make it even worse. Perhaps you and your budget council can make some progress in the interim.

It is widely appreciated that the evaluation of service from the standpoint of merit is a subjective affair and is therefore likely to be filled with controversy. When the department chair attempts to initiate an approach to the problem that might produce criteria that could be applied on an across-department basis, the dean uses his "check around" prerogative to measure interest. By formulating his inquiries to others in a way that discourages interest in pursuing the issue, he is therefore able to report back that for other departments it is "too tender to tackle." We also see a 1,1 orientation in the dean's reluctance to get involved in differences between the chair and the budget council on a within-department basis.

When the chair does challenge the dean's handling of it in this way, we see the dean proclaiming interest in the problem while at the same time tabling action indefinitely. Even though clarity is important from the standpoint of establishing operational criteria for evaluating service, the dean is unprepared to make the effort toward solving the problem.

Managing Resources

The 1,1-oriented administrator takes the path of least resistance with respect to the allocation of resources. The numbers in the columns of the budget must add up. Often the easiest way to make sure they do is to take last year's budget and update it by an inflation factor. If new funds are available, they are either applied to items on which everyone agrees, sprinkled throughout the budget, or given to those who clamor the loudest. The board meets with the president, the president with deans, deans with chairs—all of whom tell the next level what to expect this year. The 1,1-oriented administrator accepts the budget ground rules as a nonnegotiable statement of the conditions within which allocations are to be made. When cuts are mandatory, the solution is to lop off a job, program, or dollar category unlikely to be noticed or missed.

Funding allocation decisions are likely to be based on mechanical formulas because these obviate the need for exercising personal judgment. The nominal solution to salary increases is to make across-the-board adjustments, corrected for inflation, and either to let faculty go rather than meet competition or to retain faculty by matching competitive bids. The formula that applies may shift from time to time, depending on the scarcity of faculty or upon the pressure anticipated from strong and weak departments. Another practice for avoiding resource allocation decisions is to delegate the decision to others. Under these conditions the strongest and most determined get what they go after, and the weaker and more retiring become even weaker and even more unable to cope. The president can unload the problem onto deans, and deans onto department chairs.

The next conversation illustrates how resource allocation takes place under a 1,1 orientation to administration. This dean has been told to cut the budget 5 percent. Short of involvement in the problem, what can he do to minimize the clamor and hassle? He does what upsets people the least. "Faculty in general don't care about media programs. They think continuing education is lowbrow. No faculty member has a full-time investment in those efforts. The directors of these two programs are untenured. It might be better for them to get into the mainstream. How about reducing their budgets?" Thus, this administrator makes the following pitch to the two key targets of his red pen. He is conferring with the director of continuing education and the director of the community service programs.

Dean: We've got some bad news with respect to budget cuts. As you know, the governor is putting the pressure on universities to cut budgets by 5 percent. We are going to have to tighten our belts. I'm afraid that the work being done in your areas is where we are going to have to do some of the tightening.

Director of Continuing Education: Why us?

Dean: Well, we are reminded that the central function of the university is to serve students. Continuing education and community service programs are really a bonus we can no longer afford on such a wide-scale basis.

Director of Continuing Education: Most of our program is self-supporting. What is it we can't afford?

Dean: I'm under instructions to put some of the money you are making back into regular programs rather than use it for expansion. Now, of course, your positions are funded through faculty salaries and we will have to look at that too. It may be that you will be cut to half time rather than continue as full-time directors.

Director of Continuing Education: Oh, terrific! . . . right after I've made such progress in the last two years in the funding picture, I get this kind of news.

Director of Community Service Programs: We are just now getting started. We need the budget support more than ever.

Dean: Well, I've looked over the budget for the fifth time, and I just can't see other places to cut without also doing some juggling in your two areas.

Director of Continuing Education: My shop is making money for the school, and it doesn't make sense to cut back on the support you are giving me. My time, in terms of faculty salaries, comes back to us tenfold in financial returns.

Dean: That's certainly true, and I congratulate you on that. I know that you'll be able to continue this in spite of the small restriction in your budget.

Director of Community Service Programs: I think the thing we really have to tackle is our concept of education.

Dean: Well, what in the world do you mean by that?

Director of Community Service Programs: Well, the idea being expressed is that the kind of work we're doing is expendable. If you take a look at the trends in student enrollment and the nature and direction of continuing and community service education in the future, these are the growth areas. We've got to get over the idea that universities are designed only for people from the ages of eighteen to twenty-four or twenty-five.

Dean: Philosophically I know you're correct. But as an administrator I am obligated to operate within the current definition of the stated priorities of the university.

Director of Continuing Education: If you agree philosophically, it certainly is your responsibility as an administrator to exercise an influence on the academic echelons above you in order to bring about recognition of our work and alter the stated mission of the university.

Dean: What you're describing is what I would do if this were an ideal world. But unfortunately I'm a cog in a giant machine that has its own momentum. Literally there is nothing I can do to influence a shift in future direction. If your programs represent important niches that the university must fill, sooner or later recognition will be accorded the activities you are now bringing into focus.

Director of Continuing Education: What you're saying is that decisions about resources are not made on rational grounds.

Dean: Evolution may not fit your meaning of "rational," but it is inevitable that universities operate in this manner.

This 1,1-oriented dean moves along the path of least resistance. Even then he encounters obstacles from those who are to be adversely affected. At an intellectual level he acknowledges the positions being taken by the others but relieves himself from the responsibility to act on his convictions by placing his administration in the context of an academic organism that is evolving according to its own peculiar logic and that is understandable in terms of its place within a larger social system. His self-resignation is seen in his description of himself as a cog.

Supervising Personnel

Personnel decisions are among the most difficult for a 1,1-oriented administrator to deal with in a safe manner because such decisions touch on the whole host of human emotions of loyalty, dedication, pride, resentment, and competition. Being aware of the crisscross of pressures in these matters, the administrator tries to be seen as acting responsibly while maneuvering to avoid accountability. Most likely the 1,1-oriented administrator operates according to accepted traditions, precedents, and past practices. Personnel matters are allowed to remain dormant and are only reacted to when they present acute problems. Even then the decision made or solution reached is likely to be marginal in the sense that it does not really come to terms with the issue at hand.

In the following scene, a 1,1-oriented dean is asked to intervene in a dispute between a faculty member and her chair. The gripe is over pay—the lack of an adequate merit increase, according to the faculty member. The 1,1-oriented dean ends up feeling satisfied with his handling of this case. He thinks he handled the conflict just as a management textbook would dictate: "Talk to all concerned. Get the problem aired. Get the participants to take responsibility for the problem. Summarize the outcome in writing for future reference. Documentation in case of further developments later is always wise." Note how the dean distorts these lessons.

Faculty Member: I resent the harassment by my chair. I have been rated high in the teaching area for the last ten years. However, I haven't had a raise in five years. I have not put a lot of my time into research because I have spent most of my time teaching and in service and consulting. As you know, I do a lot of training of physicians through the medical association, so this is where I want to put my emphasis.

My chair is really taking it out on me because he has a mandate for pushing the research area. I know he was brought in to shape us up in that regard, but in all honesty, I feel different people have different contributions to make. He is forcing everyone to follow the model of the great researcher.

My contribution has always been in the teaching area, where I'm in demand not only within the department, but outside. Tell me, is it or is it not possible for me to progress in this department any more? I can teach elsewhere. If I'm to stay, you have to get him off my back and give me a raise.

Dean: As you acknowledge, the higher administration wanted us to bring your present chairman in to upgrade faculty research. However, I'm aware of your teaching, and I've seen your teaching evaluations.

You haven't had merit increases? Is that what you're referring to when you said you had had no increases?

Faculty Member: I haven't had a merit increase in the last five years. Sure, cost-of-living changes, but nothing above and beyond. The ultimate blow was when the chair assigned me three classes this semester, each one with a different preparation. To make matters worse, I'm teaching every day. Last year I had a Tuesday-Thursday teaching schedule, and I was able to be gone on Monday, Wednesday, and Friday to do the work in health education I am called on to do. I consider the scheduling of my classes for every day of the week a direct personal attack, a maneuver to prevent me from taking advantage of many of the opportunities through the medical association.

Dean: Now, now. Everyone has a schedule difficulty now and then. Did you say you've had pretty good schedules for several years?

Faculty Member: That's right; otherwise I wouldn't be here now. I'd have taken a job somewhere else that permitted me to juggle my schedule between the association and the campus. If he's going to put this kind of straightjacket on me, then I'll go somewhere else.

Dean: I feel he doesn't intend this as any kind of personal attack. Is he even aware of it?

Faculty Member: Oh yes, he's aware of it. I've already told him. He refused to change a thing.

Dean: What did he say?

Faculty Member: He said it was too late. Everything has already been set in motion, and it would be a real problem to make the changes.

Dean: Let's look at your teaching schedule. What course do you have on Monday-Wednesday-Friday?

Faculty Member: That beginning physiology course could easily be switched. There's another section on Tuesday-Thursday like the one I've always had before. To add insult to injury, this is the first time I've taught three classes in a long time, too.

Dean: Everyone is teaching more this year because by necessity teaching loads have gone up.

Faculty Member: Well, I'll swallow that if you can get this whole thing switched so I have a Tuesday-Thursday schedule.

Dean: Why not meet this schedule the first week? In the meantime, why don't you talk to the chair? Maybe something can be done.

Faculty Member: Absolutely not. That's what you are for. You're a dean. I've talked to him, now it's your turn.

Dean: Okay, okay. Calm down. I'll talk to him.

(The faculty member leaves. The dean calls the chair.)

Dean: One of your faculty was in here discussing her teaching schedule. She wants a schedule different from the one she's been given.

(The dean explains the encounter with the faculty member. The chair replies.)

Chair: Yes, we've had a lot of trouble with her. As you know, she's doing no research and has done none for a decade. Her teaching is popular but I'm not sure it's strong; certainly it doesn't reflect the sense of involvement and enthusiasm that comes from original inquiry. She's gone a lot, does a lot of consulting, and really, if you ask me, she's not carrying her load, particularly in terms of contact with students.

Dean: But it is important to remember that she has years of seniority and is known to be a dedicated teacher.

Chair: Dedication to teaching by no means is a measure of the quality of what is taught.

Dean: Okay, dedication and quality are two different things.

Chair: I'm pleased to know we agree on it, but in any event I apologize for her bringing this family matter to you for solution.

Dean: That's all right. That's what I'm here for, you know, as a sounding board. I've heard her and I wonder if the next step isn't for you to talk to her further. She seems a trifle edgy.

Chair: Well, I've talked with her and talked with her, and the budget council has reviewed her overall contribution. I've pretty much told her that I'm going to stick by my guns this time and that she's going to carry her fair share of the load and teach the schedule that has been worked out. We couldn't even consult her in advance because she was off campus when the assignments were being worked out.

Dean: Did you discuss her research and the merit raise issue?

Chair: We started to but ran out of time.

Dean: She may be a bit upset. I've talked to her some, and she's convinced she has a point. I suggest you spend a little more time trying to work something out.

Chair: Okay. I'll talk to her again.

Dean: I knew you'd be able to handle it.

After hanging up the phone, the dean dictates a short note to the faculty member:

> "Dear ———— : I have discussed your teaching schedule with your chair and agree that whatever the two of you work out based on your unique situation is the desirable approach.
>
> "I understand the desire for the most adequate teaching load and best schedule that can be negotiated. I hope whatever you work out for this semester will be acceptable to you as well as your chair and other faculty. In this situation the chair has final responsibility to make the decision. Although it may not be possible to work it out to your best liking this semester, I hope that in the future you and your chair will be working together on this and on the research issue and that you will be satisfied as to the best solution under the circumstances. I know you'll agree that these differences are better worked out at the department level than for the dean to adjudicate them."

This handling of a complaining faculty member bears many of the hallmarks of a 1,1 orientation. When the faculty member introduces the problem, the dean does not challenge the chair's definition of the true issue, that is, the faculty member's lack of research contribution and frequent absences from the campus, but underscores in the meeting with the faculty member that he is aware of the faculty member's preeminence as a teacher. His 1,1 orientation to administration is revealed when he inquires about the faculty member's merit treatment over the years. He accepts the faculty member's complaint about how her chair has scheduled her but does so by rationalizing that scheduling difficulties are inevitable. His basic orientation is seen further when he asks the faculty member about her conversations with the chairman and then shifts the problem back onto the faculty member by asking her to try to work it out with the chair. Rather than leaving it at that, though, the dean calls the chair and passes the message that he has a disgruntled faculty member on his hands, asking the chair to put a little more effort into solving the problem at the departmental level. The final demonstration of this orientation is in the letter sent by the dean to the faculty member—a letter that, in effect, absolves him from responsibility for solving within-department problems while encouraging the unhappy faculty member to accept what is inevitable for the current period.

The dean may be seen to have acted responsibly by talking with the faculty member, talking with the department chair, writing a letter, and in truth he has done all these things but without exerting any impact on the solution of the problem. He has done them in such a manner that the chair is unlikely to feel that he has been undercut and the faculty member is likely to feel listened to.

Coordinating Student Affairs

In the eyes of the 1,1-oriented administrator, the modern student is not to be led. Guidance is to be kept to a minimum. Students put a stop to the doctrine of *in loco parentis,* and they now pursue their personal interests and take responsibility for themselves in such a way that the university is left with little but the opportunity to respond to their whims.

When it is a question of requirements, the administrator limits advice to restating the rules and allowing the student to place his or her own interpretation on them. Sometimes this does not solve the problem, and a ruling is required. Then, a student is asked to reconsider the request for a ruling or exception. Alternatively, the problem is taken under advisement, with the administrator hoping that a delay will cause the problem to disappear or that he or she can carry the problem to a higher level to get a decision that can be passed on to the student.

The 1,1-oriented administrator is also cool to the whole idea of outside speakers. Such speakers are not responsible to the university, and since they do not have to live with the consequences of their pronouncements, they can use the campus as a podium, presenting viewpoints that range from silly to seditious. Moreover, the larger community often interprets the outside speaker's viewpoint as one with which the university's senior administrators are in explicit or implicit agreement. It is easier for an administrator to prevent such problems from occurring than to deal with the aftermath such presentations leave in their wake. As a result, he or she does little to encourage campus presentations by outsiders. The rationalization is that these activities might divert students from their academic work, but the deeper reason lies in the administrator's desire to avoid controversy.

When counseling on the editorial policy for the student newspaper, the 1,1-oriented administrator avoids taking positions as to what is right or wrong, risky or risk free, sound or unsound. It is possible to do this by pointing to the positive and negative consequences of any action and then setting these against the positive and negative consequences of no action. Sometimes it is possible to tip the balance in favor of no action and in this way to limit editorials that are critical of how the affairs of the university are being conducted. Or, at the very least, this approach may result in editorials that are bland rather than burdensome. Under these conditions, the student paper ceases to be an irritant to the administration and will be unlikely to expose its affairs for examination by the broader public.

The 1,1-oriented administrator's attitude toward student government is to let students fend for themselves. Being uninterested, he or she dampens activities, and from his or her standpoint the less active the student government the better, since awakened students can find all kinds of campus matters to apply their attention to. When this occurs, administrators have to respond one way or another. The need for a response can be avoided by keeping student government weak.

When the source of financial support for foreign students

is curtailed by international events, many of them are at a loss to know what to do. They seek, rather angrily, the aid of the student affairs office. The 1,1-oriented vice-president in the following dialogue has never coped with such a situation before and "what to do" isn't in any manual. Thus, he decides that it is not his role to do anything. He cleverly tosses the problem back to the associate dean and assumes the role of onlooker or third-party bystander.

Associate Dean: What are we going to do about the cutoff in funds to the foreign students? They need help.

Vice-President for Student Affairs: I'm not sure exactly what we can do. How many of them are really in a bad way?

Associate Dean: Well, it depends on what you mean. You know there are basically four factions within the total. Several feel as though they can't go back. Many, of course, are sympathetic with their whole national situation, but on the other hand they don't want to stop their schooling either. So I think a lot of them are torn. They'll say one thing at one time and something else the next. This is not double-talk as one might think. Many are just plain scared.

Vice-President for Student Affairs: That's not something we can do much about. I understand some are planning demonstrations.

Associate Dean: Oh great. That way we'll be unable to get any kind of help for them from private sources or anywhere. I hope we can handle this without an ugly incident.

Vice-President for Student Affairs: There's nothing I can do. If you think of anything that might ease the situation or loosen up money to tide over the ones who need it the most, it's within university policy to do so. I don't need to be consulted.

The vice-president for student affairs sees the explosive character of this situation and how the bomb might go off in his own hands. Being alert to the risks of taking sides, he quickly shifts the hot potato to the associate dean, directing him to take charge rather than participating in making the decision himself.

Managing External Relations

By virtue of the permeability of the university membrane, with everyone free to talk about it and with outsiders free to penetrate it, the idea of an effective external relationship program is absurd—or so reasons the 1,1-oriented administrator. As a result of this fatalistic attitude, the administrator extends little or no effort in the direction of creating an active external relations policy or, if one already exists, of implementing it. He or she expects other administrators and faculty to deal with their own external relations on a local-option basis, even though strong administrators and faculty members are likely to exploit this freedom, sometimes using it to attack the university or to advance the vested interests of their own department, program, or institute.

Those with a 1,1 orientation are likely to avoid situations where they would be called upon to comment on issues of interest to the public. When this is impossible and comment is required, such administrators avoid giving specific reactions that might be subject to challenge and therefore embroil them in controversy. Statements such as "The study has not yet been completed in this situation," "All the facts are not in," and "Others are in a better position to give you a reaction than I" are their stock-in-trade.

The 1,1-oriented dean in the dialogue below knows that being seen and getting around on the "outside" are expected of an administrator. He has an opportunity to educate a significant segment of the business community about the role of a college dean. Aware that to do so would mean putting his educational philosophy on the line where it might be subject to criticism or attack, the dean casts about for an uncontroversial topic when asked by a neighbor to speak to a local civic group.

Neighbor: Dean Grey . . . it has a nice ring to it. How do you like being dean?

Dean: Well, so far so good. It's really not much different from being chair.

Neighbor: I understand that, as a dean, you are called upon to make more speeches and you have to be more like a public servant, or a politician, or something like that.

Dean: Where did you get that idea? It sounds like something I didn't bargain for at all.

Neighbor: Well, that's just what one of my other friends was telling me about a dean he knew. That's how he had to operate.

Dean: He must have done all that because he wanted to; it's not really required.

Neighbor: You mean you don't have to make speeches all around? I was getting ready to ask you to speak to the Rotary Club.

Dean: Oh, well, I'm saying you don't have to; you can if you want to.

Neighbor: Our speakers committee has asked me to invite you to speak when our district director is in town.

Dean: Sounds like I'm obligated. What did you have in mind?

Neighbor: Oh, something popular and humorous like the role of a dean in the academic fishbowl, or something like that. Most of the people wouldn't care too much what you talked about as long as it was enlightening.

Dean: I'd rather talk about fishing. My experience is that academic administrators and scholars contribute more to the university in public settings when they show their light-hearted sides rather than treating the heavy stuff or the prosaic issues. Of course, entertainment can be serious, but I have thought many times over the years of what fishing might be like viewed from the fish's point of view. During my vacation this summer I fished a great deal and my mind is still there. During the no-bite periods, I crystallized a presentation that contains a good deal of dry humor related to this wet topic.

Neighbor: Why did you take this dean job anyway?

Dean: Well, to tell you the truth, so I'd have more time to fish. Kidding aside, I will speak to the Rotary, but in preference to the role of a dean in a university, I could bring them some insights as to "Comparative treatment of alternative possibilities of what a fish thinks on seeing a hook."

In this neighborly conversation we see how a 1,1-oriented administrator conceives of his role in representing the university in its external relations. He doesn't refuse to participate but rather responds to the requested activity in a way that will allow him to remain neutral with regard to actual or even possible issues of controversy regarding the operation or thrust of the university. But far more than simply keeping himself out of trouble by not dealing with significant matters, this dean is likely to create an environment in the presentation in which the asking of a serious question would be quite inappropriate. Even if such a question were to be asked, the dean would be in an excellent position to turn it off in a lighthearted way and without appearing to be irresponsible.

The dean's 1,1 orientation to planning is seen in his calculated avoidance of a serious subject that could illuminate the public's understanding of some significant aspect of public life. True to his Grid style, he introduces humor that is calculated to be playful but that comes through as rather pointless.

Assuring Basic Operations

The infrastructure is as much a part and parcel of university administration as any other aspect. This becomes particularly evident when the power plant breaks down and there are no lights in the university library, or when campus security falters in the face of a student demonstration.

The 1,1-oriented administrator delegates to experts a maximum of responsibility for operating, maintaining, and protecting the plant. The power plant is left to engineers, buildings to architects, protection to personnel with security qualifications, and dining services to nutritionists. The administrator provides little more than an office for passing messages up and down. Under these conditions there are few matters requiring the 1,1-oriented administrator's active exercise of judgment. But what if he *is* required to make a decision? At the start of the following dialogue, the phone rings in the vice-president's office. The campus police chief is calling. Note that the 1,1-oriented administrator's attitude is to rely on precedent or to redefine the problem as one belonging to somebody else.

Chief: Vice-President Moore, President Gilmore is out of town, so it's up to you to make a decision.

Vice-President: What are you talking about?

Chief: Oh, I'm sorry. Let me give you the background. We've had a bomb scare in the dorm again. This is the third time this month. I think it's just a prank, but, you know, somebody has to decide whether we evacuate or not.

Vice-President: Why me?

Chief: The policy says this kind of decision is needed from the highest level. The president is gone, so it's up to you.

Vice-President: What did he do last time?

Chief: He called for an evacuation but the weather was warmer. It's an extremely cold night tonight.

Vice-President: Well, that could put everybody out in the cold. What do we do? Send a team in to look for the thing and find nothing? Is that the usual routine?

Chief: That's what happened the last two times.

Vice-President: Well, then we should go through the same routine one more time. I'm sure the president had good reason to make the same decision each time. It seems to me he's practicing the old adage that "it's better to be safe than sorry."

Chief: If you administrators are going to make the same decision every time, I don't need to call you up.

Vice-President: Why don't we just get together with the president when he comes back, and decide that we're going to do this every time. I see no reason to make a special decision in each situation.

Chief: Better yet, why don't you let me make the decision based on my own assessment of the severity and the probability of its being a prank?

Vice-President: Well, that's a very good idea. Let me bring it up and get the president to decide on that.

Chief: Well, are you sure you want evacuation in freezing weather?

Vice-President: Did the president leave any guidelines with regard to temperature limits or offer you any guidance about what to do when the weather is beyond certain limits?

Chief: No, we've been working on problems one at a time.

Vice-President: Then I say you rely on the president's judgment.

Chief: But he's not here.

Vice-President: Give me your best estimate as to what his judgment would be or if you like I'll phone him to get his reaction.

Chief: The bomb could go off while you're trying to locate him.

Vice-President: That seems to suggest that this requires an expert decision by you based on local circumstances. After all, you're on the scene while I'm way up here in my office. What do you think the president would say and do you agree? If so, proceed as the president and you think best. If you think you and he would disagree, I'll try to contact him for an official decision. If I can't locate him I'll have to decide. I'll get back to you as quickly as possible.

Chief: I think the president would evacuate, but I personally think this is a prank.

Vice-President: Let's be safe. Evacuate but search as quickly as possible. Don't keep those students out in the cold too long.

Chief: Okay, if you say so.

This 1,1-oriented vice-president's attempt to avoid responsibility becomes clearly visible as he seeks to play the role of message passer between the president and the police chief rather than exercising direct responsibility for decision making in a crisis situation. When the police chief bucks at a solution based on a precedent that is not easy to apply, the administrator first tries to pass the responsibility on to the police chief to second guess the president, but finally appears to make the decision himself. The vice-president is covered whichever way the crisis turns out since he uses precedent as a guide and plays it safe. He may have made the "right" decision but for the wrong reasons.

Summary

Though this is sometimes difficult to see, a 1,1 orientation to administration often takes the form of a custodial approach over the long term; and an organization so managed gradually assumes the qualities of an eleemosynary institution. The administrator's goal is limited to hanging on and in this way surviving to retirement. On the negative side his or her motivation is to do enough to avoid being asked to step down.

The functions of management are supplied in a "going through the paces" kind of way. Planning is nonexistent or short term. Thinking about how to organize, if any, is last minute and superficial. Direction is avoided by delegating at the general level or by authorizing actions that have been routinized as part of the institution's traditions, precedents, and past practices. When undertaken, organizational controls are used to satisfy higher-ups that some supervision is being exercised. Staffing tends to be done in an indiscriminate way, with personnel called upon to do the minimum the institution can tolerate.

A 1,1-oriented administrator accepts whatever the organization is doing as an expression of its mission. From the standpoint of teaching, the administrator interprets this as being all right when those responsible show up at assigned class periods and turn in their grades. Curriculum decisions are left to the inclinations of individual professors. Little more than lip service is given to the importance of research. Service requests are responded to only when it would be impractical to do otherwise. Resource allocation is based on living within the constraints of what has been given in the past, with approvals that depart from the past delayed as long as possible. Academic personnel are provided the minimum of support and thereafter left on their own. Students took responsibility for themselves in the sixties, and that's where the situation remains. Because of the openness of the university, it is a practical impossibility to conduct a meaningful program of external relations. Operations are delegated to personnel with expert credentials or relevant experience, and thereafter message passing provides the necessary connection between those responsible for the operations of the infrastructure and those concerned with influencing it.

Decisions are by default. Convictions are weak, ill defined, or easily changed. Conflict is avoided by remaining neutral. Temper is not evident because an administrator who has no specific goals rarely gets stirred up. Humor is pointless. Effort is minimal.

Chapter Five

Authority-Obedience Administration: 9,1

The 9,1-oriented administrator, represented in the lower right corner of the Academic Administrator Grid in Chapter Two, has high concern for institutional performance and low concern for the people who are responsible for this performance. The administrative role is seen as a matter of making sure that others follow the "proper" course toward achievement. The performance goals of the university—teaching, research, and service, whether public, professional, or university-wide service—may be somewhat difficult to be specific about, and yet the administrator is confident that he or she perceives accurately what performance should be in each of these areas. Therefore, he or she has little or no hesitation in directing and controlling personnel in ways that move them toward realizing the administrator's standards of performance.

The positive motivation pole is domination, mastery, and control. To come out on top at all costs is the aim. Thus, this administrator feels no hesitation in pulling rank in order to impose standards on others.

Fear of failure or of not being effective represents this administrator's negative pole. Defeat comes from not receiving proper recognition; from not having put together the most prestigious combination of talent; from not placing students in the best graduate schools or employing organizations in the country; or from not having one's opinion sought out by external agencies or organizations or authorities. The ultimate blow is having the research of the faculty challenged as being quantitatively extensive but qualitatively poor. The latter is a certain signal of failure, and individuals with a 9,1 orientation seek to avoid this by putting greater and greater energy into defensive strategies that place institutional programs above criticism by outside persons or agencies.

As administrators, 9,1-oriented persons are constantly concerned with judging others. To be afraid to give a negative evaluation is a sign of weakness, and they go to the opposite extreme, demonstrating strength by "calling a spade a spade." They are preoccupied with rendering judgments of others and their work as worthy or not worthy.

A 9,1-oriented administrator privately believes that he or she is the cause of whatever success comes, regardless of the contribution of subordinates. He or she does not admit defeat, however, and either denies a given failure or explains it away as due to another's unreasonableness, blockages within the organization, factions that are traditional and hold antiquated points of view or that are not knowledgeable and competent enough to make the kind of judgments needed for progress. In short, others are pinpointed as the cause of failure. This causes the administrator to try harder and harder and to handpick subordinates in order to feel more in control of the judgmental and decision-making process.

The 9,1 Administrative Approach

When the organization rewards performance and shows little consideration for people, an administrator with a 9,1 orientation feels elated because this means that his or her attitudes are in tune with those of the organization. He or she is free to drive others in line with the ethic that "results are what count." Whenever a contradiction exists between people and performance, it is resolved at the expense of people. This administrator continually thinks about the job and the problems that he or she must solve to get performance and often wakes up in the morning with these concerns in mind. "If you don't look out for yourself, who will? The law of the jungle is what prevails in this dog-eat-dog academic life. It's survival of the fittest all the way." This determination to overcome obstacles and overpower opposition is seen by others as headstrong, yet performance results are likely to be on the plus side, particularly in the short term.

Relationships with subordinates are along the lines of *authority* and *obedience.* The administrator may exercise authority over the smallest details of subordinates' activities, and they are obligated to comply. The hierarchy is not to be questioned. Lines of accountability and responsibility are to be adhered to. If a subordinate should question a 9,1-oriented administrator about performance, the administrator might answer, "I've thought this through. It's an extremely complicated matter, and there's not enough time to go into details now. Just trust that I have examined all the ramifications and have concluded what it is necessary for you to do." The unstated message is, "You don't need to know why, and so don't question my orders."

The underlying assumption of a 9,1-oriented administrator is that externally imposed direction and control, of necessity, must be applied down through the organization. Why? First, people are thought to dislike work inherently. Therefore, they must be pushed. Second, they are likely to be seen as less than fully capable of organizing their efforts effectively at their own levels of administration in order to accomplish the institutional mission. While administrators at lower echelons are held responsible for output, the planning and organizing aspects of their jobs are thought to be done more effectively up the line where more perspective, skill, and information are present. Third, to administer otherwise would seem to weaken the structure of established authority and allow "unwilling" subordinates to contradict the institution's major thrust and to go off on tangents.

- *Planning:* "I do the planning by setting performance standards and detailing plans to achieve them."
- *Organizing:* "I design a structure where lines of authority are clear. I expect people to operate within the specified framework and to go through proper channels."
- *Directing:* "I tell subordinates what to do, how, when, and with whom. I'm inclined to leave out why."
- *Controlling:* "I keep in close touch with what's going on to ensure that what I have authorized is being followed. I ensure that schedules are met and move people along faster if progress permits. I criticize, assign blame for deviations, and impose corrective actions."
- *Staffing:* "I make the assignments."

When administrators manage in this way, resentment is more or less inevitable. They come to expect it, rationalizing that to get performance one has to give close supervision and step on toes. It is easier to keep people under control by holding each of them accountable for his or her own job. The assumption is that individuals, not groups or teams, are productivity's building blocks. But this assumption remains hidden.

Administrators with 9,1 orientations often concern themselves with the minor details of a project and other arrangements at lower levels. Jobs are defined in terms of operational requirements. People are not expected to contribute ideas; their only duty is to turn out results. The primary advantage of this kind of work simplification and division of activities into segments is that judgment and decisions that concern anything more than simple procedures are reduced to a minimum. These arrangements fragment work into mechanical units. Thus, people do not need to be relied on to think.

At higher levels, a similar kind of separation between executives can be achieved by regulating the flow of information. In one university, for example, the president meets with each vice-president separately and frowns on their meeting with one another. He does this for several reasons. One is that it gives him complete and ultimate control over all decisions and keeps him from being subject to criticism by any one subordinate because no one has a sufficiently broad perspective to know the complex considerations that will affect the final result. Another is that he avoids creating "generalists" who could go into competition with him. Needless to say, such a president is unlikely to have developed replacements and therefore is not threatened in that dimension either. When he or she is removed for whatever reason, the organization is likely to enter into a period of drift, if not crumble entirely.

We can now examine how these basic attitudes toward planning, organizing, directing, controlling, and staffing reveal themselves in the actual functions of academic administration.

Implementing Institutional Mission

A 9,1-oriented administrator who accepts a position in the academic hierarchy will push his or her version of the university's mission, whether that version is congruent with or contradictory to the mission as stated by the relevant governing bodies. He or she takes every opportunity to shape specific decisions in favor of preferred interpretations of the institution's mission. This individual has definite opinions about what programs to fund, what kind of faculty to hire, and how courses should be taught. He or she is known throughout the campus for clear convictions and the courage to stand behind them. Colleagues soon learn the administrator's preferences and give support or face wrath knowingly.

The administrator does not waiver in the effort to control decisions and propose strategies to implement his or her own version of the university mission. Those who disagree do not "understand," are "complacent," have no "integrity," or are "outsiders." Conflict is dealt with by suppression. Seldom plagued by indecisiveness or divided loyalties, this administrator takes on the image of the true advocate, the stalwart warrior, or member of the "old guard." Debating skills, power tactics, and preparedness are relied on to institutionalize his or her views and to perpetrate them in the face of counterpressures.

In the example that follows, a 9,1-oriented chair uses a

well-prepared plan, coupled with surprise, to reinforce his views
of departmental mission. He is meeting with the faculty curriculum committee, which is responsible for the design of the graduate program.

Chair: We've been asked to come up with a plan on the assumption that we will have four new faculty positions in the next
   three years. Furthermore, we will be authorized to replace
   faculty who leave. As you know, this is part of the president's effort to support our programs, given the shift in enrollment to our college. Therefore, what we have to think
   about is what this will mean for our undergraduate and
   graduate programs. In essence, we've been asked to forecast
   the number of students we can meaningfully admit to our
   graduate programs on the assumption that we will experience the possible addition of four to six faculty over a
   three-year period. So the question is, What will we be able
   to accomplish given this support to the graduate programs?
Committee Member 1: What about adding some faculty in the
   undergraduate rather than the graduate program?
Chair: The basic mission of this university emphasizes graduate
   teaching. The president and the dean's council have given us
   a guideline that if we add anywhere it is to be in graduate
   faculty.
Committee Member 2: That doesn't really make sense. Our
   undergraduate program is expanding faster than the graduate program.
Chair: Well, we need not necessarily worry about the number of
   students if we can come up with some method of organizing
   the curriculum to cover the number of students we get. But
   with the estimated increase in faculty we have a chance to
   do some things we've all wanted to do. I've had some
   chance to think about this. Let me go over what I think
   would be a reasonable proposal so you can react to it. I have
   a handout here I would like for you to read over. Note that
   it contains a graduate teaching assignment plan under three
   conditions—no new faculty, a 5 percent gain, and a 10 percent gain. Class sizes would not change for the lab courses.

There would be a 25 percent class size increase within three years for the core courses.

(The chair then proceeds to make a very persuasive argument for a highly detailed proposal that he has obviously spent a great deal of time working on. He passes out a five-page appendix to support his original proposal. The committee, after listening to a forty-five-minute presentation, is left with no alternative except to react to various features of the proposal in a halfhearted manner.)

Here we see the chair's 9,1 orientation in his attitude toward decisions and how these relate to his version of mission. He masterminds the solution of the expansion problem, putting it into place in a unilateral way that, for all practical purposes, asks of the curriculum committee no more than their approval. His goal is not to earn their involvement nor is it even to get their commitment. Rather, he wants their compliance with a *fait accompli.* Others are overwhelmed with his detailed material and presentation; they are caught off balance and can give little response other than nodding acquiescence. A 9,1-oriented administrator who can thus seize and keep control of decisions regarding university mission is hard to dislodge from the driver's seat.

In this example of a 9,1 orientation to planning, we see the play of two of the elements in the Academic Administrator Grid. One of these is that the 9,1-oriented administrator's convictions are strong—it is unlikely that he would have brought up the issue had he not had something close to a fixed position in advance. Second, we see his approach to making decisions. His attitude is that once the administrator's mind is made up, it is the responsibility of others to fall in line. This is what administrative authority is all about.

Supporting Teaching and Learning

The 9,1-oriented administrator's educational philosophy is that the student is responsible for his or her own learning and that the role of the professor is to encourage self-discipline and individual effort on the part of the student. Students are expected to learn what they need to know, not what they like or avoid what they dislike. Furthermore, they should learn according to a standard of competence and sufficiency. Grading is important in this process, and the bell-shaped curve is certainly a wrong way to go about assessment. It is not what the student knows relative to others that is important, but what all students know or do not know relative to a given standard of comprehension. Thus 100 percent may fail or 100 percent may pass, depending upon their efforts.

Classroom presentations should be designed to pack the maximum of information into the fifty-minute hour. Tests and examinations should be given frequently to keep students on their toes and to determine the extent to which they are applying themselves. The value of small classes is a myth. A good teacher can communicate as well to a hundred students as to ten. Thus knowledge can be put into a linear progression from professor to student and students in fact learn best when subject matter is presented in this way. The argument that students in large classes cannot ask questions is not valid. When one student asks a question and gets an answer, twenty other students who were about to ask the same question also get their answer.

Armed with this academic ideology, the administrator responsible for decisions about conduct of the classroom selects professors who are clear as to the importance of their subject matter and how to communicate it. A candidate who can communicate to the student the importance of rigorous self-discipline and who gives frequent examinations for self-measurement can be expected to gain student compliance and is therefore favored in the selection process.

In the next dialogue, the 9,1-oriented medical school dean is attacking "excessive" expenditures for elaborate equipment. His unstated assumption is that "hardware" is an attempt to make up for teaching deficiencies or to provide a way for the unprepared professor to hide. Since the dean considers these hardware costs as peripheral to the teaching effort, he puts heavy pressure on the "guilty" chair to cut teaching aids out of the program. The chair feels betrayed because his department made the conscious choice several years ago to spend money on equipment rather than new faculty. Thus, the chair believes that the planning and choices about teaching approaches that his department has made have not been understood or appreciated by the dean. The dean proceeds to impose his values about teaching on the chair in the name of efficiency and refuses to be convinced that the chair's own efficiency argument is valid. After all, a department that chooses equipment over good faculty must have its priorities reversed and will have to suffer the consequences, or so reasons the dean.

Dean: Explain to me why your department spends so much money on all this teaching hardware. Every year you have an unbelievable amount of money in your budget for teaching equipment—films, television monitors, cameras, slide shows, overhead projectors, movie screens. What kind of teaching situation do you have that makes all this equipment necessary? It's totally out of hand.

Chair: Well, it's for the learning resource center we set up.

Dean: What do you mean? Can you explain how your department is any different from any other department?

Chair: Well, it's a matter of our department's being more willing to utilize some of the more creative teaching techniques.

Dean: What happened to the old-fashioned idea of using teachers to teach?

Chair: It's not a matter of one or the other. It's a matter of supporting the effectiveness of teachers with sound teaching tools.

Dean: Some of the best teachers I ever had never used any of that stuff. They just knew their material, taught what they knew, and they were the best teachers in the whole college.

Chair: As you know, we have developed a lot of the materials in our department, and we also use them for in-service education programs. There are side benefits in terms of use of these materials.

Dean: We've got to put a top on this. I want you to get me the figures for the amount of money you've spent on this type of equipment over the last five years. I'm going to ask for

comparative data from a couple of other departments. I
want you to see the extent to which these budget requests
are out of line.

Chair: With which departments are you going to compare us?

Dean: Any you choose.

Chair: Well, it really doesn't matter to me. Just choose some
that are comparable in the sense of doing a lot of in-service
education programs.

Dean: They all say they're doing that.

Chair: But it's a meaningless comparison just to examine expense. You also have to measure impact. Visual aids
strengthen the students' capacity for visualization at a fundamental level. In many respects the mind is a visual instrument. Once a person can see the connections between things,
that person is in a better position to gain an understanding
of how things really fit together in an integrated way. Particularly in our ballpark when you have to deal with sur-
geons, cell biologists, and pathologists.

Dean: Yes, the eye is the visual gateway to the world. I didn't
come up through ophthalmology for nothing. A good textbook is a good visual field for the eye to play on.

Chair: I believe if you'll check, we do the most in-service education of any department on campus.

Dean: I think you have a lot of frustrated technicians over there
who like to play with gadgetry.

Chair: Now, dean, that's going a little too far. We really have a
good reputation in the service area, but you have to understand that this equipment is also useful to us in teaching in
the classroom, especially in the labs.

Dean: Of course, everybody says it's useful. But the point is,
Can we put a lid on it? It's out of hand; we simply cannot
afford these kinds of expenditures year after year. The contracts on the equipment for upkeep alone are enormous,
and I'm just going to have to put a stop to it.

Chair: All we asked for this year was one videotape recorder.

Dean: And the cost is exorbitant!

Chair: We can develop a lot more individualized instruction
with these. We haven't asked for a new faculty member in
three years.

Dean: I should hope not! You're overtenured as it is.

Chair: But we haven't asked for any new positions.

Dean: Look, let's not get into an argument as to what you have or haven't done. I'm just saying that this expense category is exceeding by far what I think is reasonable. I want you to get the figures together as to how much money you've spent on these kinds of materials over the last five years. Better yet, I'll get my assistant to pull that information together for your department and a couple of other comparable departments. I've got to put a stop to this kind of thing somehow, and I don't know how else to do it other than to show you what's going on in comparable departments.

In fact, I think one solution might be to centralize all this teaching equipment and have all departments use the same stuff. We could probably cut out a lot of duplication that way.

Chair: After we've forfeited other requests in favor of this! That's not a very acceptable alternative.

Dean: It sounds pretty reasonable to me. I'll get back in touch with you when I have the information and we can go over it.

Chair: Thanks a lot!

The control function is the basis of this interaction, and the dean takes a strong win-lose approach to the conflict between himself and the chair. This is seen in the fact that he brings the budget item up and focuses upon it exclusively, without really considering what this budget item may be contributing to the overall effectiveness of the department. His way of exercising leverage is to call for a study of comparable expenses in other departments; this will give him data with which to undermine the chair. He retracts his suggestion that the chair conduct such a study and decides that it ought to be carried out by one of his own assistants. The implication, of course, is that "he who controls the arithmetic controls the interpretation."

Comments such as "What happened to the old-fashioned idea of using teachers to teach?" reveal the dean's basic attitude toward educational innovation, and they also reveal that the dean has a narrow view of mental processes and disregards the possibility that learning can be supported by stimulating the visual capacities of the mind.

The dean is sarcastic and hurls exaggerated accusations at the chair—for example, "You're overtenured." The same kind of disrespect for the other person's point of view is seen when the dean recounts how the best teachers in his day taught. These belittling statements have the effect of undermining the chair's readiness to persist because they indicate that the dean is not arguing in a logical and reasoned way but rather to win his position. For the dean, the end justifies the means.

Establishing the Curriculum

The 9,1-oriented administrator views the curriculum in terms of "blocks" of knowledge. One way to reduce inefficiency is to be sure that course content is not duplicated in more than a minimal way. Certain kinds of content are more important than others and therefore should come first. These views may be strongly colored by the administrator's own disciplinary background. The approach to curriculum decisions is to keep them out of the hands of committees as much as possible. One's capacity to influence decisions risks dilution by committee action. When committee authorization is required by university governance, the administrator may do any one of several things to diminish committee influence. One is to appoint committee members who rubber-stamp whatever decisions the administrator requests. Another is to present a committee with decisions that are at the level of conclusions. A third is to tie a curriculum committee up in knots so as to prevent any decisions from being made. Eventually everyone will be prepared to accept a unilateral resolution in order to resolve the issues involved. Still another method is to state objectives in vague and global terms so that the process of defining them can go on and on. The particular tactic varies with the specific situation, but the administrative strategy remains the same: to make sure that in the final analysis the administrator determines the curriculum content.

In the next conversation a 9,1-oriented dean is responding to a request from two department chairs for a new faculty member to teach a given core content. It may not be immediately apparent that the dean has decided that the content should be taught in department X, not department Y, yet he makes the decision and then simply announces it arbitrarily. The apparent discussion is about faculty hiring, but the *real* discussion is about the curriculums of the two disciplines represented by the two department chairs with whom the dean is meeting.

Dean: I wanted to bring to your attention that faculty position openings in each of your departments have turned out to be similar and overlapping. Do we really need two faculty members in two different departments with such similar backgrounds and areas of expertise? Did either of you know about the request from the other department?

Chair 1: No, I didn't. We haven't had a chance to talk about it.

Chair 2: No, I didn't realize it either. We must be thinking along the same lines.

Dean: In the past this kind of thing wouldn't necessarily have come to the dean's level, but since I instituted this new system for recruitment and selection of faculty and since job announcements are now approved by this office, we catch this sort of thing more quickly.

Chair 1: Even though the job descriptions may sound similar, we can't be sure that they are until we've had a chance to talk about it. What did your department have in mind when it made that position request?

(The two chairs discuss faculty needs in the contested area. The dean listens for a few minutes.)

Dean: So far, it sounds as though the overlap is there and quite extensive. I know that you have both asked for another position. I really can't see funding both this year. Since one request is so similar to the other, even though I know the slots are in the budget for next year, I see no reason for you both to select someone. Therefore, Joe, you go ahead with your selection for this position request.

  Sam, take yours back to your department and come

up with another statement of the kind of faculty member you want, perhaps in another area for next year. Inform them that we're going to select a highly qualified person in this area for Joe's department. Let's hold up until next year unless you have a definite need. You know how much trouble we get into when we hire somebody just because there's an open position. We're usually sorry later. Think very carefully about this position and see how you really want to use it, if at all. I guarantee that we'll hold it for a year and give you time to think about it.

This is a striking example of a 9,1-oriented approach. The dean decides to determine the organization structure and chooses clearly in favor of a division of labor; he dictates which department will have the opportunity to hire in a certain area. The validity of division of labor is not at issue, but the 9,1 orientation comes out in the arbitrary way in which the division is made. The dean has a preconceived position prior to "consultation" with the chairs. He allows them to express their points of view, but his mind is made up, and they are dismissed with hardly an acknowledgment of their concerns or reservations.

Supporting Research and Scholarly Productivity

In colleges and universities where research is a significant aspect of mission, the high concern for performance leads to research being approached under the publish-or-perish doctrine. As a result, many universities that elevate research and publication to the pinnacle of academic achievement seek to stimulate faculty productivity through permitting them to teach fewer courses, granting them research leaves of absence, and making funding decisions that bring the productive professors additional financial resources.

The quality of research and publication is monitored because poor research can bring ridicule to a professor and the institution. The 9,1-oriented administrator has definite "rules," such as the following, to evaluate research scholarship. His scales weigh scholarly productivity and are tilted in the direction of quantity but tempered by the presumed quality of the publication outlet. Under usual circumstances the administrator judges quality only in the area of his or her own expertise. Otherwise, if the publication outlet is the official organ of a professional association, this probably indicates scholarship of satisfactory quality. Journals and periodicals of regional or local professional organizations are acceptable but suspect; the tendency is to grade them of lesser importance.

The same is true for books. Publication by one of the large, old, well-known houses is often taken as a certificate of importance. If the book or text is released by an unknown house, this does not necessarily disqualify it, but the unknown house does not carry the same authority of scholarship as an old-line outfit. Finally, awards, prizes, or professional acclaim on a large scale are regarded as measures of the university's strength and therefore have a high degree of credibility.

In his or her selection decisions, the 9,1-oriented administrator favors strong people and has little respect for the weak or the tentative. This attitude carries over into support of programs and research projects. This individual is also likely to downgrade innovation and new ways of approaching research and other issues as unsound or faddish. Attempts by others to change the existing organizational structure are viewed with suspicion, since the existing structure has proved itself so often in the past. He or she sees attempts to change tradition or practices as an "erosion" of the strengths of the present system. For example, this kind of administrator views the emergence of interdisciplinary research centers with suspicion. The present categories of knowledge are well bounded, and new developments can be integrated into the traditional disciplines without creating hybrids.

In the situation below, the pressure for organizing some sort of interdisciplinary support structure for innovative research is viewed by the president as an attempt to weaken what exists and as a way for some faculty to "do their own thing" without the checks and balances that the existing structure ensures. The 9,1-oriented president is expressing his dissatisfaction with the trend toward establishing interdisciplinary research centers on campus. Convinced that the existing structure is capable of absorbing the proposal at hand, he imposes a strict policy limiting these centers over the objections of several people on the special committee that he has formed to advise him about research matters. The ad hoc advisory research committee includes the vice-president for research, the chair of the faculty research policy committee from the faculty senate, and the president's assistant.

President: What I would like out of this meeting is a clearcut policy with respect to establishing interdisciplinary research institutes. We've had an overwhelming number of requests for institutes this year. I don't see how we can approve all of them. It's out of hand. Therefore, I'd like to go back to the beginning. I want to be convinced that they are really necessary. When you come right down to it, why isn't the department basis adequate?

Faculty Senate Representative: Part of the reason we have so many requests is that federal funding policy makes it easier to get money when the project is for an interdisciplinary research group. Perhaps even more important, traditional disciplines often do not truly represent some of the newest research areas. These areas create the need for some sort of structure where the usual disciplinary lines can be crossed. I think it will be a continuing problem. When it's done out of a genuine desire to do research rather than to reduce teaching load or grind out publications, it represents a definite effort toward creativity on the part of faculty who request these institutes.

Assistant to President: It creates a real paperwork load for this office when grants and contracts from the government come in. We have to set up budgeting and accounting systems for each institute. You know all the headaches. Using the existing departmental structures would avoid this and probably not make much difference to those concerned anyway.

Vice-President for Research: Some of these institutes are certainly beginning to overlap. I can see that an institute might bring interested people together, but I can't see the distinction between the special institute on gerontology and another special institute on human development through the life cycle, which includes aging. There is some overlap there. Maybe the solution is to consolidate institutes.

Assistant to President: How can faculty members be effective when they belong to several institutes? I really don't see the point at all. It produces fluff.

President: Well, you've proved what I already suspected. The situation is out of hand. We're just going to have to do something about it. I don't see why many of these grants can't be located in existing departments. That would certainly make the monitoring of funds more efficient.

Faculty Senate Representative: Once you place a grant in a department, that department becomes dominant. Anyone from another discipline comes into the project as a second-class citizen. Institutes promote equality and allow intellectual differences to appear based on people's real capacity to contribute.

President: The grant should be placed in the strongest department, and that department should be dominant. I don't see the problem.

Faculty Senate Representative: Those from allied disciplines don't feel they have as much control when it's in someone else's department. It makes it difficult for those in other departments to feel committed.

President: That's ridiculous! They are too sensitive. We're all adults. We're just going to have to make it clear that our general policy is to put research grants in given departments. Only in very exceptional cases will we okay an institute—when there is clearly no discipline that should be in control of the project, when the study area is really innovative and different, and when it's unclear as to what the dominant department should be.

Let's put that into a one-page policy statement and circulate it to all the chairs and other interested administrators. After all, the vice-president for research has the authority to approve or disapprove these actions, and the chairs need to know that these programs are not going to be approved in the future except under narrowly defined and exceptional circumstances.

Vice-President for Research: But wait a minute! Are we sure we want to go that far on this? Gene, who represents the faculty, isn't convinced, and neither am I. This will further split the faculty into haves and have nots.

President: I'm sorry, but I think that the policy I've outlined is a very generous one. If we don't take a clear position now, we'll just have more trouble in the future. It's a well-known management philosophy to build on strengths. I suggest you draft a policy summarizing what we've said. Let that be it.

This 9,1-oriented president is fixed and unbending in his thinking. He has a preconceived solution that ignores the real problem of how to mobilize human resources for research effectiveness, and he is only interested in promoting administrative efficiency. He rejects those who disagree with his own position, blocks out contradictory points of view, and listens only to the assistant who agrees with him. As a consequence of his policy, strong departments will be in a position to dominate the weak ones, which are likely to become further weakened. Interdisciplinary research will be reduced rather than stimulated; academic executives who disagree will become resentful and may then go underground to build the strength necessary to win future battles. In addition, this president favors a "survival of the fittest" solution and wants to retain the established order, thus creating no new niches in which the unforeseen might appear. He determines the policy and assigns its implementation to the vice-president for research, dictating that it be so tightly written that there will be no question of intent and no opportunity to challenge its interpretation in the future.

This 9,1-oriented president's conception of organizing demonstrates a tightly compartmentalized mode of thinking— no links, no crossing over, no gray areas. But in an era when knowledge is in a state of flux and the best way to organize it is open to serious question, this kind of predetermination can create institutional rigidities that prevent innovation and creativity—all in the name of quality.

Encouraging Community and Institutional Service

Maximum service effort is expected from everyone for whom 9,1-oriented administrators are responsible, and these administrators in turn are prepared to maximize personal effort for the sake of the campus, college, or university. However, 9,1-oriented administrators are selective in what they take on personally and what they delegate to others. They reserve for themselves those activities that carry with them the opportunity to make important contacts or to be in touch with sources of money or that involve decisions that might add to or detract from the institution's lustre in the public eye. By doing so, 9,1-oriented administrators are continually strengthening their personal power bases while delegating other kinds of service requests.

These administrators view community service as a way of gaining support for the university. It is important to make a "good impression" on outsiders and to mend any cleavages between town and gown. Thus, when a member of the university community causes controversy, the 9,1-oriented administrator feels that he or she must step in. The university community is expected to build rapport with important civic groups and outside organizations in order to strengthen the university. University members' activities are to be curtailed if they create problems.

In the following example, a 9,1-oriented dean uses a required formal performance evaluation of a chair to communicate dissatisfaction about the performance of one of the chair's faculty. The faculty member served on a local community board during the previous year. The chair was asked to serve but declined and suggested the faculty member instead. The dean had "pulled strings" to get his trusted chair appointed to the board and is angry about the substitution (about which he was not consulted). After some prominent community leaders complained about the controversial character of the faculty member's contributions on the board, the dean summons the chair to his office.

Dean: You have been on 50 percent administrative and 50 percent regular faculty time in your department this year.

That's strenuous in a department like yours. How did it work out?

Chair: Fairly tight. As a matter of fact I found myself unusually busy. I know I requested that kind of arrangement last year because I wanted to get back into teaching a bit more. I thought I could handle it, but it turned out to be a squeeze.

Dean: Well, as you know, we need to review your performance for the year, and I would like to take up your service, teaching, and research first and then move into the administrative area.

Chair: Okay.

Dean: On your annual report you identified only two significant service activities.

Chair: That's all I had time for. I had several requests, but I had to give them to others I thought could do the job. It worked out very well.

Dean: As a matter of fact one was a referral I made to you with the suggestion that you take the assignment. I must say that I was shocked, disappointed, and dismayed that you sent Sally in your place.

Chair: Oh, you mean the board appointment. She was willing to do it. I thought that worked out rather well.

Dean: Are you telling me that stirring up a hornet's nest on the board is your idea of working out rather well? That girl spreads ash like Mount St. Helens.

Chair: I know she became a very active member, but I didn't realize she was volcanic.

Dean: We got a lot of backlash. I had expected you to serve on the board because I thought I could count on you to represent the university's interests. She has mucked up and now we have problems.

Chair: I'm sorry. I didn't think I could carry the extra load.

Dean: These community positions put the whole university in the spotlight. I'm saying you were not careful when you chose her for this assignment. You should have been more aware of the implications and the consequences.

Chair: I'm sorry it turned out that way.

Dean: One of the things I learned long ago as an administrator was to read people very well and to make damn sure they have good judgment. Since you were squeezed this year, maybe you weren't giving as much thought to some of these assignments as you might have otherwise. I'm bringing this to your attention as a bad judgment call on your part.

The dean masterminded the staffing of this service request but lost control when the chair failed to follow orders. His staffing views can be seen in his selection of the chair as a person to keep the university position from being weakened. Now the dean puts it on the line with this chair, and it can be expected that the chair will toe the line and be reluctant to exercise local autonomy in the future. The dean's convictions are strong, and his decisions are intended to be final. Even now as he recalls the incident, his temper flares at the blocking of his unilateral decision by the chair.

Managing Resources

Money goes to what this administrator thinks is important, and it does not go to what he does *not* think is important, stated mission notwithstanding. If there is any difference between the two, his or her personal concept of mission replaces the stated mission. In this way, the 9,1-oriented administrator establishes or maintains mastery over university mission. There is only one exception to this general statement; that is, money goes to the loyal and not to the disloyal or antagonistic, and the withholding of money thus becomes a form of administrative punishment. Since the loyal may come from the ranks of the unimportant and the antagonistic and disloyal from the ranks of the powerful, the 9,1-oriented administrator may at times be torn, but these occasions are likely to be few and far between.

Learning how the financial management process works is almost a full-time job because it is not written up in any instruction manual. It is taught through mentors in quiet corners at five o'clock meetings. The 9,1-oriented administrator knows how the money game is played and plays it well—for the good of the university, of course.

There is one way for a university administrator to become a hero in the eyes of subordinates, to gain increased power over colleagues, and to implement his or her own views of the mission of the university in one fell swoop. That way is to get more of the available dollar pie than competitors are able to acquire in the annual budget conference. This can apply to a president competing with other presidents in a state system, to deans competing with other deans, or to chairs competing with other chairs.

The 9,1-oriented administrator is the one who comes back with the chips. He or she secures funding for three new grading assistants when all other chairs in the division are able to get only one or two. The 9,1-oriented administrator's secretarial pool holds at six clerical people, whereas other administrators, with an average of four staff members each, lose one. Since the others lose one each, an overall cost reduction is accomplished on the campus.

When such an administrator decides that one faction of the faculty is not adequately supporting the proper university or departmental mission, this faction is told that the president has refused to fund its special proposals or that summer teaching money has dried up. Since most faculty and lower-level administrators are not likely to question the decisions of budgeting conferences or the advocacy of their requests, the administrator is usually home free. Others have learned to take his or her word as final.

In the following case, the 9,1-oriented vice-president for administration and several other vice-presidents are meeting with the president to go over their administrative budgets for the coming year. The president had previously warned them to develop very conservative budget proposals. They know they are in competition for the available dollars. In previous years, the pattern had been for each to bargain independently. This time the president has asked them to meet together—group members should share information and, at least in the mind of the president, will then become more understanding and more reasonable in their requests.

Vice-President for Administration: I'm glad we're going to hear the budget proposals of everyone at the same time. It certainly can make for a lot more consistency and coordination.

President: Yes, I agree. I'm glad you made that proposal last year.

Vice-President for Administration: I would like to go first.

President: It's fine with me.

(Everyone else nods in agreement.)

Vice-President for Administration: Now, I have taken great pains to make the budget I'm proposing this year reasonable. I have followed the president's suggestions with respect to containing it as much as possible. I have only two additional expenditure areas to add to the budget beyond the basic maintenance budget that results from projecting last year to this. In other words, no other expenditures except two major projects. I've kept the staff the same size, and the other budget items are the same except for the usual inflation adjustment. I've really kept this at the bread-and-butter level.

The projects I'm adding to the budget are both year long. You're going to be absolutely jealous when you hear how clever they are. (The others laugh.) One is so innovative and so terrific that you'll be amazed. These will greatly increase the efficiency of university operations, and in the long run we'll be saving money. The efficiency savings will pay back these budget items in five years.

(He describes the project.)

Vice-President 2: Well, that first project proposal is not all that new. There are two colleges that I'm familiar with that . . .

Vice-President for Administration: You're not going to tell me that my idea has already been tried somewhere else, are you?

Vice-President 2: Well, I have heard of similar programs in two other places. It would be worth looking into.

Vice-President for Administration: Which ones are you talking about?

Vice-President 2: Purdue and Berkeley.

Vice-President for Administration: I've looked into those and they're not the same at all. If you would like, I'll be happy to detail the major differences, although I can't do it today because I've got to make another meeting. Believe me, they didn't go nearly so far as this one; what they were doing is really old hat. However, I guess there's no way you could have known that.

Vice-President 2: Well, it sounds very similar to me.

Vice-President for Administration: Of course, but that's way out of your area. You can take my word for it that my project is much different from either one of those. They're really not the same at all.

Vice-President 2: It's hard to tell from the budget statement.

Vice-President for Administration: I know. I do have the information, though, if you're interested.

(Other vice-presidents begin their presentations. The president sits quietly.)

Here we see the vacuum created by a 1,1-oriented president being filled by a 9,1-oriented vice-president for administration. The vice-president for administration's 9,1-oriented approach to budget planning is evidenced in the following: He seizes the initiative and sets the tone of the meeting, putting forth a proposal to get more money in such a positive way that it is hard for others to criticize the proposal. In doing so, he indicates that everything in the budget is the same as before except for the two projects. Then he introduces the projects, all the while emphasizing to others how clever he has been in bringing these two projects to the budget stage. In his own estimation, his convictions regarding the rightness of his request are incontrovertible.

Supervising Personnel

For the 9,1-oriented administrator, the key to productivity is to select the *right* people. Sometimes choices are wrong, and people don't live up to expectations. In such cases, the solution is simple: replace them. This kind of administrator has little tolerance for incompetence and no real conviction about being able to develop people. Seldom is the lack of productivity seen as situational—people who don't perform are either not motivated or have poor skills. The 9,1-oriented administrator first tries exhortation and then close supervision. If these fail, another person is hired to do the job. The subordinate is never asked whether the job is poorly structured, the instructions are clear, or the goals are proper or whether the rationale for the total effort makes any sense. After all, the 9,1-oriented administrator structured the job, gave the instructions, and set the goals, and he or she harbors little doubt about the directions that were set.

The 9,1-oriented administrator is known for being clear and consistent, for holding people to deadlines, and for rewarding performers. Those who can't cut it are encouraged to look for jobs elsewhere. This philosophy applies particularly to staff, since faculty have to be handled somewhat more cautiously and with more finesse.

When it comes to selecting junior faculty, the 9,1-oriented administrator relies heavily on evidence. If a candidate published as a graduate student in a decent journal, this can be taken as at least tangential evidence of promise. If he or she has been a teaching assistant or was held over a year after receiving his or her degree to serve as an instructor or lecturer, this is more evidence of ability. Much of the risk of personnel selection is removed when such clues are coupled with evidence of good personal attitudes and loyal dedication to university values.

Performance becomes even more important in the context of the tenure decision. Now the 9,1-oriented administrator goes far beyond the title to dig into the text. The candidate for tenure is seen as unworthy of tenure until he or she proves otherwise, and such study of the candidate does not stop when the administrator has reached a conclusion. If he or she decides that the candidate is not qualified, then the 9,1-oriented administrator goes much further in order to accumulate evidence and make an airtight case. The 9,1-oriented approach to the problem of nonproductive faculty members is to push, berate, and belittle them; this approach is intended to make delinquent professors so uncomfortable that they will wake up and produce or leave of their own volition. (The likely impact, though, is to make them shrivel up and intrude even less in the affairs of the campus.)

In the following example, we see this gloves-off personnel philosophy clearly. The director of data processing is not managing his staff effectively. Recently promoted to director, he has caused dissatisfaction among the keypunch operators and other technical personnel. The business manager, who operates under a 9,1 orientation, is discussing his decision to fire the director with the vice-president for business affairs.

Business Manager: I wanted to follow up on the conversation we had Saturday night.

Vice-President: Oh, yes! I wanted to talk with you about that. I'm glad you came by.

Business Manager: The director of data processing is just not doing the job we hired him to do, and I want to know how much trouble we're going to get ourselves into if we simply don't renew his contract.

Vice-President: Legally, that's certainly within your prerogative.

Business Manager: It's discouraging to pay that much money for a person and then have him turn out to be so inept.

Vice-President: It happens now and then. Staff quality is hard to predict. Sometimes we're misled by the references we get.

Business Manager: Yes, and we got really good ones on him, but he's just not working out.

Vice-President: What's he doing to cause so much trouble?

Business Manager: As you know, his background is very strong in data processing. He has about fifteen years of experience, but he has never managed a department before, although he's been an assistant manager. It was time for him to move up to a director's slot. But for some reason, since he took the job, there has been more turmoil within that department and more griping and complaints than I've seen in a long time. There's just a real problem with his management style. I've come down hard on him several times, and I've told him again and again that he's going to have to improve. So far he's just not been able to change. I can't see why somebody with all his experience can't manage people.

If I were to summarize, I think he has little or no ability to delegate. Many people in that department have been there for years. They know their jobs. He doesn't leave them alone; he stirs things up and tries to tell everybody what to do and gets into all kinds of details a manager shouldn't get into. This gets the women upset because they're used to running their own units. At any rate, we've had some serious turnover, and three of our most productive workers quit within a week. That was the last straw. I called him in and read him the riot act.

Vice-President: What was his reaction?

Business Manager: It was kind of interesting. All he did was talk about management by objectives and cite experts to justify his position. He told me how he's been able to turn the place around to meet objectives and get the work out. I just couldn't make him understand that losing personnel like that is not helping our productivity at all. I told him that he has about six weeks left, and he'd better look for another job.

Vice-President: So you already told him his days are numbered?

Business Manager: Oh, yes. I just wanted to warn you because I suspect he's going to come to talk about the whole thing with you. He still thinks he's doing a magnificent job and simply can't understand why I don't see it.

Vice-President: Do you think he'll carry this thing to a grievance committee?

Business Manager: I don't see how he could support any kind of grievance. He's not a minority so he can't claim discrimination; he hasn't been here very long, just three years, and not that long as a director. He made a good yes-man when Sam was the director and seemed not to have any kind of problems because Sam took care of all the professional management, while he took care of some of the nitty-gritty stuff

like equipment maintenance and that sort of thing. He's
actually very good mechanically and a good diagnostician.
At any rate, I think we have a situation here of a person
who is a victim of the Peter Principle. I'm ready to get rid of
him, and I wanted to make sure you would stand behind me
on this when he comes to talk to you.

Vice-President: I'm certainly glad you've informed me. I appreciate your frankness. I hate to be caught off guard by this
sort of thing. As you know, some people don't tell it like it
is, and then I get caught talking about these situations without having heard the supervisor's side of the story first. It
really puts me in a terrible situation. But if you're convinced that he has to go, I'll back you up by saying the final
decision is yours.

Business Manager: Thanks, I knew I could count on you.

The business manager's orientation is seen in the way that
he reached a conclusion in his own mind, took an action based
on it, and is now lining up the vice-president's support to ensure
that he runs no risk of being undercut. This is particularly revealing of a 9,1-oriented approach to staffing and development
—if a person doesn't have it, he or she can't acquire it. It's a
sink-or-swim proposition and this person is declared "sunk."

Coordinating Student Affairs

In counseling with students from the standpoint of degree requirements, the 9,1-oriented administrator is alert to any
attempts at departures from these requirements, and he prefers
that exceptions to university rules and regulations need not be
extended or even considered. Students are constantly testing
rules and policies for exceptions. Unless the administrator takes
a strong and unwavering stand by not winking at deviations or
granting exceptions, the erosion of rules and policies can un-
leash a flood, with the result that after a period of time standards will have been so undermined and gutted that they no
longer have any pertinence or force.

The 9,1-oriented administrator views organized student

affairs as able to bring credit or discredit to the campus and thus scrutinizes them carefully. For example, he or she is likely to exercise close supervision of the editorial policy of the student newspaper, trying to get those responsible for editorial writing to operate within narrow boundaries and to ensure that editorials will not be critical of the university. When articles are out of line, the 9,1-oriented administrator feels little reluctance in bringing this to the attention of the persons responsible.

As a representative of the administration in its dealings with the student government, the administrator seeks to limit those dealings primarily to issues of housekeeping—compiling student directories, representation on the platform at graduation, and so on. With respect to student recommendations of speakers, the administrator does not want any controversial topics to be presented under the auspices of the university. He or she reacts favorably only to those speakers whose ideological position, if not neutral, is congruent with the basic views of the board of overseers and administrators, important alumni, other benefactors, and particularly his or her own.

Just as the 9,1-oriented administrator feels that faculty conduct needs to be directed, he or she feels that student affairs require close supervision. It is difficult, however, to control many of the students' personal activities, since these are no longer considered to be the concern of the college or university. But when the 9,1-oriented administrator sees an area of student behavior that is still controllable according to a good rationale, he or she has little hesitation about laying down the law. In the following example a 9,1-oriented dean has called together members of the student newspaper editorial board for an unscheduled meeting to discuss student-written columns.

Dean: I'm going to lay it on the line right now. I want to make clear what my position is with respect to board review of student news articles and editorials. Many faculty members feel that it is good experience for the student to be involved in a research project "in the real world." A couple of the departments have courses in research where the student is able to get firsthand experience. The problem is that several such students each semester are also journalists working on the newspaper. They get their priorities mixed.

Let me tell you the kind of problems that have developed and why I'm in the process of enforcing policy. A couple of the projects done last year resulted in some very embarrassing situations in one of the state agencies. The research students were assigned to the agency and were put to work on some confidential material. A few of the students wrote up opinions based on their research and submitted it to the campus press. It was apparent from the newspaper reports that the students had had access to confidential personnel files in the agency. That turned into a big row. One member of the agency filed a grievance because of the damage done by the student leaks.

This is just one example of the kind of problems students can get into when they dabble in the real world and aren't mature enough to exercise sound judgment. So, you are going to have to live up to the policy of board scrutiny and prevent this kind of thing from happening in the future.

Student 1: I thought we did screen those submissions.

Student 2: The one he is referring to was approved in April; it's in our minutes.

Dean: The point is that you are not screening carefully. You're letting articles go that shouldn't be published. I want you to think about it, and I will meet with you again to see how you plan to increase your vigilance.

The dean is justified in pointing out that the students had breached confidentiality. His position with respect to policy is valid. But his 9,1-oriented Grid style is seen in his approach to the editorial board and his strategy for controlling the problem. He first called an unscheduled meeting without an announced agenda. He then proceeded to outline both the problem and its solution, offering the students no opportunity for discussion or for thinking through how to implement the policy.

Since he has no real authority in this instance, the 9,1-oriented administrator attempts to impose his convictions as to how the editorial board should be conducted by sheer force of presentation and argument. In other words, the administrative function of control is not abandoned simply because the administrator finds himself placed in an advisory role; instead, control is exercised through power tactics that prevent an open discussion that in turn might allow board members to coalesce against him. These tactics make it difficult for the board to resist his directives.

Managing External Relations

The 9,1-oriented administrator is aware of the university's source of support and plays external politics hard. He or she expects other campus representatives to do the same and becomes frustrated when they do not. This administrator carefully cultivates the "right" contacts and the "right" social friends, has little interest in the uninfluential and powerless, and is antagonistic to the controversial.

External relations activities are seen as indispensable in three ways. First, they are a way of helping the university in its competition for funds. Second, they are a way of making an impact on the immediate community as well as on society at large. Finally, they are a means by which an administrator can increase his or her own prominence.

Information released about the college or university tends toward propaganda. The 9,1-oriented administrator exercises censorship, but in such a subtle way that the administrator does not become subject to criticism. The administrator simply plays up evidence of institutional strengths and progress and plays down evidence of weakness or failure.

The senior university administrator is unlikely to exercise direct control and supervision over what subordinates say and do in the sense of previewing texts or speeches, as this is simply too obvious an invasion of other people's areas of freedom. Nor is he or she likely to grant or withhold approval for another administrator or faculty member to make a presentation or engage in an activity, as it would create bad public relations and hard feelings within the campus if such uses of administrative authority were to become known. Rather, he or she is likely to rely on reward and punishment in the sense of praising those that present the university in a favorable light and isolating those whose pronouncements cast aspersions on it.

As for the negative aspect of activities within the university, the administrator makes every effort to prevent them from being publicized. There is no reason to hang out dirty linen. The result is that the 9,1-oriented administrator is likely to try to plug embarrassing leaks or, when they do appear, to make every effort to reduce their impact by making them look less adverse than the facts justify.

In the example below, the president, whose orientation is 9,1, knows full well that Professor Smith is an alcoholic. He has been trying to convince the chair of Smith's department to "do something about Smith" for a long time. Since it is hard to fire tenured professors, the next best thing would be to insulate Smith and keep him from making everyone else look bad. No wonder, then, that the president is upset when he opens the morning paper and learns that Professor Smith has been arrested the night before for driving while intoxicated. The president reacts with swift and decisive action. He picks up the telephone and calls the chair of Professor Smith's department.

President: What's going on with Smith? This is the president.

Chair: Oh, I didn't recognize your voice. Professor Smith—what about him?

President: Have you seen the morning paper?

Chair: No, I haven't. What's the matter?

President: Smith has been arrested for drunk driving again. I thought you promised me you would take care of him last year.

Chair: Well, he's been to individual counseling . . .

President: Obviously it didn't work.

Chair: Well, obviously not. Do you know the circumstances?

President: I only know what I read in the paper, and it doesn't look good at all.

Chair: What time was the arrest?

President: Evidently late last night.

Chair: We were all at a party until about two in the morning.

President: You mean all of you were drunk?

Chair: No, and in fact he wasn't even drinking. I'm surprised he was arrested. I wonder what happened?

President: I don't know, but you'd better find out about it because if it gets out that all of you were at a drunken party, and the whole thing gets in the paper, it's really going to look bad to the community, to say nothing about the reactions of your students and their parents. I suggest you get in touch with everyone who was there and tell them not to talk about it. These things can really get out of hand. Tell them all to meet in my office to go over a strategy in case this party thing gets out. I also suggest you find a way to cover Smith's classes. Sometimes it's very embarrassing for the professor the next time the class meets. The last time this happened to Smith it was never publicized. That may come out too. You'd better coach everyone as to what to say if they're contacted about this. I'll have my legal man with us when we meet.

I'll see you all at three o'clock.

Chair: It's possible that there's some mistake.

President: What do you mean, mistake?

Chair: I mean like maybe he's not even guilty.

President: Are you kidding? I wasn't born yesterday. And by the way, if the dear professor is not down in the jailhouse, get him to the meeting, too.

The president's handling of Professor Smith's problem shows his 9,1 orientation. He takes the newspaper account as final, and indeed it confirms in his mind that Professor Smith's longer-term problem has not been resolved. The same orientation is seen in his effort to eliminate any leaks that might be used by the newspapers and in his deciding to bring together all who were involved, so that they can be coached on a party-line version of the problem. He has, in effect, made his initial decision and taken the next steps without learning the facts, particularly those that might not support his own point of view. The president has decided in advance what the problem is, who should be involved in containing it, and the strategy he wants applied in a coordinated way.

Assuring Basic Operations

As for operation of the physical plant, the 9,1-oriented administrator exercises close supervision to increase productivity and to reduce expenses caused by the ineptness of subordinates. He or she does, however, delegate authority to those who have proved themselves capable. This often means that a 9,1-oriented administrator consistently rewards persons in staff jobs who keep to themselves and run their own show in a business-like way. However, when a crisis occurs or an unforeseen problem arises, the administrator is likely to blame the support person in charge for not informing him or her about what was going on or not managing the unit properly. Therefore the support person is often placed in a double-bind: "Which is better, to tell and get chewed out or *not* tell and get chewed out?"

The chief of police in the following situation is a relatively innovative, open administrator. He has not yet learned to adjust to the communication pattern of his superior. Instead, he expects to discuss problems with his superior and to get help, in the form of advice, modification of policy, or at least a sympathetic ear. The 9,1-oriented superior, on the other hand, doesn't want to know what his subordinate's problems are. He expects the chief to execute his tasks without philosophical discussions. The chief is seeking the 9,1-oriented vice-president's consultation about needed exceptions to the overall university personnel policies, which do not seem to fit the campus police personnel situation.

Vice-President: Look, there's no reason in the world why you people need any kind of special consideration when it comes to a personnel dismissal policy.

Chief: I would still like the chance to talk to you about it. It's important for you to understand what kind of bind it puts us in when we have to follow some of these policies.

Vice-President: We can't make exceptions for every department around the campus. I understand that police work is different, but we still need a common set of policies, and if we make separate procedures just for you, there'll be no end to it.

Chief: We may not be able to get separate policies, but I'd like for you to understand the binds that present policies put us in.

Vice-President: The problems of following the policy are *your* problems. That's what we hired you for, and I expect you to work it out.

Chief: But . . .

Vice-President: If you have anything further to say, put it in writing.

The vice-president's 9,1 orientation becomes dramatically clear in this conversation. The vice-president is in effect saying, "We give clear directions. They are found in our policies, and policies are policies, period. Deviations are unacceptable, regardless of the reason, and I don't even want to know the reason." The vice-president sees policy as absolute, and nothing the chief says does the slightest to shake his convictions on this. The vice-president's 9,1 stance is further revealed in his parting remark: "put it in writing." Because it is time consuming to put complex problems in writing, it is likely that the chief will simply drop the matter. And the likely further consequence is that the chief of police will become less and less committed to trying to solve the personnel problems that arise in his part of the campus.

Summary

The 9,1-oriented administrator's impact is seen in his or her version of university mission; when a contrast exists between the stated mission and the administrator's view of what is important, he or she opts for the latter. A high degree of teaching competence is expected, and the use of "gadgets" such as visual aids is seen as a way of covering up inadequacies.

Research, to qualify, has to be first class, and passing the publication test is the best indication of its worth. Publication by the best houses and the official organs of professional associations is the acceptable criterion of quality.

Service is a means of increasing the power of the university and the administrator's power as its representative. Resources are applied to extend the 9,1-oriented academic administrator's version of the mission and to reward those who are loyal. The strength of the university is determined by the quality of appointments; training and development can do little to strengthen a weak or unmotivated person. Student activities are not "controlled" but are closely contained to avoid unfortunate incidents that might put the university in a bad light. External relations are closely monitored to ensure that university activities are projected in a positive manner. Operations are delegated but are closely monitored to ensure an efficient and well-run infrastructure.

The functions of the administrator are exercised in a unilateral way. Plans are formulated and then simply announced; organized efforts are carefully thought out before being revealed. Direction is exercised so that it is clear who should do what, when, and how. Control is through close monitoring to spot and correct deviation as it occurs. Staffing is lean, with everyone expected to carry a load and a half.

The key for understanding 9,1-oriented administrators is their drive toward mastery: they must prove themselves through performance. Opinions of others that might demand a shift from a preset course of action are disregarded, and these administrators tend to be impervious to criticism. Rejecting others who disagree is characteristic of them.

Most 9,1-oriented administrators place high value on making decisions that stick or on doing things in their own way: "Any way is okay as long as it's my way." "Control the terms of the discussion and you'll control the result." "When there is a problem, jump in, seize the initiative, fill the vacuum, and dictate the solution." These administrators are always ready to stand up for their own ideas, opinions, and attitudes and to press forcefully for their acceptance.

The 9,1-oriented administrator is likely to initiate action, then take the ball and run with it. Once he or she adopts a conviction, opinion, or attitude, it is likely to be adhered to tenaciously. An administrator who acts according to 9,1 assumptions is more inclined to "interpret" facts in order to uphold his or her own views rather than to modify conclusions in line with the objective situation.

The 9,1-oriented administrator finds little reason to shy away from conflict. Furthermore, he or she is a person who is determined to prove himself or herself even at the expense of friendly relations with other people. A 9,1-oriented administrator relishes competition, conflict, and tough discussions because these are seen as tests of skill, as a way to show expertise and to establish domination. The same administrator feels that there are no limits to his or her personal competence and strength. When discussions are completed and conclusions reached that he or she originally had in mind, or actions are taken that conform to his or her ideas regarding performance, this administrator is satisfied and feels in control, in charge. Little or no appreciation is expressed for what others may have contributed to the outcome.

A 9,1-oriented administrator uses emotions in a win-lose way. They are a means of attacking and putting down other persons. He or she finds performance personally stimulating and seeks out opportunities to demonstrate mastery. What effort an administrator is prepared to apply is also expected of others, and there is no hesitation about imposing pressures on others and driving them hard. Decisions are unilateral; they reflect convictions that are strongly held and not subject to influence. Tempers may flare when the 9,1-oriented administrator is crossed. His or her humor is cutting and sarcastic.

Chapter Six

Comfortable and Pleasant Administration: 1,9

The 1,9-oriented administrator, in the upper left corner of the Academic Administrator Grid in Chapter Two, has low concern for performance coupled with a high concern for those involved in the academic enterprise—administrators, faculty, students, employees, and the public. The 1,9-oriented administrator sees it as his or her role to support efforts to make the academic environment a comfortable and pleasing place. Therefore, much effort is expended to create the "proper climate." This is done through encouraging a cooperative work atmosphere.

The particular production goals of a university—teaching, research, and service—are seen as obtainable through individual effort of the kind likely to be produced only in a supportive

118

environment. The administrator does not see it as his or her prerogative to prescribe or to establish standards for performance; rather, faith is placed in the aspirations of individuals to be creative and to perform their activities without intervention, except for interventions that support efforts in a positive way.

The positive pole of motivation for the 1,9-oriented administrator is to gain the warmth and approval of others. To him or her the attitudes and feelings of others are of utmost importance. When relationships are accepting, he or she feels emotionally secure. Because of the desire to be liked, this individual is typically solicitous, attentive to what faculty, colleagues, employees, and students think. He or she seeks their approval by being interested in them, by being kind and considerate, and, above all, by being responsive to their wishes and desires. When others are pleased and reflect it in their friendly reactions, the administrator feels a oneness with them. For these reasons an atmosphere of warmth is cultivated. The 1,9-oriented administrator judges success by the extent of warm feelings exhibited by others. When strong unity is apparent, the administrator feels that he or she has earned the warmth and approval of others.

The negative pole of the motivational dimension is fear of rejection. Thus, a 1,9-oriented administrator reacts to others according to his or her built-in uncertainties rather than according to the objective properties of the situation itself. In efforts to avoid rejection he or she is likely to become ingratiating, acquiescent, and malleable.

When asked about personal approaches to management functions, a 1,9-oriented administrator may mention the same functions as someone operating under any other style: to plan, organize, direct, control, and staff. However, applications of these responsibilities are distinctive.

- *Planning:* "I suggest assignments and convey confidence by saying, 'I'm sure you know how to do this and that all will go well.' "
- *Organizing:* "Subordinates know what to do and how to coordinate with each other. If they need my suggestions, I'm ready to listen and offer whatever help I can."

- *Directing:* "I see subordinates frequently and encourage them to visit me. My door is always open. My desire is to get the things they want without their having to ask. That's the way to encourage people."
- *Controlling:* "I rarely need to check on how things are going since subordinates try their best. I place emphasis on congratulating each individual for good effort. Our discussions usually end with our talking about why we did as well as we did and how we can help things to go as smoothly or more so in the future."
- *Staffing:* "I try to ensure that subordinates are in the jobs they like best and working with those they enjoy."

Collegiality is a key concept for an administrator who sees the university, or his or her part of it, as "one big happy family." He or she is likely to go overboard to establish a spirit of collegiality, even at the expense of performance.

Meetings also are occasions for getting together, and they don't start until "everyone is present." Some topics are avoided because they might imply pressure or criticism. Under these conditions people are not antiperformance in the sense of actively resisting; however, because of the seeming lack of interest of their administrator, they tend to become less and less involved in the work itself.

Implementing Institutional Mission

When a 1,9-oriented administrator exercises leadership in the academic hierarchy, he or she does so without strong personal convictions regarding mission. Instead, mission is made operational through planning how to achieve it. Planning is a way to get everyone into the action. The 1,9-oriented administrator does not like to impose any structure in a given situation for fear of promoting feelings of constraint and "blocking" communication. Since he or she accepts all views as legitimate, ways are found to meet requests of others. This is often difficult, but it can always be argued that he or she "tried" and that someone else was the obstacle. Because the administrator's colleagues are familiar with his or her style, they *do* feel free to express themselves. They know they will be listened to and that he or she will seek to understand their problems. Because of this free-floating style, however, conversations in group discussions are likely to be unstructured. Planning meetings often turn into ventilation sessions in which different individuals express complaints or make demands. The 1,9-oriented administrator sees this as productive communication.

In the following situation, the 1,9-oriented dean is meeting with several chairs to give them instructions about how to complete a survey form that the president needs for future planning. The chairs are to report the kinds of faculty manpower needs they anticipate in their respective departments over the next several years. The dean has just been to a meeting where the issue of manpower planning was discussed and the forms were explained by the president. Now it is his job to meet with the chairs in small groups and get them to complete the forms accurately. But one chair in this group uses the opportunity to bring up a number of other problems.

Dean: There is at least one way of avoiding having to hurt people, and the other deans and I have promised to make the effort. (He pauses.) Retrenchment is inevitable over the next several years; registrations are declining, and this is the beginning of a trend. Some departments may continue to increase, but I am speaking about the big picture.

We deans want to ask you department chairs to plan your faculty recruitment and development programs contingent on your anticipated minimum requirements. Tenured faculty, who have five or so years before retirement, probably should be counted as stable, though a few may prefer early retirement. They are outside the scope of this study. They can be expected to remain.

Where you can plan best is with your assistant professors. How many do you anticipate will remain here over the next five years? Make an estimate of the chances of success of those who may go up for tenure during this period. You will also have some attrition. Assistant, and also associate, professors will leave for other appointments. All this can be put in a table. Use your current faculty as the base and project decrements related to retirement and people leaving, either because tenure is not granted or because of appointments elsewhere.

The other requirement of this planning project is to anticipate enrollment trends and then do a bit of calculating. If you come out at the other end seeing an increase in positions needed, then you will need to develop recruiting plans. I trust that retirement and other terminations over the period will be low and will keep recruitment at a minimum. I also hope we can come through this transition without having to ask anyone to leave.

Chair 1: Do we assume faculty workload is to remain stable and faculty commitments much the same? As an example, we have three faculty on half time in special administrative assignments.

Dean: That's certainly a good question, and I'm glad you brought it up. You may be able to project anticipated trends there too. The deans didn't discuss this, so I would like to jot it down and add other queries that may come up so I can check with the administration to get clarity on these things. It's important because the deans all need to define the issues in the same way across the various units or the numbers will be meaningless.

Chair 2: Are the other chairs filling out the same form?

Dean: Yes, they are, as a matter of fact.

Chair 3: Will we suffer from being honest about our needs relative to other departments? This could become a real contest between divisions before it's all over!

Dean: Oh, no, no. We're approaching this with what the president calls a PMA—a Positive Mental Attitude. There's great support and a feeling of togetherness among deans. If anything like that should arise, I am sure it can be handled if we all simply think about what is in the best interest of the students and university.

Chair 1: Well, our department, unlike many others, is experiencing an influx, and it's going to be hard to anticipate the situation three or four years from now. We're shorthanded right now.

Chair 2: Increase your grading standards. That'll reduce your student load.

Chair 1: I need help on another planning assumption. Are we going to be able to count continuing education and community service in the load? If we get assurance that public service and continuing education can be counted, we can guess what our needs may become. For example, we can probably increase our continuing education programs if faculty members see a reward for doing that, particularly from the promotion angle. As of now people get paid for it, but it doesn't count much and certainly is not considered as important as teaching or, of course, research.

Dean: Everyone here knows continuing education is very important, and that I've encouraged it as much as is humanly possible. We have done our level best to reward people who have contributed this type of service, so if you need my commitment, I am saying I believe in it. I advocate recognition for those involved in it as their promotions move up the line.

Chair 2: Then why did we have so much trouble with Joe's promotion last year? His contribution through continuing education was outstanding, but we got nowhere with his promotion.

Dean: Well, now, I know none of us wants to talk personalities, but I understand what you're saying and am certainly happy you raised it. Thank you for reminding me of that case. It's meaningful from the standpoint of an illustration.

Chair 1: What about other aspects of public service in addition to continuing education? How much can we expect them to count?

Dean: What sort of other things do you have in mind?

Chair 4: Well, like serving on commissions, professional accreditation bodies, or active community participation by being on boards of service organizations that benefit the city or the county, that sort of thing.

Dean: Well, I, for one, believe it is very important for all faculty and administrators to be active in this service. I don't know what can be done on a university-wide basis, but I think it is important for us to develop better documentation of these contributions. Some people are better documenters than others, and, as you know, human judgments are positively influenced by evidence, even though it may not be officially counted. We all know of assistant professors who fail to document these things, and it has worked against them later. Thanks for reminding me. It reaffirms that we need better documentation and some criteria for consideration of public service.

I have a number of things I need to raise with the vice-president, and I thank you for bringing them to my attention. Thanks again. I know we can have better faculty morale through sounder planning, and I thank you for your help.

Here we see the dean emphasizing the importance of staffing because of its value in anticipating human problems and avoiding them. When various controversial issues are raised—for example, pushing continuing education as a way to use surplus manpower yet not counting this kind of service toward tenure— the dean does nothing to resolve the problem. The actual conflict that does appear in this meeting is kept at a low level. The dean agrees with whatever people say and promises to get answers to their questions as if the conclusions were not already indicated. The dean's handling of conflict by smoothing over differences is seen in his pursuit of approval through rejecting nothing, promising much, and encouraging all. This attitude allows the meeting to proceed in a pleasant, if not productive, manner.

Supporting Teaching and Learning

The 1,9-oriented attitude toward teaching is that learning occurs best under conditions of warm informality. Under these conditions the student feels secure and unthreatened and therefore is able to concentrate without defensiveness or self-doubt.

Intimacy in the classroom is better able to flourish when class size is small. Professors can then know everyone on a first-name basis.

With this concept of teaching, the 1,9-oriented administrator is anxious to employ professors who place a high priority on good relations between themselves and students. In curriculum decisions, he or she favors the presentation of courses that appeal to students. Grading is seen as necessary but unfortunate, and professors are encouraged to provide extra support so as many students as possible can pass. When these conditions obtain, the campus is likely to be a warm and friendly place, untouched by the unhappy events that so many other campuses experience.

To the 1,9-oriented administrator, teaching is a "do your own thing" area. He or she subtly translates the unassailable norm—"academic freedom"—into the right to teach in any way the professor chooses as long as he or she appears in the classroom at the appointed hour and students are satisfied. The rationale is that good teaching cannot be quantified; it is a matter of individual choice. Who can prove that one way is better than another?

A 1,9-oriented administrator is likely to place emphasis upon the administrative support function to ease professional burdens, such as assigning faculty to rooms or having the secretary call in book orders so students won't complain about books not being available at the beginning of the semester. Faculty members soon learn to appreciate these services, and most are happy with the bargain that has been struck, although good teachers, now and then, become concerned when they don't see appreciation of their efforts reflected in their merit increases.

In the example below, the 1,9-oriented president has the opportunity to reward teaching excellence because a major corporation has donated a special fund for these purposes. However, not wishing to create ill feeling by rewarding faculty differentially and thus creating competition and invidious comparisons, he looks for some acceptable way to reward "all," without regard for unequal performance. The reluctance to objectively measure performance is typical of a 1,9 orientation.

Keeping performance criteria vague and fluid makes it possible to protect the faculty from unfair scrutiny or embarrassment. The president is speaking with two of his key staff members.

President: I'm really excited about this excellence-in-teaching money. We don't usually get this kind of money for encouraging teaching excellence, and I hope we can come up with some good ideas on how to distribute it. We want to use it so that we can encourage as many people as possible.

Staff Member 1: Did you have in mind giving excellence-in-teaching awards to one faculty member in each department, or what?

President: Well, the problem with that is one faculty member wins, and another two or three or so in that department get bitter. I wonder if we couldn't come up with something that encourages a lot of people without making it such a competitive thing.

Staff Member 2: Well, we could just give a certain amount to each department and let them figure out what to do with it.

President: You mean like a grant, sort of, based on the number of teachers in the department, and let them come up with a way to award it?

Staff Member 1: Yeah, something like that. Then if one department wants to use it to reward a good teacher, they can do that. If another wants to buy equipment, they can do that. I mean, we shouldn't put any restrictions on it.

Staff Member 2: What's buying equipment got to do with teaching excellence?

Staff Member 1: Well, it would encourage teaching excellence by making the classroom a richer experience.

President: I'm not sure that's what the corporation had in mind, but it's something we could talk to them about. Maybe they would be willing to broaden their concept here.

Staff Member 1: Maybe there are some other approaches. We could even take the money and develop a teaching improvement center or put it into the teaching improvement center we already have on paper. You know, that was never funded, although we have the idea and the plan.

President: That's a good idea. It would encourage teaching improvement among those people who have perhaps not been as good as others, and that would certainly be encouraging excellence.

Staff Member 2: But is that rewarding teaching effectiveness? Or rewarding teaching ineffectiveness? If you put the money into those who aren't doing so well and need improvement, is that really what we have in mind here?

President: Just because somebody needs improvement doesn't mean they're not already good. Maybe we ought to encourage a faculty member's desire to learn more and to improve regardless of how good he or she already is.

Staff Member 2: I can't imagine that those people who are the best teachers are necessarily going to need much more improving, at least it doesn't make too much sense to me. Why don't we just flat out reward people who are good to start with?

President: There are a lot of good ideas here. I suggest we turn this over to a committee that can come up with a range of proposals and recommendations. These are all creative ideas. I would not want to neglect any of them. Why don't we collect as many ideas like these as we can, and then take the list back to the corporation and see what they think? That way everybody will be in agreement, and we'll have no hard feelings when we finally come up with something.

Staff Member 1: That sounds good to me.

President: Good. Then let's do it that way. I would certainly not want to jump into anything and have a bunch of people feeling we used the money in the wrong way.

We see the president's 1,9 orientation to potential conflict in his desire to spend the money in such a way that no one will be singled out or made to feel rejected. Another aspect of this orientation is seen in his acceptance of every idea offered by his staff members and his refusal to exercise evaluative judgment as to the merits of these ideas—it might cause conflict among the two staff members if they were asked to come to a single conclusion. Finally, we see him avoiding the issue entirely by directing that a committee be appointed to develop a range of proposals to be taken back to the corporation to get its reactions. In this subtle way, the company, rather than the president, is about to become responsible for administering a significant aspect of the university.

Establishing the Curriculum

The educational philosophy of the 1,9-oriented administrator is that faculty and students alike gain the greatest benefit from campus experiences when doing things they enjoy doing. As a result, the 1,9-oriented administrator approaches curriculum development from the perspective of giving people what they want to the greatest degree possible.

This administrator knows that dabbling with the curriculum is a dangerous thing. Faculty feelings can run strong when changes are suggested. The usual situation is one in which the older, more powerful faculty members have claimed territorial rights over specific courses. They hire new faculty to fill in gaps or to support the program by adding manpower in overloaded areas. New faculty often accept their "gap-filling" function until after they have been around for a while and then they want to claim some of the prize courses for themselves. It is also to the advantage of any department to claim an area of content as being within its territory. The department can then justify hiring new faculty and at the same time keep present faculty occupied. When retrenchment pressures are strong, territorial disputes can accelerate. Everyone wants to keep his or her curriculum rights because they mean job security. Giving ground on the curriculum content issue to another discipline amounts to virtual suicide.

The 1,9-oriented administrator seeks to bring about agreements that allow the maximum number of faculty members to teach courses in line with their personal interests and preferences. This is motivated partly by the recognition that people teach best those subjects they like most and partly by the desire to avoid pressuring professors to deal with subjects not of their own choosing. The 1,9-oriented administrator also wants the curriculum to be one that is satisfying to the students. And if a majority of faculty members have the same attitude, the curriculum will come to consist of courses that students find interesting, with the subject matter presented in such a manner that it is easy for them to grasp.

In the following dialogue, a 1,9-oriented dean is meeting with an interdepartmental committee responsible for coordinating the curriculums of undergraduate courses. The dean is obliged to convey retrenchment news from the president. The vice-president is thinking about how to cut the course load in anticipation of a drop in student enrollment. Responding to a request from the academic vice-president, the dean is suggesting that the number of research methods courses offered in the college as a whole might be reduced if one department would take major responsibility for those courses that have overlapping content. The dean doesn't really want to face the financial issues or be a party to their solution if it means being the bad guy. He is looking for an out, and the chairs with whom he is conferring are most happy to supply it.

Dean: I appreciate your coming in to discuss what the academic vice-president thinks to be a very important matter. One way we might be able to reduce teaching demands is to minimize overlap in course offerings. The research methodology courses seem to have broad application in our many departments. The evidence of this is that basic research techniques and methods are taught in almost every department. There's a lot of similarity in catalogue descriptions. I would like to discuss ways we might reduce the number of courses and consolidate. Maybe we could either have one department take major responsibility for these courses or rotate them among departments on an annual basis, or something like that.

Chair 1: Do you realize what a can of worms you're opening up?

Dean: What do you mean?

Chair 1: Two big problems. Number one, the way we compute workloads, it would be a gross disadvantage to have any one department give up its teaching load in the research area. These are required courses. Number two, these are courses that many of the faculty have taught for years. They feel very close to them. So the second problem is to get faculty to give up their pet courses. These are the two big reasons why any department does not want to give up its particular courses on research methodology.

Chair 2: It may appear to the academic vice-president that there's a lot of duplication and similarity, but it's actually not so. The course I teach is specifically designed for our department. It is not easy to teach one general course that applies to all the different disciplines, even though the same basic methods may be presented. The examples that are offered, and the level at which we go into a particular topic, vary dramatically from one department to another.

Chair 3: I see we're not going to get very far in this meeting. Why has cutting down on duplication become such an important issue all of a sudden?

Dean: Well, the vice-president anticipates cutting back all along the board, and he anticipates retrenchment. He says if we don't look at these areas, somebody else will, and we may be less satisfied in the long run if others get into the act than if we take care of this situation ourselves. It's not the best possible solution, and I agree that it is better to cut and tailor the courses to the particular needs of students. I also appreciate that there are other reasons that any department wants to keep its research courses intact. I want to see to it that this happens myself. If you don't think we'll actually confront a situation of duplication, then help me understand how best to present this thesis in our next dean's council.

Chair 3: Why did the duplication issue have to come up in the research area? I can think of some other areas where a lot more duplication exists.

Chair 1: Go easy there. You're admitting that we have a thin line and that an attack may prove successful. Yes, I can think of other areas too. Should I make a list? (laughter)

Dean: Well, one of the reasons the vice-president seemed to be concerned with research methodology is that those courses tend to be so small. His thinking is that it would be less of a problem to each of you to combine these courses. It wouldn't involve huge classes as it would in some of the other areas. There are courses where combination would cause some disruption, but it wouldn't really result in putting people out of work.

Chair 2: In this area, small is beautiful. The research methods course is a more complex subject than some others. It's not easily taught in huge classes. You need a lot of lab assistance, a lot of tutoring, a lot of working with students to make sure they understand what's happening. Statistics, particularly, requires a lot of individualized attention.

Dean: Well, I certainly appreciate what you're saying. Nothing is more important to us than individualized teaching and particularly research methodology, which comes across to some people as not of immediate interest. I suspect that we may have misread the catalogue descriptions of research methodologies as taught in the different departments. It sounds to me as though there is a lot more individualization than I had anticipated.

Chair 2: The course taught in my department is just the way I like it, and I think it is a very good course. As a matter of fact, I teach it myself and get high teaching evaluations. That's pretty hard to do in the research area, and I would sure hate to blow it now, especially when I'm going up for full professor.

Dean: Yes, indeed, I understand and commend you for high evaluations on research methodology. That's not easy to do.

To sum up, however, it seems to me that while retrenchment may be in the offing, there are probably other areas than research methodology where economies can be realized. Thank you so much for helping me on this one. I will express your convictions to the academic vice-president.

This is clearly a 1,9-oriented approach to organizing the curriculum. The dean is not presenting the positions as his own but rather is using the vice-president to lean on. He reflects the concerns of the level above him and gives lip service to the idea of streamlining university course offerings. But there is no real digging in to test whether or not the "individual" differences that separate one department from another are real. There is no genuine effort to test whether tailoring subject matter is essential to student learning, and there is no real effort to uncover potential overlaps or gaps in the courses. The dean's 1,9-oriented leadership in this context protects vested interests, permits easy rationalizations, and results in shortsighted decision making.

Supporting Research and Scholarly Productivity

The 1,9 orientation to research is that it is "expected," but there is little or no direct encouragement of it because that would shift a professor's emphasis away from teaching responsibilities and social and other informal contacts with students. These latter faculty activities are seen to be of greater importance in assisting students than is research. Nonetheless, even when research is deemphasized relative to the importance of teaching and student work, the curriculum is likely to be arranged so as to provide the interested student the opportunity to study research methodology as one subject matter of organized course work.

The 1,9-oriented administrator's actual low commitment to research is seen in his or her decisions in specific cases—decisions that often undermine the efficient implementation of a university or departmental research strategy. He or she knows that the research process is not closely scrutinized by either granting agencies or other university administrators and believes that a little inefficiency for the sake of good human relations is a small price to pay.

In the following example, a 1,9-oriented chair is talking with the principal investigator of a major grant. The chair sees the research dollar as a means of solving more than just a research problem. The production goal is easily forfeited for the sake of other agendas that have to do with "promoting morale," "saving face," "sharing," and "departmental goodwill." The administrator knows that he can make a reasonable argument for asking the principal investigator to hire some extra faculty over the summer. He knows that the qualifications of the proposed faculty are sound and that they can "make a contribution" to the research effort. In his own mind, he is calling on the principal investigator to extend a favor that is perfectly legitimate and could even be helpful in furthering the research effort. He is taken aback when the principal investigator refuses to extend the courtesy. However, the 1,9-oriented administrator maintains his aplomb and gentlemanly manner even in the face of the rebuff.

Principal Investigator: I have your note about employing a couple of faculty for my summer research budget.

Chair: Thank you for coming by. I know that you will want to help on this.

Principal Investigator: Sorry about that; I came to explain why it can't be done.

Chair: Well, it was a suggestion that all department chairs were asked to explore with each principal investigator. It would really be valuable if you could help. What seems to be the problem?

Principal Investigator: Money. I need to employ people who can contribute to the goals of the project, and I can't see how people other than those I'm now employing could be of help.

Chair: Did I indicate who I had in mind? I didn't realize that was in my memo.

Principal Investigator: No, I got it through the grapevine.

Chair: That's usually a very good source of information! Seriously, however, most of the people in my department can be covered out of the summer budget. There are two or three who really need employment, though, and we could either have them teach courses or work on research. Since you have the biggest grant, I thought you might be a good person to help me figure out how to handle this.

Principal Investigator: I vote that you go the course route. The only one who could really help me is Alfred, and he's not even going to be here this summer.

Chair: Well, maybe we could take another tack. We really do have a large number of new people. I wonder if there aren't some of them who could be more helpful to you than you might imagine.

Principal Investigator: Believe me, I am familiar with the new people. More than that, though, I don't like to have to pick up and cover for people who can't really be used in my research project. I don't think that's what these research projects were intended to accomplish, so I have a bias against the whole thing.

Chair: Well, let's see. I don't know how to help some of these people who actually do need summer money. Some of the new ones were given to understand that they could probably pick up summer teaching or research funds. And since university research funds were cut back so much this year and teaching assignments actually had to be cut back too, we really could have a morale problem.

Principal Investigator: I realize that, but it's not something my research project is designed to solve. Maybe you could go to the administration or find a way to get them assignments outside the university. Have you thought about that approach?

Chair: That's an idea. I do have some industry contacts, and they might come up with something. Let me think about it, and I'll be back in touch later. Thanks for helping me think my way through this problem.

A 1,9-oriented attitude to staffing in the research context is clearly revealed here. First, the chair tries to solve the morale problem of new faculty by distorting the use of research funds. In his proposed decision to spread the work around, he is not thinking about the contribution people could make to the quality of research. He is thinking about fulfilling vague promises made to them in the past—promises that no longer have validity because other situations have changed also. The chair is taking the easiest way out rather than tackling the problem directly. Second, the chair yields in the impasse between himself and the principal investigator by accepting the suggestion that he go to friends in industry and unload some faculty members on them for the summer.

Encouraging Community and Institutional Service

Nothing is more important to the 1,9-oriented administrator than good relations on the campus and with the larger
community. Responding favorably to service activities is a certain way to cement good relationships, and key significance is
therefore given to supporting these activities. The 1,9-oriented
administrator sees service activities as an opportunity for the
university in general—and for himself or herself in particular—to
be helpful. As a result, they are responded to in a favorable
manner, and the 1,9-oriented administrator goes out of his or
her way to express appreciation to other administrators and faculty who make their time available.

The public can be served by academic institutions in a
number of ways. It is common today for faculty to be called on
to appear on radio or television. Such appearances, of course,
afford a good opportunity for the university to create community goodwill and at the same time allow the university to provide a needed service by educating the public on some topic of
interest. The 1,9 way is to bend over backwards to respond to
such requests.

The 1,9-oriented vice-president is meeting with the dean's
council in the dialogue below and is soliciting the council's aid
in identifying faculty who can speak "on camera." The general
subject is health education, and the vice-president has circulated
a list of topics that the media people feel the public is interested
in, such as "Smoking and Cancer," "The Rabies Epidemic," and
"Protecting Yourself Through Nutrition and Exercise." These
topics are not exactly broken down according to the academic
specialties of the faculty; with a little preparation, however,
most could prepare a reasonable talk on several of the subjects.
The main problem is finding faculty members with "personality." The vice-president doesn't want to use just anyone, but he
doesn't want to be the one to decide who is qualified. So he
asks the dean to help him find faculty who can "perform." He
is rather uncomfortable with discussions about performance and
treats the whole issue in a joking manner to cover his concern.

Vice-President: It is my pleasure to tell you that the station has

requested an increase in the number of public service programs. We certainly want to serve the community in this
way. What are your reactions?

Dean 1: I'm for it, but it creates problems for us.

Dean 2: One problem is that we need to continue to use our
best faculty, the ones we know can teach effectively via
public television or radio. Yet, others should also be given
the opportunity to participate in the series.

Dean 1: I've looked over the topics the station has suggested.
Some of them are in areas where we have faculty with little
expertise, or there are problems about how well those with
expertise might come across on television.

Vice-President: Anybody have a suggestion about how to handle this?

Dean 1: Maybe we could have an award for television-teaching
excellence. Not seriously. That would produce a popularity
contest.

Vice-President: Well, individual differences on television are a
matter of learning how to use that medium. Professors are
not necessarily equally skilled in all channels of communication. Possibly some sort of training to help them get into
that teaching environment is all that is really required.

Dean 1: Maybe we could indicate our own range of topics based
on people we know who will be good on television. Just remember that many stars of the silent era could not make
the transition when movies became talkies. There were a lot
of protests last year, people calling in and complaining
about the quality of several of the programs. I don't want
that sort of thing to happen. It doesn't help us.

Dean 2: How many faculty would be involved, and how many
different programs are we talking about? The dilemma is
that we want to offer topics that people are really interested
in, but we may not have people who are able to address
these topics. That's the real pickle.

Vice-President: Thirty is the number I was given. That's a big
increase over the fifteen from last year. They are talking
about maybe forty next year. With the thirty-minute-per-
session format, we also need people who can express them-

selves in that short period of time. Many professors, as all of us know, don't want to talk about a topic if they don't have time to introduce all of the essentials. But we also don't want people who overgeneralize and therefore leave misunderstandings in the wake of their presentations.

Dean 2: That idea of auditions makes a lot of sense to me. Coaching would probably help too.

Vice-President: I agree, particularly if it's done well and with discretion so that no one is embarrassed. We could couple auditions with training? That way the audition would not be a pass/fail situation but a basis for helping each individual professor teach in this new medium.

This discussion is conducted by a 1,9-oriented vice-president. He wants to arrange a situation in which everyone can participate, no one will run the risk of rejection, and all will be happy with the outcome. He can do this by converting an audition situation into a training situation and then by offering each participant helpful guidance on how to maximize his or her impact. This is a 1,9 orientation because it makes the best possible interpretation of the situation and presumes that other people will "buy in." But it is too idealistic.

What is missing? It is the recognition that some professors are likely to flunk an audition or to be so offended by the idea of auditioning that they never participate. If given advice about how to use training in communication skills, they would feel resentful and reject the notion rather than take advantage of it. This exemplifies how a 1,9-oriented administrator seeks to exercise control over a situation without imposing his will on decisions.

Managing Resources

The allocation of financial resources creates many unhappy situations for the 1,9-oriented administrator. There is never enough money to go around, with the result that not all worthy projects can be funded adequately. His or her goal in resource allocation is to please the greatest number. The technique of doing so is to spread the funds so as to give something to everyone and to reduce whatever unhappiness remains by making promises. There are two exceptions. One is that there will be somewhat more favorable funding to those who have been warm, supportive, and undemanding. But even then, the extent of this exception is limited by fear that disproportionate amounts of allocations will lead to a sense of rejection by those who received less. Another exception is the squeaky wheel. In this case the 1,9-oriented administrator is likely to be super-sensitive and to make favorable funding decisions under the premise that money is grease and will eliminate the squeak. We see a 1,9-oriented vice-president trying to mollify an aggressive dean in the following dialogue.

Dean: Our faculty feels mistreated regarding travel funds for re-search conferences.

Vice-President: I'm sorry to hear that.

Dean: The fact is our departments are not the most prestigious. The result? We don't get the money we need in comparison with other departments. How do you get better if you are treated as "no good"?

Vice-President: I can assure you, allocating scarce resources is never a very happy experience.

Dean: The committee that makes these decisions is made up of people from only a few divisions. Many in my division think that it doesn't represent the feelings of all the disciplines.

Vice-President: In other words, you feel that the committee is unbalanced.

Dean: Yes, we do, and for us visibility at conferences is ex-tremely important; maybe more significant for us than for other, more prestigious departments.

Vice-President: I know how difficult it is to say what is fair.

Dean: That's true.

Vice-President: The committee has had to whittle the requests down. It's tough to do. Not everyone can be satisfied.

Dean: But I bet that if the record were examined, we would discover that some departments are not receiving their fair share.

Vice-President: I will certainly take a look at that. How would we go about measuring a "fair share"?

Dean: One way, actually the simplest, is to measure the number of requests made versus the number granted.

Vice-President: Yes, that is simple, isn't it?

Dean: Another approach is to take the total faculty in each school and see if the proportion of travel grants to faculty in a given department is in line.

Vice-President: That's another way to do it.

Dean: Obviously, you could argue that if a department is not turning in as many requests as another, it would not get as many okays, even though the first department may have a larger faculty.

Vice-President: That is something the committee could discuss.

Dean: If we at least knew how they arrived at their decisions, we might have a better chance.

Vice-President: I certainly want your group to get its fair proportion. Perhaps I should meet with the chair of the meetings committee and review your suggestions for allocations.

Dean: Another thing. Some departments have grants that pay for travel, and so they don't put such a tax on the general college funds. But our department can't get those kinds of grants, so we're in double jeopardy.

Vice-President: That's something I really want to think about. Just let me say this: I'll do everything I can to help you. I know the committee wants to be helpful too. I'll bring this up with the chair the next time we meet. Thanks for dropping by.

This is a 1,9 orientation on the part of the vice-president to a matter of control. He is smoothing over what appears to be a legitimate complaint about how travel funds are allocated. His approach is to accept the definition of the problem as given by the dean and to accept in a nonjudgmental way all the possible solutions that the dean recommends. Then he promises to convey to the chair of the committee the concerns that have been expressed to him. The vice-president, in other words, contributes nothing to the definition of the problem, to the diagnosis of its causes, or to the strategies by which it might be solved. Within this context, the vice-president encourages and supports the dean, who may not feel that he got an answer but who cannot deny that his problem has had its day in court.

Supervising Personnel

Selection, promotion, development, counseling, and termination of personnel are the most painful decisions that a 1,9-oriented administrator is called upon to make. Not everyone who applies can be selected; not everyone who is qualified can be tenured; not everyone who is tenured can be expected to maintain peak proficiency for thirty years. To terminate a person can be destructive of a personality.

Since "not everybody can . . . ," decisions must be made that favor one person over another. The one who is favored feels wonderful, but the one who does not get the nod is likely to feel hurt and rejected. The 1,9-oriented administrator fears rejection from others as a result of having to deny them promotion, tenure, and so on. It is this that makes personnel decisions matters of such anguish.

As a result, when a choice must be made between two more or less equally qualified candidates, a 1,9-oriented administrator is likely to accept the one who is more docile, understanding, and cooperative. With respect to promotions, however, the one who might become aggressive and hostile if not chosen is more likely to be given tenure, on the assumption that the more cooperative candidate will understand and accept the delay. A 1,9-oriented administrator simply avoids facing up to the problem of faculty burnout, preferring to hope that the condition will be no more than temporary and that the professor will come around after he or she has had a chance to get away from it all.

Nothing is more difficult for the 1,9-oriented administrator than performance evaluation. It is nearly impossible for this person to openly criticize another. Important decisions about personal performance are therefore handled quite carefully. This administrator feels that people should be encouraged even if the "system" works in such a way as to reward the performance of only a very few.

A particularly crucial point in the career of a faculty member is when he or she comes up for tenure. The percentage of young faculty who can expect to be promoted has dropped considerably, and the system is especially rough on clinical faculty who carry a heavy teaching load. Clinical teaching involves many hours of contact with students. Moreover, students model themselves after the clinical professor, who demonstrates methods and coaches in practice work settings. Such a professor usually has high teaching ratings but perhaps not too much evidence of research productivity to submit at promotion time.

The 1,9-oriented vice-president in the following scene has been asked to explain his views on evaluating clinical faculty. He does not want to discourage such faculty, so he paints a rosier picture of their promotion chances than past history warrants. The promotion committee in a department comprised of clinical as well as research faculty is often stuck with having to tell the clinical faculty that they have not been promoted after many years of encouraging them in their clinical teaching. A few on the promotion committee wanted to go to the president over the issue; others didn't want to be abrasive and suggested a more cooperative approach: "Let's get them to explain their criteria to us, so at least we can predict how our recommendations will be viewed. Perhaps we can change their decision criteria if we discuss the problem openly with them." The chair of the committee suggested they call in only the academic vice-president because "he is such a good listener."

Chair: Thank you very much, Vice-President Green, for meeting with us today. Our committee has had a great deal of discussion about how to go about evaluating faculty in the research area. With your long experience in serving on the promotion committee at the administrative level, we thought perhaps your views would help us to resolve some of the conflicts we have in our own committee.

Vice-President: Well, I certainly appreciate the opportunity to discuss this most important matter with you. As you know,

I fully recognize that there are certain major differences from discipline to discipline and even from department to department. I would hesitate to say what your criteria ought to be one way or the other.

Faculty Member 1: Well, you do participate in these decisions. Surely you have some observations about what kinds of things are weighted more heavily than others.

Vice-President: Oh, yes, I can discuss that sort of thing at the level of principle. What questions do you have?

Chair: One of the major conflicts in our committee is over the evaluation of clinical faculty. As you know, in our department we have a considerable split between clinical faculty and more research-oriented faculty. Our clinical faculty feel that they are not as able to meet the standards of research performance as the other faculty are, and, indeed, with the load they carry and the kind of work they do in their central mission here, it does seem rather ridiculous to hold them to similar standards.

Vice-President: Oh, I think there have been a number of cases where clinical faculty who do not have the kind of research record that our research faculty does have received promotions. No problem there. We fully appreciate the importance of clinical faculty to graduate students; we need successful practitioners teaching clinical areas.

Faculty Member 1: Yes, but such promotions are rare events, aren't they?

Vice-President: Oh, no. We've had numerous cases like that. I don't have the exact figures, but my memory tells me it hasn't been that unusual.

Faculty Member 2: Would a faculty member who has done very little research—let's say he has not published anything but is an excellent teacher and is very well known for his clinical skills and teaching skills—would that person get tenure, in your opinion?

Vice-President: Why certainly, if a strong case is made and documented, I think the president and other vice-presidents and myself are more than willing to entertain that basis of promotion.

Faculty Member 2: Well, as you know, we've tried to get a couple of ours promoted and haven't had any luck.

Vice-President: Well, I don't know who you mean specifically because we see so many, and also remember that the promotion rate is declining. I think our expectations are going to have to be pared down, but the really good people will get through. I do believe that.

Let's approach it in another way. Why don't we discuss how we could be more helpful to faculty or promotion committees in preparing a case for faculty members that we think are worthy of tenure. I think that might be a more constructive way. I hate to be one who's always talking about what can't be done and the negatives. I would really like to put the issue in a positive light.

Faculty Member 2: I don't think it's possible to put this in a positive light, especially when you have to talk face-to-face with these people. The clinical faculty are overworked. They feel a lack of support from the larger university. It's getting to be a real issue in this department.

Vice-President: I know that. One of the things I have thought about doing to be helpful is to establish a special grant fund for research so that clinical faculty could possibly take a semester off now and then to concentrate on research. That's the only way they are going to find time.

Faculty Member 3: It's hard to get research accomplished in a semester, especially the kind we do.

Vice-President: Yes, I know. Reading the resumés and looking over the folders from your department, it takes me a semester to understand what's going on in some of these research projects.

Chair: We would appreciate it if you could give us some specific ideas on how to evaluate the chances for promotion of our clinical faculty and, for that matter, some of our other junior faculty in terms of research. We want to give them at least some targets to shoot at, and we don't have any idea at this point as to what research standards are being utilized.

Vice-President: Again, there is no one standard. We rely on individual judgments. It's very difficult to quantify that sort of thing.

Faculty Member 1: That's what we keep telling them. They don't believe it.

Vice-President: My sense is that it's hard for us to reject a nomination that is well written and fully documented. That is particularly so if one or more of us has enjoyed pleasant contacts with that candidate at parties or official gatherings and has gotten to know about his or her research efforts personally. We all know there's a subjective element that can't be escaped when spouses meet spouses—for that matter, it makes a difference to me when a faculty member shows appreciation of my efforts. There are many influences on such decisions and all are important.

Faculty Member 2: Then your conclusion is that the decision is like looking into a Rorschach card. In the absence of a bibliography, there are no quality criteria? You are really saying, "Nice guys finish first"?

Vice-President: Not really. Rather that each case is uniquely and qualitatively different and that probably each of us on the promotions committee places somewhat different emphases on different things. This way we balance out any subjective factors.

Chair: Thank you for coming by. We do have a better understanding of what is involved. The key, at least as I understand it, is well-written and well-documented recommendations by faculty who are socially mature and make good impressions in their contacts with higher administrators.

Vice-President: Possibly not with quite your emphasis, but the "whole person" notion is certainly basic.

The vice-president's 1,9 orientation to staffing decisions is evident in his vagueness—a vagueness that reduces the likelihood that others will take offense—and in his desire to be accepted by the members of the council. Were he to be decisive, others might take exception to his views. Thus, he emphasizes uniqueness and individual differences—no two people are alike, no two departments are alike, everyone needs to be appraised from the standpoint of the "whole" person. He also points out how valuable individual differences are among the various members of the promotion decision committee: in the absence of infallibility, each person's personal preferences can be modified when weighed in the balance of other people's different personal preferences. Yet the vice-president ignores the fact that different disciplines are capable of sharing uniform or comparable standards with respect to the rigor of theory formulation, research design, data gathering, data interpretation, and report writing. All that the vice-president really comes up with is the generalization that the clinical faculty is just as valuable to the teaching of the student as practitioner as is the research faculty to the student as prospective researcher.

The vice-president also exhibits other aspects of a 1,9 orientation. One of these is his acknowledging the importance of well-written and well-documented nominations. In effect, what he is saying here is that the candidate's protocol is as important as the candidate's actual performance: what is on paper counts, because anyone can point to documentation and defend decisions premised on it. Beyond that, the 1,9 orientation is to be found in the vice-president's indication that social contacts count—the more socially gracious the candidate the better—including how well the candidate's spouse relates to other spouses.

Coordinating Student Affairs

The 1,9-oriented administrator sees the positive conduct of student affairs as of first importance in creating a pleasant, harmonious campus enjoyable to students, faculty, employees, and administrators alike. He or she prefers that degree requirements be kept to a minimum. Requirements tend to stifle natural development and to reduce the student's capacity for free exploration and self-expression. The requirements that remain under 1,9-oriented leadership are largely those essential for the college or university to maintain its membership in associations, and even here exceptions are generously offered and substitutions freely approved.

The editorial policy of the student newspaper is influenced by a 1,9-oriented administrator toward the "upbeat" and the pleasant. On most campuses there are many, many positive features of administration, faculty, and student life that can be commented upon favorably. For example, there is the professor whose fourth book has recently been published, or whose address to a professional body has been appreciatively received. Or there is the administrator who has been called upon to serve as a member of an accreditation review team at another university.

Nor should the campus newspaper overlook the student who receives a graduate scholarship or some other reward of merit, or the student whose athletic performance is outstanding, or the student-inspired event that draws the positive attention of the community. These are all affirmative in character and encourage administrators, faculty members, and students to identify themselves with the college or university and to find pride in its success. An editorial policy that emphasizes the positive is far more to the liking of a 1,9-oriented administrator than one that polarizes and adds to campus tensions by creating divisions.

The 1,9-oriented administrator encourages students to sponsor campus speakers who can be expected to compliment the college or university on its success in its first seventy-five years, or the eminence of its graduates, or the contribution of its faculty, or the wisdom of its administrators. Again, this creates a sense of identification with the college or university for all the major campus groups. Dissension is discouraged because it destroys a congenial atmosphere.

The 1,9-oriented administrator encourages the student government to program activities that support campus cohesion. Traditional activities like a sports event, a winter festival, or a homecoming dance are all encouraged. The student government that takes this approach to student life can collaborate with students and faculty in enriching campus life beyond the lecture, the library, and the laboratory.

The 1,9-oriented administrator does not want to be perceived as unfair with respect to student activities. He or she values human feelings and believes that most people can perform well when given a chance. Lack of talent can be compensated for by more education. Thus, the administrator tends to favor such approaches as "open admissions," "remedial classes," "competency-based instruction," and "special tutoring programs" for the less prepared. Naturally these programs are very popular with students. The administrator views faculty members who feel differently as elitists who fail to comprehend the times or the meaning of democracy.

In the example below, a vice-president is meeting with the dean of engineering, who wants to raise admissions standards in his division. The vice-president reacts negatively to this proposal but tries to hide his chagrin by cajoling the "recalcitrant" dean. The 1,9-oriented vice-president does not want to say no, but he doesn't want to say yes either. He is hesitant and tries to gloss over the difference of opinion with vague appeals for cooperation and by mentioning the "need to talk it through" with others (not present). He skillfully masks his own position and hopes that the dean won't notice.

Dean: I thought we had agreed on this admissions standards business. Now I understand that in the faculty meeting the other day you said all divisions would utilize common standards of admission for undergraduates. From what you said in our private conversation, I thought our division could develop standards that would be more rigorous than the ones applied throughout the rest of the university. Your shift came as a real shock to me.

Vice-President: Oh, I'm sorry but it's not that way at all. Let's go over what I said again. There's a misunderstanding somewhere.

Dean: Well, what did you say? I may have taken it wrong, but I'd like to hear it directly.

Vice-President: I said our university should not get into competition among divisions as to which is most rigorous, which is most scholarly, which is the hardest on students. I said this kind of contest is one we have no desire to get involved in. Now, if there are particular needs in a department, we suggest consideration of factors other than general admissions standards. That is something we would have to work together on because we would need to consider each department's special roles and the impact that these would have on other divisions.

Dean: What about considering the impact on our division created by general or uniform standards that result in admission of unqualified students that in turn leads to more remedial work, reducing course quality, and so on, and so on?

Vice-President: What do you mean?

Dean: What I mean in a nutshell is that we are getting students who are not prepared, and the extra series of tests we are proposing could be utilized to beat this problem. For example, mathematics is important to us. We are just going to have to implement some way of keeping people out who are totally unprepared.

Vice-President: Mathematics is important. I understand that. The problem we must look at is that if you have your own standards, it appears to the public that we are favoring those from the elite high schools or from the higher social classes where they have had more help from their families. You know all these arguments, of course. And if one department uses higher standards than other departments, the others get upset because they feel they have become the dumping ground for the less qualified. If we could all arrive at a common set of admissions standards, I think it would work better for everybody, don't you?

Dean: Great! Then let's raise standards all across the board.

Vice-President: Oh, I'm afraid that would not set well with the public either. Our institution is expected to serve the community and the region. If we were to start raising standards, we would hear from all the minority groups and everyone else who thinks standards are a method of discrimination.

Dean: But that's the very point. Standards *are* a method of discrimination. I *want* us to discriminate; I want us to select those who can take advantage of what we have to contribute and to reject those who are unable to take advantage.

Vice-President: But we know that people already think we discriminate in ways that have nothing to do with ability. With all the criticism these days about testing, I'm just worried about the impact. Have you read about Ralph Nader's attack on testing?

Dean: Well, I'm here to say that I have already told my faculty we would be able to institute that testing program.

Vice-President: Oh, I'm extremely sorry to hear that. I wish you had been at the meeting. What I was trying to say is not what your representatives heard. I think you would have understood. I mentioned that we would work out specifics with some of the departments, but I didn't want it to be a rule.

Dean: Well, can we work out specifics for my department right now?

The vice-president expresses his convictions in a 1,9 way. In many respects he is trying to please everyone by arguing for admissions standards that are "low but equal." He anticipates that in this way he can ward off adverse public reactions and accusations of discrimination and also avoid creating invidious comparisons among departments. When he bumps into trouble with the dean of engineering, he works hard at sidestepping the real issue, but the dean persists in advocating his position on the upgrading of standards.

Managing External Relations

Administrators with 1,9 orientations are particularly adept at public relations. They are in tune with the current "in" phrases that help to oil the wheels of person-to-person contact, are warm and friendly, and are able to sweeten sour situations. Since public relations encounters are often short and there is little need to develop permanent relationships, these administrators find themselves in their element. Their objective is to encourage people and make sure that everyone present goes away feeling content.

In the situation below, the young reporter, just out of journalism school, is feeling good about herself. She has visions of glory as she begins to cross-examine her witness. Her quarry is a 1,9-oriented president who has survived much worse grillings than this. She relies on personal charm during the interview.

Correspondent: We're thinking about an article for the Sunday edition. First I would like to ask a question about a specific problem involving student services.

President: Fine. Fire away.

Correspondent: My question is this: What do you think about the transportation services? The city system is not sufficient. Are you or are you not in favor of special university-run buses?

President: What we have is quite good. We are looking at the alternatives for expanding this right now. I am going to be talking with city transportation people regarding modifications that might be made. I want to explore all these possibilities and several others before concluding as to the ideal system.

Correspondent: But there have been a number of studies already. Is another needed?

President: Well, on complex problems you can't be too well informed, no matter how much study has been done. The committee and I will be narrowing down the alternatives to two or three options sometime later on.

Correspondent: When?

President: We don't have any timetable; sometime later this year.

Correspondent: Isn't that going a bit slow?

President: In these problems, the slow way often turns out to be the fastest way. It's important that all sides have the maximum opportunity to present their viewpoints. We want the most efficient, the safest, and the most economical approach. It's not something to jump right into without really seeing how people feel about the various alternatives.

Correspondent: Well, what our readers would like to know is this: How do you *personally* feel? Do you think the present services are okay?

President: There is always room for improvement. The city transportation system is doing a good job. What we want is meaningful improvement. Before we go to a different system, we want to be sure we've explored all the possibilities of modifying the present one.

Correspondent: But the services have been described as woefully inefficient.

President: What study indicates that?

Correspondent: Well, there are any number of student surveys.

President: Do you have reference to the informal surveys conducted by student publications? They are very helpful, and we are already taking them into account. However, there are some limitations about the way those surveys were conducted, and it becomes particularly important to be careful in interpreting the data. Very few students were questioned, for example, and some say it was not a random sample. Let me assure you of this. Your line of questioning leads me to say that we are interested in providing these services, and you can have every confidence about our enthusiasm for expanding these services in a meaningful way. Let me reassure you that we have been applying a lot of time to this question.

Correspondent: But, there's still no solution, even if you look out on the horizon.

President: The system that will please everyone is yet to be devised. Thank you so much for coming by. We are trying for the very best for the students, and I know that is your concern too. I really appreciate your interest and look forward to your story in the newspaper. Thanks again.

The president is clearly dealing with this correspondent in a 1,9-oriented way. The correspondent may not be happy with the president's planning efforts but does not succeed in trapping the president by creating an argument. By deflecting emotional accusations, the president maintains control and never allows the correspondent to polarize the issue. Her way of reducing any tension in the situation is to imply that an agreement already exists between herself and the correspondent: they are both concerned about the problem. She, the president, wants the best solution for the students. She thanks the reporter profusely, hoping in this way to create a positive attitude. What we see is communication with a person external to the university carried out in a way that reduces conflicts and diminishes differences. Looking deeper, we see the president offering no data, no facts, no evidence as to how a better transportation system will be established. She has agreed to nothing, disagreed with nothing, and kept it all pleasant and congenial—the hallmarks of a 1,9 orientation in a potentially antagonistic situation.

Assuring Basic Operations

The first thing that a 1,9-oriented administrator wants is smoothness in the performance of the operational support divisions. When requests for personnel, equipment, and so on cannot be met, however, the 1,9-oriented administrator shows awareness of and sympathy for the problem.

He or she feels a need to touch base with each of the basic operations every few weeks or so to "check that all is well." The administrator also spends a lot of time chatting with his or her staff. He or she believes in informality—as a means of keeping communication lines open and expressing support. Sometimes, however, these informal exchanges expose problems of which the administrator had not been aware. Then he or she attempts to minimize any negative feelings that surface and to smooth over any cracks that may have appeared in the organization's infrastructure.

Next, a 1,9-oriented vice-president, walking by one of the staff offices, remembers he has not seen the equal employment opportunity officer lately and decides to drop in on her. He finds her buried in print-outs on the floor. He pulls up a chair and jokingly begins the conversation.

Vice-President: I'm delighted that your office is so busy, and only sorry we have been unable to generate the budget you say you need. Maybe you can find some more money in those print-outs . . .

Officer: Well, I do need help.

Vice-President: Of course; the grievance level has vastly increased in the last few years. Now that the ombudsman is on board, we have a source of relief, and your operation is certainly helpful. Then too, we have the personnel department. Have you met with the ombudsman and personnel to see how best to mobilize all these resources?

Officer: No, we haven't. The problem isn't quite that simple.

Vice-President: What is the problem as you see it?

Officer: Well, there's a lot of confusion about the affirmative action plan and this office and what the jurisdiction is. We get grievances that have nothing to do with affirmative action and a lot of time is spent on those cases. Unfortunately, we have to review the problem in depth before we can sort it out and see that it's not an equal employment problem. Beyond that, many times, even though a problem is not within the scope of our office, we are able to offer help with solving it; that may have a secondary positive effect on affirmative action. Therefore, I do think it's important that we spend whatever time is necessary talking with these people, even though the case is not specifically an affirmative action case.

Vice-President: How do you coordinate with the personnel office when it's a regular personnel problem? I realize that you're tremendously overloaded, but since there's no extra money, you might be able to reduce the burden via coordination with personnel. You know, burden sharing, not budget sharing. (nervous laughter)

Officer: I refer a lot of problems to personnel once I discover their nature and find they are in the general personnel category and not strictly equal employment.

Vice-President: What kinds of problems are these, typically?

Officer: Well, sometimes it's a conflict between the supervisor and a subordinate in a staff job. For example, the staff person may be a woman who simply has a conflict with her boss. The first place she comes is the affirmative action office, not personnel.

Vice-President: But why?

Officer: Maybe they feel more comfortable coming here. The personnel office is older; it's more bureaucratic, and there may not be anybody too sympathetic up there to talk with. Besides, I know a lot of the women, and they come in because they know me and can talk with me.

Vice-President: You certainly have done a terrific job. I want to encourage you to do more, and I hope that the budget will be available to strengthen your staff next year. There does seem to be a tremendous overload here, and we might be able to shift some of your burden onto personnel in those cases where it appears to belong there.

Officer: I really think I should spend my time talking to whoever comes through that door. It builds a long-term credibility for this office.

Vice-President: I agree with that, and yet it might be that we can get you some further help by transferring some of these problems to the personnel office. That's what they're there for.

Officer: That's a whole different definition of the problem.

Vice-President: What are your thoughts?

Officer: The people in personnel aren't too sympathetic, to women in particular. There are very few women there. The ones that are there tend to be rather bureaucratic. I think that's why women with problems come here.

Vice-President: But doesn't that result in your getting into things that are not within your scope? Some of the chairs and some supervisors might begin to put pressure on me to use the normal channels. At least a couple have complained that we're making affirmative action cases out of things that are not really related to affirmative action.

Officer: Now we're getting to the core. Why didn't you tell me you had received some specific complaints? We might get farther if we talk about particular cases.

Vice-President: Oh, I'm not sure it's a matter of individual cases. Anyway, I'd be hesitant to do that because some of these comments have come to me in confidence.

Officer: And the women are talking to *me* in confidence. So if we can't talk to each other about these things, who can we talk to?

Vice-President: I really think we can handle this in some way, but I don't want to be misunderstood. I think you are doing a terrific job. Keep it up. I'll think about it some more and be in touch.

The vice-president's orientation is clearly 1,9. He has an organizing problem in that the equal employment office is over-extended and moving into issues that are within the scope of the personnel office. He knows he needs to get the officer to respect the territory of the personnel department and the ombudsman, but he doesn't want to dampen her enthusiasm. He attempts to draw the line between her office and personnel but does so cautiously, almost feeling his way to see how far he can go without aggravating the officer. He works on soothing the ruffled feathers of the officer and tries to show his sympathetic understanding of the "tremendous overload" she has. To avoid making any remark that might be unsettling, he creates the impression that he's trying to help her solve her problem of overload. She "catches" him doing this, and the vice-president immediately tries to assuage any discomfort she might feel by repeating, "You are doing a terrific job."

Summary

The key to understanding 1,9-oriented personal behavior is the administrator's need to enjoy the warmth and approval of others. This leads to unending efforts to create a harmonious social atmosphere.

The 1,9-oriented administrator is committed to developing positive interpersonal relations among the faculty and throughout the entire organization. Sensitive to and fearful of conflict and criticism no matter whom it involves, this administrator often tries to prevent open conflict and to dissolve any criticism that might disturb harmony and a sense of togetherness. Rejection of others is avoided because it creates ill feelings and in turn opens the administrator up to their rejection.

The 1,9-oriented administrator places high value on reaching decisions that almost everyone can be expected to support. This means avoiding decisions that might provoke even minimal opposition. Many times the decision-making process is short-circuited, yet it appears to be functioning well to the outside observer. The administrator does not particularly care if the decisions made are good in any ultimate sense; the standard for a good decision is simply the amount of agreement that can be harnessed in support of that decision. In fact, the 1,9-oriented administrator often does not have a particular stand or position on an issue but instead takes the attitude that "no one is ever right all the time. I am willing to listen and think about all points of view. I invite discussion among others who are likely to arrive at a shared opinion." Since the 1,9-oriented administrator finds situations of conflict extremely distress producing, particularly if he or she is an active party to the conflict, he or she tends to yield to the boss, to colleagues, and even to subordinates and can often be found on all sides of an issue.

When, out of their own self-interest, or for some other reason, individuals maintain a strong stand against the prevailing view, the 1,9-oriented administrator feels that it is best to deal with them on a one-to-one basis. Sometimes these are individuals who feel rejected or in some way are not in tune with underlying trends. They need to be reassured or aided to see that the prevailing opinion is not necessarily counter to their own particular position. Private discussions make it possible to bring these persons around and to solicit their cooperation or at least to placate them. Quite often one needs simply to help them to understand and sympathize with the points of view of others. The administrator therefore spends a great deal of time empathizing with others in the working environment.

When tensions do arise, the 1,9-oriented administrator uses humor to reduce them. This individual is patient, and his or her temper is not easily triggered. The 1,9-oriented individual rarely initiates issues that call for positive leadership but does actively initiate contacts and exerts effort to establish bonds of friendship.

While a 1,9 orientation to administration can create a very pleasant campus climate, it can also be destructive of academic excellence. Whenever performance values and human values come into conflict, differences are resolved in favor of the latter, and in a way that all too often fails to solve the performance issue.

Planning tends to be short term and to be undertaken primarily for the purpose of avoiding conflict rather than to provide a framework within which sound decisions can be made. Organizing reflects the informal alliances of those who want to work together. Directing is avoided by making it possible for people to do what they want as far as possible. Control is not a real issue because people are expected to do no more than the basic minimum. And staffing tends to draw together those who are congenial and can work in a cooperative way.

The stated and actual missions of the university are likely to drift apart under a 1,9-oriented administrator, with sociability coming to the fore and production receding into the background. Teaching is informal and permissive. Curriculum decisions tend to favor what faculty or students prefer, even though there may be little coherence among course offerings.

What research is done receives praise, but the administrative approach is basically passive with respect to stimulating research effort. High value is placed on service, primarily because of the good relationships it tends to build. Resources are used to take care of one's friends and to placate critics. Personnel selection emphasizes the importance of a cooperative and friendly spirit, a readiness to accept things as they are, and a willingness to work constructively within the existing framework.

The 1,9-oriented administrator is particularly wary of hiring individuals who show any sign of becoming discontents and troublemakers. Student affairs are characterized by informality, with extensive advising and counseling to aid students to feel secure and comfortable on the campus. External relations are based on accentuating the positive and playing down the negative. Operations are seen as no less important than the primary university functions, and support is given through continuous interaction and encouragement.

Administrators with 1,9 orientations tend to yield to what others want. They find it easy to alter their convictions to bring them into harmony with the views of others. They abhor conflict and avoid it by smoothing over differences. They use humor to deflect attention from the serious side of issues. Finally, while they are eager to help others, to them "help" means making life easier and more tension free.

Chapter Seven

Combinations of 9,1 and 1,9 Approaches

As Chapter Two noted, combinations of two or more of the five basic administrative styles are possible. The most important of them for academic administration involve the coupling or alternation of 9,1 and 1,9 orientations. This chapter notes three of these combinations—wide-arc pendulum swinging, counterbalancing, and the two-hat approach—and then describes in detail paternalism/maternalism because of its particular significance to academic life.

Wide-Arc Pendulum Swings

Under the wide-arc pendulum approach, either the 9,1 or the 1,9 orientation may be operating but not at the same time. One follows the other.

The wide-arc pendulum swing can be seen when an administrator drives for accomplishment in a 9,1-oriented way, and, in doing so, arouses resentments and antagonisms. He or she recognizes these negative attitudes and then overcorrects by removing all pressures and becoming exaggeratedly interested in the thoughts, feelings, and attitudes of subordinates. Achievement falls, but relationships are restored to a smooth basis. Once again he or she reverts to a 9,1 manner of managing, only to back off again as tensions peak.

At least two circumstances can result in these wide-arc pendulum swings. One occurs before and after a representative vote or a certification election on a campus where administrators want to remain nonunion or keep an accommodating union that has been challenged by a more hostile one. The antiunion administrative forces say, "The signal is out. We want to be sure the election that's coming up results in a favorable outcome. For the next few months let up on the tough stuff. Ease up on applying the policies. Show an interest in people. Find out what's griping them. Take whatever action is required to show faculty we are interested in them." When the election is over and it went the way the administration wanted it to, the same people are told, "Now we can get to work. Cut out the soft stuff."

The other circumstance is related to cyclical movements of the economy from troughs of recession to peaks of prosperity. When hard times hit, there are feverish activities to increase productivity and reduce expenses. Included are such efforts as cost control, workload reporting, and attacks on the tenure system. Cracking down to get efficiency, then easing off to get back in the good graces of faculty members, and then pushing for increased accountability again—this is the pendulum swing from hard to soft to hard. To those whom they affect, the tightening-up actions seem cold and impersonal because they result in an increase in pressure. Sometimes the kind of efficiency improvement decisions that are made do, in fact, result in improved performance. But relationships become so disturbed that trouble can be seen brewing. As soon as an equilibrium has been restored to the campus and conditions improve, attention turns away from the kinds of efficiency moves previously taken. The administration feels compelled to ease off and to demonstrate increased concern for personnel and thus shifts to a 1,9 approach to show that it does cherish human values. Control programs tend to fade out, and inefficient practices creep back in. Without the goad associated with economic threat, practices that are in fact "soft" are likely to be overlooked or accepted. After a degree of confidence and peace has been restored, another period of hard times leads to a new tightening up to regain the losses in quality and efficiency suffered during the previous swing.

As people catch on to what is happening, these kinds of swings begin to sow the seed of their own destruction. People cease to trust the administration's word, and the union becomes progressively more attractive as a bulwark against these kinds of ups and downs. Pendulum swings are most likely to occur when administrators see human needs and performance needs as two ends of a seesaw: when one is "up," the other is "down."

Counterbalancing

Counterbalancing is another way of applying 9,1 and 1,9 approaches. Part of the campus organization, such as the classified staff structure, may be operated according to a 9,1 orientation, and this produces the usual negative reactions of frustration and aggression. To prevent such feelings from festering and breaking out with disastrous effects and crippling the entire campus, an add-on staff component is given the responsibility of keeping its finger on the pulse of these employees and providing disgruntled people the opportunity to blow off steam through ventilating their feelings. Thus, these units become a safety valve to prevent the entire system from exploding under high pressure. The members of this kind of staff department may be called "field representatives," "personnel representatives," or "employee relations coordinators." Their responsibilities are to keep in touch with what is going on and counsel with those who are antagonistic. In some settings, staff services have taken an even more elegant form. Psychiatrists, psychologists, and other professionals skilled in listening are employed for relieving pent-up feelings. The World War II management response to gripes—"Here's your card, take it to the chaplain and have it punched"—exemplifies the concept of counterbalancing, although this "solution" has been strengthened and refined since then.

An example of the counterbalancing concept in practice is described in the early studies of the Hawthorne plant of Western Electric, where nondirective counseling at the work site originated in the following way. While interviewing employees who were taking part in an experiment on the relationship between lighting and productivity, the experimenters came to understand the benefits of the interviews for the people working in the experiment; that is, these interviews allowed workers to get hostile feelings off their chests, and they thereafter began to produce more. Recognizing this, management took another step by making the interview a *part* of the management approach to the maintenance of morale. The idea was to have counselors, paid by management, available to all employees. The counselors would not report to management except to keep it apprised of trends that suggested adverse attitudes were building up toward the company. Employees could feel free to talk out their problems because when they "spilled their troubles," they would not need to worry about being reported.

There are other forms of counterbalancing in addition to balancing a "hard" 9,1-oriented line administration with a "soft" 1,9-oriented personnel department. For example, in some organizations the line organization has become fixed into a 1,9 orientation and is unwilling to make harsh personnel judgments. Then evaluation of managers for promotion becomes the responsibility of the "tough" 9,1-oriented personnel department, which exercises competency judgments and controls promotions. This is a reverse swing in which the personnel staff serves to buck up the weak line. The critical feature in counterbalancing is that responsibility for performance and for people is not seen as a single integrated aspect of managing that rests on the shoulders of those who manage. The responsibility is divided and separated into two aspects, responsibility for performance on the one hand and responsibility for people on the other.

Whether used in industry, the military, education, or elsewhere, however, counterbalancing has a serious disadvantage in that it treats symptoms rather than causes. While tensions are reduced for the moment, the 9,1-oriented administrators responsible for generating the tensions remain unchanged.

Two-Hat Approach

When using the two-hat approach, an administrator practices 9,1-oriented supervision in daily work but removes the production hat at six-month or yearly intervals and puts on a 1,9-oriented "people" hat to counsel with staff in ways that deal mainly with attitudes in general and only incidentally with issues that relate to effectiveness. Under the two-hat approach, performance appraisal is not seen as an integral part of work activity and professional development. Rather, it is scheduled activity, and it takes place only when the "people" hat is worn. Administrators are likely to engage in this kind of activity not because they think it contributes to improved work and development, but because the personnel office has placed them under obligation to conduct these sessions as a matter of organization policy.

The two-hat approach is sometimes an organization-wide practice. On Monday, for example, the chief executive officer meets with staff and discusses inefficient operations. On Wednesday, the same group meets again, but this time it discusses personnel problems, morale issues, and turnover. The actions taken on Monday are intended to solve performance problems. They are considered mainly in terms of technical aspects. Even though they may be tied in with personnel problems, they are not likely to be considered in light of their effects on other administrators, faculty, or students. The same is true on Wednesday. The "people" problems considered at that time may include leaves of absence and scheduling. They may bear significantly on performance, but they are viewed mainly in the light of human needs. On Monday, problems concerning people are set aside until Wednesday. On Wednesday, production problems are delayed for discussion until the next Monday.

The two concerns are thus viewed as separate but equal in importance. The basic assumption is that though there are two sets of problems there are no inherent connections between them. This "separate but equal" way of seeing problems is very widespread in our society, and it is widely relied upon because at a certain level it "makes sense." It is necessary to simplify problems in order to grapple with them effectively. Trying to discuss everything at once, that is, how the attitudes of personnel affect performance and how performance issues influence the attitudes of personnel, gets hopelessly complicated. Yet it is quickly recognized that both are equally important. It is just that they are different. Therefore, to split up these equally important but different issues and deal with them one at a time is a natural way of trying to grapple with problems that seem too complicated to be dealt with as interconnected issues.

Administrators with 1,9 orientations often do the same when asked to evaluate the talents of two staff members. Rather than make a comparison and identify the reasons for the promotion of one and not the other, the administrator pleads that both are equal, though different. Their competence is essentially the same, but each has a different set of unique skills. In fact, however, the administrator is trying to avoid the unwelcome prospect of making a judgment that might result in drawing criticism or might cause one staff member to feel offended and resentful at having been regarded less favorably than the other. The "equal but different" mentality permits the problem to be resolved in such a manner as to avoid real-life comparisons. This approach fails to appreciate that, seen in a broader perspective, the strengths and weaknesses of several persons can be identified and evaluated and that generalizations can be drawn that permit various levels of ability to be distinguished.

Paternalism/Maternalism

Paternalism describes a relationship between a male administrator and those with whom he deals, and maternalism that between a female administrator and those with whom she deals. In either case, it involves a 9,1-oriented concern for performance, coupled with 1,9-motivated approval giving for compliance. The administrator needs to dominate, master, and control but does this in such a way as to avoid the harshness that would produce rejection or resentment in subordinates. If these reactions were forthcoming, the administrator would lose what is also of immense importance to him or her, namely, warmth and affection. Thus this person exercises control but not in a straightforward 9,1-oriented, authority-obedience mode. Rather, control here involves creating a relationship of obligation in such a way as to gain the warmth and affection of subordinates.

A recent television commercial tells the story. In it a middle-aged woman is seen getting out of bed, having difficulty putting on slippers. After she slowly rises from the bed, she walks down the stairs to the kitchen to prepare breakfast for her children, who are young adults, and one of them is heard to say something like, "Wonderful Mom, insists on getting breakfast for us even though she suffers. But she never complains. Wonderful." The camera then focuses on their mother, and she is seen acknowledging the esteem and affection in which she is held with a slight and demure smile. The mother's refusal to be "thrown" by the illness, while she continues to do things for others at a personal sacrifice, earns the children's love and affection, as well as their readiness presumably to do her bidding when asked. In the same way, a paternal/maternal administrator retains tight control in work matters, telling staff in no uncertain terms what to do and how to do it (but often not why to do it). Yet this person is generous, kind, and supporting in a personal way when subordinates do what they have been told to do.

- *Planning:* "I think out in advance of consultation what it is that I think needs to be achieved and then seek to involve others in 'independently' coming to the same conclusion I have drawn."
- *Organizing:* "I arrange the conditions of work so that each person will feel that I appreciate his or her efforts."

- *Directing:* "I rarely give orders or make demands. Rather, I discuss problems with others to the point where they see it my way."
- *Controlling:* "I extend rewards to those who come to see things the way I do and withhold them from those who do not give cooperation or who resist."
- *Staffing:* "I tend to rely on and utilize the resources of those on whose loyalty I can depend."

The spirit of paternalism/maternalism is seen when an administrator calls a staff member over about an hour before the end of the day and says, "Helen, you've put in a good day's work and finished all your assignments early. Why don't we go and have a cup of coffee and a cigarette in the lounge?" Gratitude for compliance is expressed through personal warmth and thoughtfulness.

A paternal/maternal administrator treats staff members as part of the institutional family by telling them how to perform every activity. He or she encourages them to be responsible, but they are likely to avoid exercising initiative because the administrator is unable to delegate authority. He or she constantly checks whenever someone is involved with a problem not previously discussed. Staff members soon learn that such an administrator is never happy with them unless they are handling the problem precisely as he or she would have had them deal with it had they come for advice in the first place.

The result of this way of administering becomes painfully clear when the administrator is heard to say of staff members: "My staff won't accept responsibility. They are bright and capable, with plenty of know-how, but they check everything with me first. They won't take the ball and run. It is difficult to see how they will ever succeed." What the administrator fails to realize is that staff members want to please him or her, and yet they feel the need for double-checking because the administrator promotes a sense of uncertainty that undercuts the confidence necessary for them to act autonomously.

Paternalism/maternalism can become so widely practiced that it pervades the university. The reward for compliance with a maternalist's wish to be "mother" is economic and social security; thus, staff members come to prefer being dependent for guidance to acting on their own. Those who buckle under are given many material rewards from the administration—including increases in pay—to say nothing of personal acceptance and feelings of security. These benefits, in exchange for compliance and dependency, do tend to increase the workers' sense of well-being.

However, negative feelings can arise under a paternal/maternal administration—feelings aptly summed up by the line from a famous song: "I owe my soul to the company store." One way of understanding these negative reactions is this: 9,1-oriented supervision of work rejects or disregards the thinking and capabilities of subordinates. This generates frustration, resistance, and feelings of alienation. These feelings are difficult or impossible to express directly toward an employer who, at the same time, offers economic, social, and personal security to those who comply with unilateral demands. Reactions to indignities, as a result, may be swallowed or bottled up. But they are still there, in the form of seething resentment and unrest, however much they may be masked by the appearance of docility, devotion, and loyalty. Under these circumstances, even a minor irritation can trigger an eruption of vitriolic and hateful reactions. *The formula for producing hatred consists of arousing frustrations under conditions of dependence.* The person in this situation feels antagonized and aggressive but cannot fight back because of the fear of losing acceptance and security. Although paternalism/maternalism has failed repeatedly to solve the problem of getting people to perform, it is still a rather widespread attitude that underlies much administrative thinking.

Implementing Institutional Mission

A paternal/maternal administrator is likely to have a definite and consistent view of the university mission, with few or no doubts about priorities. Wanting to be a pillar of the community, the administrator with a paternal/maternal orientation is likely to choose a mission and set priorities among goals that are traditional and accepted by powers beyond the university. He or she is sensitive to the environment and to the prestige figures and decision makers who populate it and derives gratification from their approval. Thus, this administrator becomes a key link between the institution and its environment and articulates goals and priorities in a way that both campus and community can understand. He or she does this, however, as a means of controlling the institution.

The paternalistic administrator comes across as a warm, supportive, and gracious person unless he is betrayed or unless his goals for the institution are questioned. Then he can be hard, cold, and unfeeling toward others. Those who are aware of his wrath may even talk about it in mystical terms, as if he were an ancient volcano that could erupt and bury sinners without warning. The vengeful side of his personality may show itself only rarely, but these exhibitions are enough to frighten people for years. Then the word is "out" that this leader can be punishing and unforgiving if "his" chosen people wander too far from the proper path. Most never witness the paternalist's more negative side; yet by subtle cues they become aware of its existence, and they carefully avoid provoking it.

The president below is conferring with the chair of a committee assigned to review the performance of the university library system. We see how his paternalistic orientation is readily accepted.

President: I want to go over this report. It's a good one, but I think it needs to be revised in the light of our university mission. Remember that a number of people will read it; I want it to communicate the proper tone.

Chair: What "tone" do you mean? We worked on that for over a year. We went through all points thoroughly. We evaluated the library against the criteria set. That report is the result. As far as I'm concerned, our committee has completed its work in a satisfactory manner. We stated the situation as clearly as we could.

President: When I originally set up this review team's task, I told you about some of the things that I felt were particularly problematic. Those areas are addressed in the report, but it would benefit from further development of them.

Chair: Those three points you told us about have been addressed, not in the exact language you originally posed them, but we studied all three concerns. We came up with very little. It was the determination of the committee that the concerns were unwarranted. With so many people reading the report why do you want to focus on those problems anyway? What kind of impression will *that* create?

President: Oh, no, no. Maybe I didn't make myself clear. You know that when I go for funding I need to show how the money is related to our overall university mission. The problem areas, better explicated, would illustrate our need for more adequate funding of the library. For example, the business school library is one of the problems, remember? Well, you know the past history of the problems between that dean and the head of the main library. They've been engaged in a feud for years. Now that we have a new business dean I hope that we can start afresh, and the expansion of the business library fits in with our priorities. So I need some documentation on the deficiencies.

Chair: Why didn't you tell us all this before? And last year when you gave us this job the former dean was still on board. We had no idea you wanted to expand that library.

President: Well, now . . . I didn't want to, necessarily. I just wanted an in-depth review and I saw that as a problem area; the deficiencies I mean. And I did know that the dean was thinking of resigning. Now *is* a good time for a number of changes over there. The new dean, whom I've just appointed, will be looking for ways to improve morale. You know that library is just one of many problems, but I think with her coming in we'll see some improvements. At any rate, I had similar reasons for highlighting the other two problem areas.

Chair: Well, we sure didn't know how you were going to use this report.

President: Actually, I'm not talking about any major revisions in it. I would appreciate it if you could write about three or so pages on each of the problems. You already have the background information to do that. I'd rather not do it because I wish this to be a faculty committee report. I imagine you can assign one area to each of your committee members and then review their drafts. You all agree on the phrasing. It's strictly your report. I would just like the report to touch on those matters of concern. If you can do this for me, I will consider it a real contribution to the university. Understand, I want the report to be objective.

You don't need to go into detail with your committee about how I might use it. Just explain that a little fuller accounting on those areas would be useful.

By the way—when this is finished, maybe you and the entire committee can have dinner with me when Senator Phillips, the newly selected chairman of the state education committee, visits us for a few days at the end of the month. That would be a good occasion for us to get together. One of your committee members is an old acquaintance of his.

The president is trying to exercise control over the report of the library committee in a paternalistic manner. The chair indicates that a thorough study of the library has been completed, but the president wants to modify the report. Note that the president practically forces the chair to shift the content of the committee report to support the president's personal convictions but makes submission palatable by holding out rewards if the chair agrees to go along.

His reason for wanting to revise the report is shared with the chair on a confidential basis, and he couples his request for extra work with an attractive social and political incentive. If the chair expresses his frustrations or reservations, he might lose his reward; if he goes along with the president, he will have to maneuver the other committee members into shifting the report without revealing why.

Supporting Teaching and Learning

Paternal/maternal administrators are characteristically committed to high performance standards, as are administrators in the 9,1 or 9,9 orientations. Because they use themselves as instruments to monitor quality, it is difficult for them when the quality problem is beyond their area of expertise. Their perception is that they must "personally see to it" that high standards are maintained in all areas. On a small campus these administrators may reinforce standards by attending meetings, getting around to classes, talking with students, and in general making themselves available and visible throughout many dimensions of campus life. When the campus is large and diversified, these administrators look for ways to intervene, at least selectively, and to convey, as far as possible, a sense of "presence." They do not see "quality" as a systems problem nor seek ways to reinforce the internalization of standards in others. They do not feel that everyone can really make critical judgments in the first place. Rather, they believe that they must constantly be on guard and be the first to take action whenever an erosion of standards is detected.

The paternalistically oriented dean identifies a teaching problem in the following episode. Dissertations in one department are not up to acceptable levels. The dean believes that the faculty who are not maintaining standards will become more quality conscious if they know that the dean is interested in and watching their work. He calls in the chair of that department to discuss the problem. Note that he does not really assist the chair in solving the problem, although he says that is what he is doing. In fact, he undercuts the chair and assumes direct responsibility for monitoring the quality of teaching in the chair's department, indicating that the chair can assume a minor role in supervision too. The chair is left little alternative but to accept, in an appreciative way, the dean's strategy for what should be done to reinforce teaching standards.

Dean: All in all, your faculty is doing a marvelous job. There are, however, some important opportunities for improvement.

Chair: Thank you, I appreciate your interest. What are they?

Dean: I've been going over these dissertation abstracts we've been sending over to the graduate school to check their accuracy. There are several from your department. I need to discuss them with you.

Chair: Sure! What's the problem?

Dean: Here's one, for example, from a graduate student who states that his research results indicate little genetic variability within a highly variable environment. Is that a very typical result? Could there be some error in the way he's stated the results?

Chair: I didn't really take a look at that one. I remember seeing it go through the office. Are you questioning the findings?

Dean: No, I'm questioning the interpretation. I have a couple more examples here of either poor writing or questionable statistical analyses. I'm concerned about this because abstracts not only go out to the graduate school but get reprinted in a number of places. My basic concern is that the quality of our teaching does not give students the opportunity they need to fine tune their research skills.

Chair: Why don't you let me take them back? You can point out the other parts that don't seem to make sense and let me go back and check on them.

Dean: We need to go over these much more carefully. The dissertations seem to be uneven in quality. I know these aren't students you've personally supervised, but some of the faculty in your department probably have not been considering the dissertation as a reflection of the teaching-learning process. I'm concerned that they are not attending to their teaching responsibilities with respect to research design and writing as they are applied by the student. At least that's my feeling. What do you think?

Chair: I know that some of the faculty are much more rigorous than others. I've not ridden herd on them, but maybe I should.

Dean: Well, perhaps I can assist you. I know you've got your hands full. And you can't personally read every dissertation. I'll tell you what I think may work. One of us ought to attend every oral exam, or at least those of the students whose professors aren't cutting the mustard. Now which faculty do you think are not attending to quality?

Chair: Well, I would say Hornsby, Abbott, Wilcox, and maybe Walters. Now this is just off the top of my head.

Dean: I know, I know, but I trust your intuition. Now let's do it this way. Send me a schedule or note as to when their students are having orals this year. I will attend. I will go to some other orals too because I don't want those four to feel singled out. It would be good if you could go to a few also, but I will definitely attend most of those for the four professors you named. Later we can talk about my conclusions. I think we will discover that just my attendance is enough to make everyone more rigorous. I know you'll be pleased also to get the message across to your faculty members.

Chair: I think they'll appreciate the fact that you are showing some interest.

Dean: I have that in mind also.

The paternalistic orientation can be observed in the dean's way of trying to solve the problem, which appears to be one of faulty teaching. Reading an abstract, he picks up what appears to be a questionable finding and uses this to get across his desire for more attention to proper teaching in the dissertation courses within the chair's department.

The dean has strong convictions about the need for good teaching. His approach to quality control, however, will be to make his presence felt in the academic process by personally attending oral exams so he can apply subtle pressure on both the faculty research supervisor and the graduate student involved. By making his presence felt in this way, he will be able to communicate to the faculty members the importance he attaches to them and elicit their devotion by expressing approval of them when he sees fit.

The dean "hooks" the chair by asking him to identify the "problem" faculty and then indicating that he trusts the chair's judgment in the matter. Thus, the chair becomes an accomplice, and the paternalist knows that the chair cannot tell others of the conversation without incriminating himself.

Establishing the Curriculum

A paternal/maternal-oriented administrator seeks to exert close control, and in exchange for compliance is lavish with care and support. He wants subordinates to see him as the one to whom they can come with their problems. He wants them to ask for advice and counsel. He is warm and easy to talk with when things are going as he feels they should be going.

At times, however, even one of his most faithful subordinates fails to check with him or keep him fully informed. The paternal/maternal administrator may let things ride and not say anything for awhile, waiting to see how far his protégé will go toward autonomy. (He defines autonomy as "not being a part of the family" or "not playing on my team.") The other person in the situation may very well be doing everything that had originally been assigned or that is obviously part of the job. To the subordinate these activities may be so clearly a part of the overall effort that he or she does not even bring them up in the meetings that do occur. But the paternalistically oriented administrator, wanting to know and keep track of everything, feels hurt or left out when major aspects of the work or even some of the details go unreported. He begins to suspect that the subordinate is "not attending to his job in a conscientious manner." He wants to monitor not only the overall effort but also how everyone manages time, where they put their priorities, whom they hire, and so on. When he feels one of his people has gone too far toward an independent stance, he will let out the rope and then jerk it back unexpectedly, and in the process seek to induce guilt for disobedience in the subordinate. The subordinate can relieve his guilt only by "confessing" to the boss and will then feel increased devotion after being forgiven.

The assistant dean of medicine in the following dialogue has been working very hard over the last year and has had excellent reactions from the intern colloquium series. He is now in his second year as assistant dean and has not been calling on the paternalistically oriented dean to whom he reports as much as he once did. The dean feels it is time to pull in the rope. He does so by scrutinizing the curriculum of one of the more successful programs.

Dean: I notice Joe Goodrich is scheduled for three colloquiums this year.
Assistant Dean: Yes. You know him?
Dean: Know him! I went to school with him twenty-five years

ago. I also know his career since graduation. I want you to know he's a slick character . . . terrific bedside manner but . . .

Assistant Dean: Votes count. I've used him before. He is terrific. He has a knack for hitting the nail on the head. Everybody thinks he's great, one of the highest-rated presenters in the entire series. Great humor.

Dean: He has a knack for extending his bedside skill to an audience. What sort of fee do you pay?

Assistant Dean: Well, I'm not sure. I'll have to check on that. I recall he commands one of the higher figures. He certainly earns it. At least that's what I hear from the program coordinator.

Dean: Did you have a chance to get to the colloquium he presented?

Assistant Dean: No, but . . .

Dean: Well, the next time I advise you to go yourself. It would be even better if you could find a way to personally check out the presenters that we bring in from the outside.

Assistant Dean: Most of the time I do, but in this case I didn't. I was busy at the American Medical Association advisory committee in Chicago.

Dean: I wish you had checked with me before you invited him then. I could have steered you to some other sources to check him out.

Assistant Dean: I'll remember that next time.

Dean: Good, good. You understand that my main concern is maintaining the quality of our programs. I don't want us to get into popularity contests. I want to make sure that our colloquiums have substance. The content must be sound.

Assistant Dean: Evidently he was provocative and interesting because interns were talking afterwards. He really got a lot of discussions going, I remember that.

Dean: But I fear that he hasn't really kept abreast with the research in the areas where he projects himself as an "expert." I heard him one time. He was lively and charismatic, but his information was out of date. I worry about people like that. They can be very convincing.

Assistant Dean: We want to maintain quality. As you know,

that's one of the real difficulties—getting experts in the field who are good teachers and who can present the material well and who know what they are talking about. It's quite an art to carry a full afternoon until 5 p.m. after some of the interns have come to work at 6 a.m.

Dean: I'd like to talk to you about how we might take a better look at evaluating this series. That's a separate issue worth pursuing. Would it be a good idea for you to develop a written summary of how you evaluate your presenters before we meet? Then I would like to meet with you and two or three other staff members to discuss the entire series.

Assistant Dean: Very well.

The dean exhibits a paternalistic orientation in his drive for excellence and for proper monitoring of the curriculum. He "checks on" how the assistant dean is evaluating programs to demonstrate his concern about an individual participant and the content that person is presenting. He focuses on the curriculum as the most vulnerable aspect of this presenter's work. Regardless of the material covered, of course, he will be able to show gaps and question its appropriateness every time a discussion is in order.

He reveals his judgments in a reserved way to his assistant dean and expects the assistant dean to follow up and to "discover" that the dean is "right" about this particular presenter. The assistant dean is put on the alert about Joe and, not having really looked at more than the reactions from a previous series, can't speak to the quality issue. The dean relies on his personal judgments about the individual in question, yet he gives no explanation of the event that he mentions and doesn't tell how the circumstances of it may have been similar to or different from Joe's more recent activities.

The dean is rather gentle in his approach to the assistant dean—he doesn't tell him he can't use Joe since that would be going too far in usurping authority in the situation. However, he definitely conveys a message of displeasure and wants the assistant dean to accept his judgment of the situation. He further induces guilt by suggesting that the assistant dean could have avoided the mistake by personal evaluation or by seeking the counsel of others. The assistant dean is caught unprepared and is not able to fully support his past action. But even if the assistant dean had been able to defend his position, this would not stop the dean from questioning a future decision in an attempt to reestablish his control and the assistant dean's dependency.

Supporting Research and Scholarly Productivity

The paternal/maternal-oriented administrator tries to increase credibility through stimulting faculty research. When people do research on important topics, the administrator can stand behind it and use it to demonstrate how good his or her "family" is. Rewards—money, additional faculty, and so on—are given to departments that carry out the administrator's desires. This administrator is likely to "sacrifice" his or her own research time in order to become an administrator, and in this way take care of the research needs of others. The paternal/maternal-oriented administrator is supportive in a way that encourages dependency. It is difficult for those involved to see this when they so obviously gain something they want from their interaction with him or her.

In the next situation, a problem is developing around the administrative aspects of a research project. The chair is talking with the research group members: George, Jill, and Robert. The secretary has been slow in sending out priority mailings; and as a result, the research project is suffering. The research team is relieved of the problem of dealing with Carol, the secretary, when the chair offers to "take that load off them." At the same time, the secretary is protected from the angry faculty members by the chair, who thus gains the loyalty and indebtedness of both the faculty members and the secretary. She further centralizes communications and in this way increases her control and power. Considering the benefits that she gains, the cost in time for her is minor. The real losses are more subtle. The secretary loses performance feedback because she fails to learn the consequences of her lack of attention to her work. Faculty input and influence on administrative activities are also weakened.

George: These samples have to be mailed on time. They deteriorate if we wait too long.

Chair: Can't you get them down to the post office yourself if they're that important?

George: We can't waste our time running back and forth to the post office. The campus mail ought to be able to handle this. Isn't there something we can do about it? Those that were ruined last week were held up in this office, not in the post office, anyway. Carol decided on her own that they were not a high-priority item after I told her they had to go out as soon as possible. I've examined what happened. Since she didn't have enough stamps and there was no money in petty cash, she let them sit over the weekend and forgot about them until Wednesday. She says this happens time and time again because the kitty is too small, and the secretaries don't have time to be constantly running to the post office for stamps. Anyway, that meant five or six lost days, and we didn't even know it. We found out later that the samples just weren't any good.

Chair: Perhaps—I hate the thought—but perhaps too many people are instructing the staff. From now on, everything like that goes through me. If you have a special request, place it in my hands. There's no other way to keep things going except to have one person on top of these things. I can sympathize with you about the secretaries. They've been acting too self-confident since those raises went through.

Jill: Seems to me they'd work harder if they've just had a raise!

Chair: Well, it doesn't necessarily work that way. From now on I'll take care of this myself.

Jill: Isn't that putting too much on you? You shouldn't have to handle the mail.

Chair: It may not be ideal, but we can't take a chance with that research. I'm extremely interested in having the results for the national convention.

Robert: Maybe it would be better if you were to talk with Carol. You could get her to do it correctly.

Chair: We have a research project that requires special handling of some of the most important sample materials. We can't chance a secretary who takes it upon herself to put them aside and thus spoils the samples. She's been having personal problems and she's been distracted. I'll take care of these mailings or work with her on them until I'm sure she can handle them herself. Don't bother your heads about it and get back to your research.

The chair underlines her support for research, but her solution to the problem is to reorganize the flow of work and to take on the problem herself. She doesn't want the faculty to worry about administrative matters or deal directly with the secretary. Once the problem is brought to her attention, she quickly finds a solution without asking for input from either the secretary or the research team members.

She shows them she is willing to make personal sacrifices for them (and no doubt will expect favors in return). She indicates concern for Carol, who is "distracted," and volunteers to prop her up until the storm passes. In all likelihood she will gently inform Carol of the faculty members' anger with her, letting her know that she "understands" and that she will help her with her workload until she is feeling better. Carol will be happy with this trade, and her loyalty to her boss will be increased. In sum, the chair's power is enhanced all around. Here again, a "sacrifice" is made in such a way as to produce both increased control and increased devotion.

Encouraging Community and Institutional Service

Service within the university and to the community is quite important to the paternal/maternal administrator. Young faculty should be encouraged to accept service obligations. However, faculty are not always able to "get outside themselves" and see this when there are so many publish-or-perish pressures or when they find themselves overwhelmed by their clinical and teaching responsibilities. Accordingly it is up to the administrator to aid faculty and other staff in planning their activities and to direct their energies toward the most promising ones. Otherwise they might not "choose properly" and end up wasting their time in a misguided fashion.

In the situation below, the first dean is a paternalistically oriented administrator. The second dean has described a conference that the first dean realizes is a golden opportunity for some of his people, and he wants to make sure that they do not turn it down. Many would welcome this kind of advocate. What makes his behavior paternalistic? The consequences of turning down a paternalist are quite different from the consequences of turning down a mentor with a different administrative style.

Dean 1: Sure we'll be able to help you on that conference. What is it we can do for you?

Dean 2: I'd like to use a couple of your faculty for some of the presentations.

Dean 1: That should be no problem.

Dean 2: I was thinking of Joe Hawker, Sarah Lawrence, and Kelly Zavala.

Dean 1: Oh, yes . . . all good people.

Dean 2: I'll have to get them released from teaching their classes on the dates we have in mind. That's why I'm calling. Do you see any problem with that?

Dean 1: No. I give you my permission for them to participate. I'm really glad that you're giving them this opportunity.

Dean 2: Okay, fine. I'll call them up and ask them to participate.

Dean 1: I'm sure they'll be most interested. I presume that you're paying them to do this, some type of fee?

Dean 2: No, we're hoping to get them to volunteer their time. This is a very important conference. It will give them a lot of visibility. You know, we have some people coming from Mexico, several from the Far East, and many from South America, as well as the U.S. and Canada. It's going to be quite an international conference. I'll tell them you've okayed their participation and that should do it.

Dean 1: Well, I'm glad you want our people, and I can assure you they will be most willing to participate. I'll talk to them about this myself so I can be sure their classes are taken care of. I'll get back to you with confirmation once I've worked out the details.

(The first dean then walks over to a faculty member's office and finds her at her desk.)

Dean 1: Sarah, I want to tell you about a terrific opportunity I've arranged for you. This is something I think will really give you and the work you've been doing some international visibility. Let me describe what I have in mind and then we'll talk about logistics. And before I go into detail, I want you to know that if you turn this down I'll be upset. This is one of those service opportunities I feel our best people should definitely take part in.

Sarah: Whatever it is, it sounds good. I'm all ears.

The first dean is dealing with this problem in a paternalistic way. He is willing to do a favor for the second dean, thanking him for the invitation to his faculty members and committing himself to releasing them from teaching assignments. But he takes the initiative away from the second dean by inserting himself into the communication network. He wants to be in the middle of the negotiations between the second dean and his own faculty members. By this method he can be supportive of both his faculty and the second dean, and he can mediate the rewards on all sides, thus strengthening his power and causing himself to be viewed by both faculty and the second dean as a "prime mover" and as a person who gets things done.

He alone has made the decision that the faculty members should participate, and he sets them up carefully so that their cooperation will be inevitable. This is illustrated in the conversation between Sarah and the first dean. The dean personally goes to see Sarah in her office rather than calling her to his office—a cue that the issue is "important." He tells Sarah he has "arranged" something special for her so that it is next to impossible for her to refuse. This way of "directing" a faculty member secures compliance with an activity before the faculty member has had the opportunity to explore the full implications of the time and effort involved. Part of the cleverness of the strategy is the fact that the first dean inserts himself between Sarah and the second dean and presents himself as the source of the opportunity. In this way he increases Sarah's dependency on him.

Managing Resources

Where money is concerned, paternal/maternal administrators are on top of things. On the one hand, they are often seen as fast movers because they are willing to give support quickly and cut through red tape for projects that they consider important. On the other hand, they often count pennies and expect a total account for every expenditure, with detailed justification for the smallest purchases. They are aware of the financial rules and regulations and how to live within them.

Financial leeway is used to reward those who are performing according to expectations. Everyone knows that when something extra is needed to complete a project and there is no money in the budget, old "X" is the one who knows how to carve out those extra dollars from somewhere, provided your work is in favor.

Paternal/maternal administrators have a strong sense of the central importance of budget management. Although they may consult with their subordinates about certain details, they seldom include subordinates in preparing the budget. Discussions about the allocation of money are reserved for the real insiders, those who have been tested over the years. According to paternal/maternal administrators, few have the total picture or the long-range perspective or even the right to know the logic of final budget decisions. Their attitude is that this is the one area that cannot be relegated to open discussion. "People just get frustrated. Their limited perspectives and self-interests do not allow them to make equitable or rational decisions based on what is in the best interest of the university as a whole." Thus, these administrators do not involve even their key subordinates in the budgeting process unless the traditions of the campus dictate that they be involved.

In the university that figures in the following dialogue, the custom was for the chairs of departments to prepare a departmental budget proposal and submit it to the dean. In past years the process was automatic. The dean looked over various departmental proposals and, within the total amount allotted, made minor adjustments. He called in the chairs only if their budgets seemed out of line. In the example below, however, the dean wants to change the procedure. He realizes that zero base budgeting (ZBB) offers him the opportunity for more complete authority over expenditures, even though the authority would be more psychological than actual. His evaluative role would be enhanced if chairs had to justify more completely to *him* their proposed budgets. He is setting up a situation where each chair would have to prepare more carefully for the dean's scrutiny and red pencil. The actual decisions may be no different, but the psychological process will be changed and his central, judgmental role will be extended. He rationalizes that he is better able to explain to higher-ups what is going on in the various departments than are the chairs. In one sense, ZBB affords him an opportunity for getting an education from his subordinates. His subordinates, however, will see it as requiring much more careful accounting of their activities—an accounting for which they should be well prepared in order to "look good." Thus, the dean wants to elaborate the budgetary judgment process in order to build his reputation and image as a key figure in the distribution of rewards.

The paternalistic dean is here seen imposing his unilateral approach to next year's budgeting on a department chair. In spite of the chair's personal opinion, she goes along and conforms to the dean's wishes.

Dean: We're going to submit our budgets according to the zero base budgeting system this year. ZBB, you know. This means every cost item must be justified. Therefore, we have to go through a slightly more complicated process than in the past.

Chair: Whose idea is this? I think it's absurd. Is this another one of those monitoring or auditing things the administration has decided to lay on us?

Dean: No, as a matter of fact, it's my idea. I'm trying to cut costs, and ZBB is a procedure for that. Are you willing to try it?

Chair: I'm sorry. I should have known it was your idea.

Dean: You're forgiven. As a matter of fact, I think ZBB has inherent logic to it.

Chair: Since when has budgeting ever been logical?

Dean: Well, maybe it should be. (He laughs.) Anyway, I expect your justifications this year to serve as an example for all the other departments. In fact, I'm requesting that you get your budget in early so I can use it as a model. You attended that budgeting course last summer so you should be prepared to do it in style. I'm counting on you. When do you think yours could be ready?

Chair: How about March 1? But make it clear to the others that I am *not* a ZBB advocate. I argued against it the whole week in that seminar.

Dean: Yes, I know. I got that report from several people. I keep track. I also know that you are willing to try new things even when you don't think they will work. That's one reason I'm glad you are one of my chairmen. I need people who "dare to be different." Like that athletics plan you instigated last year. That was a stroke of genius. And you a member of foreign languages! That's what I like: people who think creatively about administration.

Chair: Well, I never would have had that idea about the athletics program if you hadn't put me on that committee. I'm glad the president liked it. I can't tell when one of my ideas is going to "hit" and when it's going to "miss."

Dean: I'll let you know when you're off base. Just keep thinking. Who knows? You may come up with a new wrinkle on ZBB.

The dean is dealing with the chair in a paternalistic way. First he introduces in an arbitrary way a new budgeting procedure to use as a foundation of the planning process for next year. When the chair belittles the proposal, revealing frustration and placing responsibility for these new demands on the administration, the dean replies by clearly identifying himself as the source of the idea.

The dean reveals his paternalistic orientation in statements such as "You're forgiven" and "I'll let you know when you're off base," reserving the judging role for himself. He mixes compliments and encouragement with pressure to get the chair not only to go along with his budgetary approach but also to become an advocate for the approach or some modification of it. He wants to make the chair a model child to hold up to her peers for emulation. His paternalistic orientation ensures that the conflict between them will be resolved his way and that in the process the chair's personal loyalty and dedication to the activity will be secured. That she may be frustrated is of no consequence to him, and she knows all too well that it is useless to argue.

Supervising Personnel

The paternal/maternal-oriented administrator feels it a part of his or her responsibility to help faculty and staff select their activities wisely. The basic assumption is that the administrator "knows best." In many ways the paternal/maternal-oriented administrator is the epitome of the "mentor" who gives parental advice, counsel, and encouragement to those just beginning or even those who are well into their careers. He sees specific "career tracks" that are proper for his protégés, and he strongly advises them to follow his prescribed formulas for their success. When he sees one of his protégés choosing the "wrong" path, he warns in a supportive way about its dangers and possible negative consequences. He is also on the lookout for opportunities for his people and stands ready to bring those who are loyal to his point of view to the attention of others. He is happy to help them advance their careers.

Expecting the staff to be loyal to *him* and to *his* organization, the paternal/maternal oriented administrator strongly identifies with the institution and its traditions. He believes that disagreement with him is, by definition, a threat to the central values of the organization. Staff members who do not go all out in behalf of administrative goals are seen as disloyal, both to him and to the organization. They are letting him and it down. There is no place in modern organizations for disloyalty.

In the following scene, the paternal administrator is angry with several faculty members whom he perceives as "deviant." They are not spending their time in the way he prefers. Therefore, he puts pressure on them to conform by clearly rewarding other faculty with better teaching assignments. When one of the "deviants" complains, the paternalistic administrator solicits the aid of more loyal faculty in "putting a stop" to the others' misbehavior. He uses the "divide and conquer" approach. To understand the motives in this situation, it is important to recognize the administrator's underlying assumption: "I know how people should spend their time for the good of the organization. If you do what I say, I will ease your burden."

At lunch, the chair is talking with Bill, a faculty member. Bill mentions Bernard's frustrations regarding his teaching assignments, and the chair uses this occasion to flatter Bill and denigrate Bernard.

Chair: How do you like your teaching schedule, Bill?

Bill: Mine is great! It's terrific, just what we had discussed in terms of my preferences. I know a few who are not too satisfied with theirs, however.

Chair: I can guess who they are!

Bill: Why did you give them extra courses?

Chair: Well, they're not doing anything much for the department, and I think people like you who contribute their time on administrative and committee work and help take the load off me should have some reward, don't you?

Bill: Well . . .

Chair: Bernard is no doubt the angriest of all.

Bill: Yes, he is. He feels you're being punitive.

Chair: Where did he get an idea like that?

Bill: Don't you think it's going a little too far to make all his teaching assignments in different areas?

Chair: It's my prerogative, and I think he needs the development. It's for his own good.

Bill: Yes, but he's never had that before. It'll be hard for him to prepare that many different courses all at once.

Chair: He's a bright young man. It may stretch him a bit but that's growth.

Bill: That's not exactly what I mean. You know, he just got a divorce.

Chair: You mean he's got to learn the domestic trades, to sew and cook, and therefore he's got no time for this?

Bill: That's not what I meant.

Chair: Look, I'll talk to him. He doesn't realize the load some of the others like you carry. You don't complain. That curriculum revision committee you chaired last year was a whopper. How much time did you spend on that?

Bill: I didn't even count. I was happy to do it. Bernard should know how hard I worked on that. He was on the committee. But he still feels the teaching should be the same for everybody. Most people in the department teach three courses with just two preparations because they usually have two sections of one course.

Chair: I try to balance the load. There are many things some people do to support me that don't show in their teaching loads. But people like Bernard don't do another *thing,* and there's no reason why he can't teach four courses. If you hear any more gripes from your colleagues, let me know and I'll ask if they'll help me with some of the office work. After they say no, they won't have much of a leg to stand on if they start agitating for lighter loads.

Bill: Okay.

The paternalistic chair is angry with Bernard because he does not pitch in when there is extra work to be done. The chair uses his prerogative to make staffing decisions as a means of rewarding those who do his bidding and of punishing those who don't. His humor takes the form of insulting comments and is a signal to Bill: play on my team and win benefits or resist and you'll suffer. This subtle threat is not lost on Bill, who indicates his willingness to oblige by the "Okay" at the end of the conversation.

Coordinating Student Affairs

According to the paternal/maternal administrator, students are to be protected and supported during their formative years, though the obvious control characterized by the doctrine of *in loco parentis* can no longer be exercised.

When it comes to the student newspaper or passing on outside speakers, he or she doesn't say no but keeps people talking until they say what he or she wants to hear. When it comes to student government, he or she plants ideas and lets them grow. In many respects the paternal/maternal orientation is sympathetic to those with less power and less experience. They can be counted on to give blind adoration. The paternal/maternal administrator often undercuts middle management in the process of supporting "the student" or "the average staff employee." He or she does this in such a way that it is hard to argue, for sentiment and morality are on the administrator's side. Who can protest when a leader takes up for the less powerful within the organization?

In the dialogue below, the dean is meeting with his associate dean, with Linda, who is head of admissions, and with a staff employee. The dean has just entered from his office, where he has been discussing a problem with a student. The dean has learned from the student that materials the student had submitted were, upon later examination, not in his file. The student is questioning the record keeping in the central office and is upset because his incomplete file has delayed his admission to a particular department.

Dean: Linda, I want you to explain to me what procedures are with respect to placing material in a student's file.
Linda: It's really very simple. We try to keep track by means of Social Security numbers, but sometimes we have difficulty putting material submitted late into the proper file. I know you have been talking to one of the students, and that is what happened in his case.
Dean: Yes, he's very upset, and I really don't want this sort of thing to happen. It delayed his admission, and I think he has a good reason to be upset.
Linda: Well, there's another problem that may be related to this. I didn't want to bring it up, but now that it's come to light, maybe you should know. The associate dean's secretary, Rose, came into my office the other day. She asked

for all the files of final applicants in the master's program. I questioned her and asked if she realized that those couldn't be taken out of the office. She said that the associate dean had asked that she get them and that she was doing so on his request. I said okay and gave her the files. I wrote a note to you indicating that she had them. There were fifty files.

I came in a couple of days later and found the files on my desk, but there were only forty-six. They were all mixed together. Some of the files had been unstapled and re-stapled, as though they had been pulled apart and put back together. I'm very concerned because they were not returned the way I gave them to her. I don't know what she was doing with them. It looked as though she had copied some of them. Anyway, I showed my anger and said, "What in the world have you done to these files? They're all messed up! They're not in the order I gave them to you."

She said, "That's ridiculous! They haven't changed at all." We got into a big, shall we say, angry dispute. I said, "I can't imagine what the associate dean wanted with these anyway." She said, "It's none of your business." The more I started thinking about it, the more I wondered just what was going on.

Dean: I'm not sure I understand. (He turns to the associate dean.) Do you know of any explanation for this?

Associate Dean: To tell the truth, I'm totally perplexed. I can't imagine what Rose was doing with those files.

Dean: I suggest we find out immediately. I think we need a full explanation. I want you, Linda, to make an appointment with Rose for me. Tell her to come into my office at two o'clock. I want to find out what's going on.

Associate Dean: Don't you think I should talk to her first? She's my secretary. She may have had some good reason for checking out those files.

Dean: There's no good reason for her to talk to Linda the way she did. I'll talk to you afterwards to let you know the upshot of this thing. Right now I need to talk to the student. I gather that his file was among those that were scrambled. Is that right, Linda?

Linda: Yes. He came in to check on his file about that time and realized that some of the material was missing. That increased my concern. I didn't know what to tell him.

Dean: Let me talk to him and I'll see if I can't handle it with him. In the meantime, make that appointment with Rose for me, and let me take a look at this student's file also. I need to look at that now, before I talk to him.

(Linda gets the file for the dean. He concentrates on reviewing the file for about ten minutes and then goes into his office to discuss it with the student.)

Dean: I have reviewed your file and what has happened. It appears that you are correct; those materials were somehow misplaced. We're very sorry that this happened and that your admission has been delayed. Don't worry, though, these things can be handled. I'll see to it that you're registered for classes. Now that you're here, we ought to be able to process the paperwork very rapidly. You probably will have to bring in those same materials again and put them in your file, but at this point I think we can go ahead and process your admission without those copies. Just make sure they are inserted some time in the next few days. Is this all right with you?

Student: Yes, dean, thank you very much. I was very upset when I received the note that my file was incomplete and that I could not be processed for admission. I would appreciate your putting everything in order so that I can enroll.

The dean acts in a paternalistic way when he requests an explanation from the associate dean and thereafter quickly moves to usurp the latter's authority in the situation. It is possible that there may be some underhanded dealings going on in that the associate dean is caught short by the episode and can offer no reconstruction for how it might have come about. However, the dean's paternalistic orientation shows up in his total trust of *his* subordinate, Linda. He buys her version of the incident without question. *She* is trusted. Rose is not. The associate dean is viewed as weak and Rose as impertinent.

The dean's interaction with the student is also paternalistic in tone. The dean quickly solves the student's problem by bypassing the usual procedures and admitting him to the program. He asks the student to overlook the mismanagement in the office in trade for a rapid admission. He does not reveal to the student what occurred in the office or that his record may have been inappropriately refiled. This would only raise the student's anxieties further. The student is satisfied with the brief explanation since his goal—getting admitted—is assured by the dean. The student has learned an important lesson that may be useful in the future: When you have a *real* problem, go to the dean.

Managing External Relations

The paternal/maternal administrator is very conscious of his or her image—the "robes of power"—and carefully cultivates it. The symbols are maintained. He or she is excellent at "staging" the social interactions important to the maintenance of the institution and has a good feel for what is "proper." When it comes to others representing the university, he or she avoids telling them what to do and yet exercises very strong control through coaching them to put their "best foot forward." This is done in such a manner that they feel free while actually being controlled.

In the following scene, the chair is planning an alumni reunion and has worked out in his mind how the event should unfold. Everyone has a role to play. He is talking with three graduate students who serve on a faculty committee dealing with alumni. They have been given important assignments to which they respond enthusiastically.

Chair: I've chosen you three as our representatives on the alumni anniversary committee, and I want to tell you how important I feel this committee service to be. There aren't a lot of fifty-year graduates left. Many are retired, in their seventies, a few even older, a few in their sixties. Remember, in those days people graduated at younger ages because they didn't go through so many years of high school. At any rate, these older folks think a lot of their college. They remember it as it was in the old days. Many of them, of course, give money to the school. I have selected you, therefore, as representing the highest standards of today's young people, and I want you to make me proud of you. You will get to attend the banquet with the president, as well as the various other activities, and of course you will also work on the committee with the alumni and students from other parts of the campus. You'll have to do some chores along with your assignments on the committee, such as registering people, taking folks to the motel, showing them around. Our old town has grown a lot since they were here, so many of them may need guidance and assistance. I really think you'll enjoy this service and get a lot out of it. This is a marvelous opportunity to make contacts that can be helpful to your careers.

Student 1: We appreciate your appointing us to the committee. We will do our best. When we flunk out of a few of our classes, will you stand up for us?

Chair: (laughing) Now, Chuck, I chose you because I know you can keep up with your studies and still do this extra work. I'm sure you can do it without any problems.

Student 2: I hope you're right.

Chair: We wouldn't want to look bad in the eyes of the other departments, would we? We have to make our department look top-notch.

Student 2: Have the faculty representatives been appointed yet?

Chair: No, they haven't, as a matter of fact. I am going to do that this afternoon at the faculty meeting.

Student 1: Have you chosen yet?

Chair: Yes, but I just haven't told them yet.

Student 1: Who are they going to be?

Chair: I wouldn't want to let out any secrets, especially since I haven't told them yet. I am selecting faculty who are outstanding and can't help but earn the respect of our alumni. You will find it an honor to work with them.

The chair's approach here is paternalistic. He has the "total" plan well worked out in his mind, but his decisions are conveyed to students in such a way as to make the students want to embrace them. Paternalism is clearly apparent in his telling them what he wants them to do and explaining to them the benefits that will be theirs as individuals and as students in the department if they offer their enthusiastic compliance.

If these students were to be asked about their participation, they would answer, "We volunteered to take part. No, we've not been told what to do; that was left up to us. Our chair is open and aboveboard and easy to talk to." The fact is that these students have been placed under tight control, and they will act according to the chairman's wishes without being aware that they are puppets. We see further evidence of the chair's paternalism in his response to the students' query about the faculty members that will be helping. The chair says that he has all that thought out too and that while he wants no suggestions from them, he is sure that once his announcement is made they will agree with his choices.

Assuring Basic Operations

The paternal/maternal administrator sees operations as an area that should present no problems. The operational system of the university exists to serve the main purposes of the institution, and it has no other legitimacy. Therefore, there is no reason for conflicts regarding the effective operation of the system itself—those responsible for operations should loyally dedicate their efforts to serving the rest of the organization.

But difficulties are inevitably encountered in administering the operational system. When this happens, the paternal/maternal administrator steps in to help. The paternal/maternal administrator sees himself or herself as the *guardian* of the system in contrast to the 9,1-oriented administrator who sees himself as the *master* of the system.

In the following scene, a chair is conferring with a secretary of a departmental office. She has been criticized by a faculty member for not getting some work done on schedule. The chair arrived just in time to overhear the faculty member's tirade.

Chair: Lola, I heard the loud voices, and I can tell you are upset. Would you tell me what happened?

Lola: I'm so angry I could spit nails.

Chair: I gather Dr. Smith criticized you for something.

Lola: He sure did, and it wasn't my fault. I tried to explain it, and he wouldn't listen. I'm getting absolutely sick of this. This is the third faculty member that's acted like this in the last three weeks. I keep trying to explain why we can't get their work out, but they simply won't listen. I'm not sure I can take this much longer.

Chair: Easy does it. Can you tell me about it, or do you want to calm down first?

Lola: No, I'll tell you about it now! I want to tell you what's going on in this office and why all this seems to be falling on me.

Chair: I'm certainly interested in correcting the situation. You are an excellent secretary, and you shouldn't have to feel this way.

Lola: I'm at the front desk. I sit where everyone turns in work to be done. I also have to answer the phone and open mail and talk to students. I handle all the traffic. Sometimes faculty just tell me about some work they want done, but they don't write it down. I don't always remember the specifics. Like Dr. White told me that there was a deadline for his paper. He says he told me, but truly I can't remember his saying that. I had no idea the work was needed today.

Chair: What happened in the other two instances?

Lola: In one case Dr. Johnson had given the work to a temporary who happened to be here for the week I was on vacation. He gave her material that needed to be typed, and he told her about using certain margins, and it had to be just so. She didn't relay all that information to me. She left; I came back. I picked it up and did the typing. I did it the wrong way. He threw a fit.

In the other situation, I caught the brunt of someone else's mistake. I took the work, made a note, and told Lucy to take the stuff to central duplicating and that we needed one hundred copies by a certain date. We got it back on

time, but then when the instructor used it for his conference, he discovered a lot of material had been assembled incorrectly. He came back and jumped all over me. That material was done at central duplicating! You could say it was
my fault since I didn't check it before I gave it to him, but
they hardly ever make mistakes over there.

Chair: It sounds as though you're catching the overload of a lot
of traffic and that it's hard to keep track of all the different
instructions you're getting.

Lola: I'm not sure I can take the stress any longer. Ulcers, you
know. That I can do without! I seem to be the one that
catches most of the complaints. The other secretaries are
more insulated since they work in the back room.

Chair: Maybe I can give you a break. How about it if I ask one
of the other secretaries to take your place at the front desk
for four hours a day?

Lola: That would really be a relief. At least for the next few
weeks while we're trying to get settled in for the semester.

Chair: Why don't you take a little time and recover from this
incident. Then I will set up a schedule so that you and the
other two secretaries can rotate on the front desk. I'll get
June to come out here now.

Lola: Thanks. I'm going to get some iced tea. Would you like
some?

Chair: Yes, thanks. I'll talk to the other secretaries, and when
you get back you can go to the back room for the rest of
the day. I think this will all settle down once the class routine is established. These professors get "hyper" at the beginning of every semester. You'll see. Everything will be fine
by the beginning of October.

This is a paternalistic orientation. In the very beginning
the chair takes the initiative by involving himself in some un-
defined problem. He does so by acknowledging that he heard
loud talk. When Lola reveals what happened, he takes the time
to console her. She is seen to be under "stress," and the dean
takes action to protect her. He then tries to diagnose the situation in an objective manner and concludes that in truth there is

a traffic problem. The problem is exaggerated by a lack of systems and procedures that could ease management of the traffic.

However, instead of trying to solve the problem as a systems and procedures issue, he translates it into a personality-caused difficulty. He is in a position to make changes so that the secretary will not feel "put upon," but he does not offer any assistance to Lola that would help her more effectively cope with pressure. Nevertheless, Lola welcomes the kind of fatherly support her boss offers. Lola's approach is to accept her dependence on him for a solution. When the chair "solves" the problem, she readily accepts the solution. She falls easily into the trap of protectiveness, and as a result there is no exploration of the underlying systems and procedures, and her competence in diagnosing problems in structural terms is not enhanced.

Summary

The paternal/maternal administrator is supportive of the emotional needs of his staff. He or she "fixes" their hurts and in the process often robs them of the opportunity to deal directly with conflict situations. This style is particularly prominent in relating to younger subordinates. The paternal/maternal administrator is strongly "protective," and his or her solicitous behaviors are called into play at the slightest difficulty. On the surface this way of operating may seem entirely appropriate and may well win the administrator the loyalty of more dependent employees. Independent employees often are not clearly aware of why they are uncomfortable with this type of leader because he or she is so apparently smooth, supportive, and open. Yet they feel a sense of increasing powerlessness that they are not able to explain unless they are adept at analyzing social interactions.

Each of the compound 9,1 and 1,9 approaches recognizes the dilemma of getting performance with and through people. Each tries in some way to handle it. However, all of them distort the basic possibility of integrating people into performance, and thus lose all the benefits that come from doing so. Their underlying limitations are that they do not seek to change the status quo; in trying to adjust to it, they deal with symptoms rather than correct underlying causes. The real solution lies in learning to apply principles of human behavior to involve people in work and to integrate their individual goals and the goals of the organization in a 9,9-oriented way.

Chapter Eight

Constituency-Centered Administration: 5,5

The positive motivation of a 5,5-oriented administrator is to belong: "I want to look good, to be 'in' with my colleagues." (Appropriately enough, this administrator is found in the center of the Academic Administrator Grid in Chapter Two.) He or she does this by finding out what the majority thinks or wants and then "leading" it. Being popular means putting together a package of qualities that are sought after in the human marketplace, including whatever is fashionable in the way of dress, neighborhoods to live in, places to go, books to read, values to espouse, theories to teach, and so on. He or she is likely to develop pleasant manners and to strive to be an interesting conversationalist. The goal is to make many friends, even though not close ones, and in this way to build a constituency that one can "lead."

An administrator who is motivated by the desire to belong tends to be superficial in convictions and careful to avoid self-exposure. This can be done by always taking cues from the actions of others. Prevailing opinions are his or her opinions. What others reject, he or she rejects. Therefore, he or she seldom has deep ideological commitments, whether political, religious, literary, social, corporate, academic, or otherwise. But when convinced that he or she has support, the 5,5-oriented administrator can be an able advocate.

This administrator experiences a sense of well-being when evaluated positively by fellow members of the university, even though the administrator may have just compromised a long-term gain for a short-term convenience, embraced a point of view only because boss and colleagues did so, withheld a vital piece of information to avoid anticipated ostracism, or winked at a shady practice because "everyone" is doing it. The ability to back and fill, to shift, twist, and turn—all within the broad limits of honesty—and yet to stay with the majority is important to a 5,5-oriented administrator's style. When he or she achieves this objective, the administrator feels "right." The motivational motto is, "If I think, look, and act like everyone else, but a little more so, I will be an administrator in good standing."

Sometimes the 5,5-oriented administrator is unsuccessful and then feels unpopular, out of step, and isolated from the group. He or she experiences embarrassment and shame for having lost the cadence. Being out of step can lead to ostracism and loss of membership in the "group." In terms of the negative side of this administrator's motivation, he or she wants to avoid looking bad and stirring resentment as a minority of one, to be separated from the mainstream, or to become an object of ridicule, even though the position he or she stands for may, in fact, be a valid one.

Administrative Orientation

A 5,5 orientation to administration emphasizes "responsive" leadership. There are many ways of moving forward and at the same time remaining in step with others. The administrator stays within the bounds of what everyone else is doing and sees this as the ultimate criterion for appropriateness or pertinence.

This amounts to a philosophy of *gradualism* in which change is by improvisation or by trial and error and there is very little goal-oriented action. The result is neither particularly chaotic nor particularly coherent. It is more likely to be conformity centered and to come out piecemeal and makeshift.

A 5,5-oriented administrator does not *command* or *direct* others to get the job done so much as he or she *motivates* and *communicates.* He or she avoids exerting formal authority. His or her approach is to suggest and to "sell" in order to get people to want to work.

- *Planning:* "I make my plans according to what I know my subordinates will accept and what they will resist."
- *Organizing:* "Before organizing the activity, I get input from everyone on how they think it should be done and take their views into account."
- *Directing:* "After explaining aims and schedules, I make individual assignments. I check to make sure subordinates think what I request is okay. I encourage them to feel free to come back if they don't understand what to do."
- *Controlling:* "I keep up with each person's performance and review his or her progress from time to time. If a subordinate is having difficulty, I try to reduce pressure on him or her by rearranging conditions of work whenever possible."
- *Staffing:* "I seek people who will 'fit in,' work at a reasonable pace, and get along well together."

Administrators of this kind think it is important to communicate, to elicit suggestions from subordinates, and to consider their points of view. Within this context, their goal is to avoid "pushing" subordinates beyond what they are ready to agree with. They seldom give an order without pretesting to see if people are ready to buy it, and they believe that people are more likely to go along if they are allowed to talk and even gripe a little.

This provides an indication of the 5,5-oriented way of dealing with what the administrator regards as inherent contradictions between academic performance requirements and human needs. Neither set of needs is ignored. He or she scales performance down to what people are prepared to accept and encourages them to offer suggestions that can be used either to reduce the effort necessary to get a result or to decrease pressure and thereby eliminate frustrations. This accommodation between performance needs and human needs involves a balancing act, giving up part of one goal to get part of another. When the administrator reduces the push for performance and considers attitudes and feelings, people will usually accept the situation and be more or less "satisfied." Acceptable performance is possible without unduly disturbing people. This orientation assumes that people are practical, that they realize *some* effort is to be exerted. The hallmark of a 5,5 approach is not to seek the maximum in terms of *performance and people* ("that would be too 'ideal' ") but to find the position that is about halfway between both. It is the commonsense approach to academic leadership.

In the 5,5 orientation an administrator often prefers one-to-one dealings with each subordinate in informal and easy-going give-and-take discussions. Through touching base with subordinates, he or she appears to embrace democratic values, and this in turn enhances his or her popularity. He or she is also likely to enjoy group sessions and to rely on group decisions, special committees, or task forces to spread around the responsibility for decisions. He or she tends to see the leader as a catalyst or facilitator, one whose procedural skills help subordinates reach agreement or at least a majority point of view. By giving formal approval to what subordinates seem ready to agree with, the administrator becomes a sensitive leader and a key member of the group.

Implementing Institutional Mission

A 5,5-oriented administrator takes the interpretations of university mission made by key opinion leaders at face value. Mission is not something that is "pure" or idealistic or theoretical, nor can the passing wants of students be a guide to its formulation. When making decisions, this administrator tries to move forward by a series of successive accommodations to the vested interests of many contending groups.

Given this "flexible" definition of mission, the best administrative tactic is to keep the big issues to one side and the actual discussions about goals and objectives at the practical level. After all, Rome was not built in a day, and a university cannot radically shift its course overnight. The danger always exists of alienating other administrators and the faculty, as well as of undermining all the hard-won agreements that have been forged over the years. There is nothing more disturbing to this kind of administrator than a faculty gripped in the fervor of an intense philosophical debate, for it can be misled by loud-mouths and malcontents.

Administrators with this orientation feel pride in their ability to cement the social fabric and to prevent too much fragmentation, thus maintaining a semblance of the whole. In order to keep people together and activities from becoming unstuck, they utilize a variety of political tactics, such as subtle arm twisting, timely buttonholing, end runs, and *faits accomplis*. Masters at finding middle ground, these individuals are adept at "ear to the ground" maneuvers that essentially bring diverging factions together long enough to reach workable agreements.

In the following scene, the 5,5-oriented vice-president is preparing ground for future, perhaps necessarily unpopular, decisions. He is meeting with the dean's council to plan a major undergraduate curriculum change, its purpose being to deal with changing enrollment patterns caused by shifts in job markets. Student enrollment patterns are bleeding the traditional liberal arts areas, while engineering and business are booming. Relative to student population, there are too many faculty in the liberal arts colleges and not enough in the professional schools.

But who wants to kill Shakespeare? The job market for students needs to be balanced against the university image of itself as the producer of the Renaissance man and, more recently, woman. How does one preserve the traditions and still stay competitive? That is the question being debated here.

Vice-President: The first item for us to deal with is required courses for the B.A. There has been a significant decrease in students in the traditional liberal arts areas, coupled with extensive and major increases in preprofessional programs, particularly business, engineering, and architecture. If we leave the curriculum as is, we face a high demand for hiring new faculty in business and engineering and an oversupply of faculty in some other departments. One way of dealing with the imbalance is to change curriculum requirements in heavily enrolled areas. I do not expect us to make such decisions today, but I would like to have your input and ideas about how we might go about spreading the teaching load.

For example, some departments, such as engineering and business, might require more hours to be taken in other departments than has been the case in the past. There is no language requirement in the engineering program. There is no math requirement in the business program outside the business department itself, yet the business school teaches courses such as statistics. Thus one way of dealing with the shifting enrollment might be to move some of the required courses into the liberal arts areas that are suffering enrollment declines.

Dean of Engineering: One of the biggest problems of requiring courses outside our own college, such as mathematics or English, is that the kinds of objectives we want achieved would not be met as well. If we teach these courses in our own college, we select the faculty and tailor the curriculum much more specifically to the needs of engineers. Engineers need a heavy dose of technical writing, specifically geared to the engineering profession.

Dean of Business: The same is true for business statistics. If statistics is taken, let's say, in the math department, or in psychology, or somewhere else, the problems studied can be quite irrelevant to the business world. And it's hard for students to make the translation. The faculty in these other departments are not always capable of illustrating concepts in the ways most useful to our business students.

Dean of Natural Sciences: Is the problem with the faculty member, or is it the limited ability of students to conceptualize and generalize? By doing it for them we may be "solving" the wrong problem. We need to help them take basic meth-

odology and develop the skills of generalizing. Then they
can utilize the concepts in a variety of applied areas.

Dean of Liberal Arts: Constantly expecting students to limit
themselves to courses that have immediate application leads
to a narrow definition of education. This is exactly what
worries me about the direction of our curriculum in many
of these areas.

Vice-President: Let's not get committed to drastic changes in
the curriculum and get too concerned about these issues in
the philosophical sense. I will be satisfied if we can solve
some real-life problems and make just one or two changes
next year to lighten the load in some departments and balance it out a little bit in others. If we narrow our scope
here, we can deal with the practical problems. In this empirical world academic philosophy is out-of-date.

Dean of Liberal Arts: Can we really avoid the philosophical
issues? Too often we take a piecemeal approach without
considering curriculum decisions in the light of our true
long-range objectives for graduates.

Vice-President: Well, you've got a point. But we have to deal
with the immediate aspects. I'm the one that gets the headaches when imbalances exist and some professors feel overworked and others have too few courses to teach. That's
real life.

Dean of Liberal Arts: Well, actually we all have headaches. It's
just a different kind of headache for each of us.

Dean of Fine Arts: Maybe what we ought to do is reassign faculty instead of redesigning the curriculum.

Dean of Engineering: We would get the faculty you don't want,
wouldn't we?

Vice-President: How about this? Why don't each of you go back
to your respective department chairs and talk about this
situation and develop proposals for what you can do to alleviate it. Then when we have something in writing, our
dean's council can discuss this whole problem area again.

   This 5,5 approach to the resolution of the conflict is
through expediency. At the heart of the problem there *is* a deep

philosophical issue about the mission of the university, but the vice-president prefers to sidestep that issue. Were he to delve into the underlying value system of education and attempt to get agreement to a solution based on a shared understanding by the council of the university's mission, the meeting would get nowhere. Thus he asks the deans to study the problem to see how they can organize the existing resources to accommodate and adjust to the current imbalance in a short-term way. By going to the "practical" issues facing the university next year, he can temporarily reorganize the existing curriculum as a way of dealing with a limited definition of the total problem. His convictions find their root in the marketplace, not in the ethereal majesty of an overriding and comprehensive conceptual structure. It is quite likely that each person can be persuaded to shift a little, so that no one feels unduly pressured. By slowly chipping away at the uneven load, the vice-president can keep things moving without open rifts or fundamental changes that upset the status quo.

Supporting Teaching and Learning

Good teaching is of first importance in the thinking of the 5,5-oriented administrator, who sees professors as the university's representatives in the classroom. This representation is important to the university's future because students pick up attitudes from their professors toward the university and pass them along to parents and other members of the community. Then, too, students become alumni, and alumni become financial supporters if they experienced an enjoyable campus life as students.

Thus, professors are sought who create comfortable relationships, who are attentive to the needs of students, and who can interpret subject matter in a way that makes it understandable to the average student. This kind of professor does not take conceptual sides, even though in a given instance the weight of evidence may be strongly in favor of one position relative to others, but instead is careful to present both sides of every issue in such a way that students are led to believe that the choice

among alternatives is theirs. For example, theories of evolution
and of creation are given equal value as explanations of the
origin of things, and the student is led to believe that both theories are equally credible. The same is true with regard to any
other debatable subject. Such professors meet the criterion of
being "reasonable," but they are never opinionated.

Academic administrators who conceive of teaching in this
way prefer to select professors who have graduated from prestigious universities. They usually favor those who have had
courses in how to teach over candidates who have demonstrated
no active interest in the techniques of teaching. Candidates who
are market oriented and who appreciate the importance of satisfying the needs of students are likely to be selected over those
with a more rigorous concept of what it is that students need to
learn or who hold high standards of what it means to be an educated person. These administrators also may be expected to
take active roles in counseling with professors to assist them in
acquiring the skills requisite for implementing a responsive, balanced approach toward subject matter and students alike.

The teaching program is important to a 5,5-oriented administrator; he or she supports the faculty and stands behind
them. As long as no one raises issues, all is well. But what if the
performance of a faculty member is questioned and the administrator is asked to "do something"? He or she often tries to
resolve the difficulty by cooling down emotions and implementing symbolic solutions. Such is the approach of the 5,5-oriented
president in the next incident. He is confronted with a student
complaint that he, as president, must handle. The student represents a larger group in the engineering department, and this
group is up in arms about some of the professors in the sophomore and junior classes who it feels are unable to communicate
effectively. The president wants the students to handle the
problem through regular channels, although they have already
attempted this to no avail. The 5,5-oriented president proposes
a solution and implements it without really thinking through
the larger problem or the possible negative consequences of his
specific action.

Student: I don't think that the administration realizes the extent to which our faculty is loaded with individuals from foreign countries who have a difficult time communicating in English. Some are excellent teachers, no question about it. However, students simply must be able to understand what's being said in class, and there are some professors who are incomprehensible. It's just impossible to comprehend their lectures or explanations of material.

President: Can you give me more information and tell me which classes?

Student: The biggest problem is with the required courses in the sophomore program. Two are taught by individuals who speak very little English, so the students are caught with two engineering courses that are taught by professors they can't understand. A lot of people are very upset about this.

President: Are they flunking the courses?

Student: Well, they struggle through, but some do flunk, yes. But the problem is that they feel they're not really prepared for the next series of courses because they don't understand what is going on in those two classes. Both individuals who teach these classes are no doubt pretty good in mathematics, but have you ever tried to understand math when you can hardly understand the numbers the person is pronouncing?

President: I gather you've talked to the dean and now you've come to me?

Student: Yes, we've talked to the dean. We didn't get anywhere.

President: What did he say?

Student: The dean said these two are fully qualified for teaching those courses, and we're just going to have to live with them. It's true that they are eminent—one is from Heidelberg and the other from Tokyo University. The dean said he will provide more student tutors, but that really doesn't seem to cut it for us.

President: Why not?

Student: The student assistants are just about as confused as we are. A lot of us took an exam last week, and the problem was we couldn't understand the complicated phraseology of the questions. Once the student assistant explained what was really meant by some of the questions, it was easy; but even then something is lost in translation.

President: Well, it seems to be a problem of communication. Perhaps the students are learning more than they think. Let me talk with the dean and see if we can't work out some sort of strategy for dealing with this. I may ask the dean to sit in on those classes for the next couple of weeks and give me a report.

Student: Terrific! I think somebody ought to see and hear what's going on firsthand. Nobody has been listening.

(The student leaves, and the president calls the dean of engineering.)

President: Dean, may I ask you to look into something for me?

Dean: Why, certainly! What seems to be the problem?

President: I've heard from some students who are upset about two of the professors in your sophomore program. The problem seems to be an inability of faculty to communicate effectively with students. The two professors are foreign, and what I'd like for you to do is sit in on the classes and make your presence felt by the students. Then later I'd like you to come talk to me. I think some show of your presence in those classes will tide this thing over.

Dean: Oh, yes, I've also talked with those students. They get upset about this time of year, after the first exams. My experience is that it will blow over after a couple of weeks.

President: Well, probably, but to keep me from reneging on my promise, please sit in on those courses a couple of times, and then later on we'll get together and talk. Perhaps next semester these two professors can be assigned graduate classes, where students are better prepared to handle the material.

Dean: I'll sit in and let you know how it goes. I've been rather curious myself.

President: Good, good. You know how terribly important it is that students see their administrators as concerned and supportive, as role models who take student concerns seriously.

The 5,5 orientation to staffing in this setting appears in the president's concern that the professors will have an adverse influence on student attitudes; he is not really concerned with how the professors are presenting their subject matter. He simply wants to patch up the status quo, appease the students, and give the appearance of trying to solve the problem without tackling the deeper issues with which the students are concerned. His convictions regarding the quality of teaching are shallow. The problem will remain even if the professors are assigned to graduate students, although graduate students are more likely to accommodate themselves to the idiosyncrasies of highly respected professors. Under these conditions a deficit may be turned into an asset.

Establishing the Curriculum

For the 5,5-oriented administrator, curriculum is the ultimate expression of democratic process. The give-and-take resulting from the clash of educational philosophies and vested interests eventually produces a series of trade-offs and compromises that, from the 5,5-oriented perspective, are likely to yield the best curriculum possible under the circumstances. When this process of trade-offs, compromises, and accommodations is well led by an able administrator, the result will usually be a reasonably high degree of general satisfaction because everyone will have had the opportunity to voice opinions and objections.

In curriculum building there is always a tension between two competing approaches. On the one hand, there are those who see academic subject matter as composed of building blocks that range from the elementary to the complex, with each step having to be mastered before the next step is undertaken. A student's deficiencies should be removed prior to admission, and students admitted should be able to follow a fixed core sequence, even though elective opportunities are provided. On the other hand, there are those who adopt a marketing orientation. The curriculum should satisfy the students, and it should be geared to the pace that most can meet. Admissions are more open under this philosophy and the curriculum much less rigid. In this view, deficiencies are inevitable, but the clever teacher can work around them.

Compromises between these poles create the curriculum.

The 5,5-oriented administrator thus views curriculum decisions as academic games, where the playing field produces bargains and compromises with few winners or losers. He or she views long struggles between unrelenting contending forces, with each side unwilling to give up even its more outlandish demands, as foolish and harmful to all concerned.

The 5,5-oriented administrator approaches such contests (in which he or she is not a direct participant) as a conciliator, a grand head of state whose desire is to bring peace through trade-offs and who appeals to the self-interest of each side. The administrator gambles that the conflict can be handled without a real conflagration—"unconditional surrender is something neither side wants." In some cases the best strategy is to get one side to "trade in" its original demands for another set of demands that the 5,5-oriented administrator has the power to grant. The administrator feels quite successful when this kind of lateral pass can be completed. This is the vice-president's approach with the dean of medicine in the following dialogue. The battle line has been drawn between two departments in a medical school, and the fight is over the human body. Who should teach the thyroid?

Vice-President: I can't believe that the chair of general surgery is still complaining about that decision on the thyroid.

Dean: You better believe he is. His whole department is up in arms.

Vice-President: I thought the whole matter was ironed out a month ago. What brought all this back up?

Dean: I wish I knew. You've got me.

Vice-President: Well, why not go back to them and do a little investigating to see what's really behind this? As far as I'm concerned, both departments can teach that part of the curriculum.

Dean: That's not the way they see it. Each side says the other is less than fully competent.

Vice-President: That's an old story.

Dean: Well, I can go back and talk with some of them again, but if I do that I probably ought to talk to the other department too.

Vice-President: Probably a good idea. I don't think you necessarily need to talk with everybody. A sample maybe.

Dean: Of course, but I'm afraid that'll stir up the ones who don't have a say all the more.

Vice-President: It sounds as though they couldn't be stirred up any more than they already are, so what do we have to lose? Maybe at the same time you can convey my concern about this. If they don't settle it pretty quickly, I'm going to have to do it myself, and I'd much rather they reach what they think is an amicable agreement.

Dean: That may be what they are really asking for. There may be other aspects we're not aware of. I hope they'll tell me what they are. From what I gather, general surgery taught thyroid for years. When they lost the faculty member who was in charge of teaching it, the other department decided that the medical school needed to modernize and that it was about time we got sensible and put thyroid in their specialty. It's a typical territorial dispute.

Vice-President: Well, I guess that's what deans of medicine are for, to resolve these conflicts. I suggest you do some scalpel work though; find out how strongly everybody feels, and whether you can see a solution that will satisfy them. We might even give the department that surrenders the thyroid something else in return. If you find a solution, go ahead and implement it. If not, and you think we need to talk again, let me know. I just feel as though, with a little neat stitching, so to speak, you will probably be able to get everyone to knit together.

Dean: Well, I'll certainly try. I'll let you know how it goes.

The vice-president's approach to this conflict exemplifies a 5,5 orientation. This is evident when he says, "We might even give the department that surrenders the thyroid something else in return." Thus, his approach to the organization of the curriculum involves a balancing act, and he thinks that anybody who gives up something should gain a benefit in return. Such an approach ignores the possibility that there may be a sound solution based on the logic inherent in the problem—for example, demonstrated competencies in the two areas—and that longer-term consequences might favor a decision different from the one that is likely to result from a negotiated agreement.

Supporting Research and Scholarly Productivity

Universities capable of "buying" scholarship are likely to search for professors with established credentials. The prestige derived from research and scholarship is important if a university wants to be judged favorably by other institutions. The emphasis is on the reputation accorded the institution rather than the fundamental nature of a scholar's contribution.

The 5,5-oriented administrator wins a lot of points if someone on the faculty achieves a major scientific breakthrough. Delivery of the research goods provides long-term insurance for continued support of the college. Board members beam when a faculty member's research is picked up by a national news service or when it is reported in a highly regarded professional journal. (The university clipping service of course reinforces this attitude, which confuses prestige with profoundness.) The administrator who can gather together a group that can talk a good research game is applauded. However, the 5,5-oriented administrator is not always sure who can cash in at the creative marketplace and so chooses the proven prizewinners when possible. The 5,5-oriented administrator pays a lot for the convincing producers in any field. If another university supports them in their lean years and this administrator bags them at their peak, so what? That's the way the system works. Where assistant professors are discouraged and the retired Nobel Prize winners are feted, a 5,5-oriented approach is likely to be operating. Isn't it healthy for the young researcher to be in contact with the outstanding? Of course! But isn't it also healthy for the already established to rub elbows with the young upstarts, that is, the young scholars who are not willing to model their thinking about research along the patterns of their more power-ful and proven colleagues?

Not according to the 5,5-oriented administrator. It is far better, in the president's way of thinking in the following dialogue, to throw in his lot with the tried and true. When it comes to making decisions about research potential, he leaves it to the professional establishment. However, he also knows enough to lend some type of encouragement to the untested or less sure bets. So he adopts a two-part strategy. Like a good gambler, he places most of his cash on the proven racehorses and some side dollars on a few long shots. The president is conferring with the vice-president for research regarding a policy statement for distributing summer research funds.

President: Even though the discretionary fund is intended to be used for summer faculty research, I feel the faculty senate has a point. We need to set some guidelines for how those decisions are reached so the faculty understands the basis for distributing the dollars. Therefore, I need some sort of policy statement we can circulate.

Vice-President for Research: What do you want from me? A statement as to what I think the policy ought to be?

President: Have any thoughts?

Vice-President for Research: My personal opinion is that research proposals from various disciplines are so different that it is too difficult to evaluate proposals in terms of comparable merit. Maybe we ought to come up with a formula that makes sure each department or division has some chance of getting something. Now, most of it goes into engineering and the sciences. I get a lot of flak from the other departments on this.

President: Well, isn't it primarily because departments in those fields have had the best proposals? You know I had a committee to advise me, and we all agreed on that.

Vice-President for Research: Probably you could get a different committee to come up with a different finding. In the final analysis it's got to be subjective. I don't think there's any way to compare a proposal in, say, chemistry, with one in anthropology. At least not in terms of the criteria applied by that committee.

President: What do you mean? What criteria?

Vice-President for Research: Well, for example, the committee favors traditional, experimental designs. I've heard that in some of the social sciences the kinds of designs coming into use are more nontraditional, and yet some of them are very creative.

President: Well, I understand your point. Another criterion relates to the ability to apply the findings to immediate problems. Some of those social science studies just don't seem to be too relevant to anything. Looking through my physics prism, it's just difficult for me to understand some of the things they do in the social sciences.

Vice-President for Research: Now you're really being unfair.

President: Okay, okay. Let's do it this way. Why don't we informally agree that at least one research proposal will be approved from each department. Beyond that, selection will be solely on the basis of merit as judged by the committee. Would that satisfy the troops?

Vice-President for Research: Well, at least it's a move in the right direction. I don't necessarily say we should go totally toward a quota formula for allocating research dollars, but I am concerned that we need to motivate across the board. Even though I favor the sciences, I see the value of other disciplines. I also see the real difficulties of the design problems they have, especially in field research.

President: As I recall, some of them had very strong designs, and we have funded one or two every year.

Vice-President for Research: But even then the ones in the social sciences that get grants are the brass instruments side of experimental psychology. What concerns me is some of the other areas like education and journalism and anthropology and even some of the liberal arts areas—English. Those don't get anywhere near their share. Over the long term I really worry about our commitment to research in those areas. To some extent it's a matter of morale. I want to be able to say we are going to support scholarly effort in those areas with some real dollars.

President: Well, I hope you work at it and get those departments to submit more proposals that seem to have merit.

Vice-President for Research: I'll do my best, but many of them, of course, are just not going to be of the same cut as some of those out of engineering and chemistry and physics.

President: Well, I'll be asked to report to the funding sources about how we used this money, and there's going to be quite a bit of it. The board and others want to see some return. We've had a good record in that regard, and I don't want to spoil it. So I'm saying I see your point and I'll do my best, but I can't go too far on this.

Vice-President for Research: I understand. I think the approach you suggest is a good one. Spread it around more but even then keep merit in mind.

The president's suggestion is for guidelines for the allocation of summer research funds. First of all, he wants guidelines to placate the faculty senate, which might presume that the only legitimate criterion for allocating funds is merit. As the problem is passed back and forth, a mechanical formula that gives something to each department and allocates the rest of the funds on the basis of something approaching merit is finally settled on. This is likely to earn the most endorsements, and therefore that's the way control is to be exercised in this situation. What these administrators fail to appreciate is that rigor is a state of mind, not a property of subject matter; hence, their convictions regarding the merit of research are easily bent.

Encouraging Community and Institutional Service

Service to the community or in broader settings that brings appreciative attention to the university is promoted by the 5,5-oriented administrator. Those assignments are favored that reinforce or reflect on the administrator's importance. Accounts of activities that appear in the campus or local newspaper, or, best of all, in the national press, are particularly relished. The same is true of radio and television interviews of prominent faculty members.

A 5,5-oriented administrator is usually skillful in parlaying one appointment into many. Having become a member of one company's board of directors, he or she is soon invited to sit on three more. This kind of service is likely to include honorary appointments that draw public attention; preferably, they will not demand technical specialization and will not be as time consuming as more substantive activities might be. Everyone gains. The corporation profits from the reputation of the board member's university and vice versa.

Those for whom this administrator is responsible are expected to engage in service activities as well. Matching the talents of other administrators and faculty members to particular service needs is one of those areas of judgment where a 5,5-oriented person usually shines.

The 5,5 way of handling questions of judgment is to substitute popular demand for critical thinking and analysis of problems. According to this philosophy, one does not second-guess the marketplace. In the scene below, the chair and executive council are meeting to establish criteria for evaluating faculty. The 5,5-oriented chairman is struggling with how to measure faculty contributions in the service area. Quality is particularly hard to judge in that area because the volume of service is not necessarily equivalent to its quality. Services often take place off campus, and this makes it even more difficult to judge their worth. Yet since service is important for forming alliances between the university and the outside world, the number of contacts or links established is certainly an important measure of success. Whether the contact, in a more fundamental sense, is a true "service" is not considered.

Chair: My big concern in the service area is that, number one, we provide guidelines with regard to documenting service. I would like to have service divided into university service—with committees and that sort of thing—and outside service. Some people mix those two together, and others do not put university service in at all. So we ought to get both kinds of service.

Committee Member 1: I agree with that. We can just ask faculty to list those two areas separately.

Chair: Secondly, and the bigger question is, how do we get a grip on the quality of service, especially when it's service to the community and none of us knows anything about what was done. How in the world do we evaluate quality?

Committee Member 2: Maybe there is no way to evaluate it. The very fact that faculty members are called on is enough at this point. If people are in demand, they must be good.

Chair: Or is it a matter of getting hold of a popular topic and riding it to death? For example, Jan Stone gave twenty-four talks on some women's issue last year. I'm not sure it had real merit to it. As far as I know, she hasn't done any research on the subject, and her invitations came from groups I've never heard of.

Committee Member 1: That shows you're not with it, George. Popularity is popularity. That is not to be denied. When you come right down to it, it's practically the same as quality. Popular people tend to be quality people, at least in my experience.

Committee Member 2: Doesn't that really confuse the issue? Some salespersons are popular with their customers, but that doesn't mean that they sell quality products.

Chair: If that's right, all we need is a nominating process. In all seriousness, how do we handle the quality issue, or do we drop it? What do the rest of you think?

Committee Member 1: First, how are we going to clarify the issue of paid versus unpaid service or is it none of our business whether they get paid?

Chair: Let's just take community service and have faculty list whether it's paid or unpaid on the assumption that paid service is questionable in terms of its service value, even though it may be of higher quality. If it's paid for once, it shouldn't get evaluated as service and be paid for twice.

Committee Member 2: We hashed that out last year. Remember, we decided that whether it's paid or unpaid—it's all still service. It's time consuming. The amount of pay—or whether the person gets paid—shouldn't make any difference because he's projecting the university's image as an active organization that is interested in helping with things beyond itself.

Chair: Well, I'm not sure I agree fully with that, but maybe at

this point in time, we've talked the thing to the quick anyway. I prefer the simplest approach. Otherwise we'll waste
tremendous energy on this, and I'm not sure it's as important as the other areas anyway. Why don't we just assume
that a large volume of requests indicates quality and let it go
at that?

Committee Member 1: I believe that will meet with faculty
acceptance almost without discussion.

The first committee member takes a typical pragmatic approach by concluding that if you can't separate things, then join
them and treat them as one. He suggests that popularity and
quality are close enough to be two measures of the same thing
and that acceptability at face value is about the same as soundness. The second committee member does much the same when
he equates volume with quality on the premise that if you can't
calibrate quality or draw distinctions, at least you can total up
the amount of service performed.

The additional issue of whether paid and unpaid service
should count equally quickly collapses into irrelevancy when
the faculty members agree that quality standards are simply not
feasible in the service area. Thus, the conflict is set aside; each
faculty member will simply be asked to provide quantity documentation, and no further judgment will be exercised. In effect,
the least controversial solution is accepted to this control issue,
and the problem will arise again next year when the faculty
members who are not necessarily considered to be among the
best turn in the longest list of service contacts according to the
documentation instructions and expect a payoff.

Managing Resources

Resource allocation can be one of the most stimulating
and exciting aspects of university administration. Funding questions are of crucial concern to administrators and faculty members alike. And there is no more opportune time than when
resources are limited for the 5,5-oriented administrator to exercise his or her political skills. Money can be used to buy support

from the most important and prestigious groups or from groups of individuals whose goodwill is needed if the administrator is to widen his or her own base of power.

The 5,5-oriented approach sees the use of resources as a way to enhance the reputation of the university in the context of nonacademic values. This might mean allocating money for sports activities if alumni think these are important, even though teaching or scholarship may suffer. Or it might mean spending money on the latest fads and trends in higher education, as these are reflected in the thinking of the administrator's colleagues in other universities and colleges.

Uncertainties give the administrator room to bargain and to turn funding restrictions or resource maldistributions into opportunities for personal and organizational advancement. Sometimes the inconsistencies and discrepancies in the administrator's many versions of a story do come out. Yet the administrator is usually forgiven for these minor infractions, and most of the time he or she tends to land straight up with both feet on the ground.

In the following exchange, a nine-lived, 5,5-oriented president is providing aid and comfort to two of his favorite administrators. Each has a problem, and the president sees a way to solve both problems with a "perfect" resource swap. He seals the bargain as the middleman and takes his commission in the form of future obligations. The president is speaking with an administrative secretary, who is reporting a telephone call.

Mary: The acting director of the nutrition project has been trying to get you all morning.
President: What's she calling about?
Mary: She needs staff right away in preparation for that big grant they got.
President: What? I don't understand.
Mary: They have to hire some people now. If they wait until the grant actually starts, it will be a bad hiring time and they won't have the lead time they need. They seem to be under the gun to start almost immediately after the grant goes into effect.

President: Don't they have staff within their present numbers?

Mary: I don't know. I guess you'll have to call her. She really didn't give me a lot of information.

President: Okay. (He calls the acting director.) This is President James. What's the problem, Henrietta?

Acting Director: This grant money has already been delayed twice by some manipulation or other in Congress. The money won't actually be here until November. I need the people I already have, and I need to hire new ones too to tide me over until it goes into effect. There are three staff members whose jobs end September 1. They are some of my best. I don't want to let them go and then hire them back two months later. That would be ridiculous.

President: What can I do to help?

Acting Director: What I need are funds to tide over the people I'd like to keep—three are critical to success under this new grant. If the grant had come in on time, they would have been put on it right away. We really need the lead time anyway. The grant requires a lot more work than people realize. The year-to-year funding business doesn't take into account the needs for staffing and long-term development.

President: But that's something we all know results from getting into these kinds of projects.

Acting Director: But there's no other source of funding.

President: Don't you have some other funds you could reallocate to cover these three?

Acting Director: I've scoured the budget. I just can't find enough. We could break the contract on some of the equipment under lease, but that doesn't make too much sense either.

President: The only thing I can think of would be to reassign the three on a temporary basis. Then when the grant becomes effective, we can transfer them back. Contingency funding? That's not what it's for, and I would be in trouble on that. However, I can certainly understand your dilemma. Why not send me some background information. I'll do my best to find temporary assignments. By the way, how are you voting in the faculty senate next week on the benefit package?

Acting Director: Well, I was leaning toward plan A. What do you think?

President: Well, of course, I favor plan B because it has many advantages.

Acting Director: Is that so? I'll certainly take another look.

President: Good. I'll get back in touch as soon as I've had a chance to look into some temporary assignments.

(He hangs up and calls the director of alumni affairs.)

President: Harry, this is President James. I may be able to squeeze here and there to get a couple of people to work on that project you had in mind. I might assign some people to you temporarily, say for two or three months, you know, just to see how your idea works.

Director of Alumni Affairs: Gee, great! I'm really impressed at how fast you move! I really appreciate it.

President: No problem. You can't be a great university unless you think big. I think your idea is good, and I want to support it. You understand that this is on a trial basis. If it works, we'll see about implementing it over a longer time period. I might have to use a different funding base for more permanent people, and we may have to switch personnel. But don't worry now; let's see what we can do on an experimental basis. You'll be hearing from me in a few days about whom we might have available.

Director of Alumni Affairs: Thanks again! I really appreciate your terrific support.

Here we see a university president building his own popularity by "solving" staffing problems through helping two university employees, neither of whom knows anything about the benefits that will accrue to the other and ultimately to the president. The 5,5 aspect of his decision making comes through his effort to disguise the actual situation. For example, the president says to Harry, "I may be able to squeeze here and there," but he's not squeezing to give Harry the needed personnel at all. He is simply taking available personnel from one director and giving them to another, putting in all the provisos about temporary, experimental, and so on, while knowing full well that these people will be withdrawn as soon as the federal grant arrives.

Supervising Personnel

The 5,5 approach to personnel management places as much emphasis on "who you know" as on "what you know." Who you know is an important measure of who you are. To this way of thinking, a candidate for assistant professor who has studied with prestigious teachers or illustrious researchers is qualified by the mere fact that important persons have placed their seal of approval on him or her. This basic proposition is extended to institutions as well. Graduates of more famous institutions already have earned some degree of distinction. A degree from Harvard, Stanford, or Yale is simply worth more than a degree from a newer institution. When it comes to actual selection, the 5,5-oriented administrator banks strongly on recommendations from colleagues who can certify that the candidate will not only fit in with other faculty but will be acceptable to students and the broader community.

Not everyone can be expected to maintain peak productivity over a thirty-year period, and therefore faculty burnout is best dealt with by recognizing that individual differences are inevitable. In any event, it may be that a "burned-out" person is simply recharging batteries and will resume a productive attitude in the next period ahead. To look at one low period and to try to extrapolate it into the future are risks this administrator seeks to avoid, partly to avoid errors and partly to avoid having to face up to the deadwood issue.

The 5,5-oriented administrator knows that the evaluation of other administrators is a delicate thing. One must approach this with care, if at all. The 5,5-oriented administrator believes strongly in supporting and encouraging those who are loyal and in making evaluations that "encourage" people to build on their strengths rather than to confront weaknesses. "Favorites" are chosen, and close relationships with administrative protégés are developed.

In the following exchange, a 5,5-oriented dean is "mentoring" one of his younger colleagues, a new department chair that the dean selected for the job a year ago. The new chair has a particularly tough assignment. The previous chair was an entrenched tyrant who had squelched most controversy within the department. Over the years, however, faculty were hired who wanted to make changes. The new chair was selected out of this up-and-coming group. The old chair and his smaller but more powerful clique remain on the faculty and are able to block most of the changes the newer faculty want to introduce. The younger chair has his chance to vent his frustration during an informal performance review with his mentor. The dean happily counsels with his favorite "son," sharing with him the accumulated wisdom of his years.

Dean: David, your first year is up. I know it's been a rough one for you. Let's review where you've been and project where you are going. What are your ideas on being a chairman?

Chair: Do you have all day for me to cry on your shoulder? This has been one hell of a year.

Dean: Remember, at the outset we talked about this as being a very difficult assignment with the conflicts that have been brewing in your department over the years following a repressive chair who finally stepped aside. You can expect a lot of uproar when people have to adjust to a new administrator. One reason you were chosen is because you're more easygoing and tolerant and willing to accept different points of view. But you can expect a lot of conflict and aggression after a period of repression. At least that's my opinion, and it's been my experience.

Chair: Well, your predictions certainly are being borne out. I have simply made no progress in straightening out the curriculum. We have two strong factions that won't yield an inch. The more they talk, the worse the whole thing gets.

Dean: I have a suggestion. Why don't you just say, "Look, this is how one side feels about the curriculum, and this is how the other side feels about the curriculum." Then take a vote to do it one way or the other for the next three years on a trial basis. The majority wins, and that's it. Tell them that you, as chairman, and with me standing behind you, have the authority to settle it this way. This can't go on any longer and they'll just have to go with it, whichever way. It's the democratic thing to do, and no one can complain that he or she had no voice.

Chair: Unfortunately, I have given the impression that we're going to talk this thing out until it is resolved and everybody agrees on the best approach.

Dean: But you know that's next to impossible unless you fire half your faculty. You're just going to have to coax them into a decision one way or the other. They're not going to like it, but the conflict is taking its toll. Students are suffering in the process.

Chair: What I'd like to tell them is that we're going to devote another month to discussion. Then we'll settle it your way if there is no agreement. How about that?

Dean: If that's the expectation and if that's preferable to your style of operating, it's fine with me. I would like to talk about your performance the first year, and maybe this is a good case in point. I think you have the potential to be a really fine administrator. That's why I chose you. On the other hand, it would be good if you could move a little more rapidly in settling some of these conflicts. They can go on and on; with an articulate faculty you'll be talked into the twenty-first century. My one suggestion for the next several months is for you to be a little firmer with respect to settling these tribal wars.

In my experience you just have to find out how most people feel on a subject and settle there. Otherwise, it'll drag on forever and you can't get anything done. It's a practical approach. I've found that if you let people know in plenty of time what you're going to do, and you give them time, they'll buy that. As I said, it's the practice of academic democracy and that's got to go back to 328 B.C. or something like that.

Chair: Okay, I'll try it your way and see how it goes. Perhaps after the former chairman, I've just gone too far the other way.

Dean: Okay, good. Your performance has been excellent. I know it's a tough situation and you're doing a fine job. Give me a call now and then to let me know how things are going.

Chair: I certainly will. Thanks for your understanding and constant support and recommendations for next steps.

A performance evaluation sets the stage for the dean to exercise control of the chair's approach to faculty. The dean thinks that the curriculum conflict between the two factions has gone on too long and recommends that it be resolved quickly by a vote. To make the decision more palatable, he suggests that the outcome of the vote be implemented only for a trial period; that provides a way to get off the hook if new troubles arise. We see the same use of majority will in another of the dean's commentaries when he advises the chairman that "you just have to find out how most people feel on a subject and settle there." What gives this attitude toward majority determination a 5,5 character is that it carries within it the concept of consensual validation. Majority thinking is confused with sound thinking. The position of the majority is determined, and that settles the question.

An additional aspect of the dean's 5,5 orientation is in his "sandwich" approach to performance appraisal. The sandwich is created by praising the chair for his performance, offering a suggestion about how the performance might be modified, and, when the suggestion is agreed to, praising him for excellent performance. The notion is that tucking a recommendation between two compliments makes it more palatable than it would otherwise be.

Coordinating Student Affairs

The 5,5-oriented administrator tends to want collaborative relations with students and tries to bring these about by negotiations in which successive approximations are worked out between what students want and what the administration finds acceptable. Limits of negotiating are reached only when accommodation to student demands would result in the university's appearing weak willed. Measuring the equivalence of a student's courses when he or she transfers from another college tends to be done in a loose way, and uncertainties are resolved in favor of the student. Other requirements are treated in a similar way. The thought is that rigidity in rules and interpretations is not in the best interests of the university or the student. Beyond that, the administrator who is capable of responding to student needs for exceptions in a flexible way soon earns a reputation as a fair administrator.

The 5,5-oriented administrator encourages the student newspaper to use an editorial approach that avoids controversial topics. Thus, an editorial commentary on "Educational Trends of the Next Decade" is a far better topic than "How Does This Administration Intend to Deal with the Student Drug Problem?" Content that presents the university in a favorable light, or even in a neutral way, is better than editorials that polarize issues or that have the capacity of turning students against the administration, one division of the college against another, and so on.

Student requests for outside speakers are encouraged by the 5,5-oriented administrator. But the premise is that those invited should themselves be noncontroversial and should be people who will have appeal to the broader community. The representatives of student government should concern themselves only with those aspects of campus life where students are in a good position to contribute, for example, intramural athletics, fraternities and sororities, student volunteer services, and campus social events. It is fine for students to sit on university committees when their advice has been requested, but for the student government to pressure for a seat on the college governing board is not realistic and is therefore discouraged.

Students get involved in an endless variety of activities, and some of these need attention from the administration. Traditionally, students have been a source of inexpensive and talented laborers in the community job market. This can create delicate situations. Many student organizations focus on public service, and students raise funds for social causes, some of which can be embarrassing to the administration. They also are often involved in political campaigns. Presidential candidates readily incorporate these eager workers into their vote-getting efforts, and this too can lead to alienation of a university's important funding sources and donors.

Below, it is a question of students having been asked to volunteer as workers to fight a coming emergency in the community. The administrators are discussing the method of coordinating the schedules of the volunteers who will be needed for flood control work. The severity of the crisis is not such as to clearly dictate the decision to close classes. But it is felt that while normal activities need not be interrupted, this is a good opportunity for the students to build goodwill in the community. The dean is asked to clarify policy regarding class schedules so chairmen can communicate a clear message to faculty.

Dean: The city fathers want volunteer help with this flood situation. I've been asked to organize campus-wide volunteering. This meeting is to alert you that we will be making public address announcements requesting student volunteers and, as a matter of fact, help from anyone else who can provide a service to reduce the potential disaster from this flood.

Chair 1: Here's a question: Will we permit students to leave classes? Do we give them authorized excuses for volunteering?

Dean: Well, I assume that classes can continue as usual and that students will volunteer for times when they are not in class.

Chair 1: Is that policy?

Dean: What do you think? I haven't really thought it out. Let's see what the issues are.

Chair 2: Boy, if we give them half a chance to leave class with an excuse, we'll never see them again. (General laughter) This disaster will last twice as long as the last one when they were not given excuses.

Dean: I had hoped we might not have class cancellation, but that's a faculty prerogative as long as the class is rescheduled for a later time. In that sense faculty are covered by policy regardless of what they do.

Chair 3: But faculty are going to want to know what we condone. Students will pressure faculty members to close classes so they can volunteer, then we will have no measure of whether they actually volunteered or did something else.

Dean: Are we making this more complicated than it really needs to be? Let's not set any precedents. Let's not even bring up the question of class cancellation. We'll simply ask volunteers to give their telephone numbers and indicate what times they are willing and able to help out. Then they can be contacted by city people. That way we're not really going to be in too much trouble one way or the other.

Chair 1: Maybe we ought to be specific about the length of time they are needed and how much volunteering help is anticipated as being necessary—that sort of thing.

Dean: Well, I'll be visiting downtown this afternoon to review that. I know they think a week at most and then it will be over with.

This dean's 5,5 orientation to administration is seen in the looseness with which he approaches this problem and in his attempt to deal with the problem under existing policy or in a general way. Setting a precedent would be too risky. He hopes that the volunteers will contribute what is needed and that there will be no inconvenience to the administration; then everyone will be happy.

The dean prefers to leave the message confused in the hope that all will be able to muddle through by relying on local option and that routines won't be disrupted. It is a case of winking at a problem rather than trying to solve it. The desire not to make a clear decision is based partly on the uncertainties of the situation. If the flood is not too bad, the dean would be right in holding to the regular schedule. But if it turns out to be worse than expected, he would be right in dismissing classes and strongly encouraging students to aid the community. "Let the faculty judge when the time comes" is the philosophy. That way he scores high on "delegation," "faculty autonomy," and "cooperative attitude." The problem is that the faculty may then have to individually reconcile conflicting pressures at a point where it may be even more difficult to determine the proper course.

Managing External Relations

Highly sensitive to the public, this administrator acts in the interest of expanding his or her own reputation while not disregarding the importance of projecting a favorable image of the university itself. He or she is keenly aware of the value of inviting important persons to the campus, and carefully calibrates the importance of visitors to determine how much of his or her time they are worth. He or she arranges for others to chaperone visitors of lesser stature. The same ground rules apply for accepting invitations sent to the university. The administrator personally accepts those invitations that will add to his or her own sense of prestige and importance. Invitations of lesser importance are not rejected but are passed on to others in such a way as to gain credit for providing them with opportunities to make contacts.

Other means for building a reputation include the editing of materials about the university that are likely to receive wide circulation. The editing entails forwarding information about university activities or events in the most favorable light possible, and yet doing so without reshaping the truth.

The administrator avoids being personally identified with unpleasantness by creating a distance between himself or herself and bad news. This is done by arranging for others to make unfavorable announcements. Sometimes the administrator appoints a spokesperson; sometimes he or she is simply unavailable for comment and thus creates a vacuum that someone else has to fill. Bad news is not actually suppressed, yet this administrator avoids tarnishing his or her own status by comments that might identify him or her with unfortunate circumstances.

The 5,5-oriented administrator is comfortable handling external relations. Being a master at image building, he or she does not hesitate to use any source available to persuade and win others over. Many of the administrator's public relations campaigns are for the good of the college and motives behind them are unselfish. Yet the administrator tends to bury the more objective truths in the campaigns styled after Madison Avenue.

The type of external relations strategy used by the 5,5-

oriented vice-president in the following dialogue is not unusual. Some would even say it is necessary for the survival of higher education. At any rate, the administrator here utilizes a ploy that is basic to advertising: "Discover what the public thinks its needs are and then announce that our product fulfills those needs." This tactic avoids the hard task of determining underlying or real needs or of admitting that the "product" satisfies only a narrow range of needs within the total spectrum.

Vice-President: Did you get the records of the legislative hearings?

Administrative Assistant: Yes.

Vice-President: What are the major areas of concern of the health committee?

Administrative Assistant: I came up with three. They were brought up again and again. I've outlined them. You might take a look at that memo.

Vice-President: Oh, yes. Good. Now what I'd like to do in preparation for the newsletter next week is to make sure we highlight faculty research in these three areas. It's amazing how many of those legislators read the newsletter. I know there are two projects in the nursing school. They are very active. Scout around and see if you can find others. Topic three may present some problems, but you might talk with your contacts over in biology or biochemistry. At any rate, send these over as very strong suggestions for the research highlight section in the publication.

Administrative Assistant: The real breakthrough in my opinion was reported last week by Dan Digs.

Vice-President: Oh, but Digs is so dull. He put his audience to sleep when he made that presentation. It was so technical that no one else could understand it, and he refuses to streamline his theories so that the typical legislator can appreciate them. If the legislature can understand we're really performing in some of these research areas, it'll be easier for all of us.

Administrative Assistant: Yeah, I know. There were three calls from the governor's office last month on that article about the engineering project.

Vice-President: By the way, I'd like the name of the author of that article. I thought it was quite well done. I want to send a note of appreciation.

Administrative Assistant: Right away.

The vice-president uses the newsletter to engender legislative support for research. The hope is that resources will be sustained by tuning the content of the newsletter to the interests expressed in the legislature. Public relations become the technique for controlling attitudes and making them more favorable to the university. Genuine contributions to research carry only secondary weight in the vice-president's scale of convictions. His approach "plays" with the truth, not by rewriting it, but by "bending" and "shaping" it to satisfy momentary needs.

Assuring Basic Operations

The planning process is at times piecemeal. Administrators often say they have too little time to finish immediate tasks, much less plan for the future. Assistants are frequently given the job of coming up with drafts or proposals of plans for scrutiny at higher levels. The 5,5-oriented administrator is a master at this kind of delegation. Key, trusted assistants are chosen to do the groundwork. Often these planning tasks require a great deal of time; data must be gathered, people must be contacted, administrative constraints must be anticipated and resolved. In the next example, the vice-president has gone over a proposal submitted by one of his aides in grounds and maintenance, and he is not particularly satisfied with the plan, even though the aide is one of his most conscientious and eager subordinates.

Vice-President: Look, Walter, you've made an excellent start on this landscaping plan. I have spent some time and gone over it with a fine-tooth comb, and I'd like you to take a look at this revision and revise it again or make any comments or additions you see fit. I think it's beginning to really sound good.

Aide: Let me take a few minutes to read it. I'll talk to you about it before I start revising it again.

Vice-President: I really don't think that'll be necessary. I'd like for you to just go ahead and work on it as best you can; use your own judgment.

Aide: Well, after seeing your modifications, I think there may be some points of difference we ought to work out before I spend time revising it again. You've shifted to a whole new concept on the trees. I'm not sure the drainage pattern will support it, and it may require a whole new sprinkler system.

Vice-President: Well, with the trustees' meeting, I'm going to be awfully busy the next couple of days. As you know, I have several presentations to make. I'd prefer to see at least one more revision by you, and then if we still have to talk about it we can get together next week.

Aide: Did you like the central thrust of my plan?

Vice-President: Yes, yes. The whole thing is excellent. I simply reorganized the presentation somewhat, but, in fact, the major ideas are all still there, and I just thought this re-organization a little better for selling it to the president.

Aide: (gives it a quick scan) Well, it looks like a whole new plan to me. Here's an idea I don't even recognize as mine.

Vice-President: Now, that's not true. After you've studied it carefully, you'll see that we're not in any way thinking in two different directions. It's just a matter of reorganizing the material to present it in the way that will be most acceptable to the president. I think it looks very good.

The vice-president is managing this apparent difference by offering a compliment on the excellence of his aide's plan and saying that his own work has been mainly that of reorganizing the sequence of presentation to make it more palatable to the president. The aide wants to sit down and review the underlying changes, but the vice-president prefers to avoid this and uses his busy schedule as an excuse. The aide's protest that the revision makes his presentation unrecognizable is blunted by the vice-president, who again states that he has done nothing beyond reorganizing the material. The conversation is terminated with a compliment: "I think it looks very good." The aide gains no benefit from this oblique way of changing the report or from the vice-president's unwillingness to engage in open discussion of his additions.

Summary

The positive motivation of a 5,5-oriented academic administrator is the desire to be in good standing with his colleagues. From the standpoint of the negative motivational pole, his or her objective is to avoid actions that might be criticized or might be embarrassing.

The administrative function of planning is carried out by touching base with those who will be affected by a plan, identifying what the broadest constituency will accept, and then forwarding the plan for others to react to. Organizing entails working with, through, and between loose alliances and factions and relying on bargaining, negotiation, and trade-offs to forge an acceptable basis of working relationships. Giving explicit directions is avoided in preference to relying on suggestions and recommendations. Controlling is seen as a matter of nudging people back into line and shaping and trimming the outline of a plan. Staffing is on a "who knows whom" and "whom can you trust" basis.

Mission is defined in terms of what is acceptable to various constituencies, and it tends to be formulated in functional and practical terms, tilting in the direction of application and utility. Teachers are representatives of the administration in their dealings with students. Teachers who can balance subject matter requirements with the need of students to enjoy a well-rounded social life are preferred. Curriculum is premised on satisfying student needs, and areas of knowledge are carved out in such a way as to give them maximum appeal.

Research on campuses where 5,5 is the dominant orientation is seen as a means of gaining promotion and prestige rather than as having intrinsic value. Service is employed to a significant degree as a criterion for promotion because it can promote widespread acceptance of the academic orientation of the college. In addition, it keeps the faculty in touch with the reality of the outside world.

Resources are managed in such a way as to broaden the administrator's base of political power. Selection and promotion of faculty members tend to be done on a highly personal basis; a professor's reputation among his colleagues is a significant criterion. With respect to student affairs, the dominant values of the students themselves are influential in molding administrative opinion. External affairs are managed according to a public relations approach, and most of the responsibilities for assuring basic operations are delegated.

As a decision maker, the 5,5-oriented administrator seeks what is acceptable to the majority point of view. His or her convictions tend to be shallow and to represent the prevailing values of the administrator's profession or other relevant institutional and collegial affiliations. Conflict is resolved by looking to tradition for guidelines or by seeking a compromise, with the majority point of view prevailing. The 5,5-oriented administrator maintains a good, steady pace and uses humor as a means of "selling" himself or herself.

Beyond this somewhat consistent 5,5 orientation is a combination of approaches that can best be termed a "statistical" 5,5 style. It is occasionally said of an administrator, "It's hard to say anything precise about his or her leadership style. He or she fits every position on the Academic Administrator Grid at one time or another." This statistical 5,5-oriented administrator employs any two, and sometimes all five, basic styles in dealing with performance and "people" dilemmas. The essential feature is that he or she manages according to what is thought effective at any particular time, that is, according to what appears to be appropriate to the demands of the particular situation.

This is an administrative orientation that ignores behavioral science principles. The administrator adjusts to every situation in the way he or she privately prefers, not in the best or soundest way. For example, if a staff member has little or no motivation or initiative, the administrator does not assign important work to that person. Rather, he or she ignores the staff member in a 1,1-oriented way. If a subordinate is easily upset, the administrator eases up on pressure and gives praise, even though rewards may not be justified, thus using a 1,9-oriented approach. If another staff member is falling behind, a statistical 5,5-oriented administrator points out that he or she is failing to carry a fair share of the load and that, unless he or she begins to do so, others will be critical and rejecting. Here the administrator relies on the 5,5 approach itself. If a staff member has high standards and is being productive, even though this may be producing conflict with others, the administrator spurs him or her on to greater effort to resolve the conflict in a way that maintains production, thus relying on a 9,9-oriented approach. If instructions are arbitrarily resisted by still another staff member, the administrator demands compliance in a 9,1-oriented manner.

The statistical 5,5-oriented administrator hopscotches all over the Grid, behaving inconsistently and treating each staff member differently. Yet the administrator sees little or no contradiction in these actions. He or she assumes that each person is different and unique; therefore, creating productive relationships based on common goals, mutual dignity, and earned respect simply is not practical. Lacking a concept of change or development, he or she "maneuvers," always trying to adjust to circumstances while staying within the boundaries of the status quo.

Most universities have no one consistent organization style. Each department or division is left to its own resources without a systematic plan for strengthening its administrative practices. In a more or less evolutionary way, these departments and divisions develop their own particular styles. One unit may be run as a tight ship, another may do just enough to meet requirements, while a third may strive for excellence. The statistical 5,5 quality in the final analysis is most probably brought about by a hands-off attitude on the part of top administrators in an organization practicing policies of extreme decentralization.

Chapter Nine

Team
Administration: 9,9

The 9,9 approach to administration, located in the upper right corner of the Academic Administrator Grid in Chapter Two, presumes an inherent *connection* between institutional needs for performance and the needs of faculty and staff for full and rewarding work experiences. Active participation leads to involvement and to commitment to standards of excellence. Performance through integrating people into university achievement means using their ideas and viewpoints in solving problems. While the end results of problem-solving teamwork are usually carried out by individuals on a one-alone basis in the classroom, in the research laboratory, or in a service activity, joint effort makes synergistic consequences possible. A 9,9-oriented administrator desires to contribute to institutional success and is committed to involving those with whom he or she works. These values promote voluntarism, spontaneity, open-

236

ness, and the sharing of responsibility with others in accomplishing clear and challenging goals.

Nine, nine-oriented management seeks to achieve full participation of members, pursuing common goals and objectives that integrate both personal and institutional perspectives. Individuals gain a sense of gratification, enthusiasm, and excitement when they are able to make important contributions. The closer they come to success, the greater their sense of emotional reward.

When an effort is judged to have failed, a 9,9-oriented administrator is likely to feel self-defeat and disappointment at betraying the trust placed in him or her by others. He or she may feel disturbed and uneasy and be prey to self-doubts about his or her capacity to meet future problems successfully. Even though such setbacks occur, however, a sense of perspective provides the foundation for persistence. Lack of success in the short term does not mean defeat. The motivational motto of the 9,9-oriented administrator is, "With caring, commitment, and versatility, we can solve even the most complex problems. That's the meaning of administration."

Administrative Behavior

A 9,9-oriented administrator thinks that it is his or her job to see to it that sound decisions are made.

- *Planning:* "I get the people together who have relevant facts and/or stakes in the outcome to review the whole picture. I get their reactions and ideas. We formulate a sound model from start to completion to provide an organizing framework for integrating an entire project. I lead by establishing goals and flexible schedules with them."
- *Organizing:* "Within the framework of the whole, we determine individual responsibilities, ground rules, and procedures."
- *Directing:* "By stimulating feedback, I keep informed of progress and influence subordinates by identifying problems and revising goals *with* them. I lend assistance by helping to remove roadblocks."

- *Controlling:* "In addition to in-progress critiques to keep projects on schedule, I conduct a wrap-up with those responsible. We evaluate the way things went and see what we can learn from our experience and how we can apply our learning in the future. I give recognition on a team basis as well as for outstanding individual contributions."
- *Staffing:* "Work requirements are matched with capabilities or needs for development in making decisions as to who does what."

Behavioral science experimentation, extensive field studies, and even observations across different cultures indicate that when people are oriented toward achieving concrete, specific, and agreed-upon goals, their behavior becomes orderly, meaningful, and purposeful. It appears that when individuals who must coordinate their activities are aware of institutional purpose and of their real stakes in performance, then they will exercise more self-responsibility, self-direction, and self-control. With this kind of leadership, individuals can mesh their efforts in an interdependent way.

Direction and control can be achieved by securing agreement with institutional purpose and the means of contributing to it. Understanding of an institution's economic health and performance goals, unity of effort, and commitment arise out of discussion and deliberation of major issues and through the mutual identification of sound objectives. In other words, those who are involved in the overall effort participate in creating the conditions under which sound performance can be accomplished. Such action can result in the autonomous regulation of action. This approach may require fundamental reorientation of administrative practices. It can no longer be taken for granted, for example, that people will accept the stated institutional purpose as a legitimate statement of actual purpose.

Principles Underlying the 9,9 Orientation

What behavioral science principles must be applied to ensure sound administration? The following are based on evidence from many applied behavioral science disciplines. As indicated in the Appendix, they are supported by research findings in the fields of social psychology, sociology, anthropology, mental health, counseling, psychiatry, political science, and history, as well as by studies of business effectiveness. They are also validated in reverse by demonstrations of the negative behavior produced by their violation; criminology, penology, and studies of colonialism and slavery all give evidence here. When these principles are brought into daily use, administrative interactions are characterized by mutual trust and respect. Trust and respect, in other words, are the end result of sound behavior. Sound behavior is also productive and creative in the operational sense.

Other things being equal, performance, creativity, personal satisfaction, and mental and physical health are best served by implementing these principles:

1. Fulfillment through contribution is the motivation that gives character to human activity and supports productivity.
2. Open communication permits the exercise of self-responsibility.
3. Conflicts are solved by direct confrontation of their causes, with understanding and agreement as the basis of cooperative effort.
4. Being responsible for one's own actions is the highest level of maturity and only possible through widespread delegation of power and authority.
5. Shared participation in problem solving and decision making stimulates active involvement in productivity and creative thinking.
6. Management is by objectives.
7. Merit is the basis of reward.
8. Learning from work experience is through critique.
9. Norms and standards that regulate behavior and performance support personal and organization excellence.

Considered from a behavioral science point of view, these nine principles undergird sound behavior, just as there are principles of physics that undergird sound engineering. Violate principles of physics in the engineering of a bridge or a building, for

example, and you court a physical disaster. Violate the principles of sound behavioral science and you invite a social disaster
—the collapse of an organization.

Taken together, these nine statements represent different
facets of a 9,9-oriented administrative strategy. Each reflects in
its own way the basic proposition that there is one best way to
manage. Learning these principles and coming to understand
how to bring them into daily use constitute the versatility
aspect of the 9,9 way of managing.

Implementing Institutional Mission

Administrators who embrace 9,9-oriented values place
the stated college or university mission at the forefront and test
decisions for whether they advance the university in the direction of the stated mission. Since the university is made up of
legitimately contesting groups with divergent interests, these administrators exercise leadership by confronting competing interests with discrepancies between their interpretations of stated
mission and their execution of actual mission. If sound decisions cannot be made because they are inconsistent with the
stated mission, they work toward revision of the stated mission
to bring it in line with valid academic practice.

The 9,9-oriented administrator evaluates specific programs or activities in terms of their relationship to overall institutional mission. When broad goals are well articulated and
understood, any particular plans and action steps proposed can
be clearly assessed both for short-term and long-range implications. Given the test of relevance, what at first appears "good"
may not actually be "good" in the larger sense. Alternatively,
what may appear as a problem may actually be reinterpreted as
a necessary disruption, given the overall purpose of the institution. It is difficult for administrators to restrain themselves
from "curing" short-term problems with actions that appear to
resolve a difficulty in the eyes of important constituencies.
These actions may be popular, but they might be the very ones
that will create spiraling economic ills over the long haul. A
9,9-oriented administrator makes decisions about specific prob-

lems or even positive events by asking, "How does this action relate to the bigger picture of what we are trying to accomplish?"

The following president is faced with such a dilemma. He is concerned about the rampant grantsmanship in one of the divisions. Many of the staff are on "soft" money, and the research has taken an applied, short-term, quick-payout bent to the detriment of the sound teaching and basic research to which the university is dedicated. The president is talking with the dean of that division. The dilemma is whether the president should condone a practice that brings rewards to faculty and to administrators when he is not convinced that the practice is in the long-term best interests of the university. The president is not even sure in his own mind what the long-term effects of heavy reliance on soft-money funding will be. Yet he is concerned enough to raise the issue with one of his deans, whose division is most involved in this type of funding pattern.

President: I'm going to put my concerns before you. I want you to tell me if you think I'm creating a problem where none exists. But if there is something to my concern, we really need to discuss it further.

Dean: Okay. What's going on?

President: My worry is this: I've been looking over the budget figures for all divisions and making some comparisons. I've studied where the money comes from and where the money goes, that sort of thing. I've been watching your division for several years now. It seems to be getting more and more into the soft-money situation. This can be seen as positive. Your faculties have been adept at acquiring government grants and foundation money. But you now have a large staff of nonfaculty researchers, and the turnover rate for some of these projects is high. I want to be assured that the basic teaching and research functions are being fully attended to; that the quality of the programs is your first concern.

Dean: I'm glad you've brought this up. It's been worrying me, too. Part of this is the matter of the attractiveness of some of these disciplines. They are simply more connected with outside agencies, the federal government, and private sources of funds than are other disciplines. Much of their research is popular right now. There's a lot of emphasis on applied problems, and these disciplines tend to be more practical and eclectic than theoretical and systematic. That's something I also worry about. Growth for the sake of growth can be disastrous. I understand that, and I would like to put the reins on some of the chairmen. But I just don't know to what extent I really have the authority to do so.

President: It may not really be a matter of authority in the sense of administrative controls. It may be more a matter of coming to some sort of consensus with these disciplines about what they are engaged in in the context of university mission. It might be important to have some good discussions about the dangers in this kind of situation.

Dean: But some who are the most guilty of this sort of thing— what shall we call it, rampant expansionism?—are building empires, and they aren't particularly interested in talking about how to slow down. After all, they feel they are evaluated partly on their ability to do this, and this is a true reading. We can't do an about-face now and tell them that they are going to be punished for it or that we want to put checks and balances on them, can we?

President: I know what all the problems are, and I'm stumped to think out the best solutions up here where the tower is really ivy. In fact, there may not be as many dangers to it as I envisage. However, it seems to me that we're repeating some cycles here that we've seen before in other departments. A better approach might be to learn from the experiences of some of those departments that underwent rapid expansion and then had to fall back.

Dean: We probably need a growth and retrenchment discussion of some sort.

President: It appears we need to create some way to learn from our institutional experiences—some approach where deans can examine pros and cons of the various rates of growth,

including problems of rapid growth that lead to later retrenchment. We're in the habit of discussing short-term
opportunities without fully examining the possible long-
term adverse consequences.

Dean: You are talking about that issue none of us ever really
comes to grips with—long-range planning.

President: Yes, I know. Perhaps now is the time to do something.

Dean: I don't think the chances of accomplishing anything with
my department chairs are too high.

President: What do you mean?

Dean: I've tried to get the chairs together to talk about planning
and some long-term goal setting, but so far all I've gotten is
negative responses and resistance with complaints about
how much time it takes.

President: In that case, why don't we spend some time thinking
about your own experiences. We don't want to make the
same mistake twice. Can we get some of the people involved
in your planning process to shed light on what their experiences have been?

Dean: Oh, sure. We can get several together to talk about it.

President: It would be helpful to me, that's for sure. I know
that we have to come to grips with the growth issue and
how to get in a position to make some long-range plans that
will steer us into the future and keep us moving in the direction of the university mission. I'd like to get a better feel for
why it's such a difficult problem to tackle.

The president is here trying to get open examination of a
problem. His concern is that soft money is buying empires at
the expense of program quality. The dean acknowledges this
possibility, indicating that the disciplines in his school currently
enjoy popularity with funding organizations and agencies because of the applied nature of the problems that they deal with.
Funding sources are often more prepared to support projects
that have a "quick" payout. This is an open acknowledgment
that the problem involves crucial questions of subject matter.
Having indicated this, the dean mentions to the president

that he, too, would like to restrain unbridled growth, and yet he is not sure his authority extends over the range of decisions essential for doing so. The president redefines the problem, not as one of authority, but as one between the dean and the pertinent chairs, who themselves have not developed a clear consensus on how division programs fit the university's stated mission. The dean agrees but then again redefines the problem as one of empire building and notes that individual faculty members have in the past been encouraged to do the very sort of thing about which the president and he are now sharing other reservations.

As a result of this kind of diagnostic and critical orientation, the problem undergoes another redefinition. It is now seen as symptomatic of deficiencies in long-range planning. Such planning would make possible operational decisions as to growth or retrenchment in a manner congruent with university purpose. As the discussion continues, both the president and the dean develop the conviction that something is wrong with overreliance on short-term opportunities rather than on long-range planning. This discussion may be the beginning of a different way of leading the university; there may be a shift from a stimulus-response approach to an attempt to build a model of what the university could become. Operating decisions would then be based on that model.

Supporting Teaching and Learning

The administrator who conceives of the instructional process according to the 9,9 orientation is likely to see the classroom situation in terms of student participation and to want to involve students in probing the deeper issues contained in a given subject matter. This means that all subjects must be taught in a dynamic way. In this view, active participation will lead to increased interest in any subject matter; dullness originates in the teaching process, not in the subject matter itself.

Grading is an essential condition of learning, but one of the primary values of an examination is the feedback it provides students. And when feedback is of the double-loop variety, it offers the professor insights for identifying the effectiveness of his or her teaching. The bell curve is an unacceptable basis for the distribution of grades, because it indicates what various students know in comparison with one another, not what every student needs to know to advance to a higher level of complexity.

Selection of a faculty member is likely to be based on evaluating, first, a candidate's spirit of inquiry and, second, a candidate's depth and breadth of knowledge of his or her own subject matter and ability to communicate it. A third criterion is the candidate's knowledge of or inherent sense of group dynamics, and how these can be utilized in the classroom to arouse interest and involvement and to stimulate commitment to learning.

The teaching process is of great interest to an administrator who believes in and encourages innovation. Sometimes this means supporting individual faculty in the face of conventional departmental norms. At other times it means supporting departmental methods. In the following dialogue, a faculty member who wishes to use a new approach to teaching is encouraged to do so in a given content area, despite the hostility of others who teach the same material. Having realized the political risks involved, the faculty member has sought the advice of the chair, whom he places in the position of having to choose to support the "crazy idea" of one person or the majority view of the curriculum committee, which is against it. The faculty member is strongly in favor of utilizing programmed instruction in teaching. At this point in time the chair is not convinced that it is the best approach, but he confronts the choice constructively.

Faculty Member: I've had another big fight with the curriculum committee.

Chair: What about?

Faculty Member: My attempt to get programmed instruction through the committee for the course on marriage and the family.

Chair: I didn't realize you needed their okay for that.

Faculty Member: Well, I don't, really. I can do it any way I want. The problem's that I am an assistant professor. If they are as strongly against it as they seem to be, and I do it, then I'll have to pay if it doesn't work. Several of them are also on the promotion committee.

Chair: What's that got to do with it?

Faculty Member: I wish that didn't have anything to do with it, but I have a feeling that in reality it does.

Chair: What do you mean?

Faculty Member: Well, I know and you know that teaching evaluations count in terms of promotion and merit increases. Programmed instruction is a completely different kind of teaching, where traditional evaluations of the teacher are almost irrelevant. My personal feeling is that a lot of the material covered in this course can be effectively taught through a programmed instruction procedure, and I would like to develop the course in that way. But there are two faculty members, both on the promotion committee, who have been teaching this course for some time. They have their way of doing it. They believe strongly in the classical method. They think that teaching this kind of content through programmed instruction is totally inappropriate. My feeling is that students learn a great deal more, and what I have tried to sell them on is the idea that we measure student gains under their method and my method, and I've said that I would be willing to live with the consequences of that comparison. In other words, if my method does not teach as much as theirs, then I will accept that theirs is better and do it their way. If my method is better, then I should be encouraged to do it my way and that should count for me when teaching evaluations come along, on the assumption that I am using the best techniques. I didn't even imply that they should change, should the comparison come out my way.

Chair: I'm not entirely convinced that teaching something even like "cost accounting" through programmed instruction would be the best way to go about it. However, we certainly should experiment with various approaches, and this is certainly a legitimate one. Let me suggest a solution. Pre-post testing of courses is a great idea. We should do that anyway, whether we're comparing two teaching methods or not. It's valuable to know how much students have learned in any course, and I can't think of a better way of going about that than measuring student gains. In any event, we need to be aware of the following: Just because the classical method of teaching is accepted doesn't mean it's best. And just because programmed instruction is new doesn't mean it's more effective. They may both be limited relative to a third or fourth alternative that is not represented in this design.

More importantly, however, you should be free to experiment and to try this or that without worrying about whether you are stepping on somebody's toes, and whether they will take it out on you later in the promotion committee. For this experimental or pilot situation, as far as I'm concerned, we can dispense with sending the teaching evaluations to the promotion committee, even though it's a bit unusual. I do think it's a good idea for you to circulate the evaluations at the end of the course just to see what kind of response you get from students. However, I can understand that they'll have much less contact with you and would be less likely to rate you highly on an item such as "stimulating lecturer." The best thing at this point will be for you and me to get together with the rest of the curriculum committee and let me give all of you at once my views on the subject. We're going to have to make room for different ways of doing things, even if the results turn out to be negative sometimes. That should not be fuel for the promotion committee. This may be a good example of where we ought to make exceptions. Who knows, maybe it will turn out as a positive. Not only that, preparing programmed instruction material may be helpful regardless of how you teach the course later. So I think using your time to do that certainly is a sound idea. I'll get notes out to the curriculum committee, and we'll meet as soon as possible.

This represents a 9,9 orientation to the situation on the chair's part. The difficulty is that conventional teaching is what most departments are prepared to evaluate. Innovative attempts at restructuring classroom methodology that don't require a stand-up performer open up entirely new channels that do not fit in with the usual ways of evaluating faculty. The result is that the professor who seeks to innovate runs the risk of poor evaluations.

The chair and professor see the issue clearly, and the chair takes the position that experimentation is a sound approach, particularly when it includes systematic evaluation of comparative gains from alternative methods. He encourages the professor to make such evaluations, and thus we see that the issue will not be decided on the basis of opinion or feelings but on the basis of impartial evidence. Furthermore, to ensure that the faculty member is not unfairly penalized, the chair arranges for the ordinary means of evaluation and control to be put aside during the period of the experiment. In this sense, the power to decide will not lie with the hierarchy of the organization or with the faculty member's colleagues; instead, the decision will be founded on interpretation of experimental data.

Establishing the Curriculum

"The college faculty is split, and a philosophical battle is on." For many administrators these words signal deep-lying administrative problems. The 9,9-oriented administrator is no different. This person too can be intimidated by deep conflicts. Academic conflicts are particularly difficult to resolve when they center on curriculum issues. Entrenched positions increase the difficulty of reaching sound agreements. Yet the 9,9-oriented administrator accepts his or her responsibility to bring major curriculum issues into focus and to seek resolution of them consistent with the university mission.

The curriculum is the expression of the college or university mission. As a result, the 9,9-oriented administrator involves curriculum committee members in evaluating their understanding of stated mission by discussing it and testing it against the actual mission as it has come to be interpreted in curriculum decisions. Once agreement is reached and discrepancies between stated and actual have been resolved, the committee will be in a position to design a curriculum consistent with its agreed-upon and shared interpretation of mission. This approach significantly reduces the play of vested interests of individual faculty members, while avoiding the pitfall of teaching students only what they may seem to want. When the catalogue makes clear the congruence between university mission and curriculum, students are able to exercise informed choice in their decisions as to whether this university is capable of satisfying their needs.

Below, the 9,9-oriented vice-president of academic affairs acts to bring a curriculum conflict into the open with the dean of liberal arts, even though it appears that it may take much effort to resolve the problem and that strong feelings will surface in the process. He prepares himself and the others involved for the long, hard discussions that will be necessary if concerted action is to be achieved.

Vice-President: We're going to have to reach a decision on remedial teaching.

Dean: I know it. It's the biggest can of worms. You would not believe it.

Vice-President: Well, there must be a creative solution somewhere on the horizon. It's wasteful to go through this again and again.

Dean: For you and me both.

Vice-President: Why don't you alert a group of, say, seven faculty members you think have the most divergent views on this issue. Let's get them together for a discussion.

Dean: You've got to be out of your mind.

Vice-President: I'm serious. The conflict can't go on and on. If we think about it long enough and we argue it long enough, sooner or later someone is going to come up with a sound solution. It's to the point where we have to agree on the best solution and then live with the consequences.

Dean: How much time are you willing to spend? Say a year?

Vice-President: However long it takes, that's how long we'll be there. I don't expect to come up with a decision in one meeting, but I expect to hear this advisory committee de-

velop some new ideas on the subject, and possibly a solution, in ways that so far have eluded us. I'm willing to go to
the entire faculty and argue for a sound policy. I'll participate in the discussion like everyone else.

Dean: Then you'd better get the director of athletics to come in
and umpire.

Vice-President: Would you say he is unbiased on this subject? I
thought the department of physical education needed the
remedial teaching as much as anybody else.

Dean: Very funny! Seriously though, I think the problem is
hopeless.

The vice-president starts by defining the problem as
solvable, a first step in finding an answer. Next, he speaks of the
importance of persistence in seeking a solution. Third, he sees
the problem as partly one of divergent views among faculty
members, and his approach is therefore to bring those with different positions together. From this may come a solution that
meets the reservations of all sides and yet satisfies the requirements of each. Finally, we hear the vice-president saying that he
is prepared to actively participate in the discussions himself and,
beyond that, to take whatever solution is achieved to the faculty and push for its acceptance.

Supporting Research and Scholarly Productivity

Aliveness to new ideas and personal involvement create a
state of mind that stimulates an attitude of inquiry. Such a state
of mind is an essential element in good teaching, since it spurs
active discussion and aids students to develop an inquiring attitude toward knowledge. As a result, the scholarly productivity
of faculty is a significant factor in resource allocation, as well as
in the selection, promotion, and discharge of faculty. The 9,9-
oriented administrator personally encourages the research effort
in a number of ways. He or she searches out sources of funding
or helps individual faculty members to do so. He or she assists
faculty in structuring their time to best advantage to produce
quality research. He or she is knowledgeable about the research

interests and skills of faculty and willing to discuss research issues, getting involved in creative, thought-provoking discussions that are conducive to the proper "atmosphere" for research.

Sometimes at higher levels of the institution the administrator loses touch with the daily research effort until an event occurs to bring him or her "back in touch." The following scene makes clear that sometimes his involvement in a research project is necessitated by a problem that has emerged and calls for intervention. Then the administrator has a double task. One is to preserve the research effort. The other is to strengthen the administrative process. The vice-president for research, consulting with a faculty member who has a major grant, is faced with both of these tasks, and he proposes a resolution that will not be easy for anyone concerned to accept. However, if the conflict is handled well, there is a chance that the research effort and the administrative system will both be reinforced.

Faculty Member: I'm really in a bind. I need advice. The dean wanted me to talk to you.

Vice-President: Okay.

Faculty Member: This is really hard to say, but as you know, I have a major three-year research grant—I have specific objectives that I have set for myself in terms of a time schedule to get things rolling. But I'm getting pressure from the dean to pick up some people in a holdover kind of situation. I'm not particularly interested in having them on my grant.

Vice-President: Yes, I'm familiar with the problem.

Faculty Member: Should I hire them?

Vice-President: Are they Small and Helms?

Faculty Member: Yes, that's right.

Vice-President: Well, don't hire them if it's not in the best interest of your research.

Faculty Member: That's easier said than done. I'm getting a lot of pressure. The dean wants me to put on two people to help solve some of his administrative problems, but it won't help my research at all.

Vice-President: Have you simply told him you won't do it?

Faculty Member: Well, yes and no. You can tell him, but sometimes he doesn't hear.

Vice-President: The principal investigator of a grant has the right to hire personnel or not hire personnel as he sees fit, and, although the dean may be asking you to hire certain people and even though it would be helpful to him, you are in no way obliged to do so. Think very carefully to make sure you're not resisting just because of some bias. What I'm saying is, there is certainly nothing wrong with putting some of those people on the grant if in fact they can contribute to the research objectives. That's a decision you should be making. Did you take the dean's suggestion as a pressure tactic?

Faculty Member: He's been buttonholing me and trying to persuade me to do it. He says it will only be for a couple of months and that the university is going to be losing two good people if we don't find something for them until some other money comes in that he's waiting for. He also has suggested that his office can take some of the accounting load.

Vice-President: Do you have positions open on your grant at the time he is talking about?

Faculty Member: Yes, I do.

Vice-President: I suggest that you simply tell him that you will consider all applicants and that these two will be given consideration, but that you expect to interview a number of people. Tell him what your procedure will be. If I were you, in order to avoid any misunderstandings in procedures, I would put your hiring procedure in writing.

Faculty Member: Remember, though, all new grant proposals go through the dean's office for approval. I'm likely to run the risk that when I send up additional proposals later he won't approve them.

Vice-President: That's a risk you're going to have to take. You have the right to stand by your guns on this, and that's just what you're going to have to do.

Faculty Member: Well, okay. I'll see if I can deal with him.

Vice-President: What I'm advising is not the easiest route, but I think it's what you're going to have to do. I'll be interested in knowing if you come up with any better solution. This is the best I can suggest for your particular situation, but the real problems are of a different character. Let me explain.

The first is that you feel the dean is pressuring you in an administratively unsound manner. If so, this is my problem since he is my subordinate and I bear responsibility for sound administration by those who report to me. Secondly, even though he suggested it, in coming to me you have gone over his head, and this does not constitute a model of good administration either.

It seems to me that we three need to discuss this whole problem, sort it out, try to solve it, and in the process perhaps reinforce sound principles of administration. If we do this in an open and candid way, we can also reduce or eliminate any hard feelings that may be building up. Are you willing to take part in such a discussion?

The vice-president responds to the staffing problem by telling the faculty member that he is under no obligation to use the research grant to help the dean handle a temporary personnel problem. Then the faculty member expresses the fear that he will receive adverse evaluations of his own performance if he fails to respond to the dean. The vice-president invites the professor to double-check his own attitudes to be satisfied that his reservations about putting the requested faculty on his budget are not a bias against individuals who in fact might be qualified. Having done so, the vice-president then confronts the faculty member with these facts: there always is a risk that deans will be fallible, and any dean may resent what he sees as lack of cooperation when future approval is requested. In effect, the vice-president is telling the faculty member that he has to be willing to put his convictions on the line.

Beyond these considerations, the vice-president deals with the dynamic issues of administration that reside beneath the surface problem. The vice-president does this by proposing a three-way discussion among himself, the dean, and the faculty member that can get to the deeper issues of the use of research funds. During such a discussion all points of view and motivations can be brought to light, and the conflict can be resolved by means of an objective evaluation of what each person is trying to accomplish.

Encouraging Community and Institutional Service

The effectiveness of the university is enhanced by members who contribute their efforts through participation in committees, advisory groups, and so on. The same is true in terms of the external community. The members of a university have skills and talents that are unusual, and many times they are able to make unique contributions to the community.

As in other aspects of university functioning, however, the service activities in which university members have the opportunity to engage can be so numerous as to prevent the pursuit of the basic responsibilities of the university, namely, teaching and research. Therefore, standards are needed to provide guidance for decisions about applying time and resources to meet service needs within and beyond the university.

For example, administrators or faculty members should not be expected to engage in a service activity if in doing so they are prevented from utilizing a skill or talent higher than that involved in the service activity. One exception is that their expertise may be contributed in a service area if others are not likely to be able to fulfill the need with the same degree of competence. Another exception is that the administrator's or faculty member's skills in other areas may be less than those that he or she can contribute in a service activity. Then the adverse impact on research or teaching would be less than the positive impact on service. In addition, it is expected that administrators and faculty members will participate actively in service activities that contribute to the institution's citizenship role.

The insurance of quality involves a number of small but significant daily efforts on the part of administrators. It is often easier not to make the effort. Sometimes, ensuring quality means extra work for everybody. Sometimes it means slowing someone down and getting him or her to be more careful and accurate in approach. Attempts to achieve quality are sometimes easy to put aside because to support them may require going against the strong preferences of more headstrong colleagues. Such is the situation in which the chair of electrical engineering finds himself in the following encounter with the director of professional and continuing education, who is responsible for organizing technical training programs for the professional community. The director wants to go full speed ahead and pursue a golden opportunity that the chair has brought to his attention. However, the chair fears that the director wants to cut too many corners, and he feels it necessary to stand his ground on the quality issue.

Chair: I got a call yesterday from the president of Johnston Engineering.

Director: What'd he say?

Chair: He wants a full-blown training program for approximately two hundred technicians.

Director: Wow, that's fantastic!

Chair: Yes, fantastic, except he wants it right away. He wants some pretty specific technical training. We have three people who would be good on that content. The only problem is that they're all tied up on their research projects. I don't know how in the world they would have time to do what he is asking.

Director: I suppose he also has the money to pay for all this?

Chair: Oh, yes, no problem about that. Any ideas?

Director: I think it would be a good idea for me to talk with him about what specific technical training he has in mind. A lot of times they will say it's extremely specialized training they want, but when you get right down to it, it's not as complex as it sounds over the phone. Thus, we may have people available to do the job other than those you are thinking of right now.

Chair: Well, we want to make sure we have good people, and it sounded like quite a job to me.

Director: I think I really need to talk with him.

Chair: Okay, but with one proviso. I would like for you to talk with him at some time when at least a couple of people I have in mind would be able to go with you. They would be in a good position to get a handle on what teaching content is required and how it can be done. Since this subject is not directly within your field, they might have ideas as to who might be of help.

Director: Well, if you want it that way, I see no problem. But we may be getting too many people involved.

Chair: At the very least take June with you. I know she's tied up in her research project, but she's got the best credentials for evaluating that particular technical area. I certainly value her opinion.

Director: I certainly think that should be sufficient. The two of us can gather enough information to see what is required.

Chair: Let me know when you speak to her about it. Then, I'll call back and tell Johnston's president that you'll be contacting him.

The director of professional and continuing education wants to mastermind the solution without technical support. The chair suggests, however, that the first definition of what the client needs may not be the ultimate definition and that experts are available who may be able to see additional ways of dealing with the problem. To further this possibility, the chair proposes that the director utilize other resources in determining what the real training objective is to which they are being invited to respond.

This 9,9-oriented chair recognizes an opportunity to organize and to provide a community service in a technically sound way. He gets the director to see the advantages of expert advice in solving the problem and of using the services of those who are best qualified.

Managing Resources

The 9,9 approach to resource allocation is more complex than that found in other orientations to administration. One reason is the importance given to determining whether a proposal for resource allocation will move the college or university toward or away from its stated mission. Another reason is that this approach tests a particular proposal by asking the questions "Is this way of spending money consistent with stated mission? Even if it is, are there alternative university needs for which this money could be spent that would exert greater impact on achieving the university's mission?"

In the following episode, the chair is proposing to broaden the base of budgetary decision making in a college where departmental committees share budgetary decisions with chairs. This chair wants to go further and to open up the process to all the faculty who up to this point have not been involved in decisions about resource allocation. The members of the budget committee are hesitant to share this authority. We see how the chair responds to their hesitations.

Chair: This is an unusual situation. We have extra money to spend.

Budget Committee Member 1: The end of the world must be near.

Chair: When Jack went on extended medical leave in October, his salary was terminated, but he was picked up on a benefits package. Because of the mechanics of the budgetary system, we have the rest of his salary for the year. This has been transferred into the operating budget to be used by us over the summer. We have a bit of a windfall we can use for the next three months.

Budget Committee Member 1: You mean we get to play around with how to spend that much for the next three months? It's a miracle!

Chair: Now we can't buy an oil well, but this gives us the chance to do some things we've been delaying because we weren't financially able. I think what we need to do is come up with a plan for how to use this money in order to make a long-term investment with it. How can we use it over this three-month summer period so that we can feel we spent the money wisely?

Budget Committee Member 2: I can think of a lot of lab equipment I could use. Could we use the money for that?

Chair: That's a possibility. But before we get into listing all our suggestions, we'd better develop a general plan for formulating a proposal to spend the money, perhaps bringing in faculty besides those on the budget committee, and coming up with a way of determining how to decide among the various ideas. At any rate, I'd like everyone's thinking on this. We ought to do it carefully and develop something really worthwhile.

Budget Committee Member 1: But, if we ask everyone what he or she thinks, you'll have a lot of hurt feelings when their pet projects are not chosen.

Chair: That may be a risk we have to take.

Budget Committee Member 1: It'll take this faculty at least three months to reach a decision on how to spend the money. By that time the money won't be here any more. The administration will have it back.

Chair: That's part of our problem. How can we involve everyone and yet do it in a short period so that a timely decision can be made. In fact, we really ought to make a decision in the next two weeks.

Budget Committee Member 2: I don't think that involving everyone is going to work too well, but I'm willing to go along with it.

Chair: Have you any other concerns?

Budget Committee Member 2: I think we're setting a bad precedent by indicating to faculty that they are going to have a say about how the budget is allocated. It reduces our authority.

Chair: Is that a problem?

Budget Committee Member 2: The next thing we know, everyone will feel that he or she has a right to vote on everyone else's salary. Then, we'll look like a real bunch of academic statesmen.

Chair: Sounds as though we have a philosophical issue to discuss with respect to how budgeting should be handled. Maybe it's not a good idea to change our usual procedures, even given this windfall profit. Should we simply handle this amount in the usual way? We need to think about how much involvement we want from faculty regarding budget matters such as this and to consider carefully the degree of participation we wish to extend to our colleagues. My general inclination is to expand the decision-making base on budget matters, although I realize this has not been the trend. I'd like to understand the pros and cons from your perspective more fully.

Budget Committee Member 2: I think you're right. We need to think about these things and not precipitously change our usual procedures given this unique situation. We need to talk about it a lot more.

Chair: Okay, agreed. I suggest we devote our entire meeting next time to this issue. Now, how are we going to go about making decisions to spend the windfall?

In the view of the 9,9-oriented chair, the windfall money now available is seen as a shared resource that the department as a whole should discuss. He suggests that everyone be involved in determining the best way to spend the money. However, others point out that he is suggesting a change in the decision-making procedure; a precedent may be established. The 9,9-oriented administrator realizes that the issue needs more discussion, which he initiates rather than hold tenaciously to his original position.

Supervising Personnel

Since personnel decisions are recognized as being of singular importance if the university is to reach its stated mission, 9,9-oriented administrators directly involve themselves in all but the most unimportant personnel decisions. This involvement may include direct contact with candidates, as well as examination of their teaching records, the relevance of their Ph.D. concentration to the purpose of a given program, the consistency and level of their grades, and their scholarly preparation for carrying out research.

High-ranking administrators in large institutions may not be able to be involved in academic appointments directly, but they nonetheless can aid deans to develop criteria and adhere to standards that make it possible to distinguish between the conceptually brilliant candidate and the verbally aggressive one.

Campus interviews provide an opportunity to become acquainted with candidates on a firsthand basis and to study how candidates deal with direct questions and controversial issues in the ideology of their disciplines. Such interviews will show whether candidates stand by their convictions, try to placate others or to ingratiate themselves with others, or simply remain neutral.

Decisions about promotions are of no less importance. The difficulty of assessing the quality of research and scholarly productivity is felt by many administrators who are not experts in a particular professor's field. Thus, committees are often asked to evaluate personnel for decisions at critical career points; for example, when a professor is up for tenure. Such a committee is expected to study a professor's research, to evaluate its basic quality, and then to consult with administrators as to their conclusions regarding the faculty member's likely ability to contribute in a long-term way to the university's pursuit of its stated mission.

The 9,9-oriented administrator recognizes burnout as a serious problem but thinks that it can be reduced in a number of ways. One is by asking the professor in question to change his habitual approach to teaching if that has trapped him or her into routine or mechanical ways of working. Teaching courses in a different way may result in renewed interest in teaching. Another approach is to offer counsel to the professor, who may have no clear insight regarding his or her problem. The initial aspect involves confronting the professor with evidence of burnout: student complaints, frequent absence from class, or a significant drop-off in research and publication. A second aspect of such counseling draws attention to the consequences for students, research, and one's own self-respect at not solving this problem. A third involves adding whatever support may be possible to aid a professor to get reinvolved in his or her work. If all these fail, the professor's problem is not ignored, but rather the administrator must face the inevitable consequences of using more extreme measures—for example, termination or forced leave of absence.

Most faculty experience feelings of failure or discouragement sometime in their careers. Yet they are not encouraged to openly admit feelings of inferiority or lack of preparedness. Rather, academic competitiveness breeds an attitude of "going it alone" when things are not going well. Admitting mistakes or failure to others simply gives "them" ammunition. In the dialogue below, a young professor has experienced a minor failure —a rejection from a committee deciding on summer grants for research. The faculty member reacts with dejection and "not wanting to talk about it." But the chair sees this as an opportunity to render support and meaningful aid to one who indeed does have areas that should be improved. The chair knows that if the faculty member can't talk about this minor failure, he is likely to have a much harder time with tougher situations. This interaction illustrates the 9,9-oriented approach to performance evaluation. Some basic assumptions of this approach are:

1. People need accurate feedback.
2. When giving feedback, don't use that as an opportunity for self-aggrandizement.
3. Give concrete aid, not just verbal support.
4. Don't assume your own assessment is necessarily accurate—get more than one point of view.
5. Convey the message that the solution to the performance problem is manageable—there is a way to improve.
6. Provide a method of testing.

Chair: I heard your research proposal for summer research was turned down by the university committee. Correct?
Faculty Member: Yes, yesterday.
Chair: Did they give you indications as to why?
Faculty Member: Well, not really. Their explanation was rather vague. It was sent in one of those form letters made to look as though they were personally written.
Chair: I read the proposal and recommended approval. I thought it was good. I'm curious as to why it was not approved.
Faculty Member: I'm on the verge of giving up on the whole thing.

Chair: Well, your idea is unusual, but that's what I think makes it interesting. I wonder if it would be a good idea to follow up with the committee? They should be willing to give you feedback. It's possible you could improve it and submit it again, either to them or somewhere else. I wouldn't give up now. You've already done the pilot work, and it looks promising.

Faculty Member: The letter says something about inadequate explanation of methodology, and a few other phrases like that, but it isn't specific.

Chair: What else does it say? Maybe that gives you a clue, at least.

Faculty Member: It questions some of the costs, but the main point about the proposal itself is the methodology.

Chair: Insufficient explanation of methodology and some questioning of the cost, is that basically it? Probably I should have caught that myself. I must have been too interested in the content.

Faculty Member: Well, take a look at the letter and see if you can make any more out of it. That's about all I can glean from it. I'll get it to your secretary, and she can give it to you sometime today. You can look it over and give me a second opinion.

Chair: I'd be pleased to do that, and I encourage you to get back in touch with the committee. I wouldn't let it rest. The proposal is well worth pursuing, and I don't like to see you drop it. The insufficient methodology problem can certainly be handled, and the budget, too, for that matter.

Faculty Member: You know, I've always felt a little weak in the methodology area, and I don't know that I want to go and face the committee and talk to them about it. I'd probably feel I'm back in my final oral exam again. Oh, the trauma of that!

Chair: Susan is strong in methodology. Why don't you get some help from her? In fact, why don't you let her read over the whole proposal, and then let's all get together and see if we can come up with something better. The methodology can be handled, and you know my feeling on methodology; you never can know enough. So, it would be a good learning experience to find out what they thought about the proposal in that regard. Susan and I can drill you, if you like, before you talk with the chair. We can certainly be more demanding than they can. It'll give you good practice.

Faculty Member: I can certainly use it, and, as a matter of fact, I'll think about sending it somewhere else if this doesn't work. Thanks for your help.

The chair here organizes a follow-up activity to bring an experience of failure into focus under circumstances where he might simply have ignored it because of potential embarrassment. Based on his conviction that the research is worthy of support, he seeks to organize action to overcome the faculty member's initial negative reaction. He listens to the faculty member's "explanation," that is, the implication that he is getting form-letter treatment, but the chair doesn't take this at face value. The chair proceeds on the assumption that the committee is not biased but rather that it is acting in a discriminating manner. Next, he indicates that he himself should have been more alert to challenge the methodology segment before it went forward. He acknowledges the faculty member's sense of weakness in the methodology area but counteracts with the observation that one can't know too much about methodology. Then he gets the faculty member involved in developing a plan of action consisting of concrete suggestions and steps as to what to do next, and he offers to contribute to the effort in an appropriately discriminating manner.

The chair shows a sense of respect for the faculty member and an awareness that everyone needs help and support at some point along the way. All these elements suggest a chair who is committed to helping faculty members develop their research capabilities. At the outset the faculty member feels defeated and resents that the committee dealt with him through a form letter. As the chair gets him reinvolved, he springs back, ready to accept help and determined to take the next step.

Coordinating Student Affairs

The 9,9-oriented administrator's approach to student affairs is to explore the underlying rationale of requirements for sound student participation. This administrator also works toward getting requirements changed when they are contradictory to the sound administration of student affairs.

When it comes to giving guidance to the student newspaper, the 9,9-oriented administrator's approach is to aid student editors to understand and to take into account the role of a newspaper within a university. The academic administrators or faculty members who represent the university in dealing with student government are expected to exercise a similar role. With regard to student invitations to controversial speakers to appear on campus under the auspices of the university, the administration neither approves nor vetoes the choice of speaker but requires that speakers and audiences conduct themselves appropriately and contribute to the spirit of free inquiry and open dialogue on campus.

Students confront administrators with all kinds of problems. Some are easily resolved. Others require a great deal of fact gathering and spadework prior to solution. Often policy guidelines are not really clear on specific points. Yet if every problem were to be handled by a specific policy, there would be an unbelievable number of policies to keep track of and individual students would find this plethora of "rules" constrictive.

In the following episode, a student takes the position that a faculty member is either unaware of the rules about "adds" and "drops" or neglects to follow them. The chair attempts to bring the situation into focus. Is it a matter of unclear policy, disregard of policy, poor communication, a student who distorts historical events in order to plead his case, or what? The chair listens carefully to the student and reiterates key facts to verify them. He reexamines policy in the process of following up on a student complaint.

Chair: Sara told me you are upset and you wanted to see me right away. What's going on?

Student: You can't get a straight answer around here. I wanted to drop a course and finally did drop it. Then I found out that the professor gave me an F, which was not my understanding of what would happen at all. There must have been some foul-up.

Chair: Did you drop the course prior to the deadline?

Student: I certainly did. I filed the card. I did everything I was supposed to do.

Chair: Well, you shouldn't have gotten an F, then, unless he made it clear to you at that point in time when you were dropping the course that your grade was an F.

Student: That's the problem. He didn't make it clear. We'd had no exams, and I don't know how in the world he could arrive at the conclusion that I deserved an F. We hadn't done any work at all on which to be graded.

Chair: You seem to know the policy. The professor has to approve your dropping the course and sign the card. On that card he gives you a grade or indicates that no grade is assigned.

Student: I left the card in his office, and he said he would sign it and send it directly to the secretary, so I never saw the card. I assumed everything was taken care of. Then I found out when I got my final course grades this semester that way back three months ago he gave me an F.

Chair: And you had no indication he was going to give you an F?

Student: Absolutely not. To tell you the truth, I don't think he knows me from Adam. I think he has me mixed up with somebody else. He won't listen to me when I explain to him that I did everything I was supposed to do. He says I didn't get the card in on time and that I dropped after the deadline. He also says I was failing the course and that I should have known that, and that I shouldn't be surprised.

Chair: Is this the first time something like this has happened to you?

Student: No, one other time I tried to drop a course, but I had a different kind of problem.

Chair: What was that?

Student: That time I was making a passing grade. I was making a B, and I found out that I didn't have to have the course on my record. I decided I didn't want to put in the extra work because it was a pretty tough course. So I dropped.

Chair: Then what happened?

Student: I got a C instead of a drop, but that time it was just a grading mistake.

Chair: What do you mean?

Student: Well, the instructor gave me the grade of C because he got me mixed up with another Smith. At any rate, we finally got it straightened out, but that was just an error on his part. He corrected it. But even then I had to go through a big hassle.

Chair: Let me look into it a bit and see if I can get information from the records and talk to the instructor and see what his version of the story is. Then I'll get back to you.

Student: I don't know what his side of the story is. He's impossible to talk with. I hope you can get further than I did.

Chair: Are you sure there was nothing upon which you were graded prior to the time you dropped the course, and that you dropped it prior to the deadline? These are very important facts to be certain about before I talk with the faculty member.

Student: I am absolutely positive.

Chair: Okay. If that's the case, and you dropped the course prior to the deadline, then the F may be a mistake. Why don't you come back—let's say a week from Friday. I'll see if I can have something more specific to tell you at that point.

We see the chair taking the student's problem seriously in order to deal with the conflict. His basic approach to this control issue is first revealed in the thoroughness with which he studies the problem. Did the student follow that part of the "drop" procedure for which he was responsible? Is he confident of his facts? Is it an isolated incident? He explores whether this is a single event for this particular student or whether it reflects a pattern. He wants to find out whether the student failed to comply with requirements or the system itself lacked the preciseness necessary for handling this problem in a proper manner. Thus, the chair not only involves himself in resolving the issue, but he also takes a systems and procedures orientation and tests how the system itself may be creating a problem. If the system is at fault, the problem will keep appearing.

Managing External Relations

The 9,9-oriented administrator attempts to inform the public in a full and effective way as to the state of the campus. He or she uses public relations to inform the public, to educate the public, and to motivate action by the public in ways that can be helpful to the university in its pursuit of its mission. The assumption is that public understanding of the university is necessary to accomplish the institution's purposes.

Those who speak for the college are often caught in a dilemma. The forums within which they must relate to the public—legislative committees, public speeches, social gatherings, and so on—do not always allow for a full explanation of problems and short- or long-term consequences of decisions or funding allocations. Efforts toward public understanding and support are viewed by the 9,9-oriented administrator as a responsibility of all interested parties; such an administrator seeks ways of involving faculty, students, staff, and other administrators in major external relations efforts.

Some aspects of dealing with outside organizations or agencies are routine and may even seem trivial. One example is writing reference letters for students. These are important to the student for they may influence whether or not the student is selected for a job. Yet, for faculty and administrators it is easy to fall into bad habits with respect to such routine obligations. The letters are so onerous a task that faculty and administrators may write them automatically without much individuality or care in their composition. Lack of diligence in preparation of such routine correspondence can, of course, make a poor impression on the recipient of the letter. The letter can reflect on the writer as well as on the university. Furthermore, if a letter is in some way inaccurate, the student may have a legal case against the writer or the university, and many of these letters are now available for inspection under the "open records laws." Some argue that these laws have led to a lack of credibility in the whole process. Others say that they have strengthened the process because people now tend to be more accurate in their comments.

In the next dialogue, a dean is asking four chairs to think

through the letter-writing process as one aspect of promoting better external relations. The process has broken down somewhat over the years, and the dean is concerned. He is searching for a more systematic approach to the problem, although he knows that too much "system" in a routine area is likely to be resisted.

Dean: I know you have been concerned with the problems we've been having with student letters of reference.

Chair 1: Boy, can I speak to that topic!

Dean: Yes, I want everyone to hear what you have to say. In fact, each of you has spoken to me about your concerns, and I would like for you to review them with each other.

By way of summary, I'd like to say that what I have gleaned so far is this. Our letters of reference are getting more and more positive and nonevaluative because of the open records laws. A student gets full disclosure with respect to the kind of letters written unless he or she signs a release. The other side of it is that faculty feel they can't say what they think about students anymore. It's a disservice to many corporations and agencies to write a positive letter about a student if there are really strong reservations.

Chair 1: You've summarized what's going on, all right, but there are one or two other aspects I'd like to add. I'd like to see us keep the reference letters we write, at least one copy, in the student's file in the dean's office. Then, if Joe Smith writes a reference letter on a student and I am asked to write a letter on the same student, I would have some knowledge of what he had said.

Dean: Because faculty keep copies in their own offices they are, therefore, unavailable to other faculty?

Chair 1: Yes.

Chair 2: There's no way to systematize this business. It's hopeless! There's no way to get faculty to make a copy for the student's files. I'm not even sure they should. One person's letter might influence what another says. If we've got to write them, it might be better that they be written without reference to one another, as we're doing now.

Chair 3: But we might be writing glowing letters about a student who is just barely adequate. It does little for the student, and it makes us look bad later.

Chair 1: We're always going to have differences among students in terms of abilities and potential. That's a given. The thing that bothers me is that I don't think we can always tell from a faculty member's recommendation who is going to do a good job in a given situation. Letters in the student's file written by others would at least give us a way of expanding our information base.

Dean: What bothers me is that we can't predict that accurately who is going to do well in a given job.

Chair 4: I'll tell you what I encourage our faculty to do. I have provided them with guidelines for writing student evaluations. It's a fifteen-item suggestion guide. I tell them, number one, to stick to information they have personal knowledge of and that they learned while the student was in the university, and not to try to project future potential. For example, we can say that a student scored in the top 10 percent of his or her class while here, but we should not say that a student is going to be one of the finest doctors in ten years. We can say that he or she showed leadership in certain specific ways, but we should *not* say we believe this person has the qualities of a future corporate tycoon. That's going beyond the data. My list of suggestions is concrete and specific. Then it's up to the faculty members to write the letter. That is their prerogative, as I see it.

Dean: How do the rest of you react to that? Your suggestion sounds like a sound approach to me.

Chair 1: I like that approach. It's consistent with teaching students to distinguish between using empirical data and going beyond the data that are given.

Chair 2: But it's inconsistent with our own convictions about setting up a hypothesis or making a prediction and then testing it.

Chair 4: It's fine to predict, but only if you provide the reader a basis for confirming or disconfirming your hypothesis. Otherwise it's a blind prediction and pretty questionable

coming from a university that is responsible for helping its
clientele distinguish between promise and performance.

Dean: The suggestion guide mentioned earlier might provide us
a real key for grappling with this problem. Let's explore
that further. We should be able to come up with an extended set of guidelines to help us deal with the problem in
a constructive manner.

This orientation to the problem on the dean's part contributes to the likelihood that useful letters of reference will be
written. Faculty are to be provided with basic and sound guidelines. In this way, inflated recommendations can possibly be
avoided, while at the same time prospective employers can be
helped to see students in a realistic light. The recommended
guidelines are a set of standards to be consulted; they are not
meant to exercise control over the letter writer. The dean pursues his conviction that the problem needs to be solved by finding a procedure acceptable to all.

Assuring Basic Operations

Problems in operations, as in other areas, provide an opportunity to analyze administrative issues and to develop principles that have general application. In some respects administrative issues are most clearly focused in the operational and
support areas and demand most immediate attention there.
People involved in operations are, of course, not responsible for
teaching and research activities. But problems or practices that
develop in the support areas can affect the teaching, research,
and service functions of faculty; when support functions are not
performed adequately, quality suffers in other areas too.

Below, the dean is consulting with a chair about one of
his problems in the support area—office administration. A conflict developed among three of the clerical staff members, and it
ended with a sex discrimination grievance being filed against the
chair. The dean helps the chair understand how ineffective administration led to his problem but does this in such a way that
the chair learns some important lessons that will stand him in
good stead on later occasions.

Dean: I understand a staff member filed a sex discrimination complaint. I want to learn more about it.

Chair: Yes, I have been filed against. It's the first time it's ever happened to me. It's certainly an unusual situation.

Dean: From your perspective, what happened and why did the situation develop as it did?

Chair: My view may be distorted.

Dean: Just tell it as it happened, how you see it. Distorted or not, we can evaluate that later.

Chair: As you know, I have three secretarial positions in the main office. Two of the women have worked there for approximately . . . well, one for six and one for eight years. The third position has been vacant until recently. It was filled in September by Lois, who subsequently filed the grievance. She had been there about seven months before I realized there was trouble.

Dean: How did you learn about the trouble?

Chair: Well, the two other women hinted subtly for awhile that they were having difficulty, that they couldn't get her to work, and so on. The next thing I noticed was that some of my work just wasn't getting done. So I talked with Marlene, who's been there the longest. She's sort of chief of staff in the outer office. With her in charge things run themselves, and all I have to do is give her support and encouragement. Furthermore, when she reports something for my attention, I tend to take her conclusions at face value. That's how good she is.

Anyway, she said that Lois had not been completing assignments. Instead of saying anything to her, the other two simply documented her insubordination. Marlene would ask Lois to do some work; she wouldn't do it, and then Marlene would place a note in her personnel file.

Dean: Did they tell you that they were filing these notes?

Chair: No. And technically I am supervisor of all three, although, in reality, I delegate most supervision to Marlene.

Dean: I see the picture.

Chair: The next thing I knew, Lois asked for a recommendation. She was applying for a position with zoology.

Dean: And up to this point, I presume you never really talked with Lois about her job from her point of view?

Chair: No.

Dean: So what happened next?

Chair: Well, given all the work I'm doing, I asked Marlene to write a recommendation for my signature, and I read it superficially, taking for granted that Lois didn't deserve a better recommendation. Lois found out about it and filed a complaint. Her complaint says, in effect, that as her supervisor I am the one responsible for evaluating her work, that I did not give her information about what I expected, that I favored the other two and allowed them to tell her what to do, which was not their job, and so on, and so on. What it comes to, of course, is a personality clash among the three, a two-against-one situation.

Dean: Sounds to me as though there may also have been some confusion on the organization chart.

Chair: What d'ya mean?

Dean: It may well be that Lois had taken the job with the understanding that she was to work for you and then discovered that, in effect, she was working for Marlene. Marlene was inappropriately given the responsibility for supervising. What do Lois' references and background look like?

Chair: Actually, they are good. That's why I hired her. She had terrific experience and high recommendations, so I guess the situation is a little traumatic for her.

Dean: Maybe you need to consider whether you can delegate the supervisory responsibility to Marlene or not. She may be just as upset by the lack of clarity as Lois.

Chair: I think Marlene and I have an excellent working relationship. I'd be surprised if she is not clear about it.

Dean: But does she have a supervisory position on paper? Does she have a title that is consistent with her actual place in the organization structure?

Chair: Well, she in fact is at a higher pay level, but I suppose in terms of supervision it isn't really clear. I try to develop a cooperative kind of atmosphere, and all those formalities are really the antithesis of my administrative approach.

Dean: Still, maybe you need to look at it from a different point of view. Are you unwilling to delegate real authority to your secretary, to make her an executive secretary to prevent this kind of problem? Then she would have been responsible for Lois, not just informally, but in actuality. A lot of people are talking team management, and yet what that often means is a large span of control and partial delegation of responsibilities.

Chair: You're trying to tell me something, I think.

Dean: Yes.

Chair: I'll talk to Marlene and see if she thinks I've been unclear about delegation.

Dean: She'll probably say everything is clear and everything is wonderful. After all, she's getting what she wants out of this situation.

Chair: What do you mean?

Dean: Well, she's getting rid of Lois, whom she doesn't like. . . .

Chair: Now you're suggesting something else. I'm not quite sure I follow.

Dean: Let me put it this way. Marlene may be as willing to have the power structure ambiguous as you seem to be. Not only that, she has your ear most of the time. If lines of authority are unclear, she may overstep the bounds of her job description by, for example, putting notes in the personnel file on the assumption that that is her obligation or responsibility. Yet she can hand you the problem if it gets out of hand. In other words, both of you may be benefiting from the ambiguity, but other parties may suffer.

Chair: I see. It's a case of having too good of a relationship with one person, causing problems for others.

Dean: Not so much "too good" as going about it the wrong way. It's always difficult to draw the line between formality and informality. I often think about the pros and cons of various ways of handling these situations. It may seem like a small matter, given the great issues we have to face all the time in this university, and yet sometimes it's little things that cause the big trouble. I personally can't quite believe the woman has a sex discrimination complaint, but she could well have a plain old personnel grievance.

Chair: You mean I'm not a male chauvinist pig, just a poor administrator?

Dean: Actually, I think you're a good administrator when it comes to the faculty issues of academic staffing, sound curriculum development, recommendations regarding tenure, and so on.

Chair: That's encouraging. Okay, I'll think about this. Would you like to see the file on this particular grievance, too?

The dean exercises initiative in bringing the grievance into focus. By confronting an issue that involves considerable tension, he demonstrates his willingness to exercise whatever leadership can be offered in analyzing the problem and in finding a sound approach for solving it. The thoroughness with which the background of the problem and the chronology of its development are reviewed stands out. The dean's diagnosis goes far beyond the matter of "personality" to examine the dynamics of the organization chart and how the assumptions of those who are operating the hierarchy interacted to generate this particular result. Finally, we see that the dean has not let himself be influenced by the "bias" notion. He avoids that, while at the same time giving the chair personal support and urging the chair to take the next steps toward finding a permanent solution to the problem.

Summary

The positive motivation of a 9,9-oriented administrator is the desire to make a difference by contribution, while the negative motivation is to avoid administrative actions that might betray the trust of others.

Planning is a key attribute of a 9,9 orientation because it provides a way of anticipating the future and of taking administrative actions that are consistent with long-range plans. This means utilizing the resources of others and doing this by making sure that those who implement actions also have a voice in planning them. Organizing is undertaken in a deliberate manner and involves thinking out in advance how best to arrange the conditions of work so as to reach performance objectives in an efficient way. Directing is a matter of setting clearly identified goals that are consistent with plans and ensuring that those who are responsible for achieving goals understand them. Controlling places reliance on feedback for ensuring that performance is consistent with goals as set and for creating the conditions under which goals that have ceased being relevant and appropriate are revised. The approach to staffing is to get those most capable of contributing to specific activities involved in those activities so that their talents can be utilized in the fullest way.

A concern with the stated mission is at the core of a 9,9 orientation to administration. In this view, other aspects of conducting the affairs of a university can be dealt with in a sound manner only when they are consistent with stated mission. If the stated mission is out of alignment with current requirements, then a 9,9-oriented administrator works toward getting those responsible for mission to make the necessary revisions. Teaching rests upon getting students to learn through active participation. Curriculum is an operational expression of mission and is administered in such a way as to avoid overlap of courses and to offer students a systematic progression through levels of complexity in a subject matter. Research is stimulated and rewarded, but the selection and execution of research activities are the responsibility of every faculty member and those administrators who continue research activities. Service is seen as a contribution to campus and community citizenship; rewards for service are based on merit. Resources are allocated in such a way as to support activities that contribute to the completion of the institution's stated mission. This means that value judgments are necessary in distinguishing the various activities on a campus that compete for support. Personnel decisions involving selection, promotion, tenure, and termination of faculty members are based on the quality of their work and on the degree to which their activities are consistent with stated mission. Student affairs are supervised in such a way as to encourage students to exercise responsibility for such activities as the student government, the student newspaper, and invitations to outside speakers. External relations are dealt with in an objective way by open and candid communication and open and candid response to queries from the outside as to the conduct of university activities. Operations are conducted as an integral part of the university system.

Decisions are reached after those who are capable of contributing to them have been consulted. Convictions are strongly held, but a 9,9-oriented administrator feels no contradiction in changing his or her mind in the light of new information. Conflicts are resolved by confrontation, which permits tensions and emotions to be fully resolved through understanding and insight. Remaining objective is characteristic of a 9,9-oriented administrator, even though he or she may be emotionally involved in the problems at hand. Effort is applied in dealing with the affairs of a university in an enthusiastic way. Humor provides a basis for putting problems in perspective.

In earlier chapters we examined other approaches to academic administration, several of which have prevented university administrators from engaging in the effective pursuit of excellence. In contrast to them, the 9,9 orientation is effective and sound. It stems from behavioral science principles and has been described in a more or less independent way in disciplines ranging from political science and psychology to business and public administration. Not only is it endorsed on the basis of research in these fields, but the great majority of administrators throughout the world opt for it as a better way of managing than the other approaches. Regardless of the religions that dominate their cultures, the languages in which their fellow citizens communicate, or the degree of industrialization, extent of poverty, or prevailing political system of their countries, administrators who have ranked the paragraphs of Chapter One, not for self-description but for their depiction of sound and desirable administration, have almost universally agreed that 9,9 is the preferred administrative orientation. Over 99 percent of the administrators who have studied these paragraphs during our seminars have made this value judgment. (Our seminars, offered in all areas of the world, are designed to aid managers and administrators to learn the Grid and to increase the objectivity of their self-appraisals.) Therefore, this approach is consistent with behavioral science experimentation and "feels" valid for administrators who rate its properties. To the extent that it is brought into daily use in university life, as described in the next chapter, the 9,9 orientation can provide the foundation needed for a university to create conditions of academic excellence in all its programs and activities.

Chapter Ten

Implementing
the 9,9 Approach

M uch is known regarding the development of a 9,9 orientation toward team administration as the basis for promoting planned change throughout an organization, but it is one thing to proclaim that a change in the direction of excellence is possible and another to take the concrete actions to bring about change. This chapter deals first with the issue of individual change and then with that of bringing about change within the university.

Where Do You Stand on the Grid?

Chapter One provided a way for you to determine your own style of administration. You ranked several paragraphs from 5, as the most characteristic description of your approach, down to 1 as the least descriptive. In addition, you selected one sentence from among five as best illustrating your approach to making decisions, holding convictions, managing conflict, controlling temper, expressing humor, and exerting effort. Now transfer your initial rankings from Chapter One to these columns:

Paragraphs Depicting Administrative Styles	*Sentences Illustrating Elements of Interaction*	
A _____	Making Decisions	_____
B _____	Holding Convictions	_____
C _____	Managing Conflict	_____
D _____	Controlling Temper	_____
E _____	Expressing Humor	_____
	Exerting Effort	_____

Now you can interpret your selection of these paragraphs and sentences in light of the Grid styles discussed in the intervening chapters. The first paragraph, A, and its A sentences illustrate the 1,1 style of Caretaker Administration depicted in Chapter Four. The B paragraph and sentences typify 1,9 or Comfortable and Pleasant Administration of Chapter Six. C epitomizes 5,5 or Constituency-Centered Administration of Chapter Eight. D portrays 9,1 or Authority-Obedience Administration of Chapter Five. And E represents 9,9 or Team Administration of Chapter Nine.

Did you come out as administering predominantly in a 9,9 orientation? If so, you are like almost 70 percent of the thousands of managers representing all types of organization and levels of administration who have evaluated their own Grid styles by choosing among these paragraphs and sentences. Less than 1 percent of these managers initially choose the 1,1 Grid style as most characteristic of them. Less than 2 percent select the 1,9 style. Nearly 15 percent choose the 5,5 orientation, and the remaining 14 percent mark the 9,1 approach.

But if you saw yourself as 9,9 oriented, is this your real Grid style, or is it possible that you have misread yourself? You may very well be accurate if you chose the 9,9 orientation, but the data indicate that there is something in the neighborhood of a fifty-fifty chance that such a choice is inaccurate. That is, many of us who think we are 9,9 oriented are really deceiving ourselves. When managers, who have rated themselves as you did in Chapter One, attend a week-long Grid Seminar similar to those mentioned at the end of Chapter Nine, many of them shift their self-assessment significantly after receiving feedback from the other participants in the seminar about their own behavior during the week. This feedback takes the form of paragraphs concerning the dominant and backup Grid styles that the participants have observed in each other's problem solving and decision making throughout the week's discussions. After reviewing these comments, the members rerank the Grid paragraphs to describe their postseminar assessment of their own Grid styles. As can be seen in Table 1, after the seminars less

**Table 1. Self-Ranking of Dominant Grid Styles,
Before and After Attending Grid Seminar**

Grid Style	Percent Before	Percent After
1,1 (Caretaker Administration)	0.3%	1.2%
1,9 (Comfortable and Pleasant Administration)	1.8	4.8
5,5 (Constituency-Centered Administration)	14.7	34.5
9,1 (Authority-Obedience Administration)	14.0	34.9
9,9 (Team Administration)	69.2	24.6

than a fourth of the participants—24.6 percent—see themselves as working with and through others in a 9,9 orientation, compared to the 69.2 percent who did so previously. Over a third now see themselves as either 9,1 or 5,5 oriented, whereas fewer than 15 percent did so before. The proportion who realize they are 1,9 oriented more than doubles, and the proportion who recognize themselves as 1,1 oriented quadruples.

These changes in self-judgment involve stripping away self-deception. How can we account for these shifts from false self-perceptions? There are several explanations:

1. *Better Understanding.* A more thorough comprehension of concepts makes it possible to be more objective. We can't see ourselves as well in a steamy mirror as in a clear one.
2. *Self-Appraisal.* When we look inside ourselves, we are likely

to misjudge what we find because we have many good intentions that correspond generally with a 9,9 orientation. But
without honest self-analysis, we are likely to overlook examples of our actual conduct that may be, and often are, contradictory to our good intentions.
3. *New Data.* When we receive feedback from others as to how
they see our behavior, we learn things about ourselves that
we previously may not have recognized. With this new information, we can see ourselves more objectively.

With this evidence in mind, if your first choice in Chapter
One was the 9,9 orientation, you may wish to rethink your rat-
ing to see if it reveals your most objective reflection now about
your administrative style.

Can an Individual Change?

Let's assume that you suspect by now that you may not
be as 9,9 oriented as you thought you were, or that you already
recognize your dominant mode of administration to be 1,1, 9,1,
1,9, 5,5, or any combination of these Grid styles, such as pater-
nal/maternal, or statistical 5,5. Is it possible to change in a 9,9
direction?
The answer is a clear yes. The specific activities of administration by a 9,9 orientation—whether planning and staffing or
implementing institutional mission and assuring basic operations
—are processes that any individual can learn. The roadblock to
this learning, however, is in the assumptions and motivations
that lead an administrator to adopt one of the other dominant
Grid styles. The assumptions that guide a 9,9 orientation are as
much subject to learning as is anything else. From the point of
view of planning, for example, the 9,9-oriented assumption is
that those who have a stake in the outcome of a plan should be
allowed to contribute to the development of the plan. Therefore, the 9,9-oriented administrative skills needed for planning
include the ability to involve others in actively thinking through
a plan and contributing to how the planning activities should be
organized and directed, as well as the ability to staff the activi-

ties in a way that will bring the most valuable resources to bear on the problem. This does *not* mean abdication by the administrator or "groupthink" by a committee. The leader as administrator continues to lead, but in a stronger way, because now, in addition to establishing the *content* of the problem, he or she leads the *process* as well.

The criteria for a 9,9 orientation are that administrators can express convictions in a strong, clear way, that the decisions reached reflect understanding and agreement, that conflicts are focused and resolved, that emotions are expressed in an open and free way, and that humor gives perspective to the situation. Because of the positive involvements created by this approach, people willingly commit their effort to achieving successful outcomes. Three conditions besides honest self-perception are necessary to aid an administrator to change from less effective Grid assumptions to those of a 9,9 approach:

Theory. The theory of the Grid can be learned at an intellectual level from reading. Many who have completed the text to this point should have a good comprehension of the options and alternatives open to administrators regarding institutional achievement and concern for people.

Discrepancy Motivation. As long as administrators think they are already administering in a sound and effective way, there is no motivation to change. They are already "doing it" correctly. The stripping away of self-deception, however, produces an entirely new motivational situation. Knowing the theory of the Grid and with self-deception reduced or eliminated, administrators come to perceive the discrepancy between the manner in which they have managed in the past and the way they would like to proceed in the future. This gap between their current dominant Grid style and the 9,9 orientation sets up the tension necessary for bringing the desired change about.

Social Support. The third critical ingredient is absent in most change programs; but for real change in administrative orientation to occur, its presence is absolutely essential. This element is social support.

Administrators carry out their job in a context. They are members of an organization and work with one another on a daily basis. If the prevailing mores say "be reasonable," "go along to get along," "you scratch my back and I'll scratch yours," and "Rome wasn't built in a day," an administrator who seeks for sound solutions and tries to confront conflicts and resolve them is unlikely to receive much support in his or her efforts to do so. Other administrators are blind to what he or she is about and therefore have no reason to offer their support.

By comparison, consider the possibility that all members of an administration know the theories of the Grid, have attended seminars where self-deception has been reduced or removed, and have come to experience the discrepancy between their current ways of administering and what would be truly desirable if excellence were to be pursued. They now come together in natural groupings and study their own traditions, precedents, past practices, and habits of administration so that all become committed to helping one another to change in the desirable direction. Under these conditions, social support is present. Now when an individual tries to get an examination of how sounder decisions might be reached, others are prepared to give encouragement, support, and assistance rather than return a challenge with a blank stare or a nasty remark.

In summary, besides honest self-appraisal or feedback from others to help pierce self-deception, three conditions essential for change to a 9,9 direction are (1) a comprehensive understanding of the Grid; (2) the experience of a discrepancy between one's current ways of administering and what one regards as the most desirable ways; and (3) the presence of social support. When these conditions are present, the probability is high that individuals can change. Individual change, however, is by no means the only necessary condition for achieving organizational excellence. Institutional change is also needed.

Can a University Change?

A university is far more than a mosaic of individuals held together within a hierarchical framework. Rather, it is an institution with its own history and characteristic expectations of itself, and with its own typical ways of doing things. Institutional culture can be a great impediment to organization change. In a particular real sense, no single individual, whether president, vice-president of academic affairs, dean, department chair, or administrative secretary, "owns" the institution's culture. It is owned by everyone, controlled by no one, and therefore its assumptions and ways of doing things are perpetuated from one administrative generation to another, with any administrator too limited in his or her capacity to shift the attitudes, norms, and values that are woven into its culture. For example, mission is a critical ingredient of organization culture. When mission as conceived is at variance with mission as practiced, the institution is faced with a major problem of institutional change. When excellence of teaching is saluted but reward goes to those who publish, it can be predicted that teaching will suffer. The same is true when research is saluted, but promotions go to those with the right connections or simply are given on the basis of seniority.

A way of bringing about institutional change is needed that can focus upon the institution's history and existing culture and that can cause its members to repudiate those practices, values, and attitudes that are outmoded or antiquated and to replace them with norms, standards, and goals that truly reflect academic excellence.

How can this be done? Certain fundamental characteristics of such institutional change are detailed below.

Individual Change. The dynamics of individual change just described are essential preconditions for organizational development. In other words, all administrators need to learn the theories of the Grid, receive feedback in order to remove self-deception, come to see the discrepancy between actual and ideal ways of administering, and develop the conditions of social support necessary for bringing about change in face-to-face groups. But these steps represent only a beginning.

Leadership from the Top. The likelihood of institutional change being brought about is practically zero if the effort to introduce change is not led by high-ranking administrators. Those highest in the hierarchy set the tone, character, culture, and climate of the institution. They do so either by what they stand for or by what they tolerate. In any event, they are the ones in the position of establishing the atmosphere that will allow administrative excellence to be pursued. It follows that change can be successfully accomplished only if those at the top of the administrative ladder understand why change is needed, and give their efforts and energy to bring it about. It is a case of the difference between "Do as I say" and "Do as I do." Verbal pronouncements of what is desirable fall on ears that have been culturally tuned by decades of institutional history, and such statements are therefore regarded as little more than talk. By comparison, when those at the top of the administrative hierarchy demonstrate their convictions by learning to lead in a more effective way and implement their convictions by demonstrating more effective administrative behavior, an entirely different message is passed through the system. The message is, "We are leading. We know the direction in which we want to develop our administrative skills, we are taking steps to increase our own effectiveness, and we encourage others to do likewise." In other words, top leadership provides the impetus to change by example.

A brief analysis of what many think to be a desirable alternative approach will serve to sharpen the issue of how change should be approached and make the need for leadership from the top even clearer. Thus, many might think that the university department would be the natural unit of change since a department is made up of members who have a common interest in a subject matter. There is some truth in this notion, but it contains a number of fallacies.

First of all, every department exists within the broader culture of the university as a whole. Its members are highly sensitive and responsive to the system of rewards that operates throughout. If rewards go to those who make more demands for recognition rather than those who contribute their energies toward helping the institution achieve its stated mission, then people will simply become more aggressive. If research funds are given to individuals by virtue of whom they know in the higher reaches of the administration rather than on the basis of a studied examination of their research competence and research productivity, then no amount of departmental effort toward excellence will arrest the tendency to play politics in order to gain research money.

Therefore, the fact that departments exist within an institutional environment means that they are controlled to a large extent by the broader culture. No matter how diligent an individual department's efforts to become more effective, it is unlikely to accomplish very much if the values that prevail in the administrative hierarchy are not congruent with the basic values of sound administration.

There is another reason, however, why the department is not the best level at which to introduce change. Throughout a university of any size, there are many invidious comparisons made between departments. These have grown up over the years, and some may be justified. But many are based upon misunderstandings, slights, or careless and thoughtless criticisms by members of other disciplines. Given this climate, it is naive to think that if an effort at departmental development were successful in one department, it would naturally spread to others. No department that has pride in itself wants to copy another department. Rather, the second, third, and fourth departments are prepared to proclaim that they are pleased to see that the first department is finally doing something to try to solve its problems because they are numerous and deep. The rationalization is added quickly, "We have problems, too, but our problems are different. If we proceed in the direction of departmental development, we will do so relying upon other theories, techniques, strategies, and tactics." As a result, the institution comes to be criss-crossed with new pressures that make interdepartmental cooperation more difficult than it was before.

By comparison, if development starts at the top and cascades down through the university, no division or department is put in a position of copying another. Rather, all departments are given the opportunity to engage in the development effort, and all can therefore make equal contributions to the successful outcome. Under these conditions, university development can proceed in a normal, healthy manner, involving total faculty participation. All faculty members shoulder two responsibilities: administrative, largely through their departments, and professional, through their own individual teaching, research, and service. To seek excellence through some departments while ignoring the faculty members elsewhere is to limit efforts at integrating the entire faculty into the university's pursuit of excellence.

Line Administration of the Change Effort. Another temptation frequently encountered in institutional change is for the administration to fund an outside or special training organization to convey the theories to be learned, conduct seminars, and oversee the change effort. This approach is not entirely unsound, but in comparison with an alternative approach it has severe limitations.

The alternative approach is that line administrators themselves take the initiative of learning what constitutes sound administrative behavior and then take the responsibility for conducting seminars in which other administrators and faculty are helped to learn the same concepts and behavior skills. This is an additional aspect of "Do as I do." When senior administrators apply the time and energy necessary for conducting seminars that help others learn the theories of the Grid, this conveys a sense of commitment to spurring change and bringing about its effective implementation.

Under ordinary circumstances no administrator would conduct more than two seminars. Much learning about teamwork results from conducting two, but learning diminishes thereafter. As a result, it has proved to be sounder to spread the responsibility for conducting seminars widely through the administrator group in order that more of them may gain the additional learning that comes from seminar teaching.

Team Building Within and Among Departments. Team building starts at the top and proceeds down through the departmental level. This step permits natural groups of the university to find out which of their traditions, precedents, and past practices are outmoded and antiquated and to replace these worn-out decision-making and problem-solving practices with sound procedures.

Promoting interdepartmental and interdivisional cooperation is the next step. Whenever two or more divisions or departments share common interests or have conflicts over equipment, space, courses, programs, and so on, the key personnel in each group can come together to investigate how to establish superordinate goals that will strengthen their commonalities, reduce competitiveness, and eliminate overlaps.

Revalidating Institutional Mission. The stated purpose of the institution may be clear but not pertinent to the unfolding needs of society. It may consist of platitudes to which nothing more than lip service is given. Or it may be so broad, ambiguous, and abstract that either no direction can be derived from it or any direction can be rationalized from it. The mission statement should thus be reassessed. If it is sound, its reexamination serves to revalidate it and give it force. If unsound, then administrative leaders, faculty members, and trustees can take steps to replace outmoded, irrelevant, platitudinous, or ambiguous statements with a functional statement of mission that can provide the direction needed to bring about change toward excellence. Only the key executives of a university actively participate in the initial effort toward revalidating or restating the university mission. Others should be called upon to participate in the process before final revision is formalized, but it is the responsibility of the administration to take the first step.

Implementation of Mission. Once the mission has been studied as a long-range plan and has earned the commitment of the entire leadership of the institution, it then becomes possible to reexamine institutional practices in the light of the model and to institute changes, corrections, modifications, and so on to bring the institution as conducted into line with the institution as designed. The basic work of implementation is carried out within the organization components of the institution— departments, institutes, centers, and so on, with each responsible for designing the optimal fit between its actual activities and the model.

Consolidation. Any change effort inevitably involves reversals, regressions, and retreats. Sometimes these are related to shifts in external funding, sometimes to calamities such as war. Whatever the cause, no university development approach is complete and constant without examination of progress being made as to whether the effort is still on track and, if not, how direction and rate of change can be reestablished so as to maintain full momentum. Critique of the effort takes place all the way along in the development sequence, but it also involves intervening to measure progress achieved. Since the completion of the sequence may take anywhere from two to ten years and because of the constant rotation and replacement of administration and faculty, periods of consolidation may be needed at various points along the way.

Applying the 9,9 Strategy

Now that the individual and institutional conditions necessary for implementing the 9,9 approach have been reviewed, the question that must be answered is, "Does the 9,9 orientation imply rigidity and inflexibility of behavior?"

The answer is a clear no. Calling to mind the nine principles of behavior listed in Chapter Nine as the bases of the 9,9 approach, the reader will note that these principles, which are constant and unchanging, define the *strategy* of the 9,9-oriented administrator. But their specific applications, or *tactics,* vary with the situation. Thus the principles are not violated or disregarded when the situation changes. Instead what shift are the tactics of application, which bring the principles into everyday use in creative and constructive ways that are unique to particular situations.

This idea of the tactical uses of a strategic approach can be illustrated by the example of nutrition. Nutritionally speaking, there is one best way of maintaining the body in a healthy condition. This strategy involves adhering to nutritional principles as they relate to the intake of protein, fat, carbohydrates, minerals, vitamins, and so on. Not all the details of how the body uses food have been worked out, but the principles are well established: intake above an optimum level produces obesity; intake beneath the optimum leads to fatigue, malnutrition, weakness, and susceptibility to a number of physical diseases.

Thus, optimum intake is a principle of sound physical health. Disregard it and health problems are imminent. However, the manner in which the ingredients of sound nutrition are acquired is a tactical matter, contingent upon the availability of various foods. For instance, protein may be acquired from a number of sources. It makes no difference from the standpoint of nutritional principles what the particular source is, but simply that certain substances are acquired. This is an example of the relationship between strategy, that is, eating behavior calculated to be consistent with nutritional principles, and the particular tactics through which these nutritional principles are met—tactics that vary with circumstances, availability of foods, and so on.

Several examples can demonstrate how the principles behind the 9,9 approach have different applications depending on the specific situation.

Regarding conflict resolution by direct confrontation of causes, it is clear that a 9,9-oriented president would not interact with an administrative vice-president of long acquaintance and experience in the same manner as he would deal with a neophyte administrator—for example, a new department chair. Although he might confront the vice-president directly, he would be far less abrupt in bringing the controversial issue to the attention of the novice chair. Abruptness with the chair would be seen and experienced as characteristic of a 9,1 orientation, whereas the same directness with a longtime colleague would simply be seen as a way of saving time. The principle remains the same, but the tactic is different.

In regard to management by objectives, a 9,9-oriented administrator would not necessarily bring up long-term career goals with a new staff member in discussing the task to be accomplished. The new employee is most concerned with tomorrow, next week, and this month. His or her goals are immediate and often narrow by virtue of limited understanding of the situation or restricted skills. In contrast, for the long-term employee, a discussion regarding management by objectives might involve the time frame of a lifelong career. The next fifteen or twenty years might be the period needed to attain the prospects facing the employee, and his or her competencies would be evaluated against objectives of this length and magnitude. In the first of these cases, it would be "bad" administration to disregard the new employee's inability to take a broad view of the situation and to "force" a consideration of career-long objectives. But in the second, it would be inappropriate to confer with the longstanding employee and limit the conversation to the immediate future. In both cases, the strategy is that of gaining the involvement of the person in setting objectives toward which he or she can strive in a committed and orderly manner. What is different is the tactic employed.

Regarding learning by critique, a 9,9-oriented administrator would show a newcomer what to do and encourage him or her to experiment and to learn from mistakes. The administrator would provide ample coaching and support while the newcomer becomes acquainted with the assignment. They would both critique the performance at the beginning of, during, and after activities. The administrator would take responsibility for assisting the subordinate to see new angles, options, and alternatives. Such learning from critique is the basis of inducting the newcomer into the organization. With a more experienced associate, however, the same administrator might honor the individual's capacity to learn by creating a climate within which the associate can practice, experience, critique, control the pace of learning, and ask for help when needed. In both situations, the administrator does not shrink from critiques, yet the approach in each is different.

Such examples illustrate consistency of principle with versatility of application. This combination is particularly important in relation to the basic characteristic of the 9,9 orientation: team administration, or shared participation in problem solving and decision making.

Tactics of 9,9-Oriented Participation in Teamwork

Participation is basic to the 9,9 orientation because participation spurs involvement and results in agreements that can be achieved or that are necessary for commitment. When participation is effective, it becomes possible to establish goals and objectives that are central to both institutional and personal achievement, as well as to set up shared standards that provide a definition of the difference between educational excellence and mediocrity. But the principle of participation does not mean that everyone participates in everything. Team administration or teamwork does not imply that everyone meets together all the time. If this were to happen, it would be wasteful of the human resources needed to implement the institution's mission.

Basic ground rules are available that can be consulted for thinking through who should participate in any given discussion under a 9,9 orientation. Teamwork can occur when a person is operating alone, with one other member, or with all other members. It can occur when one person acts on behalf of another person, or when each member is separated from the others, as well as in face-to-face situations. Consider the following examples of such teamwork, designated as "1/0" (one-alone), "1/1" (one-one), and "1/all," with "1/1/1" and "1/some" as variations of 1/all.

1/0. Certain "team" problems involve only one person in the solution. The reasoning behind 1/0 is that a given individual has the responsibility, the capacity, and the information to solve the problem. It is thus in the interest of teamwork for him or her to solve the problem alone and then to let others know of the solution as it affects their own responsibilities. Such "team" problems, in other words, are "one-alone" (1/0). Individual effectiveness contributes to teamwork by moving the team toward its goals and avoiding duplication of effort.

When there are understanding and agreement about the conditions under which an administrator does not involve others, his solo decisions are not seen as arbitrary or unilateral but as part of his responsibility. There is neither resistance nor resentment on the part of others. These 1/0's may be carried out in private or in the presence of others. The point is that although they are not joint or emergent actions, they are still an essential part of good teamwork.

A special case of 1/0 occurs whenever one team member takes an action or substitutes on behalf of another member. An example of this kind of supportive teamwork may clarify what is involved: "I know you have to go to New York to give a paper. I'm going to teach a class on Thursday right before the one you will miss. I will be happy to cover for you." Another example is this: "Bill is away on an extended foreign trip, but I can act on his behalf and give you an answer."

When this kind of 1/0 teamwork takes place, the initiative rests with whatever team member takes the supportive action, but the responsibility for outcomes remains with the member on whose behalf the second team member initiated action. In this sense it calls for trust to a degree beyond that required in many other kinds of situations.

1/1. Team problems that involve two people are 1/1 team actions. It is up to them to work out the solution and to take the actions that will move the team toward its goals. These 1/1's between the two free the other team members to use their time in dealing with other aspects of the team situation. Under 1/1 situations any member may interact with any other member according to the first member's specific area of responsibility and need for help, support, data, consultation, coordination, and so forth. Failure to bring in that other member can be expected to have adverse effects, while bringing in anyone else would be wasteful since additional members can contribute or learn nothing in this particular instance. The mode of interdependence may be simultaneous or it may be sequential.

1/All. The 1/all situation brings together everyone who reports to the same administrator in dealing with a given problem. It involves team-wide participation. Thus, 1/all includes everyone who is a member of the team. This is simultaneous teamwork. It occurs when (1) no one member has the knowledge, information, experience, breadth, or wisdom to formulate the answer but everyone working together can be expected to reach it; (2) coordination is required to get the job completed (every member has a part of the action to perform, and each member's participation is thus crucial to a successful outcome); and (3) all members must understand the overall effort so that each can fit it into his or her other ongoing activities. Planning a budget might be an example of 1/all teamwork.

1/1/1. This is a complex but not infrequent variation of 1/all teamwork. Here, each member takes an action that allows another member to take a subsequent action, and so on until everyone has contributed, in sequence, to the end result. It is one-to-one-to-one. Each team member's activity is indispensable in sequence. For example, a secretary might file a travel request. Smooth coordination is necessary from the secretary to those who receive the request, to those who approve it, to those who notify the prospective traveler of approval, who then goes to the secretary, who in turn may call for airline reservations. This constitutes a complex sequence of interdependent operations. If it is done well, the traveler completes the journey without delay and accomplishes his or her objective. Though there may be no face-to-face meetings, what each team member does links them together in a team effort. This is sequential teamwork.

1/Some. Here the work involves more than two people but not the total team. The 1/some situation falls between 1/1 and 1/all and differs in the number of members involved rather than in their character of interdependence.

Nine, nine teamwork may occur under any of the above conditions, depending upon three fundamental factors. One is related to the quality of decisions. A second is concerned with the readiness of team members to implement the action called for. The third deals with management development.

Testing Actions for 1/0, 1/1, or 1/All Teamwork

Rules that clarify when to use 1/0, 1/1, or 1/all strategies are introduced in Table 2. These guidelines answer the question "Under what conditions are 1/0, 1/1, or 1/all approaches likely to be most effective?" The left-hand column identifies criteria that help the administrator evaluate when 1/0, 1/1, or 1/all participation should be the basis of action. The conditions for 1/1/1 and 1/some are so similar to 1/all that they are not separated from it for discussion.

An administrator should act without consulting others when the criteria for good decision making and problem solving, shown in the left-hand column, match the conditions in the 1/0

Table 2. Guidelines for Approaches to 9,9 Team Action

	Action to be Done		
Criteria	1/0	1/1	1/all
1. Whose problem is it?	mine	his; both of us	ours
2. Time to contact	unavailable	available	available
3. Judgmental competence	full	low	insufficient
4. Pooling of information	unnecessary	vertical or horizontal	needed both horizontally and vertically
5. Synergy	not possible	possible	possible
6. Critique	no one else involved	problem belongs to two people	problem has implications for all
7. Significance to the team	low	low	high
8. Involvement-commitment of others	no significance	helpful-essential	necessary-essential
9. Relevance for others	none	present	present
10. Understanding by others of purpose or rationale of decision	no need can be assumed	needed	needed
11. Coordination of effort	unnecessary	vertical or horizontal	horizontal and vertical
12. Change in team norms/standards	not relevant	not relevant	relevant
13. Representation of issue in other settings	none	pertinent	pertinent
14. Delegation	impossible	unlikely	unlikely
15. Management development	none	present	present

column. Actions that involve one other member occur when the conditions match what is said in the 1/1 column. The actions taken should be 1/all when the circumstances match those shown in the right-hand column.

The first six of the fifteen criteria relate most closely to maximizing the quality of decisions by the effective and efficient use of human resources.

1. Whose problem is it? If, in viewing a problem, an individual can say, "That problem is my sole responsibility," then the action is 1/0. If, however, the problem overlaps the responsibilities of two people, it represents a 1/1 situation. If the problem is superordinate in the sense that each individual has a piece of the problem but no one has all of it, then 1/all is the best interaction for solving it.

2. Time to contact. If there is no time to involve others, for whatever sound reason, the individual takes whatever action he or she can on a solo basis (1/0). If time is available and there are advantages to involving others, then it is 1/some or 1/all.

3. Judgmental competence. A manager may have the depth and experience to exercise sound judgment. Other things equal, he or she does so in a 1/0 way. If his or her experience is insufficient, however, and only one other person is needed to strengthen the soundness of judgment, the situation is 1/1. If a sound judgment requires the participation of everyone, then it should be carried out in a 1/all team manner.

4. Pooling of information. When all the information needed to execute an action is available from one individual, 1/0 action is appropriate. If two people each have some of the information needed for total understanding of a situation, then pooling of information may be required on a 1/1 basis. This may be a boss-subordinate relationship or it may be a relationship between equal-level colleagues. One/all pooling may be required when all team members have unique aspects of information that need to be brought together to develop total comprehension.

5. Synergy. Teamwork may be desirable because of the synergistic possibilities that arise when several or all team members study or review a problem. The different perspectives team members apply to a problem and the clash of ideas that discussion can produce may result in a solution that is better in quality than any one, two, or several members might have developed. However, 1/0 is the rule if no synergy can be anticipated and 1/1 if only one other can contribute.

6. Critique. Decision quality may be strengthened by discussions that study the team skills in solving problems. If a

problem has no team-building application, it should be studied in a 1/0 way by self-critique; in a 1/1 way if two people can learn something about teamwork effectiveness from it; and in a 1/all way if the full team can benefit from studying it.

The next seven criteria (7 through 13) are related to the acceptance issue, that is, the readiness of team members to implement a decision once it has been made.

7. Significance to the team. If the action has no team implications beyond one member alone, it should be handled 1/0 unless he does not carry it out. If it has far-reaching operational significance, such as shifting the reporting lines in the organization, then the entire team should understand the issues. The greater the possibility that an action will change team purpose, direction, character, or procedures, the more desirable the participation and involvement of all members.

8. Involvement-commitment of others. Understanding of the problem and of the solution to it may be necessary to achieve acceptance from those who must implement the decision. If the action to be taken does not involve other team members, it should be made 1/0. If it affects only one other, discussion with him is necessary (1/1). When the action has team-wide implications, all should discuss the pros and cons until those whose interests are involved have full understanding of the action. Doubts and reservations are then relieved, and everyone is in a position of agreement and support.

9. Relevance for others. Those whose future actions will be affected by a decision need to think through the issue and discuss its implications to make sure that they understand it and are committed to it. The larger the number of team members who have personal stakes in an action, the greater the need for them to discuss the decision.

10. Understanding by others of purpose or rationale of decision. There are some kinds of problems to which others cannot contribute, yet they can benefit from an awareness of the rationale employed in analyzing it or solving it. When others already know the rationale or when it is not important that they understand it, then the action should be 1/0. However, sometimes the rationale behind the action will benefit at least one

other team member, and therefore it may need to be dealt with in a 1/1 way. All the other team members may not be in a position to contribute to a solution but may need to know the rationale, and under these circumstances the rationale should be communicated on a 1/all basis.

11. Coordination of effort. Often an action can and should be 1/0 because there is no need for coordination. When coordination with one other person is required, the matter should be dealt with jointly, on a 1/1 basis. Sometimes several, if not all, team members are involved in implementing a decision; in that case the strategies for coordination need to be worked out on a 1/all basis.

12. Change in team norms/standards. Norms/standards that influence performance on a within-team basis may need to be established, modified, or completely changed. All team members need to be involved in order for them to know and to be committed to the norms/standards. Because each team member adheres to team-based norms/standards, he or she is unlikely to take a 1/0 action if it would shift a norm/standard. The most favorable condition for reaching such decisions occurs when a new team norm/standard is explicitly agreed to by all team members.

13. Representation of issue in other settings. Sometimes one team member serves as a representative in settings outside his or her own team. Other team members may contribute little or nothing to reaching a decision, but because they are in a "need to know" position, they are brought in to increase their understanding of the issue.

The next two items (14 and 15) are concerned with using teamwork situations for management development.

14. Delegation. This arrangement is the opposite of 1/0, where the administrator takes the problem and deals with it in a solo way. In 0/1, we have a situation of complete delegation. Other things being equal, 0/1 should be relied upon rather than 1/0 when (1) subordinates can handle a given problem as well as or better than the boss; (2) a development result will accrue for the subordinate; (3) delegation, not abdication, is the motivation that propels the administrator in this direction; and (4) the

time mode available to the administrator permits him or her to solve another problem more important than the delegated one, under conditions where the subordinate has reasonable prospects of success.

15. Management development. Team members participate in analyzing managerial issues, even though they may have little to contribute to its quality by way of information and even though their acceptance of it is immaterial. Their participation, however, enables them to gain knowledge and to develop the judgment needed for dealing with such problems in the future. If a problem has no management development implications, it should be dealt with 1/0; if it has management development implications for only one other person, it should be dealt with 1/1. If it has management development implications for all team members, it should be dealt with 1/all.

Objections to the 9,9 Approach

These considerations that enter into determining who should participate in decisions under 9,9-oriented administration are all based on the premise that no amount of participation will result in either high-quality decisions or acceptance of the solution if effective 9,9 leadership is absent.

Some contingency theorists reject the concept that there is one best style of administrative leadership, such as the 9,9 orientation, on the basis of at least four criteria—"no time," "no competence," "no need," and "no flexibility." These objections deserve consideration and response.

No Time. It is said that many situations involve crises that allow no time to consult or to share problem solving in a participative way. This usually is interpreted to mean that the administrator should proceed in a 9,1-oriented manner. There are two answers to this reason for rejecting a 9,9 orientation. One is that most crises can be avoided or their impact reduced through anticipation. Simulations permit participants to learn to take responsible action in a self-directing way in order to avert tragedy at the time of crisis. However, some crises cannot be anticipated; they just happen. In this case, the administrator can exercise unilateral judgments to provide order and direction for others. Such action is not "arbitrary," but rather in itself is of a 9,9 character. The administrator is exercising judgment on behalf of others who, by virtue of the circumstances, are incapable of exercising self-direction.

No Competence. Another argument against the 9,9 approach to administration says that staff members may not be competent to participate in decision making. Therefore, it is necessary to tell them what to do in a 9,1-oriented manner or to abdicate in a 1,1 way and let them learn from their own errors in the school of hard knocks. The 9,9-oriented solution is to help staff members develop the competence essential for effective participation in problem solving, decision making, and implementation of plans. When this happens, the opportunity for involving others and gaining their thinking and commitment in a 9,9-oriented way replaces the need for paternalism/maternalism or 9,1-oriented supervision.

No Need. A third criticism is that there are circumstances in which the involvement of staff members would be wasteful because they have no stake in the situation and nothing to contribute. This criticism disregards basic concepts intrinsic to the 9,9 approach, which provides guidelines for when an administrator should act alone, with one staff member or several, or with all in concert. This is not shifting from one Grid style to another, and it does not mean that everybody must act together all the time.

No Flexibility. The fourth consideration presumes that a 9,9 action is mechanically the same regardless of the situation. This criticism fails to take into account how the concepts of consistency and versatility provide a basis for understanding that 9,9 leadership is based on sound principles of behavior used in creative and constructive ways that are unique to particular situations. Relying on behavioral science principles and implementing them through versatile applications is analogous to learning the principles of physics and applying them to engineering problems.

Compare different styles of administration, for example, in the same situation. As part of a new institute or center, an administrator may start with a group of individuals who have never known or worked with one another. The task is to get the unit moving. A situational or statistical 5,5-oriented leader might provide very close 9,1-oriented management if he or she assumes that even experienced staff members do not know what to do. When they comply with directions, he or she might then give them recognition. If they begin to buck, he or she might shift to a 1,9 sweetness-and-light approach of encouragement and support or turn to 1,1-oriented *laissez-faire* leadership to reduce their antagonisms.

But an administrator whose supervision is governed by 9,9-oriented principles of behavior knows that sound results are most likely to occur when he or she and staff members work as a team to achieve objectives. They can learn to analyze problems. And, even though there are no tried-and-true answers, they seek "best" solutions by confronting differences, relieving disagreements by gathering additional data, simulating a proposal before implementing it, and using frequent critiques to stimulate operational as well as interpersonal learning. The principles of behavior behind this approach include mutual goal setting, openness of communication, resolution of disagreements and conflict based on understanding and agreement, learning to change through critique, and others verified in social psychology, mental health research, clinical psychiatry, and other fields as essential for sound problem solving. And rather than being applied inflexibly, these principles are applied, as demonstrated in this chapter, through a variety of tactics depending on the conditions involved.

Chapter Eleven

From Reactive Modes to Institutional Excellence Through Organization Development

A cademic administrators have been under siege for the past twenty years. This condition can be expected to continue and even accelerate in the period ahead. One reason is that the university is no longer an organism but has become a loose collection of components with little interdependence among its units. Even at the departmental level, interdependence is minimal. Every faculty member is free, at least on an informal basis, to negotiate with any outside agency or funding source as a representative of the university, without being in a position to commit the department or the university to a decision. The system is so free that in many respects it resists management, administration, or supervision. When these conditions prevail, the management of change is almost impossible. Insufficient coherence among parts restricts interdependent action.

Universities are widely credited with exercising initiative to stimulate change. On examination, however, these changes turn out to be primarily changes in the broader culture or in their students. They are not changes in how universities conceive of themselves or in how they conduct their internal affairs. This stimulation of change comes about through breakthroughs in scientific and technological research, scholarly publications that disseminate new ideas to a broader audience, consultation by academicians regarding public and corporate policy, and the education of students who, as they mature, become direct agents of change themselves. Thus, viewed from one standpoint, universities appear to be models of change; but from another standpoint, they simply maintain the *status quo* and do not even try to change the way they conduct their operations.

As a result, universities have become targets of pressure for change by numerous external groups, to say nothing of their own members—faculty, staff, and students. The sources of these pressures for change are illustrated in Figure 6. They range from state legislatures to accrediting agencies to special-interest groups.

• From state legislative circles, we see pressure on universities to change their practices in a number of ways. Because most of the funding for public education comes from legislative appropriation and because legislatures have been feeling the pressure for tax relief from citizen groups, legislators have been attempting to restrict funds to higher education, to scrutinize more closely the justification for funds, and to explore far more carefully how funds have been spent. Another example is the recent flurry of attacks on tenure. In a number of states, bills have been proposed or passed that would do away with tenure

Figure 6. Sources of Pressure on Administrators for University Change

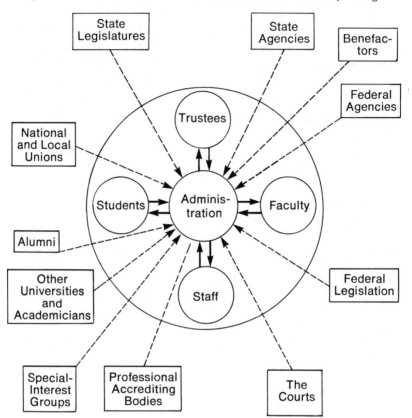

altogether or restrict it severely, while in other states legislators are just beginning to explore these possibilities. The feeling seems to be that tired old professors who have utilized the same set of lecture notes for thirty years need to be removed so that younger, fresher, more up-to-date instructors, with more dynamic teaching techniques, will have the chance to stimulate better learning in the classroom. Legislators are taking the initiative in attempting to correct this situation because university administrators have failed to face up to the responsibility for academic self-regulation and self-improvement.

• Several states have created statewide coordinating boards or governing boards to regulate higher education; and because many legislators feel that the whole educational enterprise is out of hand, they are giving these bodies more and more responsibility for making decisions that traditionally were made at the campus level. For example, some of these boards are deciding which universities within a state will be able to offer certain degree programs and which will not. They are scrutinizing the menu of courses offered on the campus to make sure the courses are within the mission of the institution, and they are deciding where there is overlap in course offerings and how to reduce it. Lacking evidence of administrative initiative, they are recommending the closing of duplicate or high-cost programs, and they are trying to control personnel costs by such policies as across-the-board personnel reductions and early retirement.

• Federal agencies are moving to tighten control over higher education. They formerly provided *carte blanche* grants to institutions, but they are now much more carefully defining the purposes for which their grants should be used. No longer are institutional grants available for the general development of departments or programs; now they come with specific goals or objectives that can be monitored and measured. The direction of research is more and more controlled by nonacademic federal administrators, with the bureaucratic value system dictating whether or not specific research projects will be funded and with professors putting more effort into projects that federal agencies are likely to fund rather than following the leads that their own thinking and interests dictate. A great deal of federal money is available for research in energy fields and engineering, while less is available in the social sciences and the social service areas. These allocations produce institutional changes over which university administrators are able to exercise only nominal control.

• Congress and the courts have set down a number of regulations for organizations, including universities, in order to correct societal ills. For example, Title IX of the Education Amendments of 1972 demanded that universities avoid discrimination in their recruitment, selection, hiring, and promotion practices. Federal court cases set precedents that now govern student admissions in regard to race, sex, age, and economic hardship. Federal regulations regarding health and safety, such as restrictions on the use of human subjects in research or on recombinant DNA experimentation, establish rules with which institutions must comply.

    • Still another source of pressure on universities comes from professional accrediting bodies. These associations usually are discipline related; they are found in such areas as engineering, psychology, nursing, and medicine. Such bodies often accredit the curriculums in programs of the disciplines with which they are associated. They send teams to a university to determine whether its curriculum, faculty, and programs are acceptable. These accrediting bodies prepare reports and recommend the changes that they see as necessary. Such accrediting bodies wield great influence, and a particular department may go through months of preparation in order to document its programs for these team visits. The team may have specific requirements that the universiry or the department is expected to fulfill in order to meet accreditation standards. Often these standards call for particular curriculums or even specific content in a designated program or course. Some administrators and faculty within universities feel that this is an encroachment on the integrity of the university and not something to which the university should respond. In any event, the pressure for change again is from an external source.

    • Special-interest groups also make demands on the university. For example, environmentalists may demand a certain kind of policy in support of nuclear power or nuclear waste disposal. Some groups have protested against trade with South Africa or investment of university funds in South African enterprises. Others have questioned the general way in which university funds are invested. Certain groups demand different testing practices at universities and sometimes no testing standards at all for admission, saying that such standards are discriminatory. Some groups protest the theories advocated by certain professors. For example, a researcher in biology who strongly advocates Darwin's theory of evolution may be subject to harassment for not giving equal attention to the Biblical creation formulation. A professor in psychology who studies racial differences in intelligence may be pressured and called a "white supremacist." A university professor who is involved in a government contract with the army may be criticized strongly for promoting militarism. One who advocates a certain political position may be pressured by citizens who hold the contrary position.

Again, the president of a university may be called on by alumni who are upset about a speech made by a professor in an open forum, and these alumni may withhold support in hopes of affecting institutional policies. Similarly, benefactors may seek to provide funds or endow chairs, such as a business school chair devoted to "free enterprise," to further a particular ideological point of view. The university may change its policies or accept the endowment, but in doing so it is responding to change induced from the outside rather than making decisions based on values that reflect its stated mission.

· Administrators are also under pressure from different factions within the university, each of which may apply pressure on the others for wanted changes. For example, because trustees have felt more and more pressures from outside groups, they are increasingly active in scrutinizing the way money is spent on campus, particularly for research facilities and equipment. On many campuses, faculty unionism is strong and growing, with faculties now bargaining collectively through national organizations. Members of the classified staff pressure administrators for changes, such as greater benefits, improved working conditions, and different personnel practices. And student pressure on administrators can range from requests for a role in formulating important policies or serving on governing boards and committees to newspaper editorials against the administration, legislative lobbying in the state capital, protest marches and other forms of activism, as well as legal pressure against the university when decisions are not in students' favor. A student, for example, may accuse a faculty member of unfair grading, an administrator of prejudice, or the institution itself of illegitimate requirements or restrictions.

Administrative Reactions

Many of these pressure tactics, which involve political trade-offs, withholding of resources or support, and surveillance, give the impression that administrators cannot be trusted to take sound actions on their own. As a result, some administrators develop strategies of defense or mechanisms of resistance to prevent invasion of their prerogatives from the outside. All of these responses are in the reactive mode. Thus budget proposals may be formulated in secrecy, and faculty appointments may be shrouded in mystery. The motives of benefactors may be rephrased in vague but sanitary terms. Special-interest groups may be placated by token changes or by technical studies that present the administration's side of the argument. And reports to trustees, accrediting agencies, and legislatures may be drafted not so much to project an accurate image of the university as to disguise problems it would be embarrassing to talk about openly. All these strategies are likely, if not inevitable, when an organization is not being led from within in a sound manner.

Some administrators may react with piecemeal efforts to improve university functioning. For example, in order to make decisions more efficiently and to better handle problems that exist on campus, they may seek to streamline administration, to write operating procedures for campus administration, to improve management through better delegation, or to change the organizational structure. They may hire outside consultants to help with technical decisions involving significant campus purchases, such as large computer systems, or even to evaluate the productivity and personnel of departments. They may employ additional staff support to help them with campus administration. To conserve resources and avoid duplication and overlap, they may cut budgets, impose uniformity across departments in record keeping, or increase monitoring and reporting requirements on different parts of the campus—thereby reinforcing the pressures for uniformity that arise from sources external to the institution.

Some administrators, recognizing that the administrative cadre is ill equipped to respond to external pressures, have set up in-service training programs to assist lower-level administrators to learn more about the nuts-and-bolts of administration. Typical topics include institutional planning, budget preparation and control, legal rights and obligations, preparing a marketing plan, individual progress review, managing the physical plant, time management, management information systems, and leadership and human relations. Legislatures and boards of regents have even allotted money for the creation of institutes for research and training on the management of higher education, feeling that most academic administrators are unprepared to handle their management functions and that the university itself is not ready to do anything about it. The motivation behind these training programs and institutes is basically sound: it is to help the university function in a better manner and to solve problems that have long resisted solution. The limitation, as evidenced by the litany of course offerings, lies in the mechanistic orientation of this training. It teaches an administrator how to do things on an individual basis rather than providing him or her with an organization development orientation. Such an orientation involves the development of solutions for problems through understanding basic values and using teamwork. For example, sending university administrators to a business school to study financial management, while it may be desirable in itself, cannot be regarded as organization development in any basic sense; rather, it is simply management development: the administrator is studying the rationale and mechanics of financial management as carried out in any organization, not analyzing the specific tactics of financial management currently in use in his or her own institution; and—more important—the training is directed at strengthening the capacity of the administrator to solve particular problems rather than at changing the culture of the institution in ways that would increase the effectiveness of all its members.

Administrative initiative is desperately needed in order to strengthen the contribution that universities can make in shaping the future directions of society. In order to apply the vast knowledge universities possess of how excellence can be achieved, something more than merely reacting to external pressures with ad hoc remedies and management development is needed. Administrators need to appreciate the extent to which the culture of their institution exercises a controlling influence over the behavior of all its members. And they need to recognize further that improvements in the effectiveness of an administration in bringing the institution to new standards of excellence are likely to come about only as the culture that controls behavior becomes itself the target of change. Administrators must adopt, in other words, a systems concept of organization development.

Organization Development

Organization development is a concrete example of applied cultural anthropology that has arisen not in anthropology itself but from research into small groups by social psychologists. It involves seeing an organization as a system—an entity of interacting parts bound together by a common purpose and maintained in a state of health when the various parts contribute to this purpose—increased profits for a business, for example, or high-quality education, research, and service for a university. Organization development focuses on practices aimed at improving the culture of the organization as contrasted with those aimed at changing only individuals. Thus, development or training activities that involve individual administrators or groups of administrators in studying operational barriers to effectiveness and in improving their effectiveness within the existing system are not organization development. Instead, they are individual or group or management development because the organization system itself remains the same as it was before the development took place, even though it may now function somewhat better. The two lists below identify the key differences between organization development and more limited approaches:

	Individual or Group or
Organization Development	*Management Development*
1. An organization is an organic entity.	An organization is a mosaic.

Organization Development	Individual or Group or Management Development
2. Individuals are interdependent, interacting within the context of the organic whole.	Persons are individual and largely independent.
3. Improvement in an organization's functioning results from: achieving a better sense of direction, strengthening the organic entity, improving the quality of interdependence, and using critique of the status quo to change the status quo.	Improvement in an organization's functioning results from adding increments of individual and small-group competence to do assigned work in a better manner.

The difference between these two approaches can be illustrated by analogy with the difference between internal change and external change in an individual, such as a change in that person's orientation, assumptions, and values versus a change in his or her situation or environment. Getting a divorce as the solution for an unhappy marriage is a situational change, but it does not mean that the person has acquired the skills essential for integrating a new marriage. Changing jobs because of problems at work may only mean that the person will leave one position and move to another where, in a brief period of time, he or she will find himself or herself experiencing the same or similar difficulties. Shifting one's place of residence may change one's physical location, but it may not affect one's way of living. Desegregation has had a profound effect in terms of increased physical proximity between blacks and whites, but by itself it does little to increase integration in the sense of promoting mutual understanding and respect. Even the women's movement, while providing greater opportunity for women in employment, has changed some of the policies and rules to make the structure more fair but has not yet altered some of the stereotypical assumptions about women.

Just as individuals need to undertake more than simple changes of a situational or environmental nature for their own development, institutions need to move beyond individual or group development for maximum improvement. Trying to change a university by shifting its structure, pleading for cooperation, changing its statement of goals, and so on is doomed to failure in assuring excellence unless the university's inherent value system—in terms of how decisions are made, convictions are expressed, and problems are solved—is sound. Certain assumptions about administration produce negative effects throughout the entire culture and operation of the institution, while another set of assumptions can have just the opposite effects. Only when administrators become aware of the way their own assumptions influence institutional culture and only when they commit themselves to actions based on sound assumptions regarding human behavior is it likely that a university will inaugurate successful organization development for the pursuit of excellence.

Approaches to Organization Development

In earlier chapters, we examined various styles of university administration that are characteristic of academic administrators at the present time. As we pointed out, most of them prevent university administrators from engaging in the effective pursuit of excellence. The best interests of the university are not well served when an administrator's dominant Academic Administrator Grid style and personal values focus on simply surviving until retirement, on enhancing his or her own position of domination, mastery, and control, on gaining the warmth and approval of colleagues and subordinates, or on serving as a father or mother figure to younger administrators, who are regarded as maturing "sons" and "daughters" and who will be expected to carry on the "parent's" traditions when he or she is no longer there to guard their interests. Each of these orientations may advance an administrator's career or increase his or her sense of security and importance, but they can produce unfortunate kinds of pressure for change both from within and outside the university because they fail to forward the best interests of the university at large. And all of them affect, largely for the worse, the university's approach to organization development.

1,1: The Do-Nothing Approach. As will be recalled from Chapter Four, the 1,1 Grid style is a custodial orientation in which the administrator holds on by avoiding any actions that might have either a positive or a negative effect. By sitting on decisions, he or she can always hope that a favorable outcome will occur once a solution is reached by others. Since "hope springs eternal," many administrators wait and wait for an outcome that will be favorable to themselves but that in fact seldom occurs. The consequence of this approach is that eventually those who see the hopelessness of it all either move in to take over or move out to apply themselves with greater effect in other situations. The resulting organizational stagnation can bring the institution to a point where it is no longer able to endure as an independent academic entity.

This orientation results in a do-nothing approach to organization development; it holds that achieving excellence in a systematic and coherent way is not a realistic possibility. Therefore it is better to do nothing than to do something that is doomed to failure or criticism. Inaction is the rule. The result is that the university tends to lurch from one crisis to another with actions forced by circumstances or based on default.

9,1: The Prescriptive Approach. As Chapter Five illustrated, the 9,1 Grid style is premised on attaining mastery, domination, and control over the administrative apparatus for which one is responsible and to do so in such a way as to avoid running the risk of failure. This can be a powerful basis for administration because it is direct, definite, and detailed. The major risk is in the consequences of the application of this approach. There are two. One is that the subordinates will buckle under and in doing so become "yes-persons." In this way the 9,1-oriented administrator is deprived of the resources that subordinates might have contributed. The other risk is that a 9,1 authority-obedience orientation on the part of the administrator will breed contempt. Though unexpressed, this kind of resentment can provoke antiorganizational resistance, with the result that underground movements aimed toward limiting the administrator's authority eventually become effective and result in his or her either being worked into a corner or being relieved from office.

The 9,1 style of administration typically results in applying a "prescriptive" approach to organization development as practiced by the great and not-so-great consulting houses; this approach tells people what they should or must do and thereby reduces their degree of freedom in making decisions. It promotes a climate of authority and obedience rather than one of openness, which would be based on participation, involvement, and commitment to stated objectives.

The prescription-oriented approach requires that administrators implement the advice of experts. For example, the prescription-oriented consultant accepts it as given that he or she has been employed to come up with answers. Difficulties in organizational functioning could have been avoided if institutional members had had the consultant's skills and understandings. The consultant assumes that he or she can see objectively what members can't, either because they are too involved in the situation or because they are too incompetent to deal with it. Whatever the circumstances, the prescription-oriented consultant's aim is to give individuals the guidance they need to take action.

Prescriptive consultation can provide the answers that members are unable to agree on or reach among themselves. Sometimes their inability to move is the result of a decision-making impasse. Sometimes it is the result of a power vacuum in which all authority has gone out of the team. Sometimes members are faced with a problem of such technical complexity that they cannot solve it. Or it may be felt that the possibilities for disorder during team deliberations make necessary an external source of "control via procedure." Thus it may come about, for example, that an organization's ranking members conduct their meetings under the egis of a long-dead prescriptive "authority" such as Robert's Rules of Order or use a manual of procedure that has been evolved, over many years, within their nation's legislative chambers.

There are three typical situations where prescriptive consultation appears to make a positive contribution. The first involves an individual who has reached an impasse where he or she is unable to influence other team members and they are unable to move without his or her concurrence. A second occurs when the solution to the problem is beyond the reach of team members, who simply don't know what to do and have thrown up their hands in despair. A third is the situation in which a team is immobilized as a result of some traumatic event that is experienced as such a total defeat that no member is able to redefine the problem in constructive terms. Under these conditions, defenses are at a low level. And, rather than resenting prescriptions, people are receptive to them because of the positive alternatives that they offer. When such client needs and receptivity are appropriately addressed by consultant prescriptions, situations that might otherwise continue to produce chronic difficulty or even tragedy can be averted. However, rather than trying to reduce the authority-obedience mode of administration and make it less arbitrary and coercive, prescription rests on the very use of authority and obedience to get a problem solved. That is, authority is exercised by the consultant, while the client's "obedience" in carrying out the consultant's recommendations is taken for granted. However, no matter how valid, prescriptions that disregard values held by members will provoke resistances that can only be overcome by unilateral actions. Such actions will, in turn, reduce trust and lower morale and, in general, cause members to turn away from rather than promote institutional involvement.

1,9: The Acceptant Approach. As described in Chapter Six, the 1,9 orientation, which is motivated by a desire to gain the warmth and approval of others on the one hand and to avoid their rejection on the other, is a way of administering the affairs of the university that is calculated to make the maximum number of people happy. This means that the administrator places low demands on others, while creating conditions under which everyone feels that he or she has been noticed and dealt with in a positive manner.

Two consequences are traceable to this approach to administration. One is that the organization's culture becomes softer and softer and, thus, less and less challenging. Administrators who need warmth and approval feel secure; but they, too, by virtue of administering in a 1,9 orientation, place few challenges before their own people, with the result that the lowering of standards is extended throughout the organization. The other consequence is that those who are strong, in either a 9,1- or a 9,9-oriented way, find this approach to administration so unchallenging that they leave for better opportunities.

This 1,9 style of administration is likely to embrace an "acceptant" orientation to organization development. This orientation is built around the premise that the greatest deficiency confronting organizations today is that the manner of operating an organization erodes the friendship that members feel toward one another. The result is that members who need to be open and accepting of one another tend to be closed and hidden. It follows that if people who are working together are closed and hidden rather than accepting and trusting, there will be an absence of communication, shared understanding, mutual help and support, and so on. When mistakes are made, they will be hidden in order to avoid further reduction of acceptance and trust rather than openly acknowledged and brought to the awareness of others in order that the problem can be rectified.

Based on this diagnosis of organization weakness, it follows that when people have learned to be trusting and accepting of one another, with the resultant transparency that intimacy can produce, the quality of friendship needed for effective administration will have been developed.

When morale and cohesion are low, people do not identify themselves with the organization, and they are not accepting and trusting of one another in a friendly manner. Thus, it is to be expected that the strategies of organization development pertinent for solving the problem of acceptance and trust are to be found closely allied to the behavioral science area of research concerned with morale and cohesion. If the organization deficit is a lack of acceptance and trust among its members, then the question becomes, "How can acceptance and trust be stimulated and developed?"

An acceptant approach is one in which members of an

organization are treated in such a way that they can feel secure in letting down their defenses, revealing hurt feelings, and unburdening themselves of tensions that perhaps have been building up for months or even years. This approach to organization development is geared to solving the problem of acceptance and trust.

One condition for the development or restoration of acceptance and trust is that those who interact with one another do so in the spirit of unconditional positive regard. Unconditional positive regard means that each and every individual is valued as a human person. When an individual is so valued, it is highly doubtful that any other person would exercise evaluative judgments of acceptance or rejection of that individual as a result of his or her actions.

Under this acceptant approach to organization development, a consultant to an institution first encourages participants to express their feelings in an unfiltered, authentic way. They can do this more easily when the consultant accepts whatever the client says in a nonevaluative, nonjudgmental manner, thereby inviting the client to put his defenses aside and to give expression to his deeper-lying feelings. Defensive kinds of behavior such as rationalizations, justifications, denials, and projections—all of which are inappropriate to the situation—tend not to be provoked because the consultant is neither "attacking" nor "prescribing." The consultant then ensures that participants in the process "share" with one another by listening carefully and appreciating what is really being said. When participants do this, they encourage the expression of feelings and emotions. Thus, the emotional expression is taken at full value—those who hear it accept it as revealing the person's authentic feelings, and they thereby come to take a less judgmental attitude than they otherwise might have done. The consultant himself, by providing an ongoing example of nondefensive behavior, helps to reduce the likelihood that others will react in ways that block cathartic release.

The purpose of acceptant interventions is to aid individuals to release the tensions that stem from feelings and emotions that they either have "bottled up" or in some other way have felt a reluctance to express. Feelings that prevent members from thinking through to decisions or solutions in objective ways have to be resolved before progress can occur. The consultant's rationale is that after pent-up emotions have been released through cathartic interventions, the causes of the problem can then be identified and rectified. A side effect, however, is that organization members come to avoid facing up to incompetency and other types of problems, preferring instead to maintain harmonious working relationships. The result is that while a spirit of harmony may prevail, the deeper and more serious problems of administration remain hidden, so that the pursuit of excellence will be little more than lip service.

The acceptant approach to organization development, as illustrated by such consultation, has much to commend it, as far as it goes. But by itself it does not address the causes of problems beyond those of mistrust and negative regard. An inherent limitation is that the promotion of love and trust often is at the expense of people turning away from the real issues of conflict that would erode trust were they to be faced. Since nothing in this approach aids participants to develop the essential skills for solving conflicts, the trust produced experientially evaporates when genuine vested interests reappear.

Paternalism/Maternalism: The Benevolent Prescriptive Approach. The paternal/maternal orientation, involving as it does a coupling of the 9,1 approach of control, mastery, and domination with the 1,9 orientation of acting in ways that are calculated to promote loyalty and warmth (see Chapter Seven), is possibly the most common and certainly the most insidious of the major approaches to academic administration. Its basic characteristic is that reward is correlated with performance only to the extent that performance is a response to demands, no matter how subtly stated, for compliance. Thus, other administrators and the faculty tend to become dependent and to engage in those activities that meet the administrator's concept of what is important rather than acting on the basis of their own autonomy and convictions as to what is important—either to teach or to engage in research or to involve themselves in service activities. As a result, many administrators and faculty learn that reward is not based upon merit but, in the final analysis, upon compliance with the paternalist's or maternalist's private standard of merit.

The paternal/maternal orientation, when exercised in the interest of excellence in teaching, research, or service, can bring the university to a position of eminence. The major difficulty is that the administration and faculty are gutted of personal convictions and the capacity to exercise initiative. When the paternalistic or maternalistic president, dean, or department chairman departs, there is an insufficient reservoir of self-motivated and spirited administrators and faculty to take over the reins and lead in the direction of greater progress. Thus, during this kind of administration, steps toward excellence can result, but these are based upon compliance rather than upon true autonomy and independent thinking.

There is a second predictable consequence of a paternal/maternal orientation. Those who submit to the requirements imposed upon them in a quiet and apparently agreeable way will eventually discover one another, and their underlying frustrations and resentments will become mobilized. This is particularly apt to happen when a faculty union appears on the scene. Union organizers are familiar with this kind of administration and know how to stimulate and motivate underlying resentments in such a way as to bring about a mobilization of the faculty, which then vents its anger on the administration.

It is not possible to specify any distinctive approach to organization development as uniquely characteristic of a paternal/maternal-oriented administrator. However, whatever approach such an administrator takes is likely to be previewed and pretested to ensure its consistency with his or her values and then pressed into use in a firm but not coercive way, with each and every reservation partially answered in the process of reducing opposition or promoting compliance to his or her exercise of will to promote development. This is a prescriptive approach in selection and in execution, undertaken in a benevolent and kindly manner, and therefore we refer to it as a benevolent prescriptive approach to development.

5,5: The Catalytic Approach. The 5,5 orientation, as described in Chapter Eight, is frequently commended as a "reasonable" approach to academic administration. And, in one sense, the 5,5 orientation is reasonable. The administrator waits until the constituency is available to support him or her in whatever new decisions are to be taken. But if these constituencies are difficult to develop or if they begin to crumble as change is introduced, then the status quo is retained as an acceptable basis of action. A consequence of this Grid style is that the administrative organization and faculty are "leveled" to an acceptable common denominator, which in the final analysis means that no one ever really wins and no one ever really loses. The deeper truth is that there is great loss in the name of "reasonableness." This loss results from the good-natured but shallow approach to teaching, the utilitarian character of research, and the popularized concept of service. For example, the student who is never really challenged to test his or her limits pays a high price, while the administrator may move up the hierarchy.

The organization development approach of choice for a 5,5-oriented administrator is "catalytic" with a "local-option" feature built in that is likely to prompt piecemeal efforts within pockets of interest. The catalytic orientation is based on the notion that what organizations need in order to increase their effectiveness is improved awareness on the part of institutional members of how they individually and collectively see situations and how each is seen by the others. When information and data are more fully shared, in other words, it should then be possible for organization members to set norms and standards to guide their conduct, and organization effectiveness should be the result.

This catalytic orientation facilitates the exchange of data and information among members of an organization, but it does not involve senior administrators in leading the institutional change effort, creating a climate for it, or giving it any basic sense of direction. With this orientation, departments, divisions, institutes, centers, and other units are encouraged to engage in their own development activities; the assumption is that any activity is likely to be beneficial. Or the favored idea of some powerful administrator determines the direction of the effort, but the soundness of the approach is not thought out or tested.

Because it is often not appropriate for members of an organization to expend time other than in direct performance of duties, it follows that difficulties in the *process* of interaction that may need to be identified, discussed, and resolved are likely not to receive the attention they merit. This approach to organization development is geared toward rectifying this deficiency by enabling organization members to suspend the routines of everyday protocol that prevent them from full and open information and data exchange.

The underlying premise is the "rational man" formulation. In effect, this premise says, "We are rational beings. But there are limits on our rationality as a result of the inadequate information on which we are expected to operate. Therefore, we must change the norms and standards in terms of which we share information and data; once this is accomplished, each of us can exercise his or her rationality in a fuller and more adequate way, and, in turn, this will contribute to the development of the organization."

The preferred method of strengthening social perception is through the mechanism of feedback. If people have information that they have not shared, then by introducing feedback it should be possible for this withheld information to become an ongoing aspect of institutional interactions.

This approach, which seeks to focus on the norms and standards of conduct in an organization as the points of intervention, is entitled *catalytic*. We might recall that, in chemistry, a catalytic agent, when placed in conjunction with certain other substances, causes a change or reaction to happen—one that either would not have occurred had this agent not been present or would have occurred more slowly. The term can also be used to describe a particular way of bringing about changes in teamwork. A consultant enters a situation with the intention of catalyzing a new "process" or of increasing the rate at which a "process" is presently occurring. The client's situation is taken at face value by the consultant. Rather than working toward any fundamental alteration of the status quo, he or she tries to assist those operating within it to be more effective in their customary team activities.

The catalytic approach concentrates the attention of

team members not so much on theory that permits current problems to be seen in new ways or on the emotional undercurrents in their relations as on their need to increase their shared understanding of a situation and one another. Greater understanding can be facilitated through gathering data about the situation itself and about the reactions of each individual to the others. These empirical facts, summarized and presented with logical analysis, are the "agents" that the consultant uses to catalyze the client's situation and facilitate his or her change efforts. Such data often consist of *social* facts—for example, the existing state of the client's attitudes and emotions. Bringing into awareness empirical facts that presently are not shared or have been "misunderstood" aids in *perceptual* clarification. The catalytic assumption is that once team members "see" their shared situation more objectively, they can then take the needed steps to improve it.

When this catalytic approach to organization development is applied, pockets of interest are likely to appear throughout the institution. Individuals, small groups, or units of the institution begin to engage in development activities as they see fit. But these atomistic efforts rarely are capable of dealing with the institution-wide problems that detract from institutional excellence.

A department, for example, can engage in catalytic team building or in survey research conducted along anonymous lines, so as to increase the flow of information in the system. This can have some beneficial results in that now people have a better understanding of where others stand. The insidious impact is likely to be that people yield convictions in the name of cooperation. The consequence may be that decisions are watered down rather than improved in quality. Furthermore, it is now well known that catalytic approaches to institutional change based on pockets of interest simply do not spread. Even at their best, positive effects within one department are resisted by other departments, which do not wish to copy what others have done. Of even greater importance is the fact that positive effects do not flow upwards. It is a simple matter of social gravity. Change processes flow down from the top, not up from the bottom.

An additional limitation in the catalytic approach is that it produces an adverse "sleeper effect." That is, at the beginning it raises expectations that "finally we're going to do something to solve our problems," but because it deals with surface tensions rather than deeper issues of administration, the problems remain. As time goes on, participants tend to become negative or disillusioned and are unprepared to give further effort, even to a sounder approach.

5,5: The Statistical Approach. Just as no institution-wide approach to systematic organization development is possible under a simple 5,5 administrative style—involving a value-free orientation to issues with resolution of problems based on taking positions consistent with what one's constituency might wish—such an approach is equally impossible under what Chapter Eight identified as the "statistical 5,5" style. The administrator who hopscotches over the Grid, dealing with one situation according to a 1,1 orientation, another according to a 9,9 orientation, a third in a 1,9 way, a fourth in a paternalistic/maternalistic manner, and a fifth in a 5,5 way, may be a "flexible" administrator, but others are apt to see his or her behavior as inconsistent and slippery. They see neutrality one minute, harshness the next, and, not long after, favoritism or compromise. The administrator who applies whichever approach seems likely to aid in achieving whatever his or her purposes may be at any particular time comes to be seen as an unsafe or unreliable person whom one cannot trust over the long term. Under this administrative style, organization development is unlikely even to be catalytic; rather, it will probably be quixotic, intermittent, contradictory, and ineffective. Whatever development occurs is likely to be opportunistic rather than systematic.

9,9: Theory-Based Confrontation. The 9,9 orientation, reflecting basic principles of behavior and conduct derived from the behavioral sciences, is the strongest and most profound approach to administration and offers the surest basis for organization development. This is so because it mobilizes human resources and strengthens the readiness of members of an organization to commit themselves to the pursuit of excellence.

Because the principles of behavior that underlie the 9,9

orientation have major implications for effective organization development, it seems appropriate to repeat them here from Chapter Nine:

1. Fulfillment through contribution is the motivation that gives character to human activity and supports productivity.
2. Open communication permits the exercise of self-responsibility.
3. Conflicts are solved by direct confrontation of their causes, with understanding and agreement as the basis of cooperative effort.
4. Being responsible for one's own actions is the highest level of maturity and only possible through widespread delegation of power and authority.
5. Shared participation in problem solving and decision making stimulates active involvement in productivity and creative thinking.
6. Management is by objectives.
7. Merit is the basis of reward.
8. Learning from work experience is through critique.
9. Norms and standards that regulate behavior and performance support personal and organization excellence.

These principles lead to a theory-based approach to organization development. This approach sets forth a value system or conceptual basis that permits institutional members to see and develop sound methods for interaction and for resolution of differences. It is an organic approach in that the institution is seen as an organism rather than as a mosaic of fragmented or loosely linked pieces, each of which acts independently of the rest. And it is a multiphase approach that allows institutional members to engage in a series of experiences that have the prospect of culminating in organizational excellence.

The basic assumption behind this approach is that values are at the core of organization malfunctioning and that the great majority of people in the organizational hierarchy are unaware of their personal values and of how deeply embedded they may have become. Therefore, individuals are unable to diagnose the consequences that follow from their values or assumptions. Sometimes these assumptions allow things to go smoothly, and their results are good. But at other times, these assumptions cause trouble. For instance, some of the most important value-based assumptions underlying organizational hierarchy, segmentation, and specialized responsibilities involve the uses and misuses of organizational power in problem solving and decision making. These range from deference to the authority of the boss regarding what should be done, even when he or she is wrong, to an underlying rebelliousness that crops out whenever the boss uses his or her rank to control subordinates' behavior, no matter how "right" his or her actions may be. If such difficulties are to be solved, these value-based assumptions must be explicitly identified, understood, and confronted.

Theory-based confrontation subsumes diagnoses that lead to prescriptive, acceptant, and catalytic approaches, but it permits these diagnoses to be seen in a new and different light. For instance, as with the prescriptive approach, it acknowledges that expert judgment may be essential for solving certain problems. But it avoids the unilateral exercise of authority in bringing a prescription into use. An organization development consultant who operates in a confrontational mode identifies to individuals, in a way they can understand, the extent to which their value-based assumptions are either invalid and unjustified or valid and sound, but he or she stops short of prescribing the values by which they should interact. His or her purpose is to aid members to break through their rationalizations, justifications, explanations, or the unspoken and unwritten "rules" of behavior that keep them from having an objective view of their situation; at the same time, the consultant wants to avoid creating defensive behavior through his or her interventions by causing team members to feel they are being attacked.

The necessary factor in effective confrontation is for an expert who has no "vested interests" to be able to pierce participant defenses in a way that precludes rationalization or justification and prevents members from falling back on their prerogatives. Thus, a confrontational consultant's strategy takes

cognizance of the likelihood that a given member will rational-
ize and justify his or her present value-based assumptions, thereby explaining away difficulties, rather than actively setting
about to discover in a factual way what his or her presently un-
perceived problem is. Organization members can be helped to
see their value-based assumptions in a more objective light if
they are challenged to explain the "whys" of their present behavior. If the consultant can point to here-and-now examples as
they occur in interactions among team members, it is likely that
defenses can be pierced.

A confrontational approach to organization development
is useful in focusing conflict; but if this approach is not based
on behavioral science principles and theory, the result may be
the polarization of destructive conflict rather than the resolution of differences. Theory-based confrontation provides administrators with a scientific system of values for organization development. It can be contrasted with a commonsense or
prescientific approach for bringing about change, whereby
administrators or consultants try to get results based partly on
"feel," partly on hunch, partly on data and information, partly
on past methods that may have "worked" without anyone's
knowing why, partly on avoiding actions that antagonize or
frustrate others, partly on prescription, and partly on getting
others involved and committed to achievement based on inner
convictions. The end result of this way of trying to work with
and through others is an eclecticism that lacks consistency and
is often at deep variance with the kind of behavior that would
be expected were administrators working with one another in
terms consistent with sound principles of behavior.

Thus theory-based confrontation as an approach to
organization development seeks to aid administrators to shift
from a reliance on unexamined values and assumptions to the
use of an applied behavioral science orientation to management.
By it, administrators are aided in learning scientific theories of
behavior, such as the principles underlying the 9,9 administrative style, and then, with adequate theory in hand, in experi-
menting with administrative behaviors based on these principles.
This approach rests on the premise that behavior, like any other

aspect of human experience and conduct, can be understood in a systematic way. By making alternative actions comparable in terms of predicting "less" and "more" favorable consequences, theory constructs enable members to operate in a more effective manner. Thus, members are able to integrate their efforts more effectively than if these conditions were not present or were only assumed.

In contrast to the acceptant approach, which views lack of trust as the cause of organization problems, theory-based confrontation may lead to the conclusion that the deeper issue underlying lack of trust is faulty exercise of authority. Therefore the problem of mistrust can only be solved by strengthening the exercise of authority through bringing behavioral science principles of sound administration into daily use. As with the catalytic approach, theory-based confrontation recognizes that pluralistic ignorance through lack of shared data and perception may be a problem, but it may see the cause of the problem as the misuse of authority. Therefore, its approach to solving the perceptual problem is to resolve authority issues as a prior condition. As with the prescriptive approach, theory-based confrontation acknowledges that expert judgment may be essential for solving certain problems. But it avoids the unilateral exercise of authority in bringing a prescription into use through earning the involvement and commitment of participants. Thus theory-based confrontation subsumes the diagnoses that lead to acceptant, catalytic, and prescriptive approaches and permits these diagnoses to be seen in a new and different light. It holds that attempts to solve problems without resolving the administrative leadership issues that are their cause are unlikely to contribute to the genuine pursuit of excellence.

How These Theories Can Be Used. The use of theories pertinent for solving everyday kinds of problems blossomed after World War II as academicians, researchers, and practitioners alike began to learn how to use theories for problem-solving purposes. The approach is contrary to the classical teacher and classroom model of didactic instruction in which concepts are presented and evaluated with no regard as to how these concepts apply to the individual. Instead the administrators test their own assumptions, beliefs, and values against systematic theories to learn how theories predict their own behavior. In other words, administrators become experts in how the theories apply to themselves as administrators.

What caused this shift toward the actual use of theory? There are many explanations, including these: (1) Techniques for "internalization" of theory. In ordinary classroom learning, the teacher may tell a student how things should be while giving little insight as to how the desired conditions can be achieved. The current difference is a distinction between theory taught in the abstract and theory learned by the client and internalized for applied use as the basis for practice. Internalization permits the client to actually apply the theory to given situations and thus to test such theories against more characteristic ways of thinking—trial and error, hunch and intuition, and so on. In this way, poor practices can be replaced with better ones. (2) Strategies for helping a client understand theory sufficiently to be able to apply it in given situations are different from traditional classroom methods. These learning strategies involve several fairly basic steps. The following steps are quite widely employed by theory-oriented consultants in assisting clients to shift their thinking to a theoretical basis.

Step 1: The client is presented with some typical situations likely to be encountered in daily activities. Reactions, either written or acted out, are called for; such reactions define "natural" responses. This activity is completed before any theory is introduced.

Step 2: The client then studies pertinent theories of behavior, either through a textbook or lecture approach, by the use of audio cassettes, or by viewing a movie that introduces the theoretical orientation. Questions and test examples are provided to enable the client to check his or her understanding of theory.

Step 3: The client participates in simulated problem situations where "best" solutions can be reached by using theories learned in Step 2.

Step 4: Post-simulation critiques enable the client to evaluate the degree to which the theories are understood and how

effectively they were applied. These critiques also help to identify any inaccurate assumptions that may have been made and
any limitations in the theory itself.

Step 5: Through an additional series of simulations, the
client is repeatedly provided with the opportunity to compare
"natural" reactions to situations against theoretical specifications. By such self-confrontations the client comes to understand theory in a personally useful way and recognizes the
extent to which second-nature assumptions take over when
pressure for action is present. Confidence is built and the client
comes to appreciate one use of theory when applied in an effective manner.

Step 6: When theories have been internalized, further
practice is provided to enable the client to perfect the capacity
to identify and execute actions and practices that the theory
requires for breaking out of self-defeating cycles.

Step 7: Theory is then employed to reevaluate how to
solve problems in comparison with the natural inclinations revealed in Step 1.

Step 8: Generalizations regarding natural bent are further
clarified and differentiated to prevent the client from slipping
back into habitual ways of responding. This step further equips
the client for approaching new situations that can be handled
from a theory-based perspective.

Step 9: Consultant support and implementation for using
a theory-based approach as the foundation for everyday academic administration are available to assist the change from intuition and common sense to a theory-based approach to problem
solving.

Though educational tactics vary, these steps are helpful in
bringing a theory into use in guiding daily administrative practices. Without them, theory remains hypothetical and irrelevant
to solving real-life problems of administration. Successful theory intervention is likely to include each of these basic steps.
Some organization development uses of theory, however, bypass significant elements of this internalization process with the
result that the theory is rejected by the client because it has not
been applied practically. The acceptant, catalytic, and prescrip-

tive approaches bypass this educational step of learning theories and principles of behavior and inevitably remain at the commonsense level.

There are a number of reasons why behavioral theory approaches to administration are such powerful aids to changing behavior toward improvement along personal and team dimensions. One is that theories can be written out and can then be tested for their validity in predicting consequences—consequences that become discernible through research and experimental evidence and thus qualify as "objective" in the sense of being based on external proof. Their authority, in other words, is derived from empirical evidence. Persons engaged in theory-based organization development use these models to observe their own conduct and to predict its consequences instead of engaging in intuition-oriented exchanges. Theory aids behavior changes in the following ways:

1. Theory, with its explicit formulations, brings individuals face-to-face with their subjective *values*.
2. Theory-based understanding of personal modes of managing and the consequences of them reduces or eliminates *defensiveness* since a person can now see that what he or she previously took for granted as "right" or "sound" or "valid" is untenable.
3. Theory provides individuals with *perspective* through supplying a social microscope for seeing what is actually going on in the present, as well as a social telescope for seeing how the past and possible future are affecting here-and-now behavior.
4. Theory-based language enables people to *communicate* with their subordinates, colleagues, and bosses in definite, mutually understood terms as to the best approaches for getting results through people.
5. A model of excellence can be designated by theory that makes it possible for a person to see what is possible and to strengthen the *motivation* to want to do better.
6. *Creativity* is stimulated when theory aids people to be more curious and more imaginative in pursuing solutions to managerial problems.

7. An individual's capacity for self-direction and *autonomy* can be increased by theory because it becomes less necessary to consult with others when a person can consult with himself as to the implications of the various actions being considered.
8. Theory specifications for sound team management provide criteria for evaluating whether or not *teamwork* is synergistic in the sense that the different perspectives that administrators apply to complex problems and the clash of ideas that discussions can produce may result in a solution that is better than any one person or group might have developed. As a result, $1 + 1 = 3$.

The above are general statements as to why theory is an important basis of intervention. But not all theories are of equal significance. Some are overly simple in the sense that they use so few categories that dissimilar behaviors are artificially grouped together; the predictive value of these theories then becomes severely limited. Others are so elaborate that people lose their way in attempting to understand them, and as a result dismiss theory as "academic" and therefore irrelevant. For still other "theories" are little more than philosophical speculations as to the nature of man. To serve as an adequate basis for organization development, a theory must show how to overcome whatever problems of effectiveness are barriers to organizational achievement; and such theory, combining high concern for people with high concern for institutional performance, underlies the 9,9 approach to administration.

Conclusion

The 9,9 orientation to academic administration is relatively rare in today's academic institutions, compared to 1,1, 1,9, 5,5, 9,1, and paternal/maternal orientations. Yet it is the soundest approach to university management. With it, principles of behavior become the basis for administrative action. Administrators become motivated to contribute in a way that makes a difference to the institution. They make themselves open to all points of view, resolve conflicts by confrontation of their causes, reward contributions on the basis of merit, and use other strategies stemming from behavioral science principles.

The 9,9 orientation results in valid decisions based upon strongly held and openly expressed convictions. It is the approach in which emotions are least likely to clog the wheels of administrative decision making or institutional achievement. And effort is most likely to be aroused in the direction of pursuing stated institutional objectives.

The extensive independent validation of this approach to administration in other disciplines, as illustrated in the Appendix, offers considerable confidence that the approach is sound for conducting university affairs. A university that moves in the direction of 9,9 administration may witness improvements on at least four criteria for evaluating the impact of different strategies of organization development:

The first criterion is productivity, whether measured directly by indicators that are easily quantifiable, such as numbers of research publications or rate of attrition of faculty members, or indirectly by indicators of educational quality or numbers of grievance complaints. In the final analysis, it is the character of how people work with and through one another that results in a university's level of performance, and only a 9,9 orientation emphasizes high concern for people as well as for performance.

The second criterion is creativity, that is, finding new things to do or discovering new ways to do existing things. The exceptionally brilliant person is able to bring forth many unique and innovative ideas, but everyone can be creative to some extent when the environment is right—when openness of communication and candor produce synergistic effects that mobilize the creative resources of individuals.

A third criterion is satisfaction—in particular, the degree of satisfaction derived as a result of membership in an organization. If a person finds little satisfaction from work, it is unlikely that his or her contribution to the institution will be as great as if work were a major source of personal satisfaction.

A fourth criterion is mental and physical health. We know that modern industrial societies are plagued by what are called diseases of civilization—diseases such as heart attacks, asthma, ulcer, cancer, and hypertension that were rare in earlier periods and even now are rare in so-called "primitive" societies. These diseases seem related to personal stress; and if stress is produced as a result of institutional maladministration, then better management such as the 9,9 style can be expected to have an impact on health through reducing stress. Being under less stress, individuals may not only be more effective in their work but may be less vulnerable to these diseases. Even if assessments of the impact of administrative styles on the health of institutional members may be difficult to make, indirect evidence of the benefits of the 9,9 approach may be gained from such indicators as absenteeism and amount of sick leave.

The time is ripe for universities to apply to themselves the vast knowledge they possess of how excellence can be achieved. Granted that tremendous pressures are exerted today by groups seeking to control universities, it is still possible for these institutions to do more than merely react to pressure. They can assume leadership and control over their own destinies. The answer to external pressure lies in improving the exercise of administrative authority and power so that university programs of teaching, research, and service achieve their goals in a truly excellent manner. The first step requires, as Chapter Ten explained, that top administrators honestly think through their own administrative assumptions and motivations, recognize their current Grid style, observe how their own values find expression in their daily practice of administration, and then begin to take positive action toward implementing the 9,9 value system. Effective administrative leadership can be restored through this value system and an organization developmental effort that is theory-based, led from the top, and carried out by the line administration. Without this system and approach, there is no realistic prospect of bringing the present erosive trends against the university under control, to say nothing of reversing them. With this system and approach, it is possible to

Leadership

Theories of leadership that attributed effective leadership strictly to particular traits or properties of individuals, such as intelligence or achievement motivation, have been superseded by theories that stress relationships among individuals and between leaders and their environment. Three different kinds of these relationship models warrant discussion here. The first is premised on a "monistic" or "subtractive" relationship between a superior and subordinates, usually in terms of sharing power. The second presumes a "dualistic" relationship that allows addition or subtraction between two independent variables, one dealing with control and the other with social-emotional aspects of relationships between a superior and subordinate. The third, of which the Grid is an example, is based on "integrative" interaction between interdependent variables. The differences among these three models are of great importance in analyzing leadership theory and practice in a systematic and valid way.

Monistic or Subtractive Models of Leadership. The Tannenbaum-Schmidt leadership behavior continuum (1958) exemplifies the monistic or subtractive formulation of the exercise of leadership. This continuum extends from boss-centered control at one extreme to subordinate-centered control at the other. Its basic premise is that the boss has 100 percent of the ability to exercise authority but the actual exercise of authority by the boss is reduced when subordinates influence decision making. It is a subtractive concept of leadership because power exercised by the boss is inversely related to the freedom or participation of the subordinate. The boss-centered administrator exercises authority and gives subordinates no freedom, but when the subordinate-centered leader permits subordinates freedom to function within defined limits, his or her capacity to influence events is automatically reduced. In other words, it is a theory of leadership based on one continuum—the amount of authority exercised by the boss.

A similar approach is that of Fiedler (Fiedler, 1967; Fiedler, Chemers, and Mahar, 1976), who uses a continuum to define two leadership positions. At one end is the human relations-oriented leader; at the other is the task-oriented leader. These are equivalent to the 1,9 and 9,1 Grid orientations, although defined by a measure derived from a questionnaire in which an individual describes the co-worker whom he least prefers in order to determine his own individual leadership style. An individual who describes his least preferred co-worker ("LPC") in relatively favorable terms receives a high LPC score and tends to be considerate, permissive, and oriented toward human relations —typical of the 1,9 approach. At the opposite extreme is the person who describes his least preferred co-worker in more unfavorable ways—thereby getting a low LPC score—and who tends to be task-centered, to manage closely, and to be less concerned with human relations—in other words, the 9,1 orientation. In research contrasting these two leadership styles, Fiedler has found that neither is superior to the other in terms of producing results and that either can be effective under certain circumstances. He thus concludes that the degree of effectiveness of the two styles depends upon the favorableness of the situation. His theory is a subtractive model since it permits variations in the range of behavior from 1,9 to 9,1 but eliminates from consideration other leadership styles such as 9,9, paternalism/ maternalism, 5,5, and 1,1. It is therefore unnecessary to agree with Fiedler that there is no one best way to manage when all but two leadership styles have been excluded from evaluation by the character of his theory and research design.

Dualistic or Arithmetic Models of Leadership. Dualistic models are exemplified by the Ohio State Leadership studies, most significantly in the work of Fleishman (1953, 1973), which represents leadership behavior as a summation of two magnitudes. One dimension, "initiating structure," is similar in concept to the Grid's dimension of concern for institutional performance. The other dimension, "social-emotional support" or "consideration," is similar in concept to concern for people. In this dualistic system, two different and unconnected measures of behavior are used to determine a person's leadership style, that is, he or she receives one score on initiating structure and a second score on consideration. Thus, the two dimensions result in an arithmetic concept of leadership. The leadership style defined by high initiating structure *plus* high consideration is equivalent to paternalism/maternalism in Grid theory, or 9 + 9 because it reflects the 9 of control from the 9,1 Grid style added to the 9 of consideration of the 1,9 approach. Thus, in this arithmetic model of leadership the possibility of a 9,9 formulation is eliminated, since by definition there is no basis of interaction or integration between the two variables; only addition or subtraction. The fact that high scores on initiating structure and social-emotional support yield paternalism/maternalism rather than a 9,9 orientation explains why Korman's 1966 study of research on the Ohio State dimensions of leadership failed to demonstrate paternalism/maternalism as the single best style across a range of situations: it casts no light on the soundness of other theories of leadership such as 9,9 or 5,5 since they are unmeasurable within the Ohio State arithmetic mode of concept formation.

The situational approach to leadership as described by Hersey and Blanchard (1977) is also a dualistic or arithmetic model similar to the Ohio State model since it uses the same two axes and combines them in an arithmetic way. Thus a 9,9 orientation is impossible within their system because when the 9 of task behavior—high control of other persons, telling them by one-way communication what to do and when, where, and how to do it—is combined with the 9 of social-emotional support—as in showing acceptance by being interested and listening —the resultant combination is paternalism/maternalism, not the 9,9 orientation.

Another variation on the arithmetic model is the Leary cross (1957) of X and Y axes. Leary's X axis ranges from hostility at one end point through neutrality to affection at the other end. The Y axis ranges from one end point of dominance through neutrality to the other end of submissiveness. Both axes intersect at neutrality. Using this formulation, Leary describes the quadrants as combinations of two variables. This arithmetic formulation of the connection between two dualistic or independent variables not only results in a neutral midpoint, which eliminates the 5,5 orientation as a leadership style, but also results in the combination of domination and affection in

paternalism/maternalism. Lefton's use of the Leary cross (Buzzotta, Lefton, and Sherberg, 1972) suffers the same basic weaknesses from a conceptual point of view, that is, no 5,5 or 9,9
orientations, and in addition Lefton incorrectly describes the
combination of domination and affection as the 9,9 orientation
of the Grid.

Another arithmetic theory, that of Spence and Helmreich
(1978), involves the two variables of masculinity and femininity. Many individuals are described as appropriately sex typed,
that is, high on one variable and low on the other as either
"masculine" or "feminine," yet others are best characterized as
androgynous—either high in both masculine and feminine characteristics, or low in both and thereby "undifferentiated." However, Spence and Helmreich also include a masculinity-feminin-
ity scale which is subtractive in nature, in that it ranges from
masculine traits on one end to feminine on the other. Thus their
data suggest that the combination of both dualistic and monistic measures yields the greatest predictability of behavior.

Integrative Models Based on Interdependent Variables.
The Grid (Blake and Mouton, 1978) is an example of the integrative model of concept formation. Its two dimensions, concern for performance or production and concern for people,
are indispensable for characterizing the exercise of leadership because both variables must be present in some degree before the
exercise of leadership is possible. Placing these variables at right
angles to each other permits any magnitude in one dimension to
be described in relation to any magnitude of the other, and the
point of any X,Y intersection denotes the *interaction* of the
two dimensions. The commas between the two magnitudes define the interaction between the variables, as is standard in
systems that employ Cartesian coordinates.

An analogy from chemistry to the interactive relationship
between these two Grid variables is that of a chemical compound in contrast to a mixture of two elements. In a compound
such as H_2O, the resultant liquid has a different character than
the gaseous elements that compose it, whereas two elements
that are mixed together retain their distinctive character. The
two Grid variables of concern for performance and concern for

people are abstractions useful for conceptual analysis of leadership, but people exercising leadership do not think in terms of one axis and then the other. Rather, their thought process is unitary in character. This model of how the mind works is consistent with experimental literature related to the psychology of cognition. Its importance for analyzing leadership behavior can be seen by the difference between the 1,9 and the 9,9 Grid styles in terms of what the second 9 represents in these two contexts. The 9,9 concern for people in the context of high concern for performance is a very different way of thinking about people than it is in the context of low concern for performance, as in the 1,9 orientation. In the 9,9 Grid style, the second 9 stands for openness, respect, learning, involvement, and resolving conflict by confrontation in the interest of achieving mutually agreed-on productive outcomes. In the 1,9 Grid style, the second 9 stands for sweetness, fawning, and yielding one's convictions for the sake of harmony and warmth even in disregard of adverse impact on productivity. Both 9s are of the same *magnitude* of concern. Their differences result from their interactional context.

The third dimension involving the Grid, introduced in Chapter Two, is a bipolar system useful in differentiating the motivations that underlie each major Grid style. As with the interaction of the other two variables, so with this third dimension. The + of the 9,9 orientation is of the same intensity as the + of the 1,9 style but the character of these positive motivations is vastly different. The concept of motivation represents another useful abstraction in analyzing leadership, but it too should be regarded as an aspect of a unitary process.

Two models that attempt to introduce a different third dimension, designated "effectiveness," to a Grid-like structure have been presented by Reddin (1970) and Hersey and Blanchard (1977). The difficulty inherent in these models is that they confuse dependent and independent variables, with both becoming aspects of the theory. Because effectiveness should be treated conceptually as the empirical outcome the theory is designed to predict, the Reddin and the Hersey and Blanchard models violate a basic consideration in systematic theory building. In addition, effectiveness as a third dimension results in a logical as well as an empirical fallacy. It requires demonstration of the conditions under which 1,1 or 1,9 orientations, for example, are effective in achieving institutional performance with and through others. There simply is no sense in which a 1 in a 9-point system, or low orientation to achieving performance, can be effective. This critical limitation in logic applies to both the Reddin and the Hersey and Blanchard models.

Contingency Approaches Versus One Best Way. Theories which are subtractive or arithmetic in character lead to the conclusion that there is no one best way to lead and that any style of leadership is best determined by the situation. These result in the contingency approaches to leadership exemplified by Fiedler and by Hersey and Blanchard.

The opposite conclusion is reached by other theorists. McGregor (1960) holds that Theory Y leadership is more effective than Theory X. Likert (1967) proposes that System 4 is the soundest approach as opposed to Systems 1, 2, or 3. Argyris and Schön (1974) contend that Model II behavior is a more effective basis for relationships than Model I. And Blake and Mouton (1978) maintain that the 9,9 Grid style is a more effective leadership orientation than other Grid styles. The Likert, Argyris, and Blake and Mouton conclusions are supported by substantial research.

The issue of versatility in employing these approaches leads to a distinction between strategy and tactics. The question is, "How can a consistent or all-purpose style which is best for all situations be applied in an effective way when obviously there are individual differences among leaders that are legitimately characterized as being equally effective?" This apparent contradiction can be resolved by an example (Blake and Mouton, 1981): An individual employs a 9,9 administrative orientation when he or she understands behavioral science principles and uses them in a consistent way as the basis for achieving institutional performance with and through people. But versatility is involved in applying the *same principles* under varying conditions, situations, or circumstances. In other words, the strategy of exercising leadership remains consistent with behavioral science principles, but how this strategy is applied in specific situations is tactical, depending on circumstances themselves. This is versatile leadership in that a leader can apply the principle in an appropriate manner to a particular situation. In contrast, the premise behind contingency theories such as those of Fiedler or Hersey and Blanchard leads to the concept of flexibility, whereby tactics become all-important and where commonsense assumptions replace behavioral science principles in attempting to deal with given situations.

The constancy of principle applied in a technically sound manner can be illustrated by the principle "management by objectives." In situational management such as proposed by Hersey and Blanchard, a flexibility-oriented boss sets no goals with an immature subordinate but simply gives specific directions without any interaction about what, where, when, and how to do a task. The idea of jointly setting goals is not even considered until the subordinate reaches a higher level of maturity. In contrast, a versatility-oriented manager sets goals with an immature subordinate, but these goals are near term, attainable within an hour, day, week, or month, and concerned with accomplishing simple tasks. As the subordinate's maturity increases, the time frame of goal setting is extended and the tasks become more complex. At highest levels of maturity, the time frame may be indeterminate and the tasks to be accomplished of unknown difficulty. In other words, for the versatile manager, the principle that the best way to organize and motivate subordinates is through setting goals with them remains constant as a strategy regardless of subordinate maturity. What is dealt with in tactical terms is relating the goal difficulty and the length of time frame in which goal attainment is conceived to the skill and maturity of subordinates.

Another example of the versatile administrator's concern with applying a given and sound principle in appropriate ways depending on the situation involves differences of opinion. In dealing with a new employee, one handles discrepancies in opinion that might lead to conflict in a far different manner than conflict arising with a long-term employee. For instance, the administrator might first examine with the new subordinate the events leading to their differences. In this way causes can be identified that otherwise both of them might fail to recognize, or each take for granted that the other understands. By comparison, a long-term employee understands the activity being undertaken quite well. It would be wasteful to engage in the same tracking of antecedent events as is desirable with the new person. It is possible to come more quickly to the core of the differences and to explore the causes that are likely to explain its origin. In both cases the principle remains constant: the administrator relies on a confronting orientation as the basis for reaching a meeting of minds. But the application varies with the unique circumstances involved.

Behavioral Science Frameworks for Analyzing Effective and Ineffective Behavior. The original use of the Grid to analyze the interaction between significant variables of administration involved in achieving results with and through people occurred in our efforts as consultants to understand a basic conflict in a top management group. One faction of the group maintained, in effect, "If we don't put the pressure on for higher production, we're going to sink." The other contended, "We must ease up on the pressure and start treating people in a nicer way." Thus, a 9,1 orientation met a 1,9 orientation. This way of conceiving the problem as *either* production *or* people eliminated perception of other possibilities such as getting people involved in the importance of being more productive. But by treating these variables of production and people as interdependent yet interacting, we came to see many alternative ways of managing: not only 9,1 and 1,9 but also 1,1, 5,5, 9,9, paternalism/maternalism, counterbalancing, two-hat, statistical 5,5, and facade approaches as presented earlier.

A way of thinking about human relationships that permitted such clear comprehension and comparison of alternatives led us to believe this formulation to be of general significance for understanding other human relationships. Thus we evaluated in greater detail how other authors and researchers had dealt with the same kind of question. We found no systematic use of a two-dimensional geometric space as the foundation for conceptual analysis of assumptions about how to manage, but we were struck by the extent to which other behavioral scientists were using such a basis of analysis either implicitly or statistically. Theorists who used two variables implicitly, without identifying the variables involved, included Horney and Fromm. Other theorists who examined variables statistically, without explicitly analyzing how assumptions and therefore behavior may change as a function of the character of the interaction of these variables, included Likert and Fleishman.

Table 1 shows the various implicit and statistical approaches for comprehending leadership and human relationships that can be fitted into a Grid framework. As shown in Table 1, regardless of their field of specialization, and with but a few exceptions, all these investigators describe behavior as if relying on a two-dimensional framework. Factor analytic approaches have reinforced such conceptual analyses in that most meaningful variance in behavior can be accounted for by two factors. And because three-dimensional formulations have added little to understanding beyond that already available from the use of two, we conclude that a framework for analyzing behavior that results from two variables is a sound and sufficient basis for comprehending managerial assumptions and practices.

Leadership in Higher Education

The following sections of the Appendix examine leadership problems and styles in the literature specific to higher education. They include perspectives of investigators who have firsthand experience on the college campus but who may not be familiar with the Grid approach or other literature on leadership as summarized in the previous pages.

Problems of Academic Administration. Munitz (1976), Riesman (1978), and Dressel (1976) are among those who have charged that effective leadership is scarce or lacking in higher education. Munitz, himself a university chancellor (equivalent to a campus president), asks, "Are we establishing a system that ultimately filters out some of the persons most capable of enhancing the quality and service of America's colleges and universities? Have we allowed conditions to evolve in this last decade that threaten the quality of leadership for higher education in the decade to come?" (p. 1).

Riesman (1978, p. 71) states that the struggles and difficulties of administration in academe have made able candidates for the presidency unwilling to serve, and thus there is a lack of strong and visionary leadership. Instead "many institutions wind up with conciliatory, faceless presidents, incapable either of vision or of the imaginative kind of planning required. . . ." He also sees structural factors in the social context, as well as in the universities, as problematic. He discusses the increase in and the changing composition of the student body, federal support for education along with the complex funding mechanisms of the federal bureaucracy, competing interests of students, staff, and faculty, lack of planning on a national level, a decline in the preparation of students (falling SATs), and a general "leveling" of quality as public campuses grow and multiply in terms of their impact on the administrative role. He summarizes, "The very nature of the office has changed; indeed, it may no longer be a job for an educator" (p. 61).

Dressel describes the difficulties of higher education management with a sociological formulation of the problem. He points to difficulties resulting from the structural peculiarities and complexities of organization design, decentralized governance patterns, protracted policy-setting mechanisms, ambiguity in the authority vested in positions, and the multitude of outside pressures with which administrators must contend. His summary of these difficulties as well as Cohen and March's text (1974) are useful overviews for the reader with inside knowledge of campus life. In addition, Bennis (1976) and Mooney (1965) discuss the problems of leadership in the university and the difficulties academic leaders have in leading. Kleiman (1976) reviews issues related to the public confidence of leaders in education. Hill and French (1967) discuss the leader as a representative. Anderson (1966) and Hagstrom (1964) cover leadership and teamwork. Jencks and Riesman (1977), Henry (1975), Handlin and Handlin (1970), and Rudolph (1965) provide historical perspective on college administration, while Hodgkinson (1979) projects "future history" by forecasting what the histor-

Table 1. Approaches to Leadership and Human Relationships by Grid Categories

Investigator	Source	Field	9,1	1,9	1,1	5,5	9,9	Statistical 5.5	Facades	Paternalism/Maternalism	Other
Argyris, C.	*Management and Organizational Development: The Path from XA to YB.* New York: McGraw-Hill, 1971.	Organization Behavior	xi, xii, 6-15, 66-70. 73-74, 77-78, 85-88 105, 107, 134, 135, 138-140			13-14, 30-34, 56-57	xi, 15-20, 21-22, 24 42, 57-61, 67-70, 85-89		19	3,62	
Argyris, C. & Schon, D.A.	*Theory in Practice: Increasing Professional Effectiveness.* San Francisco: Jossey-Bass, 1974.	Business Administration	66-84 101-102, 104, 105-106, 107-108, 149-155				85-95, 101, 102-104, 105, 106-107, 108-109				
Arkava, M.L.	*Behavior Modification: A Procedural Guide for Social Workers.* Missoula: U of Montana, 1974	Social Work	16-66					1-11		1-82	
Bach, G.R. & Wyden, P.	*The Intimate Enemy.* New York: William Morrow and Company, Inc., 1969.	Psychology	8-9, 45-46, 48-49, 71-73, 75, 83, 109-117, 129, 141-150, 256-257, 311, 312, 314	5, 48, 71-73, 84-85, 97, 102-108, 311, 314, 321-322	31-32, 312	5, 53-54, 135-136	36, 43 53, 91 119-123, 137, 161-165, 257-258, 343-348		7, 10, 13, 19, 36, 103, 120, 159, 196-197, 222-223, 253-254	113	Sick 9,1 112-113, 151, 158, 160, 260, 331 Distorted 1,9:75, 112, 154, 158, 160, 260, 331 Change 173-174

Bakan, D.	*Duality of Human Existence.* Boston: Beacon Press, 1966.	Philosophy; Social Psychology	14-15, 16-17	14-15, 188	192		14-15, 153				Psychosomatic 50,70, 124,156-164, 175,179-196 Androgynicity 108-109, 150-151 Suicide 130-131 Longevity 131,150-151 Sadism/masochism 167
Bales, R.F.	*Personality and Interpersonal Behavior.* New York: Holt, Rinehart & Winston, 1970.	Sociology	193-199, 213-219, 220-229, 230-237,	200-207, 252-257, 313-319, 320-326, 369-376	289-296, 332,339, 340-346, 347-353, 354-360, 361-368, 377-386	191, 258-264, 265-272, 327-331	208-212	190, 273-281,			Balance 5.5:191 Machiavellianism 238-241
Barber, J.D.	*The Presidential Character.* Englewood Cliffs, N.J.: Prentice-Hall, 1972.	Applied Politics Political Science	12-13,17-57,58-98, 99-142, 347-395, 413-442, 446-448	13,91, 173-206, 448-450	13,145-163,165, 166-167	170-173	12, 209-343, 452-454	79,86, 92-93	83	60,91	Two Hat: 86,87 Critique: 277-278, 331
Bell, G.D.	*The Achievers.* Chapel Hill, N.C.: Preston-Hill, Inc., 1973.	Business	23-38, 39-59, 132-152	73-83, 164-171	60-72, 153-163		104-124, 181-187		84-103, 172-180, 188-195		
Benne, K.D. & Sheats, P.	"Functional Roles of Group Members." *Journal of Social Issues* 4, no. 2 (1948): 41-49.	Clinical Psychology	45,46	44,45, 46	45	44	44		46		

Investigator	Source	Field	9,1	1,9	1,1	5,5	9,9	Statistical 5,5	Facades	Paternalism/Maternalism	Other
Bennett, D.	TA and the Manager. New York: AMACON, 1976.	Business Consultant	14,19,26-27,30-32, 122,145 146-150, 161-162, 164-165, 230	14,26-27,32, 122,160-161,168-170,230-231	79,80, 145, 153,154, 160-161	18-19, 79-82, 129-137, 145,150-153	26-27, 81,82, 83,139-140,145, 154-157, 178,194-196,230		81,82, 91-116	231	Dom/Backup: 151-152, 181 Wide Arc: 230
Berne, E.	Games People Play. New York: Grove Press, 1964.	Psychiatry	27,112, 113	25-26			27, 178-179, 180-181, 182-183, 184		48-168		
Biestek, F.P.	The Casework Relationship. Chicago: Loyola U Press, 1957	Social Work	106-107	33-47	108	48-66	67-99, 100-119	23-32			
Bion, W.R.	Experiences in Groups. New York: Basic Books, 1959.	Psychoanalysis	152-153	147-150	152-153	150-152	156-158, 169				Dom/Backup: 160-165
Blake, R.R. & Mouton, J.S.	The Grid for Sales Excellence: Benchmarks for Effective Salesmanship. New York: McGraw-Hill, 1970.	Social Psychology	45-58	59-69	70-79	80-94	95-118	187	125-136	188	Dom/Backup: 13-15
Blake, R.R. & Mouton, J.S.	The Grid for Supervisory Effectiveness. Austin: Scientific Methods, Inc., 1975.	Social Psychology	11-28	29-43	44-58	59-78	79-107				Dom/Backup: 8-9

Citation	Field	16-40	41-57	58-74	75-94	95-120	85,126-128	14,15, 37,54-55,73-74,89,90,114	34,53, 121,164	Dominant/backup 60, 205-207 Flexibility vs. Versatility 128,130
Blake, R.R. & Mouton, J.S. *The New Managerial Grid.* Houston: Gulf, 1978.	Social Psychology									
Branden, N. *The Psychology of Self-Esteem.* New York: Bantam Books, 1969.	Psychiatry	188-190	150,151	194-195	185-188	109-139, 146				
Burns, T. & Stalker, G.M. *The Management of Innovation.* New York: Barnes & Noble, Social Science Paperbacks, 1961.	Organization Behavior	96-125				96-125				
Buzzotta, V.R., Lefton, R.E., Sherberg, M. *Effective Selling Through Psychology: Dimensional Sales and Sales Management Strategies.* New York: Wiley Interscience, 1972.	Clinical Psychology	36-53, 99-100a, 120-121, 127,264-270,285-286,301-318,319, 320-324, 338-339, 344-347, 357-358, 358-359	68-82, 99-100a, 122,124, 127,274-277,287-288,301-318,319, 327-331, 340-341, 344-347, 358,359	54-67, 99-100a, 121,122, 127,270-274,286-287,301-318,319, 324,327, 339-340, 344-347, 358,359		83,98, 99-100a, 124,125, 127,199-224,277-283,288-289,301-318,319, 331-334, 341-343, 344-347, 358,359-360		113-117, 291-292		Dom/Backup: 101-112, 289-291
Durkheim, E. "On Anomie." In C.W. Mills, ed. *Images of Man: The Classic Tradition in Sociological Thinking.* New York: George Braziller, Inc., 1960, pp. 449-485.	Sociology	455-461	460	460-461	449-461					

Investigator	Source	Field	9.1	1.9	1.1	5.5	9.9	Statistical 5,5	Facades	Paternalism/Maternalism	Other
Etzioni, A.	*A Comparative Analysis of Complex Organizations.* (Rev. ed.). New York: Free Press, 1975.	Sociology	xxiv,5-6, 8,12,15 27-31,56-59,60-61, 66-67,75-82,84,106, 115,116-118,133, 287,455-460,471, 479,486-490,500-504		28,289	xxiv,5-6 6-8,12, 15,40-54, 56-59,61-72,78,81-82,89,92, 106,114-117,169, 305-311, 426-427, 455-460, 471,479 486-490 500-504	471	433-436, 437-438		xxiv,5, 6-8,12, 15,31-39, 62-67,72-75,78-82, 84-87,89, 106,112-113,116, 271,389-391,426-427,455-460,471, 479,486-490,500-504	Machiavellianism: 387
Fiedler, F.E.	*A Theory of Leadership Effectiveness.* New York: McGraw-Hill, 1967.	Industrial Psychology	12,45, 105,114-115,120, 147,156, 169,180, 182-185, 194-196, 203,209, 232,233, 234,254	12,45, 79,94, 96,101, 104-105, 114-115, 120,142-143,147, 156,169, 180,182-185,194-196,201-202,208-209,230, 232,233, 254		102,255, 265				6,12, 29-30	Contingency theory or situationalism (flexibility) 13,32-33,80, 142,145-148, 151,247-248, 254-260,261 Teamwork 18-19

Fiedler, F.E., Chemers, M.M., & Mahar, L.	*Improving Leadership Effectiveness: The Leader Match Concept.* New York: John Wiley, 1976.	Industrial Psychology	9,11, 12,17, 18,134, 135,136, 178,179, 181	9,10, 11,15, 16,19, 20,134, 135,136, 153,154, 177,179, 181		11,21, 136,181					
Fleishman, E.A.	"Twenty Years of Consideration and Structure." In E.A. Fleishman and J.G. Hunt, eds., *Current Developments in the Study of Leadership.* Carbondale: Southern Illinois University Press, 1973. pp. 1-40.	Industrial Psychology	25-26, 26-27, 29,32	23,25, 26-27, 29	26-27, 29,32, 36,37	29	23-24, 24-25, 26-27, 27-29, 32,35, 37	37			
Fromm, E.	*The Art of Loving.* London: Unwin Books, 1957.	Psychiatry	23,25, 31,43, 54-55	9,23,25, 42-43, 55-56	15-16, 23,83-84	10-11, 18-22, 25,74-76,80	24,26-28,29, 42,53-54,87, 104-109			82-83	
Gordon, T.	*Leadership Effectiveness Training L.E.T.* New York: Peter H. Wyden, 1977.	Counseling Psychology	6,150-152,257	6,94, 153-155	165	6,19-21, 42-43, 193,198				8,37-38, 156-158, 174-175	Resistance to change 37 Teamwork 40-44 Active Listening 56-91,258 Psychosomatic 168-169,257 Dominant backup 205-206

Investigator	Source	Field	9,1	1,9	1,1	5,5	9,9	Statistical 5,5	Facades	Paternalism/Maternalism	Other
Gordon, T.	*Parent Effectiveness Training.* New York: Peter H. Wyden, 1970.	Counseling Psychology	10-11,41-44,83-86, 110,112-113,151, 152,153-159,174-183,195, 207,248, 260-261, 263,280, 321-322, 323-324, 325,326-327	11,13-14, 43-44, 151,152, 154-155, 159-161, 184,190-193,248, 251-253, 324-325, 326	44,152, 183,185, 327	42-43, 110,113, 184,289, 322,323, 324,325- 326,327	12,30-31,33, 47-61, 194-264, 280-282, 305-306	261-263	22-25	11,166, 168-169, 177-178, 190-191	Wide Arc: 11,161-163
Gordon, T.	*T.E.T.: Teacher Effectiveness Training.* New York: Peter H. Wyden, 1974.	Counseling Psychology	27-29,48-49,80-84, 84-85,86-87,184-185,186-189,191, 192-194, 198-206, 211-216	49,85-86, 184,186-188,189-190,191, 206-207	49,87, 206-207, 208-209	208	220-282			194-195, 213	Dom/Backup: 23-24 Wide Arc: 190-191
Hardman, D.G.	*Authority Monograph.* National Council on Crime & Delinquency	Social Work	219,245, 246,248	215-217, 219,249			249-255, 245-254	217,221, 247, 249-255			
Harrington, A.	*The Immortalist.* Millbrae, Calif. Celestial Arts, 1977.	Philosophy	114,117, 118,119, 123-127, 137,139		117,118, 129-130	100-101, 114-115, 117,118, 127-129	136-139		144-145	120-121	

Author	Title	Category									
Harris, T.A.	*I'm OK—You're OK.* New York: Avon, 1969.	Psychiatry	72-73, 263	67-69	69-71, 142-143, 152	143-146, 153	74-77, 151-152, 153.302-304		75-76, 146-151, 152.262-263		
Heath, R.	*The Reasonable Adventure.* Pittsburgh: The University of Pittsburgh Press, 1964.	Clinical Psychology	ix-x, xii 5-6,20-24,38,39 63-67	28-29		ix,xi,4-5,10-11, 14-20,37-38,39, 57-63	ix,x,7, 8-10, 30-36, 39	x.xii-xiii,6-7,24-28, 38,39, 67-69			
Hersey, P. & Blanchard, K.H.	*Management of Organizational Behavior: Utilizing Human Resources.* (3rd ed.) Englewood Cliffs, N.J.: Prentice-Hall, 1972.	Education	169,194-195,204-205,246-248,251,258-271,307-322	169,198	169,199-203	74-76				169,195-196,250-252,258-271,307-322	Machiavellianism: 92-93 Wide Arc: 125 Change: 149-171 Dominant/backup 234
Horney, K.	*Neurosis and Human Growth.* New York: W.W. Norton & Co., 1950.	Psychoanalysis	17-39,76,97,191-213,214-215,304-306,311-316	76-77.97-98,215-238,239-243,316-324	43-44,77-78,259-290,304,324-328			312-315			Dom/Backup: 232-234 Sick 9.1: 247-256 Distorted 1.9:243-256
Horney, K.	*The Neurotic Personality of Our Time.* New York: W.W. Norton & Co., 1937.	Psychoanalysis	39,81-82,98,162-187	36,85-87,96-98,102-161	99,191-192,212-213,237	28,96-97	104,107,108,109,113,163,273-274	100-101			Distorted 1.9:259-280
Horney, K.	*Self-Analysis.* New York: W.W. Norton & Co., 1942.	Psychoanalysis	44,47-48,56-57,57-58,58-59	54-55	48-52,55-56,57,58,59-60,62,108	58,108					Wide Arc: 44

Investigator	Source	Field	9,1	1,9	1,1	5,5	9,9	Statistical 5,5	Facades	Paternalism/Maternalism	Other
James, M.	*The OK Boss.* Reading, Mass.: Addison-Wesley, 1975.	Adult Education	10-11,16-17,20-21, 35,36,39, 40,54,55, 56,57,59, 61,62,75, 76,77, 131,139,	13, 18-19,37, 39-40,75	14-15, 35,55, 56,57-58,59-61,62, 75-76, 135, 139-140	19,37, 77,132, 144	17,21, 54,55, 56,57, 59,61, 62,69, 76-77, 132-133, 139, 144-145, 161-163	27,38,64,	106-121, 124-127	12-13, 35,36, 39,73-75	Dom/Backup: 8-9
James, M. & Jongeward, D.	*Born To Win: Transactional Analysis with Gestalt Experiments.* Reading, Mass.: Addison-Wesley, 1971.	Education	18,36,68-100,101-126,230	18,37, 127-159, 230-231	37,50, 56-57	18,57-58, 58-59, 224-226	18,36, 56-62, 235-238, 263-274	2-3, 227-228	29-35, 58	86, 229-230	
Jennings, E.E.	*The Executive: Autocrat, Bureaucrat, Democrat.* New York: Harper & Row, 1962.	Business Education	2,4,20-21,25,66-70,75-77, 83-86,86-90,114-163			2,4,90-91,91-97, 105-106, 164-195, 228-232	2-3,4, 59-61, 97-106, 196-234	77-80, 256-266	85,250	25-26, 149, 157-160	Dom/Backup: 117
Jung, C.G.	*Psychological Types.* Princeton: Princeton University Press, 1971.	Psychiatry	346-354, 383-387		385-386, 388-391, 395-398, 401-403, 403-405	334-335, 354-355, 356-359, 363-366		368-370	384		Dom/Backup: 355-356, 362-363, 405-407

Author	Title	Subject									
Kangas, J.A. & Solomon, G.H.	*The Psychology of Strength.* Englewood Cliffs, N.J.: Prentice-Hall, 1975.	Psychology	7-9,10-11, 14,15-17, 55-56, 56-57, 135-136	18-19,22, 24,78	20-21, 21-22, 23	11-12, 19, 57-58	3,9,12, 21,23- 24,24- 25,68- 69,117, 130-135, 136-141, 142-145, 146-150, 151-168	26-27	13-14,17- 18,19-20, 24-25,29- 30,56,77		Wide Arc: 136
Kovar, L.C.	*Faces of the Adolescent Girl.* Englewood Cliffs, N.J.: Prentice-Hall, 1968.	Adolescent Psychology	11-12, 73-83, 103-106	9-10, 53-68	79	10-11, 35-51, 83, 148-149	4-9, 107-125, 148-149				
Kunkel, F.M. & Dickerson, R.E.	*How Character Develops: A Psychological Interpretation.* New York: Charles Scribner & Sons, 1946.	Psychology	68-81	60-67	80-82		125-140, 157-159, 176-178				
Leary, T.	*Interpersonal Diagnosis of Personality.* New York: Ronald Press, 1957.	Clinical Psychology	19,64-65, 104,105, 135,137, 233,269- 281,324- 331,332- 340	64-65, 104,105, 135,233, 292-302, 303-314	19,23-24, 64-65,95- 96,104, 105,135, 233,282- 291	19,64-65, 135,202- 203,233, 315-322	65		181-186, 188-191, 282-283, 284-285, 316,317, 318,324, 325,326	64-65, 93	Dom/Backup: 225-227 Distorted 1,9-284- 286,288- 289,367 Sick 9,1: 341-350, 364,372
Likert, R.	*The Human Organization: Its Management and Value.* New York: McGraw-Hill, 1967.	Organization Behavior	3-12, 13-46			3-12, 13-46	3-12, 13-46, 47-100			3-12, 13-46	

Investigator	Source	Field	9.1	1.9	1.1	5.5	9.9	Statistical 5,5	Facades	Paternalism/Maternalism	Other
Likert, R. & Likert, J.G.	New Ways of Managing Conflict. New York: McGraw-Hill, 1976.	Organization Behavior	19-40, 59-69			19-40	16-17, 19-40, 49-51, 51-56, 71-324			19-40	
McClelland, D.C.	Power: The Inner Experience. New York: Irvington Publishers, 1975.	Individual Psychology	7-8,8-12, 13-21,27, 49-51,52-76,77-78, 249,252-254,255-256,257, 258,260-261,264, 266,274-275,295-297-324, 326,328	27,104-122,255, 264,274, 289,322-323,325, 328		27,155, 157-158, 249	27,257, 258,260-261,261-263,263-266,269, 288,301-302,324, 325,329		301-302	35-36, 142-144, 260,289-290	Distorted 1.9:102, 104 Sick 9,1: 255 OD:254, 255
McGregor, D.	The Human Side of Enterprise. New York: McGraw-Hill, 1960.	Psychology	33-43				45-57, 61-246				
McGregor, D.	The Professional Manager. New York: McGraw-Hill, 1967.	Psychology	59-63, 79-80, 117-118, 118-125, 136-137, 138-140, 148-149	59-63	59-63	59-63, 144-145	29-30, 59-63, 79-80, 118,127-130,130-133,140, 162-182, 191-195			7-10, 142-144	Dom/Backup: 60
Maccoby, M.	The Gamesman. New York: Simon & Schuster, 1976.	Psychiatry	34,47-48, 76-85, 181-182, 183-184, 187-189, 212-213	183-187	94	34,35, 46-47, 48,50-75,86-97,189-209	179,212, 213-217	100,149	48-49, 91,92-93,98-120,121-171	240-241	

Author	Title	Category									
May, R.	*Love and Will* New York: W.W. Norton & Co., 1969.	Clinical Psychology	45-48, 57-59, 276-278	278-279	27-33	40-45, 279	55-56, 91-92, 146,283-286,303-304,306, 310-311	66		153, 160-161	Wide Arc: 66 Change: 132-139, 194-204
Meininger, J.	*Success Through Transactional Analysis.* New York: New American Library, 1973.	Business Consultant	26-27, 28-29, 33,39-40,43-44,64-67,73-75,87-90,128-129	29-30, 34-36, 38,43-44,45-46,67-71,75-76,90-92,105-106,166-170,186-190	36,39-40,40-42,43-44,56-57,100-101,105-106,110-113,153, 157	30-31, 57-60, 76-77	26-27, 36-37, 63-64, 101,113-114,129-130,158-160,165-166,175-177,178-185,186-206		7-10,60-63,78-99, 106-109, 173-175		
Metcalf, H.C. & Urwick, L.	*Dynamic Administration: The Collected Papers of Mary Parker Follett:* New York: Harper & Bros., 1940.	Government and Administration	31,50-58, 96-101, 272-277			31-32,35, 210-213, 239	31, 33-49, 58-70, 111-116, 198-202		213-225, 240-246, 260-269, 279-281		
Missildine, W.H.	*Your Inner Child of the Past.* New York: Simon & Schuster, 1963.	Psychiatry	77,85-100,103, 106,108-109,125-126,130-133,138-139	77,133-136,157, 166,171-191,259-260,266-267,271-272	78-79, 101-103, 104-105, 107-108, 109-111, 121-124, 145-155, 156-159, 165-166, 166-167, 243-252, 254-259, 261						

Investigator	Source	Field	9.1	1.9	1.1	5.5	9.9	Statistical 5.5	Facades	Paternalism/Maternalism	Other
Missildine, W.H. & Galton, L.	*Your Inner Conflicts— How to Solve Them.* New York: Simon & Schuster, 1974.	Psychiatry	35-36,37, 38-39,39- 40,62,72- 74,76,77, 81-82, 83-86, 131-133, 145-146, 154-155, 171-172, 172-180, 187-191, 196-201, 205-207	36,37- 38,61, 76-77, 130	37,39, 53-59, 60,60- 61,62, 62-63, 77, 120-127, 157-160, 162-163, 184-187		33-34, 262-263, 308-313				
Moment, D. & Zaleznik, A.	*Role Development and Interpersonal Competence.* Boston: Harvard University Press, 1963.	Business Administration	20,38,56, 62-63,67, 72,77,80, 85-86,87- 88,89, 104-105, 122-123, 158-159, 160	20,39, 56,62- 63,67, 72,77, 78-79, 80,83, 86-87, 89, 105-106, 123-124, 159-160	20,36- 37,39, 56,62- 63,67, 72,80, 83,87, 89-90, 106-107, 124-125		19-20, 36-37, 38,41, 53,56, 62-63, 68,72, 77,80, 85,89, 104, 120-122				
Mouton, J.S. & Blake, R.R.	*The Marriage Grid* New York: McGraw-Hill, 1971.	Social Psychology	41-67	97-113	123-137	151-169	181-201	80-85	76-80	69-74	Dom/Backup: 15-17
Reddin, W.J.	*Managerial Effectiveness 3-D.* New York: McGraw-Hill, 1970.	Business Administration	27,28-29, 31-32,42, 47,73-74, 94-95, 161,177,	27,28-29, 31,42,68, 73,94, 194,215- 219	43,48, 54,194, 209-212, 258-259, 263,264,	27,28-29, 30-31,41, 42-43,48, 72-73, 93-94,	27,28- 29,32, 41,48, 74-75, 94,95,	52,53-54, 139-140, 149-150, 159-160, 169-178,		42,47	Dom/Backup: 46-47,48, 49,152 Change: 163,307

Author	Title	Discipline											
Reid, W. & Epstein, L.	Task-Centered Casework. New York: Columbia U Press, 1972.	Social Work	192,194, 194-195, 221-227, 262,263, 268-269	155-156			194,205-209,213, 231-233		192,194, 230-231, 233-234	181-185, 256-257			
Riesman, D., Glazer, N., & Denney, R.	The Lonely Crowd. Garden City, N.Y.: Doubleday & Co., 1953.	Sociology, Political Science, Economic History	23,28-32, 41,57-63		278,281	23,24-28, 33,34-40, 41-42, 63-74, 278	136-138	1-260	33,278, 282,286-298,328		302-305, 305-307	303	
Roberts, R.W. & Nee, R.H.	Theories of Social Casework. Chicago: U of Chicago Press, 1970	Social Work	181-218	33-75, 131-179					77-128, 313-351				
Schutz, W.C.	The Interpersonal Underworld (originally titled FIRO: A Three Dimensional Theory of Interpersonal Behavior). Palo Alto, Calif.: Science & Behavior Books, 1966.	Psychology	29,41,46, 47-48,89	31,36,41, 47,48,89	25-26, 28-29, 30-31, 41,42, 45-46, 47,48, 89		26-27		27,29-30,31, 37,41, 43,48, 87-89			43	Sick 9,1: 43 Distorted 1,9:42-43
Spence, J.T. & Helmreich, R.L.	Masculinity and Femininity. Austin, Texas: The University of Texas Press, 1978.	Psychology	21,23,27, 28,56,57, 67,75,82, 83,93,96, 109-129	21,23,27, 28,56,57, 67,82,83, 93,96, 109-129	21,23,27, 28,56,57, 67,82,83, 93,96, 109-129				21,23,27, 28,56,57, 67,82,83, 93,96, 109-129				

Investigator	Source	Field	9,1	1,9	1,1	5,5	9,9	Statistical 5,5	Facades	Paternal-ism/Mater-nalism	Other
Steiner, C.M.	*Scripts People Live: Transactional Analysis of Life Scripts.* New York: Bantam Books, 1974.	Therapy	53,54-46, 78-81, 115-119, 188-193, 197-198, 231-234, 236-237, 253-261	54,56, 76-78, 198-201, 211-213, 222-224	92-95, 115-119, 178-181, 218-220, 243-245		3,85-86, 352-361, 362-370, 382-383, 384		44-50, 121, 175-178, 304-305		Wide Arc: 39 Dom/Backup: 37-38
Tannenbaum, R. & Schmidt, W.H.	"How to Choose a Leadership Pattern." *Harvard Business Review.* 36(2), 1958, pp. 95-101.	Industrial Psychology	95,96,97, 98		95,96,97, 98	95,96,97, 98	95,98, 100,101		98		Flexibility (situational-ism) 99,101
Thomas, W.I. & Znaniecki, F.	"Three Types of Personality." In C.W. Mills, ed. *Images of Man: The Classic Tradition in Sociological Thinking.* New York: George Braziller, Inc., 1960, pp. 405-436.	Sociology	427			407-408, 409,411, 418-419, 421,423, 425,427, 428,434, 435-436	408,409, 411,418, 423,435, 436	408-409, 418,423, 433,435, 436		420	
Wheelis, A.	*The Quest for Identity.* New York: W.W. Norton & Co., 1958.	Psychiatry	18,85			18-19, 48-49, 85-89, 91-93, 126	19,20	85			

| White, R. & Lippitt, R. | "Leader Behavior and Member Reaction in Three 'Social Climates'." In D. Cartwright and A. Zander, eds., *Group Dynamics: Research and Theory.* (2nd ed.) Evanston, Ill.: Row, Peterson, & Co., 1960, pp. 527-553. | Social Psychology | 528-529, 529-532, 537,540-541,541-546,549-553 | | 528-529, 530,531, 533-534, 539-540, 549-552 | 528-529, 530,531, 532-538, 539-541, 546-549, 549-553 | | | | |

Source: "The Grid as a Comprehensive Framework for Analyzing Human Relationships." Austin, Texas: Scientific Methods, Inc., 1977.

ian will write about these problems in 1985, and Mood (1973) projects administrative issues into the year 2000.

Financial Difficulties. Many writers are now emphasizing financial difficulties as a central problem for present and future administrators. Inflation, unemployment, enrollment declines, loss of soft money for research, and similar trends are creating constraints. Glenny and others (1976) surveyed 1,227 administrators to gauge how they viewed the economic pressures and discuss adjustment strategies. Scott (1977) discusses the impact of retrenchment on middle level managers and gives advice on how to be a successful staff manager in a university, such as to develop forecasting, planning, and budgeting skills that will be sorely needed in a period of financial hardship. Bess and Lodahl (1969) also discuss the problems of middle managers in the university environment. Kemerer and Satryle (1977) discuss adaptation and financial decline. And to cope with the financial squeeze, Topping (1979) recommends considering the expansion of continuing education programs, increased tuitions, tuition insurance (wherein parents pay into a college tuition insurance program), more cooperative efforts between junior/ community and senior colleges, student retention efforts, better planning, and more clarity with regard to mission.

Others evaluating the impact of financial belt-tightening in higher education and some of the causes of these trends include Anderson, Bowman, and Tinto (1972), who discuss patterns of college attendance, accessibility, student migration, costs, and the relationship of student ability to access, among other issues related to college attendance and finance. Cohn (1979) and the Carnegie Foundation for the Advancement of Teaching (1975) also cover issues of higher education finance, cost, and related planning matters, as well as policy development. The latter text also provides enrollment projections for the years 1975 to 2000 and discusses the possibility of universal access to higher education by the year 2000.

Bowen's book (1977) is one of the most valuable texts on relating the cost of higher education to its benefits. Bowen discusses the goals of higher education with respect to individual goals and societal goals and relates efficiency and accountability to these goals. For example, he lists as *individual* outcomes cognitive learning, emotional and moral development, competence for citizenship, return in terms of economics, productivity, competence in family life, consumer behavior, leisure and health, and the value of education for the whole person. In terms of *societal* impact, he reviews higher education's contribution to social progress, social change, research and service, and human equality, and then discusses the issue of whether the economic return on the investment in higher education is worth it. Froomkin, Jamison, and Radner (1976) discuss educational productivity in terms of standard measures, whereas Heiss (1973) covers more innovative measures in reviewing the attempts of institutions to adjust to new demands and create alternatives to the dilemmas that face them.

Litigiousness in Society. Other authors identify the trend toward a litigious society as having a severe impact on universities as well as every other institution. For instance, Vago (1979, p. 42) says that "the sense of the traditional academic community is rapidly disappearing and is being replaced by an increasingly legalistic mentality of educational consumerism." Kaplin (1979) provides a good overview of the legal issues in this movement.

A major problem facing administrators is the growth of faculty unionism. Angell, Kelley, and Associates (1977), the Carnegie Council on Policy Studies in Higher Education (1977), and Shulman (1972) all review this area, and Ladd and Lipset (1973) have also authored a useful text on faculty unionism. In discussing effective academic administrators in collective bargaining situations, Jacobs (1979, p. 26) identifies three important factors: (1) preparation or better training for bargaining and psychological adjustment to the reality of bargaining, (2) a team approach to decision-making/participatory skills (to prevent isolation of administrators), and (3) careful planning for dealing with faculty, including political strategy development, hard work, timing, and "careful preparation when selling ideas in the faculty marketplace." Much of this type of discussion seems 5,5 in orientation because the team approach is often designed to bring about cohesion *among* administrators in order to confront the faculty in an intergroup "contest" or power struggle. Wolk (1965) and Hartman (1977) portray universities in conflict. The issue of unity is addressed by Wallis (1975).

Federal Intrusion. Federal encroachment is another source of pressure for administrators. The federal role and its impact on university policies is summarized by the Carnegie Council on Policy Studies in Higher Education (1975). Another Carnegie study (Carnegie Foundation for the Advancement of Teaching, 1976) discusses five major concerns—the dynamism of universities, parochialism, the preservation of the private sector, coordination and control, and institutional independence—and the role of federal, state, and private support in these matters. It also discusses the patterns of state governance of higher education and the impact of varying patterns of statewide coordination on higher education in the states.

Bok (1980) also provides a good analysis of the inappropriate and appropriate kinds of government interventions that an administrator may encounter. For example, he labels as inappropriate governmental attempts to regulate the content of ideas and research, and he warns of the federal tendency to overrule university decisions about academic matters because governmental officials believe they can do a better job than the professors.

Threats to Academic Freedom. Others are also concerned about pressures toward conformity and constraints on academic freedom. Parker (1979) notes that the federal bureaucracy, accrediting bodies, and even mindless imitation and disciplinary loyalties of faculty prevent adaptation to changes and the emergence of creative administrative solutions to many of these problems. Gross and Grambsch (1974), in one of the most intensive studies of university goals, found that academics' primary goal in the early 1970s was the protection of academic freedom, and this goal is probably still the central concern and core value in academe. Administrators who violate this principle quickly lose the support of their major constituency, the faculty. Thus administrators must use proper types of power to maintain faculty support (Bachman, 1968).

Liberal Education Versus Vocationalism. Another serious

issue within higher education has to do with the tension between liberal education and what is often called vocationalism or career education. Cheit (1975) discusses this tension and the growth of professional preparation in agriculture, engineering, business, and forestry within colleges and universities. Hughes and others (1973) discuss the education of professionals in terms of the histories of the professions—particularly medicine, law, theology, and social work—the changing clienteles and educational emphases of these professions, and the outlook for the future. Glaser (1975) specifically covers the problems of medical schools.

Approaches to Academic Administration. In discussing the chances for significant alteration in the way higher education responds to such problems as these, the Carnegie Commission on Higher Education (1973, p. 45) analyzes the forces for and against change, including the "survivalist mentality" of administrators as a force against change. This mentality is a 1,1-oriented tendency "to hang on to as much of the past as possible to avoid trouble, to follow the political adage of the Third Republic in France that you can survive in public office provided you do nothing." This "maximin" principle leads boards of trustees to select consensual administrators rather than builders. In this sense, consensual administrators represent a 5,5 or 1,1 orientation. For example, "The rational approach for a consensual administrator, who wants to hold on to his job, is to take no risks, to assume a posture of low visibility, to say nothing but to say it well—while still being 'with it.' He does often face a delicate balance of forces, many negative veto groups, and a situation where little can be done that will not upset somebody. The graceful protection of the status quo is the course of action for survival."

The literature offers other models of leadership that represent differing ways of resolving the conflicts and pressures that academic administrators experience. For example, Hodgkinson and Meeth (1971) and Bennis (1973) offer stylistic options for administrators that are similar to Grid styles, although they do not relate these approaches to the Grid dimensions of "performance" and "people" concerns. Hodgkinson and Meeth list four dean types: autocrat, servant of the faculty, academic

leader, and change agent, while Bennis (1973, pp. 71-77) lists
these:

1. *The Problem-Solver Manager.* This 9,9-oriented manager in-
    volves important constituencies in solving problems that he
    identifies, such as by calling on a number of people in deal-
    ing with a crisis.
2. *The Low-Profile Technocrat.* This 1,1- or 9,1-oriented man-
    ager attempts to develop systems that prevent or transcend
    human error. Such a manager is a pragmatic individual who
    because of his callousness in dealing with moral and ideo-
    logical issues may soon have the faculty and students lined
    up against him.
3. *The Leader Mediator.* This 5,5-oriented style is based on
    the labor relations model. Often this individual can't help
    but make one side angry on an issue and eventually accu-
    mulated anger overtakes goodwill. He must couple his
    mediating skills with charisma and keep himself personally
    above conflict in order to be successful over the long haul.
4. *The Collegiate Manager.* This 9,9- or 5,5-oriented individual
    assumes the role of president as a colleague of the faculty.
    He or she is a representative leader in the community of
    scholars—an insider who, if not presently on the faculty, is
    usually an individual with past experience in the institution
    or one of equal stature.
5. *The Communal-Tribal or Post-Modern Leader.* This 9,1-
    oriented rebel leader identifies strongly with students. He
    not only backs them, he joins them. He is an activist, yet
    possesses academic credentials, is candid and imaginative,
    perhaps to the degree that he is shocking, and often his ap-
    peal is to the unorthodox in the academic community.
6. *The Charismatic Leader.* This 5,5-oriented individual leads
    through personal attractiveness, and is able to capture the
    enthusiasm and support of others by instilling commitment
    in them.
7. *The Law-and-Order President.* Not described in detail, this
    individual is presumably the epitome of the 9,1-oriented
    dictator.

8. *The Absentee Pluralist.* This 1,1-oriented approach is losing favor but was highly regarded in the past. The person who adopts this style sees his primary job as raising money for buildings and other needs and appointing competent subordinates. He hires good deans, spends a great amount of time on ceremonial functions, and lets things "happen." This style is often effective when the university is in a good financial position and students and faculty are relatively docile and homogeneous. It fits in with the style of governance that the faculty often prefers, "legitimized anarchy," where the locus of decision making is the individual faculty member. It is more the absence of style rather than the presence of one.

9. *The Bureaucrat-Entrepreneur.* This 9,1-oriented administrator drives the faculty to despair and runs the university more like a railroad than an academic institution although financial pressures and an over-supply of professors may make his "toned-down profit motive" style appealing to trustees.

10. *The Interregnum Solution or Style.* This benign paternalist/maternalist is a good temporary person who fills in between more permanent appointments. He or she tends to be near retirement and willing to sacrifice personal or professional goals to the requirements of the institution without any assurance of long-term rewards. He or she knows the territory, and is trusted as competent without being threatening.

11. *The Renaissance or Protean Man.* This 5,5-oriented or facades-oriented elusive superman is all things to all people. With a seductive style, this person can role play any other style listed above, and others never know exactly what to expect of him. He is remarkably adaptable and probably a low-level psychopath.

Other writers have formulated structural governance models to describe the organizational milieu in which the administrator must function. Baldridge (1971, 1978) describes the organization structure of universities as more political than hierarchical or bureaucratic and argues that an understanding of the political model (which is congruent with a 5,5 orientation) is basic to understanding and evaluating the leaders one encounters on any college campus. He outlines the key assumptions of the political model as follows:

1. *Inactivity prevails,* in that most people don't participate in the policy-making process, and decisions are made by small groups of elites.
2. *Fluid participation is characteristic,* in that people move in and out of the decision-making process, leaving elites with the power to influence major decisions.
3. *Fragmentation into interest groups with different goals and values is characteristic,* leading to armed co-existence when resources are plentiful and the environment congenial and to conflict when resources are tight, outside pressures exist, and internal groups try to take over.
4. *Conflict is considered normal* and promotes healthy organizational change.
5. *Authority is limited,* in that decisions are usually negotiated compromises between competing groups with the administrator in the middle.
6. And *external interest groups are significant* in influencing the policy-making process.

A stirring example of a university in political turmoil is described by Cooper (1979). Other good texts describing the organizational structures and patterns of governance of universities include Corson (1975), Lee and Bowen (1971), Axelrod (1965), Clark (1972), Corwin (1974), Engel (1970), Gross (1963), Deferrari (1947), Dimock (1970), Duryea (1973), Holdaway (1975), Knowles (1970), Livingstone (1974), Millett (1962), Parsons (1971), and Perkins (1965, 1973). Many authors who discuss university governance point out the importance of collegial decision making and the expression of peer influence that this usually complex and slow process typifies. Examples include Dunwell (1976), Hammons (1976), Hanson (1976-1977), Marcson (1962), Pfeffer and Salancik (1974),

Platt and Parsons (1970), and Pollay and others (1976). In addition, many write about the structure of university departments —considered the key unit on the campus; for example, Adkison (1976), Biglan (1973), Euwema (1953), Hobbs and Anderson (1971), Kingston (1972), O'Hanlon (1976), Ryan (1972), Smart and Montgomery (1976), Twaddell (1940), and Williams (1956), Yeo (1970), and Machlup (1978). It is no wonder, therefore, that many see the solution to poor management in reorganizing, restructuring, and improving decision making, such as Bess (1977) and Hiraok (1975). Others attempt to relate organizational structure to productivity, for example, Ben-David (1960), Child (1972), Eberle (1972), and Huber (1972). Some contrast the organization and management of universities with other types of institutions, contending that their governance and decision-making patterns should not be like a business organization—among them, Besse (1973), Corson (1973), and Brien (1970). Others recognize that different universities are managed differently (Millett, 1973); that patterns of university administration are changing; that different disciplines are often managed differently (Lodahl and Gordon, 1973; Blau, 1973); that academic professions are managed differently from traditional disciplines (Light, 1974); and that organizational conflict plagues universities (Darkenwald, 1971).

Richman and Farmer (1974) focus on strategy, not tactics, in urging more effective management. They argue that the key task of management, especially the president, is to (1) define, articulate, operationalize, and ensure the effective implementation of goals and priorities, (2) understand and use power wisely, (3) minimize conflicts, and (4) increase productivity and efficiency without hindering quality. In terms of governance they review the bureaucratic, collegial, political, and organized anarchy models and then adopt an open systems model coupled with a contingency approach. Many of the behavioral science principles advocated in this book are seen by Richman and Farmer to be part of the "open systems" framework, yet they couple this with a contingency philosophy of leadership, that is, good management depends on the situation. They go so far as to say, "There will never be one universally applicable theory of management" (p. 33). Their book is an excellent treatise on the internal and external constituencies surrounding the higher education administrator. Lumsden (1974) also discusses these inside and outside constituencies and how to improve efficiency within the framework of the four main functions of universities —(1) repository and promoter of civilization, (2) resource for research, (3) place for information storage, and (4) source of general and professional education.

Evaluation of Administrators. The evaluation of administrators in higher education must take into account the problems and pressures outlined above. However, it is evident that leadership is exercised in quite different ways within this milieu. Variations in administrative style among individuals, and even by the same individual (statistical 5,5 orientation), are conspicuous. More pressure on administrators may result in producing a wider range of Grid styles rather than in more consistency in implementing any given leadership approach. The literature on administrator evaluation is significant in this regard because it provides important insights as to how qualities of leadership are viewed both by academic administrators themselves and by their constituencies. This literature identifies what is regarded as good leadership and what is regarded as unacceptable or ineffective and examines the critical assumptions underlying these judgments. In other words, it presents a view of how university and college administrators are seen and how observed variations are evaluated.

For overviews regarding the evaluation of administrators, Fisher (1977) provides an historical perspective as well as a definition and a rationale for administrative evaluation, and Fisher (1978) brings together a variety of recent papers on the subject. Munitz (1977) has prepared a helpful workbook for conducting evaluations of administrators, although it, like most other materials on the topic, does not develop a comprehensive model or framework for evaluation based on behavioral science research on leadership. Instruments based on the Grid, as well as information about procedures for using them for administrative evaluation, are available from Scientific Methods, Inc. (1980).

In terms of criteria by which administrators are judged,

For example, Skipper (1978) used factor analysis to describe two important dimensions of the effective leader at a college or university: (1) *administrative skills* and (2) *specific personal characteristics.* He notes that these characteristics had been shown, in earlier studies, to have significant reliability and to distinguish between effective and ineffective leaders. *Administrative skills* included seven qualities: planning ability, knowledge about position, organization and management, leadership, judgment, human relations, and quality of performance. *Personal characteristics* included nine qualities: responsibility, integrity, self-control, intellectual efficiency, personal relations, leadership, motivation to achieve, avoidance of problems, and creativity. In studying twenty leaders representing two extreme groups—"most effective" and "most ineffective"—as judged by two different groups of fellow administrators, Skipper found three components clustered to define administrative skills: (1) *knowledge of position*—the leader's knowledge and understanding of his or her job in relation to the broad field of higher education; (2) *planning ability*—the leader's skill in establishing goals acceptable to the academic community; and (3) *human relations.* A cluster of three components made up the personal characteristics factor: (1) *willingness to act,* best described as strong motivation, ambition, clear goals, confidence, ability to make decisions, and willingness to take responsibility for decisions; (2) *thoughtful/ethical,* including personal relations, integrity, responsibility, tolerance, tact, dependability, honesty, and sincerity; and (3) *flexibility,* such qualities as insight, confidence, and assertiveness. The most effective administrators were defined as persons who developed well-defined patterns of organization, who opened channels of communication, who articulated goals, who kept morale high, and whose relationships with others were characterized by mutual respect and warmth. All of these attributes in one way or another identify qualities associated with the 9,9-oriented or, depending on assigned meanings, aspects of the 5,5-oriented administrator. Least effective administrators were characterized as persons who were the poorest in defining patterns of organization, who did not open channels of communication, who negatively influenced morale, and who were not trusted by their colleagues and subordinates—attitudes of 1,1- or 9,1-oriented administrators.

Hillway (1959) surveyed faculty attitudes regarding the importance of various characteristics of "desirable" and "undesirable" presidents. One characteristic of desirable presidents, for example, was "democratic" (the 9,9 or possibly the 5,5 orientation), whereas undesirable presidents were undemocratic (either dictatorial, interpretable as the paternalistic or 9,1 orientation; or vacillating, interpreted as statistical 5,5). Integrity and honesty versus dishonesty and insincerity were seen as central, perhaps a clue that "facades" of any sort are held in low esteem and that unexplained shifting of one's ground (the statistical 5,5 orientation) is characterized as undesirable.

Dressel (1976, pp. 389-390) has pictured the competent versus incompetent administrator as described by behaviors listed in Table 3. When complex behavior is stripped down to one-word descriptions, it is difficult to identify the Grid style

Table 3. Characteristics of Administrators

Incompetent Administrators		Competent Administrators	
Behavior	Grid Styles	Behavior	Grid Styles
Expects strong personal loyalty and support	Paternalism/ maternalism	Approachable	5,5; 9,9
		Articulate	9,1; 9,9
Cannot or will not tolerate lengthy discussion or dissent	9,1	Charismatic	5,5
		Decisive	9,1; 9,9
		Deliberate	9,1; 9,9
Ignores or bypasses others without clearance or explanation	9,1	Empathetic	9,9
		Fair	9,9
		Firm	9,1; 9,9
Depends overly much on the advice of a few	Paternalism/ maternalism; 9,1	Flexible	5,5; 9,9
		Persuasive	5,5; 9,9
		Sympathetic	1,9; 9,9
Basks in praise and does not differentiate between the university and one's self-interest	9,1	A morale builder	9,9
Blames others for errors or weaknesses	9,1		
Does not encourage or assist individuals to advance	1,1; 9,1		

involved. Therefore in this table the most likely interpretations of individual words are characterized by one or more Grid styles.

In a study by Ehrle (1975), less competent administrators are characterized as being most deficient in "interpersonal skills" (9,1- or 1,1-oriented). From his wide academic experience, Eble (1978) discusses positive administrative characteristics such as compassion, courage, and confidence, and explains why college administrators should be selected for such traits. He states that authoritarian (9,1-oriented) administrators are resented most by academics and proposes a self-administered series of questions to test overuse or underuse of authority. For example, a high need for authority (9,1-oriented) may be revealed by agreeing with "Do you welcome opportunities to set people straight?" On the other hand, reluctance to take or use authority (1,9-oriented) may be indicated by agreeing with "Do you find it necessary to talk to someone about every decision you make?"

Tucker and Mautz (1979) question whether systematic evaluation of presidents is possible based on the qualifications required in the past, since the job is changing, and they suggest more careful matching of an individual's abilities to the job as it is likely to be in the future. They also suggest fixed terms and informal reviews by trustees as ways to ensure more effective leadership.

Enarson (1979) summarizes four different ways of viewing academic leadership requirements—task, problem, skill, and attribute approaches. Tasks are the familiar functions of planning, organizing, staffing, directing, reporting, and budgeting. Problems involve context-related challenges and issues that a university administrator must address, such as faculty unionism, rising costs, program revision, and increasing state regulation and control. Skills cover such things as time management and mediation. And personal attributes (related to the "trait" approach to analyzing leadership described earlier) that an academic administrator must possess in order to be effective include such qualities as wisdom and shrewdness.

Lutz (1979) has conducted one of the few longitudinal

studies of administrator assessment in higher education in his examination of the search processes for thirty-two deans' positions in liberal arts, business administration, and nursing programs. When members of the search committees were asked to identify qualities that they valued in a candidate, their expectations in descending order of importance were as follows: previous administrative experience, the ability to lead and initiate, energy and intellectual ability, ability to relate to the field, personal appearance, practical field experience, research and publication record, recommendations from persons within the employing institution, recommendations from persons at other universities, personal values, and national reputation (pp. 266-267). Judging the chosen candidates against such criteria two years after their selection, over half of the respondents refuted the positive assessments they had made two years earlier. The most common criticism leveled by committee members related to the poor manner in which the dean treated people, particularly faculty members and students. Deans were criticized for being abrasive, dogmatic, insensitive, and unethical (9,1-oriented or paternalistic/maternalistic). None was criticized for being too humanistic or too faculty oriented (1,9, 5,5, or 9,9 orientations). A fair assumption might be that the committees' selection criteria did not pick up the attributes of Grid style behavior that are of significance in actual performance as evaluated at a later time.

Kauffman (1977) reports the effect of administrator style on leadership succession, based on interviews with thirty-two newly selected campus presidents or chancellors. Many of these chief executive officers had been selected because they could offset their predecessor's weaknesses. Thus if the previous executive had engendered bad relations with the faculty, his successor was selected to overcome this problem. After one president had severely limited faculty involvement in university governance, a new president had to teach the faculty to assume policy-making responsibility and placed top priority in restoring faculty morale and self-respect. Another president purposely set about changing the assumptions on his campus regarding the presidency by letting people know that he was friendly, open, and accessible (1,9- or 9,9-oriented) in contrast to his predeces-sor, whom many people viewed as remote and disinterested (9,1- or 1,1-oriented). The pattern seems to be a 9,1-oriented style followed by 1,9- or 9,9-oriented behavior, or from 1,1 or 1,9 to a 9,1 orientation. Thus articles about President John Silber of Boston University suggest that he exemplifies a return to a 9,1 orientation after a series of 1,9- or 1,1-oriented presi-dents and that his style has been welcomed by trustees believing that they needed someone who could rescue the university from the financial crisis that previous presidents had evidently re-fused to face.

Other writers who provide insights into the presidential role include Wells (1964), Peterson (1973), Glenn (1975), Gib-son (1966), Cole (1976), Cohen and March (1974), Burke (1977), and Benezet (1962). Writers about the vice-presidential or dean role include Enarson (1962) and Gould (1964). And those who discuss the department chair include Leslie (1973); Brann and Emmet (1972); Doyle (1953); Heimler (1967); Nicoll (1971); Montgomery, McLaughlin, and Smart (1974); Petersdorf (1971); O'Grady (1973); Porter (1961); Smart (1976); and Young (1974). For information on department chair's role conflict in being torn between faculty desires and ad-ministrative pressures, see Buder (1975); Carroll (1974, 1976); McLaughlin, Montgomery, and Malpass (1975); Podemski (1973); and Ehrle and Earley (1977). Regarding motivation, selection, retention, and evaluation of chairs and related person-nel concerns see Ehrle (1975), Checker (1977), Mobley (1971), and Snyder and others (1978).

Departmental Administration. Ehrle (1975) notes that the department chairmanship is one of the most important posi-tions in academe, both because it is a testing ground for wider institutional leadership and because it is the most common aca-demic administrative position and where key decisions about teaching, research, and service are made. In suggesting ways to reduce role conflict and job dissatisfaction on the part of chairs, Carroll (1976) recommends goal definition or designation, insti-tutional structural improvement, and improved communica-tions. He notes that one problem in role conflict is that people tend to cope by decreasing their level of communication (1,1- or 9,1-oriented) with the conflicting sources of pressure, and he advises open and forthright communications (9,9-oriented) so that a normative consensus can develop and conflict can be diminished.

Dressel, Johnson, and Marcus (1969), after studying over 100 departments and associated units at fifteen universities, defined the basic administrative process of the chair as one involving persuasion, influence, reciprocated confidence, and exploitation of confidence, approaching a swindle. They found two different kinds of departmental chairs that faculty prefer, given the nature of how department funds are obtained. In those departments heavily dependent on university funding, faculty preferred a department chair, typically from their group, who had a powerful personality and who could represent their interests to the central administration. They were willing to entrust such a person with virtually complete authority in all matters except changes in the curriculum. At the other extreme—in departments that received extensive outside funding, that therefore displayed little concern and even disdain for deans and central administrators, and that based research priorities on national and international concerns and agencies—chairs maintained the confidence of their faculty colleagues by virtue of strong national credentials and ability to guide young faculty into prominence on the national scene. In all departments, chairs who had the confidence of both faculty and administration were guaranteed a long tenure in office, but in order to maintain this confidence from both sides, they had to proceed democratically (9,9- or 1,9-oriented) to satisfy the faculty and yet be decisive and consistent enough to achieve results (9,9- or 9,1-oriented). If chairs are honest brokers, interpreting accurately to both department and the dean the concerns and dissatisfactions of the other, they will be effective (9,9-oriented). However, if they play one against the other to enhance their own position or attempt to cater to the dissatisfactions of one by enforcing demands on the other, they will be ineffective (5,5- or 9,1-oriented).

Hill and French (1967) provide a measure of the power

of departmental chairs from their study of 375 professors in five state colleges, in which they used a five-point modified Likert-type scale to obtain an index of power with respect to a number of tasks and sources of influence available to the chair. They found that professors are most satisfied when their chair has considerable personal influence (9,9-, 9,1-, or possibly 5,5-oriented) and the power to speak effectively on behalf of the faculty (9,1- or 9,9-oriented).

In a study of the relationship between chair leadership style and faculty satisfaction, Washington (1975) found that faculty were significantly more satisfied with their jobs when they perceived the chairperson's leadership style to be above the median in "initiating structure" and "consideration" on the Leader Behavior Description Questionnaire. Using the Brayfield-Rothe index of job satisfaction, faculty job satisfaction was significantly higher in departments whose chairs were appointed, either with or without their approval, than in departments which chose their own chairs; but when job satisfaction was measured by the Academic Concerns Issues instrument, it was found to be significantly higher for faculty who chose their own chairs.

Bloomer (1980) discusses desirable qualities of department heads based on workshops with school teachers. The teachers clearly preferred a democratic (9,9- or 5,5-oriented) to an autocratic (9,1-oriented) or laissez-faire (1,1- or 1,9-oriented) type of leader, as evidenced by such characteristics as maintaining a cooperative team effort, ensuring effective communication of information and ideas, promoting discussion and achieving consensus, cooperative team planning, securing support for innovation, considering experimentation with alternative strategies of teaching, and support and development of the faculty.

Montgomery, McLaughlin, and Smart (1974), from a survey of 1,198 respondents, suggest three ways to help improve the effectiveness of department chairs by giving them (1) more autonomy and resources, (2) greater administrative assistance in order to relieve them of administrative detail, and (3) more learning opportunities with respect to the nonacademic aspects of their jobs. Few of the respondents had had any professional training in management or administration; the majority mentioned a lack of technical management knowledge and acknowledged a need for more proficiency with regard to administrative skills. Orientation or training activities could include familiarization with rules, regulations, and policies; an overview of the administration of the total institution; a review of expected leadership activities such as assigning work, living within the budget, and assessing performance; and training in small group leadership, discussion techniques, and ways to increase motivation and resolve conflicts.

Smart and Elton (1976) show through factor analysis that training programs designed to enhance administrative effectiveness must take into account distinctive differences among departments, such as between "pure" and "applied" disciplines, as described by Biglan (1973). These differences have an effect on department chair administrative responsibilities regarding their *"faculty" role* (recruiting, selecting, and evaluating faculty; encouraging professional development and research and publication efforts; and maintaining a healthy department climate through conflict reduction and informal faculty leadership), their *"coordinator" role* (soliciting ideas to improve the department; planning and reviewing the curriculum; and assigning teaching, research, and other duties to faculty), their *"research" role* (managing grants, gifts, and contracts; recruiting, selecting, and supervising graduate students; and overseeing facilities, equipment, and finance), and their *"instructional" role* (teaching and advising students; managing professional, technical, and clerical personnel; and assuring the maintenance of student and departmental records).

Torgerson and Taylor (1974) have developed a computer-based simulation game, "The Academic Department Head Game," under a grant from the Exxon Educational Foundation as an orientation and training device for new or aspiring department heads. And Booth (1978) advocates discussions with more experienced chairpersons on a regular basis, retreats, more effective selection procedures, diagnostic evaluation methods, and consultants for chairs as other development activities to improve chairperson effectiveness.

Organization Development

The literature on organization development is large and diverse, and a comprehensive analysis of it through 1975 is available elsewhere (Blake and Mouton, 1976). But certain references are particularly relevant to the origins and history of organization development and to the major approaches of organization development described in Chapter Eleven, and this part of the Appendix reviews them. Its first section identifies important early literature; later sections note sources related to "acceptant," "prescriptive," "catalytic," and "theory-based confrontation" approaches.

Origins of Organization Development. Organization development as a systematic, multiphasal approach to changing organizations can be traced to two papers published in 1962 (Blake and Mouton, 1962; Blake, Mouton, and Blansfield, 1962). Both represented a break with the traditional way of trying to improve organizations prevailing at the beginning of the 1960s. This traditional approach involved individual-centered learning experiences in workshops or sessions for groups of strangers. It held that individuals, on returning to their organization from meetings attended by others whom they did not know, would be in a position to apply what had been learned about effective organizations. But because of the failure of many participants to apply this learning, these two papers described efforts then underway to rectify the inherent weakness in "stranger" learning. The solution involved training members of intact teams, who shared real working relationships, in behavioral science theories of effectiveness and in the skills necessary for successfully implementing these theories to bring change about. This departure from training individuals among strangers demonstrated that the natural teams of an organization are the proper target of development. Individuals in their working interrelationships are the carriers of organization culture as epitomized by prevailing goals and objectives, norms and standards, morale and cohesion, expected uses of power and authority, and implicit agreements for dealing with conflict. Only when a development effort permits team members to bring to awareness and systematically analyze these culturally anchored expectations by seeing them in a theory-centered way and changing them to whatever degree is necessary, is it possible to improve institutional performance. Furthermore, when this happens, new knowledge can be put into use rather than promoting resistance to change, as happened under the individually centered stranger approach to training.

The weakness of individuals rather than work teams as the target of organization change has been recognized by Katz and Kahn (1966, pp. 391-392) in these words:

> To approach institutional change solely in individual terms involves an impressive and discouraging series of assumptions—assumptions which are too often left implicit. They include, at the very least, the assumption that the individual can be provided with new insight and knowledge; that these will produce some significant alteration in his motivational pattern; that these insights and motivations will be retained even when the individual leaves the protected situation in which they were learned and returns to his accustomed role in the organization; that he will be able to adapt his new knowledge to that real-life situation; that he will be able to persuade his co-workers to accept the changes in his behavior which he now desires; and that he will also be able to persuade them to make complementary changes in their own expectations and behavior.
>
> The weakness in this chain becomes apparent as soon as its many links are enumerated. The initial diagnosis may be wrong; that is, the inappropriate behavior may not result from lack of individual insight or any other psychological shortcoming. Even if the individual diagnosis is correct, however, the individual approach to organizational change

characteristically disregards the long and difficult linkage as described. This disregard we have called the psychological fallacy.

The first major book concerned with applying a systematic behavioral science oriented approach to developing organizations appeared toward the end of the decade (Blake and Mouton, 1968).

It held that significant organization development must start at the top and encompass the entire organization rather than simply components of subsystems, or "pockets-of-interest" within it. The reason is that pockets-of-interest exist within the larger culture of organizational expectations and these may represent such severe constraints that even improved performance within one pocket-of-interest may have little or no impact on the capacity of the organization to function in a stronger or more effective manner.

Prior attempts at organization improvement did not involve organization development in this way. For example, Dickson and Roethlisberger (1966) attempted to increase organizational harmony by enabling individuals who chose to do so almost on a one-by-one basis to vent their frustrations and tensions in a harmless way, but they did not aid organization members to learn behavioral science theories and apply their learning for changing the organization in systematic, step-wise terms. And Jacques (1951) introduced consultation in a unionized factory in order to clarify and change its conventional authority structure by opening up communication between levels and increasing the degree to which decisions between the union and management were based on joint consultation, but no effort was made to introduce organization members to behavioral science theories related to the effectiveness or ineffectiveness of exercising authority. Instead, both projects sought improvement by helping people within pockets of interest clarify the existing situation, based on their own current common-sense understandings. Much of what is currently called organization development is actually similar to these two organization improvement efforts.

The 1970s saw popularization of organization development by the six-volume Organization Development series of Addison-Wesley (Beckhard, 1969; Bennis, 1969; Blake and Mouton, 1969; Lawrence and Lorsch, 1969; Schein, 1969; and Walton, 1969). Each of these books presented a particular point of view with regard to one facet or another of this still unfolding field. Since the early 1970s, a number of books and articles concerned with organization improvement in educational institutions have appeared, including three in which Schmuck has been the senior author (Schmuck and Miles, 1971; and Schmuck and others, 1972, 1977).

Once popularized, organization development evolved in a number of different directions, some of which recentered on individual development within pockets-of-interest rather than on a systematic, theory-centered development of institutional culture. In a certain sense, then, the insights of 1962 that shifted the emphasis away from the individual as a sole agent toward seeing individuals and groups as embedded within the context of the organization culture were lost. Conventional approaches to improvement were repopularized under the rubric of organization development. As the field of organization development and improvement differentiated, each of the approaches alluded to in Chapter Eleven began to develop its own leaders, language, and literature.

The Acceptant Approach. Dickson and Roethlisberger (1966) are basically acceptant, but those authors most clearly identified with the acceptant approach are Gibb (1978) and Rogers (1977). Their efforts to solve problems of organization functioning concentrate on the reestablishment of love, trust, and harmony. An excellent description of this approach with a case illustration of its use within a school system is available in Gibb (1972).

The Prescriptive Approach. The prescriptive approach derives from the doctor-patient model with the change agent as expert and the university as the patient. A prescriptive intervention that involved a massive organization redesign at the State University of New York at Buffalo has been described by Bennis (1972, 1973). Because of resistance to the prescription, it ended in disaster within four years.

The Catalytic Approach. The catalytic approach has produced the largest body of literature. Important writings illustrating it include work on process consultation (Schein, 1969), the use of survey research to diagnose perceptions by organization members (Baumgartel, 1959; Mann, 1951), and interviewing for perceptions as the basis of feedback (Ferguson, 1968; Fordyce and Weil, 1971).

The catalytic approach as applied in school systems is described in a series of publications from the Center for Educational Policy and Management at the University of Oregon. Examples of applications in colleges and universities are from the Higher Education Research Institute and Stanford University (Baldridge and Deal, 1974) and the National Training Laboratory Institute Higher Education Laboratories (Sikes, Schlesinger, and Seashore, 1974). Daw and Gage (1967) assessed how a catalytic intervention was utilized to change the relationship between department chairs and faculty members. Aldefer (1973) used this approach to give feedback to faculty regarding how they are perceived by students. Varney and Lasher (1973) used survey feedback to increase cooperation between students and faculty within a college department. Derr (1972) provided an example of catalytic intervention in a metropolitan school system premised on consultant information-gathering interviews followed by feedback and process consultation. Though this project was unsuccessful, his report is instructive, for the project's failure was related to weaknesses characteristic of the catalytic approach. The intervention was too weak to overcome the rigidities built into the system itself, and it demonstrated the devastating effect on change efforts when top leadership absents itself from the change process. Caplan (1970) has described an unsuccessful attempt to aid in the reduction of tension between a community and its school system. And Duffin and others (1973) used a catalytic approach when several schools were merged within one system to aid participants to develop patterns of collaboration where none had existed before.

A catalytic effort to promote individually centered organization improvement in university settings is sponsored by the American Council on Education through its Higher Education Management Institute (HEMI). HEMI's basic premise is that improvement results from increasing the effectiveness of individuals and working groups on a pockets-of-interest basis. "The main objective is to improve institutional operation by improving individual functioning. Related objectives are recognizing the value of work group based activities and developing work groups into competent management teams" (Webster, 1979, p. 242). This formulation disregards the cultural context within which individual or group performance takes place and which shapes, constricts, and dictates such performance. For example, HEMI's training modules do not focus directly on clarifying university mission, developing standards of organization excellence, or shifting values and attitudes, all of which are fundamental dimensions of institutional culture. Nor is its change effort focused on organization members learning behavioral science theories of effectiveness. "Training modules and development manuals emphasize management practices and skills as opposed to management theory" (p. 249)—an example of the catalytic assumption that common sense, along with open discussion of the development of action plans, is sufficient as a basis for promoting excellence. Trainees may incidentally learn some theory through readings listed in the modules, but there is no guarantee that they will integrate this knowledge usefully into action plans. Furthermore, groups select some modules based on felt needs, and they may not read the theory material most relevant to their real problem. Because action plans get much more attention than theory, actions or activities may become palliatives—emotional reassurances—and therefore random and ineffective in terms of achieving goals.

HEMI's felt needs approach is illustrated by its use of survey research instruments that assess individual perceptions of need rather than the real needs which often are hidden from investigation by self-deception. Managers and work groups of faculty members, other staff, and students "complete the surveys helping to determine what should be improved" (Webster, 1979, p. 245). With organization members the primary source of diagnostic effort, this approach is analogous to patients rejecting medical expertise in preference to diagnosing their own illnesses, or students rejecting faculty advice regarding learning needs for pursuing complex academic objectives and relying instead on their own self-prescriptions. A patient or student should of course be involved in the diagnosis of needs, but the medical expert or the professor has significant contributions to make based upon deeper knowledge and wider experience.

Another assumption underlying HEMI is seen in its emphasis on anonymity as the basis for generating data. "The needs assessment survey can work only if each person is assured that his or her perception of institutional functioning will be used constructively, professionally, and anonymously. The program's confidentiality policy which participating institutions agree to follow states that individual anonymity will be protected, work group reports will be confidential unless the group chooses to share them, and that institution-wide data will be reported only in summary form" (Webster, 1979, p. 248). By this hiding of personal ownership while revealing convictions, the HEMI approach does not solve but rather bypasses the development of openness and candor which is so basic to confronting and solving organization issues that are barriers to organization excellence.

Through HEMI, chief executives may engage in development of their own team but do not directly lead organization development of the institution at large apart from approving the development budget and appointing an institutional coordinator and task force. "The task force typically numbers from four to eight or ten people who represent various levels and areas of the college or university. The task force, trained by the institute's program center staff members [HEMI], becomes one of the institution's primary resources for management training and development" (p. 245). In this sense, chief executives delegate leadership for the process of change. It follows that whatever is subject to change involves aspects of university administration beneath the level of the whole system. Development is left as the responsibility of whoever completes the survey research instruments and participates in the exercises.

These catalytic strategies and tactics of organization development appear to fit a 5,5-oriented status quo institutional culture rather than aiding institutional members to develop a 9,9 orientation that can bring about academic excellence.

Theory-Based Confrontation. The most extensive treatments of theory-based confrontation are in sources that depict how the Grid has been used to strengthen institutional performance (Blake and Mouton, 1964, 1968, 1969, 1976, 1978). Descriptions of the underlying educational technology involving instrumented confrontation are available in Blake and Mouton (1964). Theory-based confrontation in situations where a consultant rather than instrumentation provides the basis for aiding administrators to identify their assumptions has also been described by Argyris and Schön (1974).

Recent surveys of organization development in higher education conclude that the impact of a systematic approach remains essentially unknown, since most efforts to date have been of the pockets-of-interest variety and limited to lower levels of administration (Alderfer, 1977; Kurpius, 1979). Systematic efforts to improve universities are underway in many countries, as in the Philippines, where President Manuel Soriano of the University of the Philippines has evolved a systematic planning effort that involves all units of the university through workshops on general strategy. References to school and university applications are available in "A Topical Bibliography on Consultation" (1978), and an overview of organization development in academic settings concludes that it should be significant in bringing about needed changes (Coughlin, 1979).

References

Ableson, P. "Justifying Academic Research." *Science,* 1967, *157,* 759.

Adkison, J. "The Structure of Knowledge and Departmental Social Organization." ERIC Document Reproduction Service No. 138223. Washington, D.C.: Educational Resources Information Center, 1976.

Alderfer, C. P. "A Video Assists a Student Faculty Dialogue on Teaching and Learning." *Social Change,* 1973, *3*(2), 6-8.

Alderfer, C. P. "Organization Development." *Annual Review of Psychology,* 1977, *28,* 197-223.

Allen, D. B. *Heterogeneity of Research Interests and Effectiveness of University Departments.* Washington, D.C.: Office of Education, Department of Health, Education, and Welfare, 1972.

Allison, P., and Stewart, J. "Productivity Differences Among Scientists: Evidence for Accumulative Advantage." *American Sociological Review,* 1974, *39,* 596-606.

Anderson, C. (Ed.). *Administrative Team Leadership in Concept and Practice.* Athens: Institute of Higher Education, University of Georgia, 1966.

Anderson, C. A., Bowman, M. J., and Tinto, V. *Where Colleges Are and Who Attends: Effects of Accessibility on College Attendance.* New York: McGraw-Hill, 1972.

Angell, G. W., Kelley, E. P., Jr., and Associates. *Handbook of Faculty Bargaining: Asserting Administrative Leadership for Institutional Progress by Preparing for Bargaining, Negotiating and Administering Contracts, and Improving the Bargaining Process.* San Francisco: Jossey-Bass, 1977.

Appleby, E. "The Role of Teaching in Higher Education—Its Decline and Revival." *Liberal Education,* 1973, *59*(4), 449-463.

Arden, E. "Faculty as Teachers: Improving College Teaching." *Educational Forum,* May 1968, *32,* 441-452.

Argyris, C. *Management and Organizational Development: The Path from XA to YB.* New York: McGraw-Hill, 1971.

Argyris, C., and Schön, D. A. *Theory in Practice: Increasing Professional Effectiveness.* San Francisco: Jossey-Bass, 1974.

Arkava, M. L. *Behavior Modification: A Procedural Guide for Social Workers.* Missoula: University of Montana, 1974.

Arrowsmith, W. "The Future of Teaching." *The Public Interest,* 1967, *6,* 53-67.

Ashby, E. *Adapting Universities to a Technological Society.* San Francisco: Jossey-Bass, 1974.

Axelrod, J. "New Patterns of Internal Organization." In L. Wilson (Ed.), *Emerging Patterns in American Higher Education.* Washington, D.C.: American Council on Education, 1965.

Bach, G. R., and Wyden, P. *The Intimate Enemy.* New York: Morrow, 1969.

Bachman, J. G. "Faculty Satisfaction and the Dean's Influence." *Journal of Applied Psychology,* 1968, *52*(1), 55-61.

Bakan, D. *The Duality of Human Existence.* Chicago: Rand McNally, 1966.

Baldridge, J. V. (Ed.). *Academic Governance.* Berkeley, Calif.: McCutchan, 1971.

Baldridge, J. V., and Deal, T. *Managing Change in Academic Organizations.* Berkeley, Calif.: McCutchan, 1974.

Baldridge, J. V., and others. *Policy Making and Effective Leadership: A National Study of Academic Management.* San Francisco: Jossey-Bass, 1978.

Bales, R. F. *Personality and Interpersonal Behavior.* New York: Holt, Rinehart and Winston, 1970.

Barber, J. D. *The Presidential Character.* Englewood Cliffs, N.J.: Prentice-Hall, 1972.

Baumgartel, H. "Using Employee Questionnaire Results for Improving Organizations." *Kansas Business Review,* 1959, *12*(12), 2-6.

Beard, R. "On the Publish or Perish Policy." *Journal of Higher Education,* 1965, *36*(8), 455-459.

Becker, W., Jr. "The University Professor as a Utility Maximizer and Producer of Learning, Research, and Income." *Journal of Human Resources,* 1975, *10,* 107-115.

Beckhard, R. *Organization Development: Strategies and Models.* Reading, Mass.: Addison-Wesley, 1969.

Bell, G. D. *The Achievers.* Chapel Hill, N.C.: Preston-Hill, 1973.

Ben-David, J. "Scientific Productivity and Academic Organization in Nineteenth Century Medicine." *American Sociological Review,* 1960, *25*(6), 828-843.

Benezet, L. "The Office of the President." In G. P. Burns (Ed.), *Administrators in Higher Education: Their Functions and Coordination.* New York: Harper & Row, 1962.

Benne, K. D., and Sheats, P. "Functional Roles of Group Members." *Journal of Social Issues,* 1948, *4*(2), 41-49.

Bennett, D. *TA and the Manager.* New York: Amacom, 1976.

Bennis, W. *The Leaning Ivory Tower.* San Francisco: Jossey-Bass, 1973.

Bennis, W. *The Unconscious Conspiracy: Why Leaders Can't Lead.* New York: Amacom, 1976.

Bennis, W. G. *Organization Development: Its Nature, Origins, and Prospects.* Reading, Mass.: Addison-Wesley, 1969.

Bennis, W. G. "Who Sank the Yellow Submarine?" *Psychology Today,* November 1972, pp. 112-120.

Berne, E. *Games People Play.* New York: Grove Press, 1964.

Bess, J. "Breeding New Faculty Through Organizational Restructuring." *Improving College and University Teaching,* 1977, *25*(2), 97-99.

Bess, J., and Lodahl, T. "Career Patterns and Satisfactions in University Middle-Management." *Educational Record,* Spring 1969, pp. 220-229.

Besse, R. "A Comparison of the University with the Corporation." In J. A. Perkins (Ed.), *The University as an Organization.* New York: McGraw-Hill, 1973.
Biestek, F. P. *The Casework Relationship.* Chicago: Loyola University Press, 1957.
Biglan, A. "Relationships Between Subject Matter Characteristics and the Structure and Output of University Departments." *Journal of Applied Psychology,* 1973, *57*(3),
  204-213.
Bion, W. R. *Experiences in Groups.* New York: Basic Books,
  1959.
Blake, R. R., and Mouton, J. S. *The Managerial Grid: Key Ori-
  entations for Achieving Production Through People.* Hous-
  ton: Gulf, 1964.
Blake, R. R., and Mouton, J. S. *Corporate Excellence Through
  Grid Organization Development.* Houston: Gulf, 1968.
Blake, R. R., and Mouton, J. S. *Building a Dynamic Corpora-
  tion Through Grid Organization Development.* Reading,
  Mass.: Addison-Wesley, 1969.
Blake, R. R., and Mouton, J. S. *The Grid for Sales Excellence:
  Benchmarks for Effective Salesmanship.* New York: McGraw-
  Hill, 1970.
Blake, R. R., and Mouton, J. S. *The Grid for Supervisory Effec-
  tiveness.* Austin, Texas: Scientific Methods, 1975.
Blake, R. R., and Mouton, J. S. *Consultation.* Reading, Mass.:
  Addison-Wesley, 1976.
Blake, R. R., and Mouton, J. S. *The New Managerial Grid.*
  Houston: Gulf, 1978.
Blake, R. R., and Mouton, J. S. *The Versatile Manager: A Grid
  Profile.* Homewood, Ill.: Dow Jones-Irwin, 1981.
Blake, R. R., Mouton, J. S., and Blansfield, M. G. "How Execu-
  tive Team Training Can Help You." *Journal of the American
  Society of Training Directors,* January 1962, *16*(1), 3-11.
Blau, P. *The Organization of Academic Work.* New York: Wiley,
  1973.
Bloomer, R. G. "The Role of the Head of Department: Some
  Questions and Answers." *Educational Research,* 1980, *22*(2),
  83-96.

Bok, D. C. "The Federal Government and the University." *The Public Interest,* Winter 1980, *58,* 1-22.

Booth, D. B. "Department and Chairperson Development." In C. F. Fisher (Ed.), *New Directions for Higher Education: Developing and Evaluating Administrative Leadership,* no. 22. San Francisco: Jossey-Bass, 1978.

Bowen, H. R. *Investment in Learning: The Individual and Social Value of American Higher Education.* San Francisco: Jossey-Bass, 1977.

Branden, N. *The Psychology of Self-Esteem.* New York: Bantam Books, 1969.

Brandis, R. "The Rehabilitation of Undergraduate Teaching." *Educational Record,* 1964, *45,* 56-63.

Brandt, T. "The Professor: Educator, Scholar, or Both." *School and Society,* November 1966, 381.

Brann, J., and Emmet, T. (Eds.). *The Academic Department or Division Chairman: A Complex Role.* Detroit: Balamp, 1972.

Bresler, J. "Teaching Effectiveness and Government Awards." *Science,* 1968, *160,* 164-168.

Brien, R. "The 'Managerialization' of Higher Education." *Educational Record,* 1970, *51*(3), 273-280.

Buder, L. "What Is a Department Head?" *New York Times,* April 16, 1975, p. 52.

Burke, J. C. "Coping with the Role of College or University President." *Educational Record,* 1977, *58*(4), 388-402.

Burns, T., and Stalker, G. M. *The Management of Innovation.* New York: Barnes & Noble, 1961.

Buzzotta, V. R., Lefton, R. E., and Sherberg, M. *Effective Selling Through Psychology: Dimensional Sales and Sales Management Strategies.* New York: Wiley Interscience, 1972.

Caplan, G. *The Theory and Practice of Mental Health Consultation.* New York: Basic Books, 1970.

Carnegie Commission on Higher Education. *Priorities for Action: Final Report of the Carnegie Commission on Higher Education.* New York: McGraw-Hill, 1973.

Carnegie Council on Policy Studies in Higher Education. *The Federal Role in Postsecondary Education: Unfinished Business, 1975-1980.* San Francisco: Jossey-Bass, 1975.

Carnegie Council on Policy Studies in Higher Education. *Faculty Bargaining in Public Higher Education.* San Francisco: Jossey-Bass, 1977.

The Carnegie Foundation for the Advancement of Teaching. *More Than Survival: Prospects for Higher Education in a Period of Uncertainty.* San Francisco: Jossey-Bass, 1975.

The Carnegie Foundation for the Advancement of Teaching. *The States and Higher Education: A Proud Past and a Vital Future.* San Francisco: Jossey-Bass, 1976.

Carroll, A. "Role Conflict in Academic Organizations: An Exploratory Examination of the Department Chairman's Experience." *Educational Administration Quarterly,* 1974, *10,* 51-64.

Carroll, A. B. "The Role Conflict Phenomenon: Implications for Department Chairmen and Academic Faculty." *Improving College and University Teaching,* 1976, *24*(4), 245-246.

Centra, J. A. *Determining Faculty Effectiveness: Assessing Teaching, Research, and Service for Personnel Decisions and Improvement.* San Francisco: Jossey-Bass, 1979.

Checker, A. "Continuity Among Department Chairmen in U.S. Medical Schools." *Journal of Medical Education,* 1977, *52*(9), 766-768.

Cheit, E. F. *The Useful Arts and the Liberal Tradition.* New York: McGraw-Hill, 1975.

Child, J. "Organizational Structure, Environment and Performance—The Role of Strategic Choice." *Sociology,* 1972, *6,* 1-22.

Clark, B. "The Organizational Saga in Higher Education." *Administrative Science Quarterly,* 1972, *17,* 178-184.

Cohen, M., and March, J. *Leadership and Ambiguity: The American College President.* New York: McGraw-Hill, 1974.

Cohn, E. *The Economics of Education.* (Rev. ed.) Cambridge, Mass.: Ballinger, 1979.

Cole, C. C. "The Reeling Presidency." *Educational Record,* 1976, *57*(2), 71-78.

Cole, S., and Cole, J. "Scientific Output and Recognition: A Study in the Operation of the Reward System in Science." *American Sociological Review,* 1967, *32,* 377-390.

"College Clash—Things Are Never Dull at Boston University with Silber in Charge." *The Wall Street Journal,* May 8, 1980, pp. 1, 25.

Cooper, S. E. "Who Rules Higher Education?" *Social Policy,* 1979, *9*(5), 34-38.

Corson, J. "Perspectives on the University Compared with Other Institutions." In J. Perkins (Ed.), *The University as an Organization.* New York: McGraw-Hill, 1973.

Corson, J. *The Governance of Colleges and Universities: Modernizing Structure and Process.* (Rev. ed.) New York: McGraw-Hill, 1975.

Corwin, R. "Models of Educational Organizations." In F. Kerlinger and J. Carroll (Eds.), *Review of Research in Education.* Vol. 2. Itasca, Ill.: Peacock, 1974.

Coughlin, P. J. "Understanding and Evaluating the Organization Development Process." *Journal of the College and University Personnel Association (CUPA),* Winter 1979, *30*(4), 59-68.

Crane, D. "Scientists at Major and Minor Universities: A Study of Productivity and Recognition." *American Sociological Review,* 1965, *30,* 699-714.

Darkenwald, G. "Organizational Conflict in Colleges and Universities." *Administrative Science Quarterly,* 1971, *16,* 407-412.

Daw, R. W., and Gage, N. L. "Effective Feedback from Teachers to Pupils." *Journal of Educational Psychology,* 1967, *58*(3), 181-188.

Deferrari, R. *College Organization and Administration.* Washington, D.C.: Catholic University of America Press, 1947.

Derr, C. B. "Organization Development in One Large Urban School System." *Education and Urban Society,* 1972, *4,* 403-419.

Dickson, W. J., and Roethlisberger, F. J. *Counseling in an Organization: A Sequal to the Hawthorne Researches.* Boston: Division of Research, Graduate School of Business Administration, Harvard University, 1966.

Dimock, M. "Endemic Administrative Feudality." In L. Netzer and others, *Education, Administration, and Change.* New York: Harper & Row, 1970.

Doyle, E. *The Status and Functions of the Departmental Chairman.* Washington, D.C.: Catholic University of America Press, 1953.

Dressel, P. L. *Handbook of Academic Evaluation: Assessing Institutional Effectiveness, Student Progress, and Professional Performance for Decision Making in Higher Education.* San Francisco: Jossey-Bass, 1976.

Dressel, P. L., Johnson, F. C., and Marcus, P. M. "Departmental Operations: The Confidence Game." *Educational Record,* 1969, *50*(3), 274-278.

Dressel, P. L., and Reichard, D. "The University Department: Retrospect and Prospect." *Journal of Higher Education,* 1970, *41*(5), 387-402.

Duffin, R. A., and others. "Increasing Organization Effectiveness." *Training and Development Journal,* 1973, *27*(4), 37-46.

Dunham, E. A. *Colleges of the Forgotten Americans.* New York: McGraw-Hill, 1969.

Dunn, R., and Dunn, J. J. *Administrator's Guide to New Programs for Faculty Management and Evaluation.* West Nyack, N.Y.: Parker, 1977.

Dunwell, R. "Humanistic Modes of Academic Decision-Making." *Colorado Journal of Educational Research,* 1976, *15*(3), 47-52.

Durkheim, E. "On Anomie." In C. W. Mills (Ed.), *Images of Man: The Classic Tradition in Sociological Thinking.* New York: Braziller, 1960.

Duryea, E. "Evolution of University Organization." In J. Perkins (Ed.), *The University as an Organization.* New York: McGraw-Hill, 1973.

Eberle, A. "Academic Structure and Instructional Improvement." *Journal of Research and Development in Education,* 1972, *6*(1), 21-25.

Eble, K. E. *The Art of Administration: A Guide for Academic Administrators.* San Francisco: Jossey-Bass, 1978.

Ehrle, E. B. "Selection and Evaluation of Department Chairmen." *Educational Record,* Winter 1975, *56*(1), 29-38.

Ehrle, E., and Earley, J. "The Effect of Collective Bargaining on

Department Chairpersons and Deans." *Educational Record,* 1977, *57*(3), 149-154.

Enarson, H. "The Academic Vice-President or Dean." In G. Burns (Ed.), *Administrators in Higher Education: Their Functions and Coordination.* New York: Harper & Row, 1962.

Enarson, H. "Leadership." In Mississippi Council of Presidents, *Final Report of the Mississippi Council of Presidents.* Leadership Development Work Sessions, November 30, 1979, Mississippi State, Miss.

Engel, G. "Professional Autonomy and Bureaucratic Organization." *Administrative Science Quarterly,* 1970, *15*(1), 12-21.

Etzioni, A. *A Comparative Analysis of Complex Organizations.* (rev. ed.) New York: Free Press, 1975.

Euwema, B. "The Organization of the Department." *Educational Record,* 1953, *34,* 38-43.

Farmer, C. H. *Administrator Evaluation: Concepts, Methods, Cases in Higher Education.* Richmond, Va.: Higher Education Leadership and Management Society, 1979.

Fenker, R. M. "The Evaluation of University Faculty and Administrators: A Case Study." *Journal of Higher Education,* 1975, *46*(6), 665-686.

Ferguson, C. K. "Concerning the Nature of Human Systems in the Consultant's Role." *Journal of Applied Behavioral Science,* 1968, *4*(2), 179-193.

Fiedler, F. E. *A Theory of Leadership Effectiveness.* New York: McGraw-Hill, 1967.

Fiedler, F. E., Chemers, M. M., and Mahar, L. *Proving Leadership Effectiveness: The Leader Match Concept.* New York: Wiley, 1976.

Fisher, C. F. "The Evaluation and Development of College and University Administrators." *ERIC/Higher Education Research Currents,* March 1977, pp. 142-145.

Fisher, C. F. (Ed.). *New Directions for Higher Education: Developing and Evaluating Administrative Leadership,* no. 22. San Francisco: Jossey-Bass, 1978.

Fleishman, E. A. "The Measurement of Leadership Attitudes in Industry." *Journal of Applied Psychology,* 1953, *34,* 153-158.

Fleishman, E. A. "Twenty Years of Consideration and Structure." In E. A. Fleishman and J. G. Hunt (Eds.), *Current Developments in the Study of Leadership.* Carbondale: Southern Illinois University Press, 1973.

Fordyce, J. K., and Weil, R. *Managing with People.* Reading, Mass.: Addison-Wesley, 1971.

Fromm, E. *The Art of Loving.* London: Unwin, 1957.

Froomkin, J. T., Jamison, D. T., and Radner, R. (Eds.). *Education as an Industry.* Cambridge, Mass.: Ballinger, 1976.

Fulton, O., and Trow, M. "Research Activity in American Higher Education." *Sociology of Education,* 1974, *47*(1), 29-73.

Geiger, D. "College Professors—Are They Teachers?" *Educational Record,* 1970, *51*(3), 320-325.

Genova, W. J., and others. *Mutual Benefit Evaluation of Faculty and Administrators in Higher Education.* Cambridge, Mass.: Ballinger, 1976.

Gibb, J. R. "Trust and Role Freedom: A TORI Innovation in Educational Community." *Journal of Research & Development in Education,* 1972, *5*(3), 76-85.

Gibb, J. R. *Trust: A New View of Personal and Organization Development.* Los Angeles: Guild of Tutors Press, 1978.

Gibson, R. "The President—A Synthesizer." In C. Anderson (Ed.), *Administrative Team Leadership in Concept and Practice.* Athens: Institute of Higher Education, University of Georgia, 1966.

Glaser, R. "A Note on the 'University Troubles' and Their Impact on the Medical Schools." *Daedalus,* 1975, *104*(1), 254-258.

Glenn, J. R. "A Note on Attrition Among College Presidents, 1971-1974." *Research in Higher Education,* 1975, *3,* 323-328.

Glenny, L. A., and others. *Presidents Confront Reality: From Edifice Complex to University Without Walls.* San Francisco: Jossey-Bass, 1976.

Goldstein, R., and Anderson, R. "Attitudes of Faculty Toward Teaching." *Improving College and University Teaching,* 1977, *25*(2), 110-111.

Gordon, T. *Parent Effectiveness Training.* New York: Wyden, 1970.

Gordon, T. *T.E.T.: Teacher Effectiveness Training.* New York: Wyden, 1974.

Gordon, T. *Leadership Effectiveness Training.* New York: Wyden, 1977.

Gould, J. *The Academic Deanship.* New York: Bureau of Publications, Columbia University, 1964.

Graf, E. R., and others. "An Evaluation of Department Head Performance." *IEEE Transactions on Education,* November 1979, *E-22*(4), 180-183.

Gross, E., and Grambsch, P. V. *Changes in University Organization, 1964-1971.* New York: McGraw-Hill, 1974.

Gross, N. "Organizational Lag in American Universities." *Harvard Educational Review,* 1963, *33*(1), 58-73.

Hagstrom, W. "Traditional and Modern Forms of Scientific Teamwork." *Administrative Science Quarterly,* 1964, *9,* 241-263.

Hagstrom, W. "Inputs, Outputs, and the Prestige of University Science Departments." *Sociology of Education,* 1971, *44*(4), 375-397.

Hammond, P., and others. "Teaching Versus Research: Sources of Misperceptions." *Journal of Higher Education,* 1969, *40*(9), 682-690.

Hammons, J. "The Functional Responsibility Chart: Key to Effective Organizational Decision Making." *College and University,* 1976, *52,* 12-13.

Handlin, O., and Handlin, M. F. *The American College and the American Culture: Socialization as a Function of Higher Education.* New York: McGraw-Hill, 1970.

Hanson, M. "Beyond the Bureaucratic Model: A Study of Power and Autonomy in Educational Decision Making." *Interchange,* 1976-1977, *7*(2), 27-38.

Hardman, D. G. "Authority Monograph." Unpublished paper, National Council on Crime and Delinquency, n.d.

Harrington, A. *The Immortalist.* Millbrae, Calif.: Celestial Arts, 1977.

Harris, T. A. *I'm OK—You're OK.* New York: Avon, 1969.

Hartman, J. D. "Change and Conflict in the University." *Journal of Educational Thought,* 1977, *11,* 3-15.

Hartnett, R., and Centra, J. "The Effects of Academic Departments on Student Learning." *Journal of Higher Education,* 1977, *48*(5), 491-507.

Hayes, J. "Research, Teaching and Faculty Fate." *Science,* 1971, *172,* 227-230.

Heath, R. *The Reasonable Adventure.* Pittsburgh: University of Pittsburgh Press, 1964.

Heimler, C. "The College Department Chairman." *Educational Record,* 1967, *48,* 158-163.

Heiss, A. *An Inventory of Academic Innovation and Reform.* Berkeley, Calif.: Carnegie Commission on Higher Education, 1973.

Hemphill, J. "Leadership Behavior Associated with the Administrative Reputation of College Departments." *Journal of Educational Psychology,* 1955, *46,* 385-401.

Henry, D. D. *Challenges Past, Challenges Present: An Analysis of American Higher Education Since 1930.* San Francisco: Jossey-Bass, 1975.

Hersey, P., and Blanchard, K. H. *Management of Organizational Behavior: Utilizing Human Resources.* (3rd ed.) Englewood Cliffs, N.J.: Prentice-Hall, 1977.

Hill, W. W., and French, W. L. "Perceptions of the Power of Department Chairmen by Professors." *Administrative Science Quarterly,* 1967, *11,* 548-574.

Hills, R. "The Representative Function: Neglected Dimension of Leadership Behavior." *Administrative Science Quarterly,* 1963, *8*(1), 83-101.

Hillway, T. "What Professors Want in a President." *School and Society,* June 20, 1959, pp. 306-308.

Hillway, T. "How Trustees Judge a College President." *School and Society,* February 11, 1961, *89,* 51-53.

Hillway, T. "Evaluating College and University Administration." *Intellect,* April 1973, pp. 426-427.

Hiraok, L. "Reorganization—Prescription for Higher Education." *Education,* 1975, *95*(4), 368-372.

Hobbs, W., and Francis, J. "On the Scholarly Activities of Higher Educationists." *Journal of Higher Education,* 1973, *44*(1), 51-60.

Hobbs, W. C., and Anderson, G. L. "The Operation of Academic Departments." *Management Science,* 1971, *18*(4), B-134—B-144.

Hodgkinson, H. J. "Education in 1985: A Future History." *Educational Record,* Spring 1979, pp. 129-136.

Hodgkinson, H. L., and Meeth, L. R. (Eds.). *Power and Authority: Transformation of Campus Governance.* San Francisco: Jossey-Bass, 1971.

Holdaway, E., and others. "Dimensions of Organizations in Complex Societies: The Educational Sector." *Administrative Science Quarterly,* 1975, *20,* 37-58.

Hoover, K. H. *College Teaching Today: A Handbook for Postsecondary Instruction.* Boston: Allyn & Bacon, 1980.

Horney, K. *The Neurotic Personality of Our Time.* New York: Norton, 1937.

Horney, K. *Self-Analysis.* New York: Norton, 1942.

Horney, K. *Neurosis and Human Growth.* New York: Norton, 1950.

Hoyt, D. "Interrelationships Among Instructional Effectiveness, Publication Record, and Monetary Reward." *Research in Higher Education,* 1974, *2,* 81-88.

Huber, J. "University Organizational Unity and Faculty Role Specialization." *School and Society,* 1972, *100,* 106-109.

Hughes, E. C., and others. *Education for the Professions of Medicine, Law, Theology, and Social Welfare.* New York: McGraw-Hill, 1973.

Hutchinson, W. "Yes, John, There Are Teachers on the Faculty." *The American Scholar,* 1966, *35*(3), 430-441.

Ikenberry, S. O., and Friedman, R. C. *Beyond Academic Departments: The Story of Institutes and Centers.* San Francisco: Jossey-Bass, 1972.

Jacobs, K. J. "Collective Bargaining—Its Impact on Maturing Administrative Thought." In R. E. Lahti (Ed.), *New Directions for Community Colleges: Managing in a New Era,* no. 28. San Francisco: Jossey-Bass, 1979.

Jacques, E. *The Changing Culture of a Factory.* London: Tavistock, 1951.

James, M. *The OK Boss.* Reading, Mass.: Addison-Wesley, 1975.

James, M., and Jongeward, D. *Born to Win: Transactional*

Analysis with Gestalt Experiments. Reading, Mass.: Addison-Wesley, 1971.

Jencks, C., and Riesman, D. *The Academic Revolution.* Chicago: University of Chicago Press, 1977.

Jennings, E. E. *The Executive: Autocrat, Bureaucrat, Democrat.* New York: Harper & Row, 1962.

Jung, C. G. *Psychology Types.* Princeton, N.J.: Princeton University Press, 1971.

Kammerer, G. "The State University as a Political System." *Journal of Politics,* 1969, *31,* 289-310.

Kangas, J. A., and Solomon, G. H. *The Psychology of Strength.* Englewood Cliffs, N.J.: Prentice-Hall, 1975.

Kaplin, W. A. *The Law of Higher Education: Legal Implications of Administrative Decision Making.* San Francisco: Jossey-Bass, 1978.

Katz, D. "Faculty Salaries, Promotions and Productivity at a Large University." *American Economic Review,* 1973, *63,* 469-477.

Katz, D., and Kahn, R. *Social Psychology of Organizations.* New York: Wiley, 1966.

Kauffman, J. F. "The New College President: Expectations and Realities." *Educational Record,* 1977, *58*(2), 146-168.

Kemerer, F. R., and Satryle, R. P. *Facing Financial Exigency.* Lexington, Mass.: Heath, 1977.

Kingston, G. "The Problems of Academic Departmental Management and a Ray of Hope." *Journal of the College and University Personnel Association,* 1972, *23,* 48-68.

Kleiman, M. D. "Public Confidence in Educational Leaders." *Intellect,* 1976, *105,* 161-162.

Knowles, A. (Ed.). *Handbook of College and University Organization.* New York: McGraw-Hill, 1970.

Kolstoe, O. "On Professoring: Teaching and Research." *Today's Education,* September-October 1975, pp. 80-86.

Korman, A. K. "Consideration, Initiating Structure, and Organizational Criteria—A Review." *Personnel Psychology: A Journal of Applied Research,* 1966, *19*(4), 349-361.

Kovar, L. C. *Faces of the Adolescent Girl.* Englewood Cliffs, N.J.: Prentice-Hall, 1968.

Kunkel, F. M., and Dickerson, R. E. *How Character Develops: A Psychological Interpretation.* New York: Scribner, 1946.

Kunkel, R. C. "Toward Applied Leadership Development: Gamblings of a Rookie Dean." *Journal of Teacher Education,* January-February 1980, *31*(1), 31-34.

Kurpius, D. J. "OD: A Theory and Process for Influencing Human and Organization Development." *Improving Human Performance Quarterly,* 1979, *8*(4), 217-226.

Ladd, E. C., Jr., and Lipset, S. M. *Professors, Unions, and American Higher Education.* Berkeley, Calif.: Carnegie Commission on Higher Education, 1973.

Lahti, R. E. *Innovative College Management: Implementing Proven Organizational Practice.* San Francisco: Jossey-Bass, 1973.

Lannutti, J. "The Fictitious Conflict Between Research and Education." *Educational Record,* 1973, *54*(1), 83-88.

Lawrence, P. R., and Lorsch, J. W. *Developing Organizations: Diagnosis in Action.* Reading, Mass.: Addison-Wesley, 1969.

Leary, T. *Interpersonal Diagnosis of Personality.* New York: Ronald Press, 1957.

Lee, E., and Bowen, F. *The Multicampus University: A Study of Academic Governance.* New York: McGraw-Hill, 1971.

Leslie, D. "The Status of the Department Chairmanship in University Organization." *AAUP Bulletin,* 1973, *59,* 419-426.

Lewis, L. "Publish or Perish: Some Comments on a Hyperbole." *Journal of Higher Education,* 1967, *38*(2), 85-89.

Light, D., Jr. "The Structure of the Academic Professions." *Sociology of Education,* 1974, *47*(1), 2-28.

Likert, R. *The Human Organization: Its Management and Value.* New York: McGraw-Hill, 1967.

Likert, R., and Likert, J. G. *New Ways of Managing Conflict.* New York: McGraw-Hill, 1976.

Linsky, A., and Straus, M. "Student Evaluations, Research Productivity, and Eminence of College Faculty." *Journal of Higher Education,* 1975, *46*(1), 89-102.

Livingstone, H. *The University: An Organizational Analysis.* London: Blackie & Son, 1974.

Lodahl, J., and Gordon, G. "The Structure of Scientific Fields

and the Functioning of University Graduate Departments."
American Sociological Review, 1972, *37*(1), 57-72.

Lodahl, J., and Gordon, G. "Differences Between Physical and
Social Sciences in University Graduate Departments." *Research in Higher Education,* 1973, *1*(3), 191-213.

Lumsden, K. G. (Ed.). *Efficiency in Universities: The La Paz Papers.* New York: Elsevier, 1974.

Lutz, F. W. "The Deanship: Search and Screening Process."
Educational Record, 1979, *60*(3), 261-271.

McAllister, R. "Service, Teaching, and Research: Old Elements
in a New Academic Melting Pot." *Journal of Higher Education,* 1976, *47*(4), 471-480.

McClelland, D. C. *Power: The Inner Experience.* New York:
Irvington, 1975.

Maccoby, M. *The Gamesman.* New York: Simon & Schuster,
1976.

McGregor, D. *The Human Side of Enterprise.* New York:
McGraw-Hill, 1960.

McGregor, D. *The Professional Manager.* New York: McGraw-
Hill, 1967.

Machlup, F. "A Recipe for a Good Graduate Department."
Chronicle of Higher Education, 1978, *17*(7), 80.

McKeachie, W. "Memo to New Department Chairmen." *Educational Record,* Spring 1968, pp. 221-227.

McKeachie, W. J. "Reactions from a Former Department Chairman." In J. C. Smart and J. R. Montgomery (Eds.), *New
Directions for Institutional Research: Examining Departmental Management,* no. 10. San Francisco: Jossey-Bass,
1976.

McKenzie, R. "The Economics of Reducing Faculty Teaching
Loads." *Journal of Political Economy,* 1972, *80,* 616-619.

McLaughlin, G. W., Montgomery, J. R., and Malpass, L. F.
"Selected Characteristics, Roles, Goals, and Satisfaction of
Department Chairmen in State and Land-Grant Institutions."
Research in Higher Education, 1975, *3,* 243-259.

Mann, F. C. "Changing Superior Subordinate Relationships."
Journal of Social Issues, 1951, *7*(3), 56-63.

Marcson, S. "Decision-Making in a University Physics Department." *American Behavioral Scientist,* 1962, *6,* 37-39.

Martin, T., and Berry, K. "The Teaching-Research Dilemma: Its Sources in the University Setting." *Journal of Higher Education,* 1969, *40*(9), 691-703.

Maslow, A., and Zimmerman, W. "College Teaching Ability, Scholarly Activity, and Personality." *Journal of Educational Psychology,* 1956, *47,* 185-189.

May, R. *Love and Will.* New York: Norton, 1969.

Meininger, J. *Success Through Transactional Analysis.* New York: New American Library, 1973.

Metcalf, H. C., and Urwick, L. *Dynamic Administration: The Collected Papers of Mary Parker Follett.* New York: Harper & Row, 1940.

Miller, R. I. *Evaluating Faculty Performance.* San Francisco: Jossey-Bass, 1972.

Miller, R. I. *Developing Programs for Faculty Evaluation: A Sourcebook for Higher Education.* San Francisco: Jossey-Bass, 1974.

Millett, J. D. *The Academic Community: An Essay on Organization.* New York: McGraw-Hill, 1962.

Millett, J. "Similarities and Differences Among Universities of the United States." In J. Perkins (Ed.), *The University as an Organization.* New York: McGraw-Hill, 1973.

Missildine, W. H. *Your Inner Child of the Past.* New York: Simon & Schuster, 1963.

Missildine, W. H., and Galton, L. *Your Inner Conflicts—How to Solve Them.* New York: Simon & Schuster, 1974.

Mobley, T. A. "Selecting the Department Chairman." *Educational Record,* 1971, *52,* 321-327.

Moment, D., and Zaleznik, A. *Role Development and Interpersonal Competence.* Cambridge, Mass.: Harvard University Press, 1963.

Monson, C. "The University of Utah's Department Chairman Training Program." In J. Brann and T. Emmet (Eds.), *The Academic Department or Division Chairman: A Complex Role.* Detroit: Balamp, 1972.

Montgomery, J. R., McLaughlin, G. W., and Smart, J. C. "A Role Analysis of Department Chairmen at State Universities." ERIC Document Reproduction Service No. ED089626. Blackburg, Va.: Office of Institutional Research, 1974.

Mood, A. M. *The Future of Higher Education.* New York: McGraw-Hill, 1973.

Mooney, R. "The Problem of Leadership in the University." *Harvard Educational Review,* 1965, *33,* 56-57.

Mouton, J. S., and Blake, R. R. *The Marriage Grid.* New York: McGraw-Hill, 1971.

Munitz, B. "Presidential Evaluation: An Assessment of Institutional Leadership." Unpublished report, available from author, University of Houston, 1976.

Munitz, B. *Leadership in Colleges and Universities: Assessment and Research.* Oak Brook, Ill.: Johnson, 1977.

Munitz, B. "Strengthening Institutional Leadership." In C. F. Fisher (Ed.), *New Directions for Higher Education: Developing and Evaluating Administrative Leadership,* no. 22. San Francisco: Jossey-Bass, 1978.

Nicoll, G. "Implications for Role of College Department Chairman." *Education,* 1971, *92,* 82-84.

O'Grady, J., Jr. "The Department Chairman." *Improving College and University Teaching,* 1973, *21,* 270-272.

O'Hanlon, J. "Organizing a College of Education." *Journal of Teacher Education,* 1976, *27*(2), 132-135.

Page, C. "Teaching and Research—Happy Symbiosis or Hidden Warfare." *Universities Quarterly,* 1972-73, *27,* 102-118.

Parker, P. C. "Access and Mobility in Higher Education: The Search for a Common Currency and a Gold Standard." Paper presented at annual meeting of the Association of American Colleges, Washington, D.C., February 3, 1979.

Parsons, T. "The Strange Case of Academic Organization." *Journal of Higher Education,* 1971, *42*(6), 486-495.

Perkins, J. "The New Conditions of Autonomy." In L. Wilson (Ed.), *Emerging Patterns in American Higher Education.* Washington, D.C.: American Council on Education, 1965.

Perkins, J. (Ed.). *The University as an Organization.* New York: McGraw-Hill, 1973.

Petersdorf, R. "The Role of the Departmental Chairman in Schools of Medicine." *Journal of Medical Education,* 1971, *46,* 1069-1073.

Peterson, M. W. "The Academic Department: Perspectives from

Theory and Research." In J. C. Smart and J. R. Montgomery (Eds.), *New Directions for Institutional Research: Examining Departmental Management,* no. 10. San Francisco: Jossey-Bass, 1976.

Peterson, W. "Critical Incidents for New and Experienced College and University Presidents." *Research in Higher Education,* 1973, *44*(7), 495-513.

Pfeffer, J., and others. "Publication and Prestige Mobility of University Departments in Three Scientific Disciplines." *Sociology of Education,* 1976, *49,* 212-218.

Pfeffer, J., and Salancik, G. "Organizational Decision Making as a Political Process: The Case of a University Budget." *Administrative Science Quarterly,* 1974, *19*(2), 135-151.

Platt, G., and Parsons, T. "Decision Making in the Academic System: Influence and Power Exchange." In C. Kruytbosch and S. Messinger (Eds.), *The State of the University: Authority and Change.* Beverly Hills, Calif.: Sage, 1970.

Podemski, R. "Leadership Behavior, Role Conflict, and Role Ambiguity: The University Department Chairman." Unpublished doctoral dissertation, State University of New York, Buffalo, 1973.

Pollay, R., and others. "A Model for Horizontal Power Sharing and Participation in University Decision Making." *Journal of Higher Education,* 1976, *47*(2), 141-157.

Poque, F. "Students' Ratings of the 'Ideal Teacher.'" *Improving College and University Teaching,* 1967, *15,* 133-136.

Porter, K. "Department Head or Chairman." *AAUP Bulletin,* 1961, *47,* 339-342.

Quick, A., and Wolf, A. "The Ideal Professor." *Improving College and University Teaching,* 1965, *13,* 133-134.

Reddin, W. J. *Managerial Effectiveness 3—D.* New York: McGraw-Hill, 1970.

Reid, W., and Epstein, L. *Task-Centered Casework.* New York: Columbia University Press, 1972.

Richman, B. M., and Farmer, R. N. *Leadership, Goals, and Power in Higher Education: A Contingency and Open Systems Approach to Effective Management.* San Francisco: Jossey-Bass, 1974.

Riesman, D. "The Changing American Campus: Beyond the '60's." *The Wilson Quarterly,* Autumn 1978, pp. 59-71.

Riesman, D., Glazer, N., and Denney, R. *The Lonely Crowd.* New York: Doubleday, 1953.

Riesman, D., Gusfield, J., and Gamson, Z. *Academic Values and Mass Education.* New York: McGraw-Hill, 1970.

Roberts, R. W., and Nee, R. H. *Theories of Social Casework.* Chicago: University of Chicago Press, 1970.

Rogers, C. "Personal Power at Work." *Psychology Today,* April 1977, pp. 60-62, 93-94.

Rossi, P. "Research, Scholars, and Policy Makers: The Politics of Large Scale Research." *Daedalus,* 1964, *93,* 1142-1161.

Rudolph, F. *The American College and University: A History.* New York: Random House, 1965.

Ryan, D. W. "The Internal Organization of Academic Departments." *Journal of Higher Education,* 1972, *43*(5), 464-482.

Sample, S. "Inherent Conflict Between Research and Education." *Educational Record,* 1972, *53*(1), 17-22.

Schein, E. H. *Process Consultation: Its Role in Organization Development.* Reading, Mass.: Addison-Wesley, 1969.

Schmitt, H. "Teaching and Research: Companions or Adversaries?" *Journal of Higher Education,* 1965, *36*(8), 419-427.

Schmuck, R. A., and Miles, M. B. *Organization Development in Schools.* Palo Alto, Calif.: National Press Books, 1971.

Schmuck, R. A., and others. *Handbook of Organization Development in Schools.* Palo Alto, Calif.: National Press Books, 1972.

Schmuck, R. A., and others. *The Second Handbook of Organization Development in Schools.* Palo Alto, Calif.: Mayfield, 1977.

Schutz, W. C. *The Interpersonal Underworld.* Palo Alto, Calif.: Science & Behavior Books, 1966.

Scientific Methods, Inc. "Description of Products and Services." Available from Scientific Methods, Inc., P.O. Box 195, Austin, Texas 78767, 1980.

Scott, R. "Middle-Level Collegiate Administration in a Period of Retrenchment." *College and University,* 1977, *53*(1), 42-56.

Shapiro, E. "The Effects on Teaching of Changes in Relative

Rewards for Research and Teaching." *Research in Higher Education,* 1978, *9*(1), 43-67.

Shattock, M. "A Changing Pattern of University Administration." *Universities Quarterly,* 1970, *24*(3), 310-320.

Shulman, C. H. *Collective Bargaining on Campus.* Washington, D.C.: American Association for Higher Education, 1972.

Siegfried, J., and White, K. "Teaching and Publishing as Determinants of Academic Salaries." *Journal of Economic Education,* 1973, *4,* 90-99.

Sikes, W. W., Schlesinger, L. E., and Seashore, C. N. *Reviewing Higher Education from Within: A Guide for Campus Change Teams.* San Francisco: Jossey-Bass, 1974.

Skipper, C. E. "Factor Analysis of the University Leaders' Behavior." *College and University,* Spring 1978, pp. 330-334.

Smart, J. C. "Duties Performed by Department Chairmen in Holland's Model Environments." *Journal of Educational Psychology,* 1976, *68*(2), 194-204.

Smart, J. C., and Elton, C. F. "Administrative Roles of Department Chairmen." In J. C. Smart and J. R. Montgomery (Eds.), *New Directions for Institutional Research: Examining Departmental Management,* no. 10. San Francisco: Jossey-Bass, 1976.

Smart, J. C., and Montgomery, J. R. (Eds.). *New Directions for Institutional Research: Examining Departmental Management,* no. 10. San Francisco: Jossey-Bass, 1976.

Smith, R., and Fiedler, F. "The Measurement of Scholarly Work: A Critical Review of the Literature." *Educational Record,* Summer 1971, pp. 225-232.

Snyder, R., and others. "Mid-Career Change in Academia: The Decision to Become an Administrator." *Journal of Vocational Behavior,* 1978, *13,* 229-241.

Spence, J. T., and Helmreich, R. L. *Masculinity and Femininity: Their Psychological Dimensions, Correlates, and Antecedents.* Austin: University of Texas Press, 1978.

Sprunger, B. D., and Bergquist, W. H. *Handbook for College Administration.* Washington, D.C.: Council for the Advancement of Small Colleges, 1978.

Startup, R., and Gruneberg, M. "The Rewards of Research." *Universities Quarterly,* 1976, *30*(2), 225-238.

Steiner, C. M. *Scripts People Live: Transactional Analysis of Life Scripts.* New York: Bantam Books, 1974.

Stiles, L. "Publish-or-Perish in Perspective." *Journal of Teacher Education,* Winter 1966, *17,* 464-467.

Tannenbaum, R., and Schmidt, R. H. "How to Choose a Leadership Pattern." *Harvard Business Review,* March/April 1958, pp. 95-102.

Tebutt, A. "Teaching Versus Research: A Reconciliation." *Improving College and University Teaching,* 1973, *21*(3), 192-194.

Thomas, W. I., and Znaniecki, F. "Three Types of Personality." In C. W. Mills (Ed.), *Images of Man: The Classic Tradition in Sociological Thinking.* New York: Braziller, 1960.

"A Topical Bibliography on Consultation." *Personnel & Guidance Journal,* 1978, *56*(7), 442-447.

Topping, N. *To Be or Not to Be.* Los Angeles: Pullias Lectureship Endowment Fund, Department of Higher and Postsecondary Education, School of Education, University of Southern California, 1979.

Torgerson, P. E., and Taylor, R. E. "The Department Head in Facsimile." *Engineering Education,* January 1974, *64,* 245-249.

Tucker, A., and Mautz, R. B. "Presidential Evaluation: An Academic Circus." *Educational Record,* 1979, *60*(3), 253-260.

Twaddell, W. "Departmental Organization at the University of Wisconsin." *AAUP Bulletin,* 1940, *26,* 196-200.

Vago, S. "Consumer Rights in Academe." *Social Policy,* March/April 1979, pp. 39-43.

Varney, G. H., and Lasher, J. "Surveys in Feedback as a Means of Organization Diagnosis and Change." In T. H. Patten, Jr. (Ed.), *OD—Emerging Dimensions in Concepts.* Washington, D.C.: American Society for Training and Development, 1973.

Voeks, V. "Publications and Teaching Effectiveness." *Journal of Higher Education,* 1962, *33,* 212-218.

Wallis, W. "Unity in the University." *Daedalus,* 1975, *104*(1), 68-77.

Walton, R. E. *Interpersonal Peacemaking: Confrontations and Third Party Consultation.* Reading, Mass.: Addison-Wesley, 1969.

Washington, E. M. "The Relationship Between College Department Chairperson's Leadership Style as Perceived by Teaching Faculty and That Faculty's Feelings of Job Satisfaction." Unpublished doctoral dissertation, Western Michigan University, 1975.

Weber, C., and others. "Academic Authority and the Administration of Research." *Educational Record,* 1966, *47,* 218-225.

Webster, R. S. "A Management Team Approach to Institutional Renewal." *Educational Record,* 1979, *60*(3), 241-252.

Wells, H. "How to Succeed as a University President Without Really Trying." *Educational Record,* 1964, *45*(3), 241-245.

Wheelis, A. *The Quest for Identity.* New York: Norton, 1958.

White, R., and Lippitt, R. "Leader Behavior and Member Reaction in Three 'Social Climates.' " In D. Cartwright and A. Zander (Eds.), *Group Dynamics: Research and Theory.* (2nd ed.) New York: Harper & Row, 1960.

Williams, L. "Democracy and Hierarchy: A Profile of Faculty Meetings in Department 'X.' " *Journal of Educational Sociology,* 1956, *30,* 168-172.

Wilson, J., and Wilson, R. "The Teaching-Research Controversy." *Educational Record,* 1972, *53*(4), 321-326.

Wolk, R. "Today's Multiversity: An Institution Torn by Conflicting Pressures." *Atlanta Economic Review,* 1965, *15*(8), 3-6.

Yamamoto, K., and Dizney, H. "Eight Professors—A Study on College Students' Preferences Among Their Teachers." *Journal of Educational Psychology,* 1966, *57*(3), 146-150.

Yeo, R. "Departmentalization—Solution or Problem." *Educational Forum,* 1970, *35*(1), 39-44.

Young, E. T. "A Study of the Opinions of Deans and Faculty Members Toward the Effectiveness of Women Department Chairmen in Higher Education." Unpublished doctoral dissertation, University of Southern Mississippi, 1974.

Zion, C. "Role Definition: A Focus for Administrative Growth and Evaluation." *Journal of the College and University Personnel Association,* Summer 1977, *28,* 5-12.

Index

413